Jesuit Studies

Contributions to the arts and sciences

by members of the Society of Jesus

Jesuit Studies

JESUIT STUDIES

The Wagner Housing Act

A CASE STUDY

OF THE LEGISLATIVE PROCESS

Timothy L. McDonnell, S.J.

LOYOLA UNIVERSITY PRESS

Chicago, 1957

© 1957

LOYOLA   UNIVERSITY   PRESS

Printed in the United States of America

Library of Congress Catalog Card Number: 57-12416

P-PELN-P-O-E

IMPRIMI POTEST: Daniel H. Conway, S.J.
Provincial of the Missouri Province
March 13, 1953
IMPRIMATUR: ✠ Samuel Cardinal Stritch
Archbishop of Chicago
August 6, 1957

The purpose of this case study of the federal legislative process is to expose as completely as possible in depth and extension all the activities that are involved in the making of a law. The Housing Act of 1937, which is the subject matter for this case study, was introduced in three successive sessions of Congress before it was enacted into law. The long and complicated struggle for the enactment of this law brings forth all of the activities of the lawmaking process except the presidential veto and subsequent congressional action. The law involved the development of an entirely new program and of special financial plans and administrative structures to implement the program. The study of the development and technical expression of these provisions of the law as they were formed under the pressure of the powerful lobby groups who represented the interests of the executive agencies, the real-estate organizations, and the labor unions and welfare groups offers a vivid example of modern representative government in action. Although the law was passed before the Legislative Reorganization Act of 1946, the changes in procedure and structure brought about by that law were not so fundamental as to change substantially the traditional and major activities of the legislative process as it is here described.

It was a happy coincidence for the author that at the time when the White House Papers of President Franklin D. Roosevelt, the office files of Senator Robert F. Wagner, and the files of various lobbies and of the executive department agencies which contained material essential to this study were made available, every major participant in the work of drafting and pushing through Congress the Housing Act of 1937 was still active and available for consultation and interview. Although President Roosevelt had died and Senator Wagner and Secretary Ickes were in retirement when this research was done, this does not leave any lacunae in the history of the law; for the documents in their respective files, together with the information supplied by their assistants, clearly manifest the role of these top-level leaders of the New Deal in developing broad legislative policy. The specific provisions of the law were drafted by their assistants. It is not the claim of the author that every individual maneuver in the legislative process is accounted for in the sources mentioned, for certain agreements and compromises were made in private conversations that never became the matter of record.

It is impossible for the author to list his debt of gratitude to the many librarians, directors, secretaries, and clerks who gave him valuable, gracious, and often anonymous assistance. The footnotes acknowledge the assistance of the participants in the drafting of the Housing Act to whom a special acknowledgment is due. The author feels that he must express in a special way his gratitude to Professor Paul G. Steinbicker, of St. Louis University, who was director of the doctoral dissertation that started him on this research project, and to John Taylor Egan, formerly commissioner of the Public Housing Administration, who gave invaluable assistance and technical advice during the years this work was in preparation.

T. L. McD.

August 1, 1957

CONTENTS

CHAPTER I

Housing,
the Perennial Problem

The late Senator Robert F. Wagner, Sr., of New York introduced the first public-housing bill in the United States Senate on March 13, 1935, but a thorough study of this housing bill must start at a much earlier date. No piece of social legislation so revolutionary in its philosophy and in its specific provisions as the Wagner housing bill is drafted in a week or a month by a legislator and his technical assistants, or without the guidance of previous experience and experiments. Public housing involves a social philosophy and administrative and financial provisions to implement the objectives of this philosophy, the sources of which are to be found in past experiences and experiments with social legislation in the United States. Some of the ideas and provisions of the bill, however, are derived from English and European experiences.

This case study cannot trace all these ideas to their specific sources. It is sufficient for an understanding of the bill that only those ideas and provisions that had a direct influence on the development of the bill be studied.

Housing has long been a problem in the United States. There has not been a sufficient number of adequate dwellings to shelter decently all the people of the nation. The people most seriously affected by this shortage have been the people in the lower

1

income groups. More precisely, the situation has two sides
which together make one large problem. First, single families
were not able to finance the building of new dwellings or to
find adequate existing dwellings within their economic range;
thus these families were forced to live in dwellings in blighted
areas or in slums which did not meet the minimum standards
for health and safety. Second, this economic necessity forced
two or more families to "double-up" in a unit originally
designed to serve only a single family.

In the rugged pioneer days of the development of this country housing was a personal problem. Each family provided itself
with housing as best it could. Friendly neighbors in the town
or on the frontier would help prepare the land and set up the
dwelling. In the larger towns that were to become the great
urban centers housing very early became a less simple matter.
The provision of housing, however, was still a personal problem, though it was necessary for the local government to establish certain regulations concerning housing in order to provide
for the safety and the sanitation of the town. William Karlin
has traced back such regulatory legislation to the year 1647,
when the Dutch in the town of New Amsterdam enacted a law
to set up building standards that would prevent chimney fires.[1]

With the growth of industry in the United States and the
great flood of immigrants into New York and other cities during
the first half of the nineteenth century housing became an acute
problem. There were never enough dwelling units to take care
of the large number of new families moving into industrial
centers like New York City. The result of this situation was an
overcrowding of the existing dwelling units and a conversion
into living rooms of space that had never been built or intended
for such purposes.

---

[1] William Karlin, "New York Slum Clearance and the Law." *Political Science
Quarterly* 52:242, June 1937.

In 1834 Gerritt Forbes, then sanitary inspector for New York City, made a report on the unsanitary and overcrowded conditions of New York City's fast-growing slums.[2] In the following years similar reports were made. Dr. John Griscom made an important one in 1842.[3] These reports represented an attempt to solve the housing problem in an indirect way. By condemning the unsanitary and disease-breeding slum quarters these pioneer public-health officers and social workers hoped that they would be able to force *someone, somehow,* to build better housing *somewhere.*

These pioneers discovered that the problem could not be solved at the local level of government, and so they made an appeal to the legislature of New York; but it was not until 1867 that the legislature, responding to the pressure brought to bear upon it by health groups and socially conscious citizens, enacted the first tenement-house act.

This law, like most first attempts at social or welfare legislation, was ineffective, especially as it did not make provision for its enforcement. The realization of this defect resulted in a reform movement led by Dr. Felix Adler and in the law of 1887, which provided for the establishment of a permanent Tenement House Commission. In 1901 Lawrence Veiller led a movement to revise the law so as to provide for a Tenement House Department in the New York City government which would administer the law. These laws, especially the last one, proved effective in making a start at cleaning up the unhealthy conditions of the slum areas.[4] All these laws were concerned with the establishment of standards for decent, sanitary, and safe housing. They made no direct attempt to increase the supply of dwelling units.

---

[2] Edith Elmer Wood, "Housing in the United States"; in *Encyclopaedia Britannica,* 1943 edition, Vol. 11, p. 840.

[3] *Ibid.,* p. 841.

[4] Karlin, "New York Slum Clearance and the Law," p. 241.

Before speaking of further developments in this type of legislation, it will be helpful to describe the public reaction to such legislation. Some persons who were affected by the provisions of the legislation considered its regulations to be beyond the powers of the state, and they refused to comply with them. They brought their case to the law courts. The first important case involved a certain Trinity Church of New York City, which owned some houses on Charlton Avenue and which refused to comply with the Health Department order made pursuant to the statute of 1887 requiring sufficient water to be stored on each floor of a dwelling which was to be occupied by one or more families. The counsel for the church argued that the legislation was not a proper exercise of police power. The case was decided against the church and was appealed to the higher court. The Court of Appeals of the State of New York sustained the constitutionality of the legislation in a decision given in 1895.[5]

In 1904 the Court of Appeals was called upon to rule on the constitutionality of the statute of 1901, which contained among its provisions a requirement that new plumbing was to be installed in place of older unsanitary plumbing. Here again the issue was the scope of the police power, and again the court sustained the legislation as a proper exercise of the police power of the state.[6]

While in the city of New York those interested in the housing conditions of the working people were gaining a point here and a point there, the Supreme Court of Massachusetts handed down a decision that crushed any hope that social workers might have had for a direct attack on the housing shortage by means of state loans to finance construction of dwelling units.

---

[5] *Health Department of New York City* v. *Rector, etc., of Trinity Church of New York City*, 145 N. Y. 32 (1895).

[6] *Tenement House Department* v. *Moeschen*, 179 N. Y. 335 (1904).

In 1872 large sections of Boston were devastated by fire. A statute was passed authorizing the city of Boston to issue bonds for the raising of money to be loaned to the owners of real estate for the purpose of replacing buildings which had been destroyed in the fire. The validity of the law was challenged in the courts in the case of *Lowell* v. *Boston*. The decision which was given declared the law to be invalid. The court exposed its philosophy by setting forth the following principles:

> The promotion of the interests of individuals, either in respect of property or business, although it may result incidentally in the advancement of the public welfare, is, in its essential character, a private and not a public object. However certain and great the resulting good to the general public, it does not, by reason of its comparative importance, cease to be incidental. . . . It is the essential character of the direct object of the expenditure which must determine its validity, as justifying a tax, and not the magnitude of interests to be affected, nor the degree to which the general advantage of the community and thus the public welfare may be ultimately affected by their promotion. The principle of distinction is fundamental. It underlies all government that is based upon reason rather than upon force.[7]

This was the prevailing philosophy of government elsewhere in the United States up to World War I. At that time those interested in a solution of the housing shortage and in slum clearance could have no hope of attacking the problem by employing funds derived from taxes or government borrowing.

While there was no hope of the state's doing anything to increase the supply of housing, some efforts were made by philanthropists and limited-dividend corporations to bring better housing to people living in slums or blighted areas. The aim of this program was not to solve the housing shortage but to provide better housing for the laboring people. Mr. Alfred T. White, to mention but one philanthropist, built model tenements

---

[7] *Lowell* v. *Boston*, 111 Mass. 461 (1873).

in Brooklyn between 1878 and 1890. There were a number of limited-dividend corporations in the larger cities that did excellent pioneering work in experimenting in the field of housing construction and slum clearance. The Boston Cooperative Building Company was organized in 1871; City and Suburban Homes Company of New York was incorporated in 1896. Two of the most successful corporations, in terms both of slum clearance and of sound finances, were the Washington Sanitary Improvement Company (1897) and the Washington Sanitary Housing Company (1904). These two companies were organized by progressive citizens in Washington who were interested in getting the citizens of the national capital out of the alley slums. These two companies, which cooperated with each other in this work, had built by 1930 a total of 878 apartments, and the companies paid out an average dividend of 5 per cent. Many citizens of Washington joined the corporations for philanthropic reasons, but discovered over the years that they had made an economically sound investment.[8] These examples of private enterprise were steps in the direction of a solution to the entire housing problem, but unfortunately not enough corporations were organized. Those who were later interested in the housing problem, however, learned much from the experiences of these groups.

The housing problem was recognized as being too big a problem for local government to solve. It was now admitted to be the concern of the state government. During the period from 1865 to 1914 no effort was made to have the Federal Government enter into the field of housing; the Federal Government, however, did recognize that there were slums and a housing shortage. In 1892 Congress appropriated $20,000 for the investigation of slums in cities of 200,000 or more population.[9] A

---

[8] Edith Elmer Wood, *The Housing of the Unskilled Wage Earner, passim.* New York: The Macmillan Company, 1919.

[9] J. Res. No. 22, 52d Cong., 1st Sess.; 27 Stat. 399 (1892).

report of the investigation prepared by the commissioner of labor contained detailed data on conditions in four cities.[10]

The outbreak of World War I brought many changes in the traditional "American way of life." One of these had to do with housing. The shipyards, the munitions factories, and allied industries expanded during the war. Thousands of laborers and their families moved to these critical war-industry areas and attempted to crowd into the already congested housing facilities. Rents for slum quarters reached new heights. Conditions were bad. The war effort was slowed down as a result of a shifting labor force. It is estimated that the labor turnover was as high as 700 per cent,[11] and this turnover was directly related to poor housing conditions. Individual corporations and employees were helpless in this wartime situation.

Finally, during May and June of 1918, the Federal Government took action toward a solution of the very unsatisfactory housing conditions for war workers. Congress appropriated funds (after Senator Warren G. Harding had proposed an amendment to the bill that the rents charged by the government would provide for a profit of 6 per cent on the investment),[12]

---

[10] Carroll D. Wright, "The Slums of Baltimore, Chicago, New York, and Philadelphia"; in *Seventh Special Report by the Commissioner of Labor*. Washington: Government Printing Office, 1894.

[11] John Nolen, "Governmental Housing," *New Republic* 13:213, December 22, 1917; "Government Housing Chaos," *Nation* 108:84, January 18, 1919.

[12] Harding's comments on the housing situation are of interest in view of the fact that some two years later when he was president of the United States he was called upon to take some action to solve the housing shortage. At that time he refused to take any action (see *supra*, p. 15). At the time that this bill was debated in the Senate Harding made this comment: "There could have been provision made for a prompt supply of temporary houses, but everyone connected with the idealist movement, which is back of the thing, was opposed to anything of the sort. You could not get anyone connected with the Labor Department to consent to any temporary relief of this situation. This is a bit of idealism fitted into the emergency of the Government for a paternal housing program in this country" (*Congressional Record*, April 17, 1918, p. 5206). Harding's amendment and the record of its passage are given on p. 5212.

and two corporations were chartered to provide housing for war workers.[13]

The United States Housing Corporation was under charter from the state of New York as the executive agent of the Bureau of Industrial Transportation and Housing of the Department of Labor. It was authorized to provide housing for workers in the munitions factories and allied industries. The Emergency Fleet Corporation of the United States Shipping Board was organized to provide housing for the workers in the shipyards. Both of these corporations did a good job of planning and constructing model industrial villages and housing units.[14] They also developed large-scale housing architects—Kohn, Ackerman, Dunning, Stein, and others.

Immediately after the armistice there was quite a battle over the future activities of these corporations.[15] Those whose philosophy of government denied to the government the right to engage in any type of activity that could be termed a business enterprise or that was carried out by a business enterprise, such as providing housing, demanded that the Congress liquidate the housing projects of the government corporations. Projects which were not 75-per-cent complete should be abandoned and sold for whatever they would bring. Housing units completed and to be completed should be sold to the war industries or to the workmen then living in them.

---

[13] Congress appropriated $75,000,000 for the use of the Emergency Fleet Corporation and $100,000,000 for the use of the United States Housing Corporation. See "Towards a Federal Housing Policy," *Survey* 39:552, February 16, 1918; James Ford, "Housing for War Workers Engaged on Army and Navy Contracts," *Annals of the American Academy of Political and Social Science* 79:270, September 1918.

[14] *Report of the United States Housing Corporation*, 2 vols. (Washington: Government Printing Office, 1919) ; A. Merritt Taylor, *Report of the Housing Division, Emergency Fleet Corporation* (Washington: Government Printing Office, 1919) ; Edith Elmer Wood, *Recent Trends in American Housing*, Chap. 1, "War Housing," pp. 66-82 (New York: The Macmillan Company, 1931).

[15] *New York Times*, December 13, 1918 and January 9, 1919.

Others, who were of the opinion that the government could and should engage in welfare activities and other enterprises that private enterprise could not carry out, demanded that Congress make provision for these corporations to continue their work in the housing field in order to experiment and to demonstrate the possibility of large-scale housing. Some heated hearings were held on the subject, and it was finally decided that the government corporations should sell all the facilities that were not to be turned over to other government agencies.[16] The immediate result of this government experience in housing was the study and discussion of the question of a permanent place for the Federal Government in the field of housing.[17]

The American Federation of Labor was a pioneer in attempting to get the Federal Government to take an active and effective interest in providing housing for the workers. As early as 1914, in the thirty-fourth annual convention at Philadelphia, a resolution was presented by Henry Nolda and accepted by the convention calling for "the passage of laws that will bring about a system of Government loans of money for municipal and private ownership of sanitary houses, and that we request the United States Government at Washington to pass such legislation as will serve as a model to the various cities of this

---

[16] *Ibid.*, January 18, 1920 and January 20, 1920; John Ihlder, "Uncle Sam as Auctioneer," *Survey* 41:659, February 8, 1919; Curtice N. Hitchcock, "The War Housing Program and Its Future," *Journal of Political Economy* 27:241, April 1919; "Housing Post-Mortem in the Senate," *American City* 22:110, February 1920; "Housing Corporation and the Senate," *Outlook* 124:394, March 3, 1920.

[17] John Ihlder, "Card Houses: Can the Federal Government Afford To Abandon Its Industrial Villages?" *Survey* 41:519, January 18, 1919; Robert D. Kohn, "Housing in a Reconstruction Program," *Survey* 42:341, May 31, 1919; John Ihlder, "The Housing Situation," in *Proceedings of the National Conference of Social Work at the Forty-ninth Annual Session*, pp. 278-81 (Chicago: The University of Chicago Press, 1922); "Government Duty in the Housing Crisis," *Literary Digest* 67:20, October 23, 1920; George Holden Tinkham, "The Urgent Need for a Federal Bureau of Housing and Living Conditions in the Department of Labor," *American City* 22:222, March 1920.

country."[18] This resolution was inspired in part by the European experience with housing, as Mr. Nolda mentioned in the preliminaries to the resolution.

The next year, at the San Francisco convention of 1915, the Executive Council reported to the convention pursuant to the resolution of the previous year:

> Bills were introduced for this purpose by Representative Borland of Missouri and Senator Pomerene of Ohio. They were each referred to the respective committees on the District of Columbia. Hearings were held and general discussion indulged in, but the subject being a new one in the United States, no definite progress can be reported. This is one of the subjects that will require considerable discussion and agitation before legislators in Congress, state assemblies, or municipal councils will pay serious heed to the need of the information or the plans suggested to solve the evils which everybody recognizes, and which few undertake to remedy.[19]

The Committee on Local and Federated Bodies that had been established, in making a report on the resolution (Resolution No. 61), stated:

> Your committee suggests that the subject should be brought to the attention of city and State governments by those interested. Before Congress will become convinced that the people desire such legislation it must be brought before that body in tangible form as coming direct from the people, and municipal and State enactments seem to be the most feasible method of getting the subject started.[20]

During the war years the American Federation of Labor, through its Committee on Labor of the Advisory Commission to the Council of National Defense, secured adequate housing

---

[18] *Report of Proceedings of the Thirty-fourth Annual Convention of the American Federation of Labor*, p. 355. Washington: Law Reporter Printing Company, 1914.

[19] *Report of Proceedings of the Thirty-fifth Annual Convention of the American Federation of Labor*, p. 113. Washington: Law Reporter Printing Company, 1915.

[20] *Ibid.*, p. 467.

for war workers by urging the creation of the two government
housing corporations.[21]

In 1919, at the thirty-ninth annual convention in Atlantic
City, the convention adopted a resolution for the creation of a
permanent housing board with labor representation. This resolution was not so specific as that of the 1914 convention.[22] At the
fortieth annual convention in Montreal in 1920 no new resolution on housing was submitted, and the Executive Council reported that Congress had failed to act on any housing bill.[23]

A very interesting resolution was offered at the convention
of 1921, when the forty-first annual convention was held in
Denver. Some of the "radicals," making an appeal to Carl [sic]
Marx and Henry George, demanded "that under present conditions all state and local governments should use their taxing
power [single tax on land] to relieve the terrible housing shortage." This resolution was referred to the Executive Council for
further study. It was never seriously considered.[24]

The Executive Council made a sad report on the progress of
housing legislation at the Montreal meeting in 1920:

> Shortly after the close of our report on better social and indus-
> trial conditions of last year, the Congress seemed to lose interest
> in all questions of housing. Out of eighty or more housing projects
> begun during the war, a few of them were continued and some fin-

---

[21] *Report of Proceedings of the Thirty-eighth Annual Convention of the American
Federation of Labor*, p. 105 (Washington: Law Reporter Printing Company,
1918). Samuel Gompers, president of the American Federation of Labor, was
the labor member of the Council of National Defense. He was influential in
directing the attention of the government to the need for housing workers.

[22] *Report of Proceedings of the Thirty-ninth Annual Convention of the American
Federation of Labor*, p. 384. Washington: Law Reporter Printing Company,
1919.

[23] *Report of Proceedings of the Fortieth Annual Convention of the American Federation of Labor*, p. 113. Washington: Law Reporter Printing Company, 1920.

[24] *Report of Proceedings of the Forty-first Annual Convention of the American
Federation of Labor*, p. 243. Washington: Law Reporter Printing Company,
1921.

ished without any special legislation being needed. In this year's Congress a bill was introduced by Congressman Tinkham, of Massachusetts (H. R. 7014), to create a permanent Bureau of Housing in the Labor Department, giving it power to investigate, collect information and assist by advising, etc., various housing projects that might be begun in the future; another bill by Senator Calder, of New York (S. 1469), proposing to make loans to building associations to assist in the work of construction; a third bill by Senator Kenyon, of Iowa (S. 168), proposing a commission to investigate and report, recommending legislation on the subject. Hearings were held on the Tinkham and Calder bills and there was great hope at one time that something constructive would be done. However it appeared to be beyond the powers of the present Congress to pass constructive legislation of any kind whatsoever, and these bills all died in committee. If nothing else had been done it would have been wise to institute the committee on inquiry and get definite recommendations for the next session of Congress.[25]

As was to be expected after the war, the housing shortage was worse than ever. Estimates of this shortage ranged from a conservative figure of one million and a quarter dwelling units to five million, or a high figure of ten million, dwelling units. No one really knew how many units were actually needed because an accurate real-estate inventory had never been taken for even one city, still less for the entire country.[26]

During this period immediately after the war housing was real news. Numerous articles appeared in the technical journals, and housing was discussed at various conventions of social workers. Within seven months the *Saturday Evening Post* carried two articles on housing. A year later it carried a feature

---

[25] *Report of the Fortieth Convention of AFL*, p. 113.

[26] John Ihlder, "Extent of the Housing Shortage in the United States—Its Economic and Social Effects, Resources Available in Dealing with It," in *Proceedings of the National Conference of Social Work at the Forty-eighth Annual Session*, p. 331 (Chicago: The University of Chicago Press, 1921) ; "Who Will Build Five Million Homes?" *Literary Digest* 66:17, August 28, 1920; Charles Harris Whitaker, "Wanted—Ten Million Houses!" *Saturday Evening Post* 192:23, May 8, 1920.

editorial on the housing problem.[27] Opinion magazines, such as *Survey, Nation,* and *New Republic,* carried many articles on various phases of housing. A check of the *Reader's Guide to Periodical Literature* shows that during the period from 1915 to 1918 there were seventy-one articles on this subject. Thirty-four of these articles were concerned with housing for war workers, and none of them were concerned with direct government participation in a housing program. During the period from 1919 to 1921 ninety-seven articles are listed under the title housing, and of these articles twenty-six, or more than a fourth, are concerned *pro* and *con* with the question of government participation in the housing program.

An analysis of this material shows that the government experience had evoked various reactions. Harlean James, director of the American Civic Association, speaking before the National Conference of Social Work at its forty-eighth annual meeting in Milwaukee in 1921, urged that the Federal Government restrict itself to research and information, as was done in the Department of Agriculture.[28] Mrs. Edith Elmer Wood delivered a speech to the delegates to the fiftieth annual meeting of the National Conference of Social Work, held in Washington from May 16 to 23, 1923. Mrs. Wood spoke of Federal Government aid as a means of working toward a solution to the housing problem. After telling the social workers of the progress that had been made in the European countries, she offered a specific proposal for the United States.

> The housing division of Secretary Hoover's department figured that a man with a $2,000 income might venture to build a $4,000 house if he had $1,000 and borrowed the rest from a building and loan association at 6 per cent. It foots up, according to the housing

---

[27] "Plans for More Homes." *Saturday Evening Post* 193:38, September 25, 1920.

[28] Harlean James, "Lessons Learned from the Government Experience in Housing"; in *Proceedings of the National Conference of Social Work at the Forty-eighth Annual Session,* p. 312.

division, to $550 a year, including taxes and upkeep, a rather heavy burden for a $2,000 income, and certainly impossible for lower incomes. Reduce the interest to 2¼ per cent [the interest the government was getting for its Postal Savings funds located in the banks], and you save at once $112.50 on the annual charges. Increase the time for repayment to twenty-five years, and you cut down the yearly instalment of principal by $60. This is a total reduction of $172.50, leaving an annual charge of only $377.50. On the same proportional basis that would open the chance for home ownership clear down to the $1,400 income group. The chief trouble with this proposal is that the amount of the postal savings deposits is comparatively small—only $138,000,000. There is not enough to go around. But surely a piece of a loaf is better than none at all. If half of the deposits were invested in mortgage loans averaging $3,000 each, that would mean 23,000 new homes and home owners.[29]

Mrs. Wood did not claim any originality for her idea. She mentioned that certain bills had been introduced in Congress, and Secretary Hoover himself had made the suggestion about the Postal Savings funds. But Mrs. Wood told the conference that there was no public interest in such practical proposals. She urged the delegates there present not to say to themselves, "That's a good idea!" and then go away and do nothing. She urged them to make practical plans during this meeting for implementing this financial scheme.

Three years before Mrs. Wood made this address to the National Conference of Social Work, Herbert Hoover had been called before the Senate Committee on Reconstruction and Production to give his ideas on the housing situation. This was in September of 1920. Hoover told the committee that he wanted a federal commission to coordinate the work concerning housing that was now performed by nine agencies. He was also in favor

---

[29] Edith Elmer Wood, "Must Working People Live in Frayed-out Houses?" in *Proceedings of the National Conference of Social Work at the Fiftieth Anniversary Session*, p. 352. Chicago: The University of Chicago Press, 1923.

of diverting the billions of dollars now in deposit in savings institutions and a percentage of the Postal Savings System's millions to home building rather than to commercial purposes. He admitted that there was "no panacea" for this problem. It was necessary "to get to the bottom of the whole matter," "to develop efficiency," and "to eliminate waste."[30]

Hoover was asked by the editor of *Industrial Management*, a technical magazine for engineers, to contribute to a symposium on housing. Mr. Hoover responded with a letter in which he first stated that there was a housing shortage of one million houses. He briefly stated that the war, labor difficulties after the war, increased demand, and high prices were all contributory causes to this great shortage. He urged cooperation of all economic, construction, and materials organizations. His letter ended with these remarks:

> While I am no believer in extending the bureaucratic functions of the government, I am a strong believer in the government intervening to induce active cooperation in the community itself. Furthermore, I believe we must at least examine the question of governmental assistance in credits to home builders on some plan similar to the Farm Loan Board.[31]

In May of 1921 Secretary Hoover appointed seven engineering experts to aid the Commerce Department in overcoming the housing shortage.[32]

Senator William Henry King, Democrat from Utah, asked President Harding in January of 1922 to call a housing conference to deal with the critical problem.[33] Some three weeks later President Harding replied that he would not call a meeting at that time.[34]

---

[30] *New York Times*, September 24, 1920.
[31] *Industrial Management* 60:425, December 1, 1920.
[32] *New York Times*, May 16, 1921.
[33] *Ibid.*, January 28, 1922.
[34] *Ibid.*, February 16, 1922.

While the Federal Government was investigating ways and means to a solution to the housing shortage, a progressive governor of the state of New York was attempting to convince the state legislature of the necessity of enacting a practical housing law. Immediately after he was elected to the office of governor, Alfred E. Smith appointed a Reconstruction Commission which was to investigate what it was necessary to do in the state of New York as a result of the war and the wartime emergencies and economy. A special committee on housing was working under the direction of the commission. This committee was to get the facts for Governor Smith so that he could present a realistic program to the legislature. After getting preliminary reports from the committee Governor Smith asked the legislature to enact some housing legislation during the regular session of 1920. When the legislature failed to enact any law during the regular session, Governor Smith called them into extraordinary session and placed before them a practical program. Smith proposed that all new building would be exempt from local taxation for a period long enough to balance increased postwar costs and thus keep rents low. This was a generous inducement to private enterprise to put money into building and provided governmental aid for the purpose of keeping rents within reach of the lower income groups. The governor wanted to develop further the state land banks, and if necessary have the state purchase the bonds to develop the banks into home-building banks. He went even further in his special message to say that, if voluntary capital was unwilling to do the job, municipalities, through the exercise of their police power, should build or lend money for home building. He remarked that the establishment of a state system of credit might require a constitutional amendment, and that such an amendment would require careful study; but he warned conditions were such that "we must be prepared." Under his proposals housing boards were to be established which would investigate conditions and advise the legislators at the state and municipal levels with regard to housing.[35]

This was the most comprehensive plan set forth at the period, and it brought forth much editorial comment. The *New York Sun* and the *New York Herald* took the conservative position that the laws of supply and demand would work out the problem. They were opposed to Governor Smith's plan. The *Philadelphia Evening Bulletin* took a progressive position, supporting Governor Smith's plan. It observed that the state regulates food and public service by law. Then it went on to declare that a home in which to live was essential to real "living" of the people and that, when the home market became a market of speculation and "profit-grabbing," there was equal reason for the state to interfere, at least to the extent of seeking out possible relief and remedy. The *Saint Louis Globe-Democrat* stated that the provision of adequate housing for the people was a matter of such importance that it should not be left to the unaided law of supply and demand.[36]

These editorial comments show that there was, even then, an inclination in the United States on the part of a number of citizens to accept government aid in solving some of the more acute social and economic problems. The English plan and various European plans were being carefully studied by the new group of "professional housers" that developed from the ranks of the architects, economists, social workers, and public-health officers who had devoted their time and study to a solution of the housing problem.

---

[35] Alfred E. Smith, "A Housing Policy for New York." *Survey* 45:3, October 2, 1920.

[36] All this editorial material is gathered together in "Who Will Build Five Million Homes?" *Literary Digest* 66:17, August 28, 1920. Governor Smith in a conference with Ernest J. Bohn stated that much credit for his housing legislation should go to Belle Lindner (later Belle Moskovitz), a Cleveland-born social worker. She had been an adviser to Smith since she was appointed by Sheriff Smith as the first woman deputy.

It was not, therefore, a total surprise to find the following statement in the report of the Committee on Housing created by the mayor of Milwaukee, because that city and the state of Wisconsin had early achieved a reputation of being "progressive":

> In approaching the housing problem in its broader aspect, we must not fail to appreciate the gradual change in the concept of government which has been manifested so conspicuously in England and on the Continent during the last decade or two and to some degree in this country. Legislation relative to transportation, to land improvement and development, and to public health has expanded the functions of government far beyond the older concepts of government [which concerned themselves largely with restrictive legislation], and has more fully organized nations to achieve prosperity and stability because it has put the welfare of the whole above the welfare of groups or individuals. Without the acceptance of this newer view of the functions of government, housing reform is not possible of accomplishment.[37]

After the war there was a great amount of "rent profiteering." In order to protect tenants and to bring order out of chaos a number of cities passed legislation prescribing maximum rents to be charged and prohibiting landlords from evicting tenants until certain conditions had been fulfilled. Rent laws were first passed in the state of New York during the regular session of the legislature in 1920, but these were temporary and were to run out by October of that year. During the special session called by the governor in September of 1920 more efficient rent laws were enacted, and they were to continue for a period of two years.[38] These laws were soon contested by the real-estate interests, and a great number of cases involving them were brought to the courts during these years.

When one of these cases came before the Supreme Court of the State of New York, Robert F. Wagner was one of the associ-

---

[37] *Report of the Mayor's Committee on Housing, City of Milwaukee*, April 1918.
[38] N. Y. Laws '20 (Reg. Sess.), c. 130-39, 209-19; (Extra. Sess.), c. 942-53.

ate justices hearing the case. He delivered an opinion sustaining
the constitutionality of the laws which forcefully illustrated this
new political philosophy.

> The appalling conditions of family life in certain sections of
> this community have already been the subject of judicial discussion
> and concern. A public menace threatening wholesale evictions has
> been overhanging thousands of tenants in this city; exorbitant and
> extortionate demands for rent had been met with impossibility of
> compliance; the consequent congestion which these conditions lead
> to become perilous to public health, safety and morals. The condi-
> tion was a breeder of discontent, and such a stalker of unrest as
> to become an object of apprehension as to the future good order
> of society. . . . The very reason for the existence of a representative
> government such as ours is the protection of the welfare of the
> people, who form its component parts, and who in fact, constitute
> the state. That philosophy underlies our whole system, as evidenced
> by the avowed intention of its creators at the time of its birth. I
> see no question of public interest superior to that appearing in the
> case at bar. Surely the sovereign people are not helpless in a
> situation fraught with such eminent danger. Government is more
> than an empty form.[39]

The social climate had changed greatly between the year
1873, when the Supreme Court of Massachusetts declared invalid the plan of the city of Boston for loans for housing construction, and the year 1921, when the Supreme Court of New
York declared constitutional a statute limiting rents and the
conditions for the eviction of tenants. Though the issue in the
two cases was not the same, still the important fact to note is
the difference in the fundamental attitude of the court toward
the function of government. The attitude that had been earlier
expressed in Wagner's opinion favoring a "welfare" govern-

---

[39] Quoted by Wagner in a speech at Yorkville, July 16, 1937; in Collected Papers
of Senator Robert F. Wagner (unpublished), Vol. 3, Sec. 3, No. 52, preserved
at Georgetown University, Washington. This opinion not published in *N. Y. S.
Reports.*

ment was the attitude of a fairly large and increasing number of people in 1921.[40]

There were many other citizens and groups of citizens interested in the welfare of the people who did not want the "welfare" activities of the government to change the traditional system to a "socialistic" and "paternalistic" form of government with consequent damage to liberty and infringement upon natural and civil rights.

In the present case the National Association of Real Estate Boards and the building and loan groups were representative of this attitude. The NAREB was opposed to government participation in a public-housing program. This group opposed the continuance of the government corporations in the field of housing after the armistice.[41] They fought the New York rent laws in the courts,[42] and they attempted to demonstrate to the people that laws providing for government housing and rent regulation were unconstitutional.[43] The position that was taken by the NAREB had solid arguments in its favor. As regards the constitutionality of the rent laws, the Supreme Court upheld their constitutionality by a five-to-four decision.[44]

The philosophy of NAREB is that widespread home ownership is necessary for the growth and continued welfare of America. Encouragement should be given to the ideal that each American family should own its own home, this ideal being one of the chief marks distinguishing American society from the social forms of older European countries. The association realized that there were millions of families in the nation that

---

[40] "Property Rights and Human Welfare, A Supreme Court Decision," *Outlook* 128:10, May 4, 1921; "Supreme Court and the Rent Laws," *Review* 4:430, May 7, 1921; Edward L. Schaub, "The Regulation of Rentals during the War Period," *Journal of Political Economy* 28:1, January 1920.

[41] *New York Times*, December 15, 1918.

[42] *Ibid.*, March 10, 1921.

[43] *Ibid.*, April 19, 1921.

[44] *Marcus Brown Holding Company* v. *Feldman*, 256 U. S. 170 (1922).

had incomes so low they could not afford to pay the economic rent for decent housing. Advocates of public housing held that those who were living in substandard conditions could be taken care of only by federal subsidy, and that the only practical and efficient way to take care of them was to provide quarters in new buildings. The real-estate group, on the other hand, felt that it would be extremely dangerous if large segments of the population came to have the government as a landlord, and that the objectives of public housing ran directly counter to the ideal of ultimate home ownership.

For these reasons the real-estate group actively fought any attempt to enact into public policy the philosophy of the public-housing groups. There was also a fundamental difference of opinion between the opposing groups concerning the type of housing to be provided for those who belonged to the lower income brackets. The NAREB felt that housing was of long life and should be used throughout that life by persons in descending income brackets, and that for this reason new housing facilities should not be built for the bottom economic levels of the population.[45]

On this last policy there was a sharp difference of opinion between the opposing groups as to how long a dwelling could decently shelter a family, especially in a society with constantly improving health and sanitary facilities and health and sanitary standards. This difference of opinion was the basis for divergent estimates as to the extent of the housing shortage. In October of 1922 the real-estate groups stated that the housing shortage was ended,[46] but another statement by Mr. Herbert Hoover, then secretary of commerce, announced that there was an existing shortage of one million homes.[47]

---

[45] Statement of Herbert U. Nelson, executive vice-president of NAREB (personal interview).
[46] *New York Times*, October 14, 1922.
[47] *Ibid.*, October 29, 1922.

The real-estate association carried on its own campaign to improve housing in line with its own philosophy. In 1915 the association spearheaded a national campaign for city planning and zoning as a means of protecting housing against blight. In the late 1920's the association started a nationwide movement to reduce interest rates on housing of all types, and NAREB has campaigned for the reduction of the real-estate tax. The association was thus attempting to reduce the costs involved in purchasing or in owning a home.[48]

In the years following World War I the battle for some kind of a permanent housing program administered by the state and federal governments was hard fought, and the real-estate association defeated these early attempts to enact housing legislation. Soon after the war, certainly by 1924, a certain apathy seized the people who formerly were so interested in housing. Discussions about housing were now relegated to technical journals for architects, municipal officials, and social workers. The general public seemed to accept the inevitability of a housing shortage and slums. John Ihlder foresaw this apathy, and in an address before the National Conference of Social Work expressed alarm over the fact that the middle class was willing to accept substandard housing.[49] But despite this apathy on the part of the general public certain definite changes had taken place in the thinking of the people concerning the housing problem. The Federal Government was now considered to have a definite part to play in any kind of program that eventually would be worked out. The experience of the Federal Government in operating war housing projects, brief though it was, and the European governments' experiments in housing (which, incidentally, were financed by American investors who pur-

---

[48] Material pertaining to the policy and program of NAREB was taken from the files of the association in their Chicago offices.

[49] Ihlder, "Extent of the Housing Shortage," p. 331.

chased European municipal bonds) had changed the thinking of a great number of people about the constitutionality of government participation in a housing program.[50]

While practically all the states forgot about the housing problem or gave up any hope of ever solving it, the state of New York under the progressive leadership of Governor Alfred E. Smith continued its efforts to work out an effective and practical solution. In 1926 Governor Smith presented his "annual" housing bill to the legislature.[51] This bill of 1926 was a carefully drafted bill based on the factual situation that was presented to him by the investigating committees of the state legislature. It was the most practical and comprehensive plan that had up to that time been proposed in the United States.[52] Smith began with the principle, "If it doesn't pay private enterprise to build homes for the poor, then the state must step in to aid and encourage building for the lowest income group." It is to be noted that the group here under consideration was unskilled labor, regularly employed. This group was not a pauper group, nor an irresponsible or chronic-relief group. To make his program work Governor Smith set up a state board of housing composed of five members appointed by the governor, who received no salary but did receive actual expenses. This board was to plan and supervise the construction of dwelling units. The actual construction was to be done by limited-dividend corporations. These corporations, composed of at least three

---

[50] "Legal Aspects of the Housing Problem," *Monthly Labor Review* 12:925, May 1921; *Report of the Senate Committee on Reconstruction and Production* (Washington: Government Printing Office, 1919). For comment and discussion of this report see *New York Times*, January 2, 1921; January 16, 1921; and March 28, 1921.

[51] *New York Times*, January 6, 1926.

[52] Alfred E. Smith, "To Stimulate Low-Cost Housing: A Proposal for Limited Dividend Housing Corporations, Aided by Public Credit and with Power of Condemnation," *American City* 34:127, February 1926. This article is a section of Governor Smith's annual message of January 6, 1926.

members, were chartered by the state. The corporation would be able with the specific authorization of the state board to exercise the powers of condemnation. Capital was to be furnished through a state housing bank which was the depository of public funds and which would have power to issue bonds against specific projects of the state board. Dividends were to be limited to 6 per cent; and if the company made enough profit to give a larger dividend, then the rents were to be reduced proportionately to keep the dividend at 6 per cent. Rents were to be limited to a maximum of $12.50 per room per month in New York City, the bathroom not being counted as a room; in other sections of the state rents were to be proportionately lower. The corporation was to be exempt from all state fees and taxation, and it was recommended that municipalities exempt the corporation's property from local taxes.

This financial plan was stricken out of the bill by the legislature, and was replaced with a plan which did not involve the state government in banking activities. The legislature passed the bill with the changed financial plan.[53] New York City under a local law of 1927 provided for tax exemption for a period of twenty years on all buildings approved by the State Board of Housing.[54] Some good work was accomplished under this plan. The Amalgamated Clothing Workers under the leadership of A. E. Kazan formed a housing cooperative and with state aid put up three housing estates totaling 628 living units. The Metropolitan Life Insurance Company put up another project which offered apartments at a rent of $9.00 per room per month. Six other cooperative limited-dividend corporations put up a total of 1,956 living units. The average cost in the various proj-

---

[53] "New York Housing Law," *Monthly Labor Review* 23:77, July 1926; "Housing of the Future: New York Housing Legislation," *Nation* 122:570, May 26, 1926.
[54] Local Law No. 9 of the City of New York, approved by the mayor on June 22, 1927. A copy of the law is printed in the appendix of the *Report of the State Board of Housing of New York*, February 29, 1928.

ects was approximately $11.00 per room per month. This construction increased the supply of dwelling units for people in the middle income bracket, but it did not help the people in the lowest income group, the group that Governor Smith and the other professional housers proposed to help.

Governor Smith's plan drew editorial comment from all parts of the country, both favorable and unfavorable. The *New York Herald Tribune* called it "state paternalism and socialism." The *Rochester Democrat and Chronicle* called it a "housing heresy." The *Spokesman-Review* in Spokane accused the state of New York of "flirting with State landlordism."

The *New York World* agreed with Governor Smith and with the fact of the housing shortage. The *New York Sun* also supported the governor's plan. The *Brooklyn Citizen* stated that the state has no reason for existence unless it seeks the comfort and happiness and well-being of the people. The *New York Times* commented that the United States was far behind Europe in the matter of solving the housing problem.[55]

The president of the Real Estate Board of New York, J. Irving Walsh, told the state that this plan would dampen the efforts of private enterprise in the same direction. He also claimed that "if the Governor's theory is based on a housing shortage, it is at variance with common observation and facts in the case."[56]

The housing program in New York state was getting under way when the economic structure of private enterprise crashed. The United States was plunged into the depression that began in 1929. As times went from bad to worse in the dark days of 1930 and 1931, the building-trades industry was at a standstill. Millions of workers were unemployed. The housing shortage

---

[55] All this editorial material is presented in "Shall the State Help Build Homes?" *Literary Digest* 88:5, January 30, 1926.

[56] *Ibid.* See also "Paternalism or Slums?" *New Republic* 45:230, January 20, 1926.

became even more critical as all housing construction stopped; the slums got worse, mortgages were in default. The seriousness of the situation demanded action.

The President's Conference on Home Building and Home Ownership was held in Washington during 1931. It was a privately financed conference, but it had the official sanction of President Hoover. Some 3,700 experts in all phases of housing came to Washington to contribute their knowledge and experience toward a solution of the problem.[57]

After months of work eleven volumes of reports were prepared for publication. The most important and immediate result of the conference was its endorsement of President Hoover's recommendation for a system of home-loan discount banks. This was a plan that the president had been thinking about for almost twelve years. It was the basis for the legislation providing for the Federal Home Loan Bank Act of July 22, 1932.[58]

For the purposes of this study Publication No. 3, containing a series of reports entitled "Blighted Areas and Slums," "Large-Scale Housing Operations," "Business and Housing," and "Industrial Decentralization," is of interest and importance. Dr. Ray Lyman Wilbur, secretary of commerce and chairman of the conference, stated in the introduction to this volume that the primary responsibility for producing a remedy to the deplorable slums rested with American citizens—businessmen and men of industry. He further declared that there was need of enabling legislation providing for condemnation for slum clearance and for adequate capital for limited-dividend corporations. Dr. Wilbur then warned that, if private business and industrial and financial groups failed to remedy the evil, American cities would be forced to adopt the measures of the European coun-

---

[57] James Ford, "The President's Conference on Home Building and Home Ownership." *Journal of Home Economics* 23:924, October 1931.

[58] 47 Stat. 725 (1932).

tries and to remedy the evil through governmental ownership and actual management of housing.[59]

All the possible solutions for the problem, ranging from complete governmental control to complete private financing of large-scale housing, were discussed at some length in the report. No specific and generally accepted recommendation was given by the conference. Each of the experts was left free to submit his own report.

The last attempt of the Hoover administration to deal with the stagnation of the building industries and the housing shortage, and directly in line with the recommendations of Chairman Wilbur, was the provision in the Emergency Relief and Construction Act of 1932 which authorized the Reconstruction Finance Corporation to make loans to corporations formed for the purpose of providing housing for families of low income or for the reconstruction of slum areas. These corporations were to be subject to state and municipal laws as to rents, charges, capital structures, and rate of return. The loans were to be for self-liquidating projects.[60] President Hoover personally framed the original draft of the paragraph that made this radical change in government's attitude toward housing.[61]

On July 21, 1932, when this act became law, the New York State Board of Housing was the only agency fulfilling the conditions of the law.[62] Under the provisions of this plan, which demanded a substantial amount of private capital, only one

---

[59] John M. Gries and James Ford, editors, *Slums, Large-Scale Housing and Decentralization* (President's Conference on Home Building and Home Ownership Publication No. 3), pp. xi, xii. Washington: President's Conference, 1932.

[60] 47 Stat. 709 (1932); "Federal Aid Now Offered for Low-Cost Housing and Slum-Clearance Projects," *American City* 47:82, August 1932.

[61] James Ford, "Housing"; in *Social Work Yearbook, 1935*, edited by Fred S. Hall, p. 188. New York: Russell Sage Foundation, 1935.

[62] "New York's Law, the Only One under Which R.F.C. Aid Can Be Had, Fits Only New York Conditions. . . ." *Business Week*, No. 172, December 21, 1932, p. 18.

urban project was developed. It was the Knickerbocker Village in New York City. Knickerbocker Village received a loan of $8,059,000 from the Reconstruction Finance Corporation. It also received tax exemptions from the city of New York under the 1927 law, the only project to receive tax exemption under that law. The completed project comprised 1,593 apartments containing 6,030 rooms. The average rental per room per month was $12.50. The only other housing loan given by the Reconstruction Finance Corporation was for $155,000 to finance rural farm homes in Ford County, Kansas.[63]

---

[63] James Ford and others, *Slums and Housing*, Vol. 2, p. 727. Cambridge: Harvard University Press, 1936.

CHAPTER II

The New Deal
and the Housing Problem

During June of 1933, when the Democratic party leaders were holding special night meetings to work into shape their National Industrial Recovery Act, two influential and respected civic leaders paid a visit to a special caucus of Democratic congressional leaders and presented to the group a plan that would permit the building of dwellings as a part of the public-works program. These two "professional housers" were Mrs. Mary Kingsbury Simkhovitch, director of Greenwich House of New York City, and Father John O'Grady, secretary of the National Conference of Catholic Charities with offices in Washington. More details on the activities of Mrs. Simkhovitch will be given later in the chapter dealing with pressure groups. Mrs. Simkhovitch had prepared her plan in New York; and when she arrived in Washington, she asked Father O'Grady to accompany her and add his support to the proposal.[1]

The proposal was formally submitted to Senator Wagner, who took the appropriate measures and worked out the provision for including housing in the public-works program.[2] The

---

[1] Statement of Father John O'Grady (personal interview).

[2] Statement of Leon Keyserling, legislative assistant to Senator Wagner at the time this legislation was drafted (personal interview).

section as it was finally adopted contained the following provisions pertinent to an over-all economy:

TITLE II

Sec. 202   The Administrator, under the direction of the President, shall prepare a comprehensive program of public works,
which shall include among other things: . . . the following: . . .

(3) construction, reconstruction, alteration, or repair under
public regulation or control of low-cost housing and slum-clearance projects; . . .

Sec. 203   (a) With a view to increasing employment quickly
(while reasonably securing any loans made by the United States)
the President is authorized and empowered, through the Administrator or through such other agencies as he may designate or create,
(1) to construct, finance, or aid in the construction or financing
of any public-work project included in the program prepared pursuant to section 202; (2) upon such terms as the President shall
prescribe, to make grants to States, municipalities, or other public
bodies for the construction, repair, or improvement of any such
project, but no such grant shall be in excess of 30 per centum of
the cost of the labor and materials employed upon such project;
(3) to acquire by purchase, or by the exercise of the power of eminent domain, any real or personal property in connection with the
construction of any such project, and to sell any security acquired
or any property so constructed or acquired or to lease any such
property with or without the privilege of purchase: *Provided,* That
all moneys received from any such sale or lease or the repayment
of any such loan shall be used to retire obligations issued pursuant
to section 209 of this Act, in addition to any other moneys required
to be used for such purpose; . . . The provisions of this section
and section 202 shall extend to public works in the several States,
Hawaii, Alaska, the District of Columbia, Puerto Rico, the Canal
Zone, and the Virgin Islands.[3]

When these sections of the bill were being debated in the
Senate, seated in the gallery was a labor leader from Philadelphia, John Edelman of the American Federation of Hosiery

---

[3] 48 Stat. 195 (1933). See also "Housing Features of the National Industrial Recovery Act," *American City* 48:5, July 1933.

Workers. Edelman was in Washington to see how things were progressing with regard to the labor provisions of the NIRA. He was quite surprised to hear this unexpected provision of funds for a housing program, for it was good news to the hosiery workers, who were then interested in a housing project.[4]

The story of the hosiery workers' plans for a housing program began one Sunday afternoon when a group of trade-unionists were gathered at a picnic for the purpose of discussing the possibility of setting up a trade-union party. During the course of the afternoon there was consideration of the Full Fashion Hosiery Workers and their policies, problems, and grievances. This union had the best-organized and highest-paid members in the area. They had quite a grievance about the housing situation. Just before the depression the union as a group had accepted the slogan, "Buy your own home!" The workers had in numerous cases purchased their homes without sufficient equity, and so they were carrying heavy mortgages. When the depression came these workers suffered serious losses: mortgages were foreclosed; they lost everything, even their furniture; and they could not buy another home according to the then-existing law in Pennsylvania. Hence the workers in this group were more vocal than those of other groups. They had had a taste of decent living, and they refused to live contented in the slums. They had heard of the Amalgamated Clothing Workers' Project in New York, and they talked about a housing project for themselves. An architect named Oscar Stonorov, who had seen what the workers had done in Europe, encouraged this group to start their own housing project.

Dr. Susan Kingsbury, at nearby Bryn Mawr College, conducted a housing survey of the Full Fashion Hosiery Workers

---

[4] Statement of John Edelman (personal interview). The details of the Hosiery Workers' Housing Project outlined in this chapter were all given by Mr. Edelman unless otherwise stated.

group. It was probably the first complete scientific survey of the housing needs of a definite group of individuals. When this study was completed the union had a statistical report of just what it was that they needed in the way of housing facilities, and they were told in what area the project should be located in relation to their place of work.

Governor Gifford Pinchot was supported in his campaign for office by the union. He and his wife were sincerely interested in the welfare of the workers. Through their efforts a bill was introduced in the Pennsylvania legislature to provide for aid for limited-dividend housing corporations. This bill, unfortunately, failed to pass. As a result the hosiery workers' plans for a housing project were at a standstill in mid-1933.

This was the situation when John Edelman was sitting in the Senate gallery. When he heard the NIRA provisions for housing, he returned to Philadelphia and spoke with the architect and Michael Francis Doyle, the attorney for the union, about the possibility of the hosiery workers' making application for a housing loan under the provisions of the new bill, presupposing its passage.

Doyle drafted a corporation charter. The firm of Stonorov and Kastner was employed to prepare blueprints for the housing project. The corporation was to be called the Juniata Park Housing Corporation, and the project was to be named the Carl Mackley Houses in honor of a union worker killed in a strike. Edelman and Stonorov contacted Mr. Robert D. Kohn, the newly appointed director of the Housing Division of the Public Works Administration, and explained to him their plans. When they left his office in Washington, they had his promise for a loan of $1,000,000.

The hosiery workers, therefore, were the first corporation to get a loan of money under the provisions of NIRA, and their project is officially listed in the PWA Housing Division files as Docket H-1.

Doyle had bought up mortgages on land in South Philadelphia, but according to Dr. Kingsbury's study the best location for the housing project was in North Philadelphia. Doyle therefore arranged to trade the South Philadelphia parcels for a section of land in North Philadelphia. There was only one hitch, and that was $17,000 in back taxes on the land in South Philadelphia. The union officials talked with William Jeanes, a graduate engineer and a member of a wealthy Philadelphia Quaker family who was doing volunteer housing work during the depression. Jeanes persuaded his family to advance $17,000 for the taxes. With this help the way was clear for the project to begin. The building trades of Philadelphia, under the leadership of James McDevitt, became very interested in the project. McDevitt for the building trades and the Housing Corporation signed a no-strike agreement for this construction job. This was the first such agreement on record, and it made labor history.[5]

As the work on the project progressed and word of this new cooperative enterprise spread to labor groups throughout the country, hundreds of requests for information came into the Housing Corporation office. There was such an intense interest in this housing project on the part of labor groups that John Edelman and John Phillips of the Pennsylvania State Federation of Labor decided that the formation of a labor housing conference was both necessary and opportune.[6] The place of this conference in the campaign for housing will be described in the next chapter.

The day that the NIRA became law (June 16, 1933) President Roosevelt appointed Colonel Donald Sawyer temporary administrator of the Federal Emergency Administration of Public Works, which was the agency created to carry out the public-

---

[5] Statement of James McDevitt (personal interview).

[6] Statements of Catherine Bauer, John Edelman, and James McDevitt (personal interviews).

works program set forth in the NIRA.[7] On June 23 a housing division was organized to carry out the program provided for by Title II, Section 202 (d), of NIRA.[8] Robert D. Kohn, an eminent architect during World War I who had been associated with the United States Housing Corporation, was appointed director of the Housing Division of FEA of PW on July 8, 1933.[9] Kohn immediately set to work to get a housing program under way. In addition to the new applications for loans, such as the one from the American Federation of Hosiery Workers, the Housing Division received all the applications for loans made to the Reconstruction Finance Corporation.

During the months from July of 1933 to February of 1934 over five hundred applications for limited-dividend loans totaling $1,005,461,630 had been received and reported on. Twenty-one projects involving loans of $50,450,100 received favorable recommendations, but only seven, amounting to a total cost of $10,971,600, ever became projects.[10]

The first loan, for $1,039,000, was made to the Juniata Park Housing Corporation (American Federation of Hosiery Workers) for the Carl Mackley Houses. It was listed as Docket H-1, August 17, 1933. The complete list of projects constructed by limited-dividend corporations under the provisions of NIRA is given in Table 1 on page 35. The reason why only seven of twenty-one approved projects were actually constructed was the

---

[7] Executive Order No. 6174, June 16, 1933; in *Presidential Executive Orders*, edited by Clifford L. Lord, p. 512. New York: Books, 1944.

[8] Harold L. Ickes, "Report on Activities of Housing, Division of F.E.A. of P.W." (report submitted to Senate Committee on Banking and Currency, April 14, 1937); in *Hearings before Senate Committee on Education and Labor on S. 1685*, 75th Cong., 1st Sess. (1937), p. 21. Washington: Government Printing Office, 1937.

[9] Executive Order No. 6198, July 8, 1933; in Lord, *Presidential Executive Orders*, p. 515.

[10] Ickes, "Report on Activities of Housing Division"; in *Hearings on S. 1685*, pp. 21, 28.

TABLE 1

Statistics on Limited-Dividend Housing Projects

Project	Number	Units	Rent	Rentals Include	Allotment
Boulevard Gardens Woodside, L. I., N. Y.	H-F (R-266)	967 in apts.	$11 per room per month	Equipment: but gas, electricity, paid for by tenant	$3,071,000
Boylan Housing Corp. Raleigh, N. C.	H-29	54 in apts.	$11 per room per month	Equipment: but gas, electricity, paid for by tenant	$ 198,600
Euclid Housing Corp. Euclid, Ohio	H-L (R-610)	100 row houses	For sale		$ 500,000
Alta Vista Alta Vista, Va.	H-278	50 row houses	$3.73	No equipment: only water, heat, shelter	$ 84,000
Hillside Homes New York City	H-J (R-262)	1,416 in apts.	$11 per room per month	Equipment: but gas, electricity, paid for by tenant	$5,060,000
Carl Mackley Houses Philadelphia, Pa.	H-1	284 in apts.	$9.50	Range only: tenant pays for gas, etc.	$1,039,000
Neighborhood Gardens St. Louis, Mo.	H-37	252 in apts.	$8.92	Equipment: but gas, electricity, paid for by tenant	$ 640,000

Source: Ickes, "Report on Activities of Housing Division"; in *Hearings on S. 1685*, pp. 28, 29.

lack of equity on the party of the limited-dividend corporations. The reason why only 21 applications out of a total of 531 were approved was a lack of stipulated equity at the time that the loan was requested, or the fact that the loan was requested for a project that was a commercial venture, such as a hotel or store, rather than a housing project.[11]

In February of 1934 Mr. Ickes, the administrator of FEA of PW, decided to abandon the program of loans to limited-dividend corporations because he considered it an unsatisfactory means of providing low-rent housing.[12] The administrator decided to concentrate on the direct federal construction of housing, pending the enactment of adequate state legislation. After consultation with Kohn, Ickes decided that the corporation system was the most efficient way to administer the new program. On October 28, 1933 the Public Works Emergency Housing Corporation filed application for a certificate of incorporation in the state of Delaware.[13] President Roosevelt allocated $100,000,000 to the Housing Corporation and by executive order of November 29, 1933 designated and established the Public Works Emergency Housing Corporation as the agency through which the federal housing projects were to be constructed.[14]

As there was no state or municipality in 1933 which had legal authority to engage in slum clearance or low-rent housing construction, Mr. Ickes had elaborate plans for his new housing corporation. Ickes was ready to start the construction of large-scale housing on a nationwide basis; but he had not reckoned with Comptroller-General John Raymond McCarl.

---

[11] *Ibid.*, p. 21.

[12] *Ibid.*

[13] Harold Robinson, "Some Problems Confronting the Public Works Emergency Housing Corporation." *Cornell Law Quarterly* 19:548, June 1934.

[14] Executive Order No. 6470, November 29, 1933; in Lord, *Presidential Executive Orders*, p. 538.

On January 11, 1934, when Mr. Ickes tried to draw some funds from the $100,000,000 allocated to the Housing Corporation, McCarl refused to countersign money to the corporation. The comptroller-general considered that this administrative organization was unconstitutional.[15]

No one in the Housing Division of FEA of PW knew just what to do. At first there seemed to be some hope of getting the comptroller-general to change his mind because on February 19, 1934 Colonel Horatio Hackett was appointed general manager of the Housing Corporation.[16] A short time later, however, President Roosevelt had some meetings with various officials concerned with public works, and on April 12, 1934 he approved a resolution calling for an alternate system. Funds for federal projects were allocated "for construction by the President through such other agencies as he may designate or create, including the Public Works Emergency Housing Corporation, for five cities: Atlanta, Georgia (two projects); Cincinnati; Cleveland (two projects); Indianapolis; and Milwaukee."[17] These were the first projects approved for construction by the Federal Government. This was direct construction by the Federal Government, and is to be distinguished from the limited-dividend projects which were constructed with government loans by private corporations. The Housing Division of FEA of PW began to expand. On June 15, 1934 Horatio Hackett replaced Robert Kohn as director of the Housing Division. The division was reorganized and the increase of personnel commenced.[18] The Housing Corporation was inactive. After the legal difficul-

---

[15] *New York Times*, January 12, 1934; Robinson, "Some Problems Confronting the P.W.E. Housing Corporation," p. 548.

[16] Harold Ickes, "Final Report of the Housing Division of F.E.A. of P.W., 1937" (mimeographed), Vinton Papers, Washington.

[17] *Ibid.*

[18] Ickes, "Report on Activities of Housing Division"; in *Hearings on S. 1685*, p. 22.

ties that are to be described in the following paragraphs, the corporation was to be abandoned, and finally dissolved on August 14, 1935.[19]

In July 1934 the Housing Division of FEA of PW was condemning land for a slum-clearance project at Cedar and Central avenues in Cleveland. When the owners of a small parcel of land necessary for the completion of the site refused to sell at a negotiated price, condemnation proceedings were instituted under Section 203 (a) of the NIRA and Executive Order No. 6252. The case was brought to court and the decision was rendered in favor of the United States. It had been the contention of the property owners that this action was not condemnation for "public use" and that the United States was not a proper and legal party to the suit, which party should be the Public Works Emergency Housing Corporation. Counsel for the property owners stated:

> That there is no authority in the United States of America as such to acquire this property as public property under which it should be taken off the tax duplicate of the city of Cleveland, to the detriment of all other property in the city and county and state, but that the same should be acquired in the name of the Public Works Emergency Housing Corporation.[20]

The first question in the Cleveland case concerned the authority of the Federal Government to operate a housing program. The point at issue was whether slum clearance and low-rent housing construction were operations for a "public use" for which federal funds could be spent and land condemned. This question was by-passed in the opinion of the court in the Cleveland case, but it was to be directly decided in another case some months later.[21]

---

[19] *Ibid.*, p. 21.

[20] Quoted in William Ebenstein, *The Law of Public Housing*, p. 28. Madison: The University of Wisconsin Press, 1940.

[21] The Louisville case, discussed later in this chapter (p. 45).

The policy of the Housing Division of loaning money to limited-dividend corporations and exercising a general control as to construction costs and rent in the projects was a partial solution to the legal problem; but both PWA Housing Division[22] and the general public were not satisfied with this arrangement. Moreover, the limited-dividend corporations themselves did not entirely approve of the financial arrangements of the program. They found it too difficult to raise 30 per cent of the total cost, and they also found the interest rates too high and the amortization period too short.[23]

In addition to these legal difficulties the housing program had other problems. The hope that some housing authorities entertained, that by building for the middle income group this group would be able to move to the new dwelling units and thus open up vacancies in decent dwelling units for the lowest income group, was not fulfilled.[24] The middle income group was living in substandard quarters, or families in this group were "doubled up," and the housing shortage was so great that vacancies opened up by newly constructed units failed either to fill the current demand or to relieve the shortage that had developed over the past years. Another difficulty was that the people in the lowest income group were not getting the housing that certain federal and state officials announced was being constructed for them. As a consequence they and their representatives in Congress were dissatisfied with the program.

Another difficulty that made the Housing Division skeptical about its limited-dividend program was the danger that it might

---

22 Hereafter the Housing Division of the Federal Emergency Administration of Public Works will be referred to as Housing Division of PWA or PWA Housing Division.

23 Flo Pryor, "Housing and the Hosiery Workers." *American Federationist* 42:734, July 1935.

24 Edith Elmer Wood, "Is Government Aid Necessary in the Financing of Low-Cost Housing?" *American City* 40:99, March 1929.

be used by certain new corporations whose main desire was to saddle the government with land and unprofitable ventures by exaggeration of their equity value.[25]

During the summer of 1934, on June 27, the National Housing Act became law.[26] It created the Federal Housing Administration, which was a government mortgage-insurance agency. Most of the provisions of the act were concerned with the financing of private homes and with insurance for the mortgages on private homes, but there was one provision in the new law that was definitely concerned with public housing. Little notice was taken of this section at the time, and little use was made of its provisions.

TITLE II
MUTUAL MORTGAGE INSURANCE
Sec. 207 Low Cost Housing Insurance

The Administrator may also insure first mortgages, other than mortgages defined in section 201 (a) of this title, covering property held by Federal or State instrumentalities, private limited dividend corporations, or municipal corporation instrumentalities of one or more States, formed for the purpose of providing housing for persons of low income which are regulated or restricted by law or by the Administrator as to rents, charges, capital structure, rate of return, or methods of operation. Such mortgages shall contain terms, conditions, and provisions satisfactory to the Administrator but need not conform to the eligibility requirements of section 203. Subject to the right of the Administrator to impose a premium charge in excess of, or less than, the amount specified for mortgages defined in section 201 (a), the provisions of sections 204 and 205 shall be applicable to mortgages insured under this section: *Provided,* that the insurance with respect to any low-cost housing project shall not exceed $10,000,000.[27]

---

[25] Statement of David Krooth, at the time (1935-1937) a member of the legal staff of PWA (personal interview).

[26] 48 Stat. 1246 (1934).

[27] *Ibid.* This section was included in the bill because of the efforts of the National Public Housing Conference.

Actually, the provisions of this section were not used to construct housing for those in the low income group, but the administrator of the FHA program and other officials in the executive branch of the government favored this type of program for aiding the lowest income group over the type of program that Ickes was administering.[28] More of this fight within the president's Cabinet for control of housing was to come into the open as time passed. It was to flare into a public fight when Wagner's bill came up later for official consideration.

After the summer of 1934 the Federal Government entered into the third phase of a public-housing program. The Housing Division undertook to encourage the states and municipalities to set up housing authorities so that they would be eligible to take advantage of the loans and capital grants offered to them by the housing provisions of NIRA.

In December of 1934 President Roosevelt wrote to the governor of every state (at this date, New York, Ohio, Illinois, Michigan, and Kentucky had already enacted legislation) suggesting the enactment of state legislation that would facilitate the prompt consideration of public works to relieve unemployment, and also to provide an effective method of undertaking locally a low-rent housing program.

Administrator Ickes, who was instrumental in getting the president to write this request to the governors, set up machinery to help the state legislators. The legal staff of PWA drafted a model housing-authority law and a model housing-corporation law. Whenever state legislatures convened in session after De-

---

[28] James A. Moffett, "Back to Prosperity with Housing," *Scientific American* 152:234, 292, May, June 1935. See also a series of four articles in *Literary Digest* on NHA and FHA and Administrator Moffett's program by Wayne W. Parrish: "New Deal's Far-Reaching Housing Program," *Literary Digest* 118:4, July 14, 1934; "A Real New Deal for the Home Owner," *Literary Digest* 118:6, July 21, 1934; "Housing Campaign Moves into High Gear," *Literary Digest* 118:8, July 28, 1934; "Housing Program Faces Serious Obstacles," *Literary Digest* 118:28, August 4, 1934.

cember of 1934, PWA submitted to the governors drafts of such housing legislation as was needed in the states so that there would exist state and/or local public bodies authorized to construct housing projects.[29]

The necessity of so much encouragement and pressure on the state governments by the federal agencies demonstrates an important feature in the history of housing legislation in the United States. The movement was not a mass movement, a so-called grass-roots movement. Despite the fact that shortage of dwelling units was a local problem, and that the slums were under local jurisdiction and were the source of many local problems both economic and social, it was necessary for the Federal Government, which was primarily interested in public works to relieve unemployment, to bring pressure to bear upon the state legislatures to get some action with regard to housing legislation. It is true that the National Association of Housing Officials (NAHO), located in Chicago, was rendering local officials a service of technical assistance in law drafting. It is also true that there were housing groups in New York and Ohio that were interested in setting up local housing bodies, but these groups were small and select. They could not be said to constitute a mass or grass-roots movement in favor of public housing. There is a statement attributed to the pioneer houser, Ernest J. Bohn, who is said to have remarked: "If we wanted to have a convention of all those working for public housing in 1934, we could have held it in a telephone booth."[30]

Although the federal housing program at this time (December 1934) was centralized at Washington, and although the Housing Division of PWA was undertaking a direct program of federal construction that would involve fifty projects by

---

[29] Statement of David Krooth (personal interview). Copies of these model laws are in the files of the PWA Housing Division, now preserved by the Legal Division of the Public Housing Administration.

[30] Statement of Warren Vinton (personal interview).

November of 1935, still the legal division of PWA was working for a local program with federal participation in the form of loans and grants. Despite this change of policy the program still had to be carried on as a direct one because of the absence in most states of legislation creating housing authorities and because of the restrictions and limitations in the various state constitutions regarding indebtedness by the state or its political subdivisions. The desire on the part of the legal division of PWA to discontinue such a direct federal program was based mainly upon a fear that the federal courts would rule adversely against the authority of the Federal Government to operate such programs under the law as a "public use" of land and tax money.[31] This would bring all types of housing-construction programs under the suspicion of being unconstitutional. Thus all types of programs would be blocked.

At the end of 1934 only seven states had passed legislation which provided for housing authorities: New York, Ohio, Michigan, Kentucky, West Virginia, South Carolina, and Illinois. Authorities were actually in existence in certain cities of only four of these states: New York City and Schenectady in New York; Cleveland, Toledo, Columbus, Dayton, and Youngstown in Ohio; Detroit in Michigan; and Columbia in South Carolina.[32]

To increase its effectiveness in cities that did not have a housing authority, the PWA Housing Division had appointed advisory committees of interested citizens and local officials. Such committees had been named in Richmond, Atlanta, Birmingham, Indianapolis, Miami, Louisville, Milwaukee, Montgomery, Nashville, New Orleans, Philadelphia, and Chicago. The PWA Housing Division hoped that these committees would evolve into authorized and legally constituted authorities.[33]

---

[31] Statement of David Krooth (personal interview).
[32] *National Municipal Review* 24:45, January 1935.
[33] *Ibid.*

During late 1934 and 1935, while the Federal Government
was committed to a program of direct construction and management of public-housing projects, the legal division of PWA was
attempting to work out a series of relationships with the state
and municipal governments so that operations could be undertaken on the cooperative basis provided for in the sections of
the NIRA. On September 3, 1934 Administrator Ickes wrote to
Mayor La Guardia of New York and outlined what seemed to
the PWA Housing Division to be a proper set of relations between New York City and the Housing Division of PWA.[34] The
general plan was to be one equitable to both the Federal Government and the city, and providing for low-cost housing that
would be both socially desirable and economically sound.

In order to carry out this general plan each particular housing plan was first to be approved by the PWA Housing Division,
and then to be under the joint supervision of PWA Housing
Division and the local housing authority in a manner satisfactory to the PWA Housing Division. The Federal Government
was to acquire the land necessary for the projects and lease it
to the municipal housing authorities. Loans and grants were to
be advanced to the authority by the PWA Housing Division for
projects and improvements on agreed terms until the authority
was able and willing to assume full financial responsibility and
control. The city was to put into the housing projects various
assets for equity, such as city-owned property, and it was to
maintain adequate schools, sewers, and ordinary municipal
services. The city was to advance sufficient cash for administrative costs of its housing authority. Certain tax exemptions were
to be authorized.

Involved in the PWA housing program to be undertaken
by PWA Housing Division and New York City were two projects already proposed and the expenditure of some $25,000,000

---

[34] *New York Times*, September 3, 1934.

allocated for New York City by the PWA. With all this money involved, Mr. Ickes could afford to lay down the conditions to the mayor of New York City. Mayor La Guardia replied in a letter of September 11 that the conditions proposed by the administrator were satisfactory with the single exception of a tax exemption. Mayor La Guardia informed Mr. Ickes that some legal restrictions concerned with the status of the Water Department would prevent a water-tax exemption.[35]

In January of 1935 the federal program of public housing, so far as it concerned the federal condemnation and ownership of land, was contested in the federal courts, and such ownership and condemnation were declared by the court to be unconstitutional. The case in question is known as the Louisville case. The Federal Government was engaged in slum clearance and low-rent housing in Louisville, Kentucky. Much of the land for the project had already been obtained by purchase from the owners, but there were certain parcels of land in the proposed site that the owners refused to sell. The Housing Division of PWA instituted condemnation proceedings, and the case was tried before the District Court with a decision adverse to the Federal Government.[36] The case was appealed by the government and was tried before the United States Circuit Court of Appeals, Sixth Circuit, with a decision by a divided court upholding the lower courts rendered on July 15, 1935.

The line of argumentation in the opinion of the court contained the following principles: the national government possesses eminent domain as an attribute of sovereignty; eminent domain can be exercised where property is taken for a public use; the article of the Constitution empowering Congress to lay and collect taxes, pay debts, and provide for the defense and

---

[35] *Ibid.*, September 11, 1934.
[36] *United States* v. *Certain Lands in City of Louisville, Jefferson County, Ky. et al.,* 78 F. (2d) 684 (1935).

general welfare is held not to authorize an act for the condemnation of private property for low-cost housing and slum-clearance projects; public use as applied to the Federal Government's power of eminent domain is not susceptible of precise definition, but it includes property needed for use by the public through its officers and agents in the performance of their governmental duties; a decision dealing with condemnation proceedings must be considered in the light of the powers possessed by the sovereign seeking to exercise that right, since what is "public use" under one sovereign may not be "public use" under another sovereign; the state and the Federal Government are distinct sovereignties, each independent of the other and each restricted to its own sphere, and neither can invade or usurp the rightful powers or authority of the other; in the exercise of its police power a state may do those things which benefit the health, morals, and welfare of its people, but the Federal Government has no such power with the states; therefore the NIRA, insofar as it attempts to authorize the national government to condemn private property for low-cost housing and slum-clearance projects and for the purpose of reducing unemployment, is held unconstitutional, since such use is not a "public use."[37] The ruling of the Court of Appeals in the Louisville case was subsequently adopted by the United States District Court of the Eastern District of Michigan in the case of the *United States* v. *Certain Lands in the City of Detroit,* when it was decided on October 23, 1935.[38]

These decisions, however, did not scuttle the federal housing program. Immediately after the Louisville decision Administrator Ickes made a statement to the press in which he stated that the federal program would continue along lines which

---

[37] *United States* v. *Certain Lands in City of Louisville, Jefferson County, Ky. et al.,* 9 F. Supp. 137 (1935).

[38] *United States* v. *Certain Lands in the City of Detroit,* 12 F. Supp. 345 (1935).

would be in accordance with the restrictions imposed by the decision. Further, the United States appealed the decision to the United States Supreme Court, and the case was assigned to be argued on March 5, 1936.

Three possible plans of action were open to the Housing Division of PWA after the Louisville decision. The first plan was to get housing legislation enacted in the states whereby the Federal Government would be given the right to institute condemnation proceedings. This plan was carried out in those states where such legislation had been enacted, notably New York. A second plan open to the Federal Government was to purchase the land by negotiated sale and agreement without condemnation. Of the fifty federal projects developed by the PWA Housing Division, the land sites for forty-one were obtained by this method. A third plan, which was never used, was to condemn land by virtue of a special state statute which would empower the Federal Government to condemn land for public-works projects and low-cost housing and slum-clearance projects.

The housing groups had an entirely different solution to the problem. Their idea was to enact a new federal housing law which would leave construction to the local authorities and financing to the Federal Government. It would be a permanent long-range program authorized by substantive law and not part of a public-works effort.

The Housing Division of PWA and all those interested in public housing were given assurance that the public-housing program was legally possible within the framework of existing state legislation by the pioneering decision of the court in the case of *New York City Housing Authority* v. *Muller*. This decision upheld low-cost housing and slum clearance as "public uses" for which the state or an authority created by the state could exercise the right of eminent domain.[39]

---

[39] *New York City Housing Authority* v. *Muller*, 279 N. Y. S. 299 (1935).

This decision was rendered on April 12, 1935, shortly after the decision of the lower court in the Louisville case. Had this decision of the New York Supreme Court been adverse, it is questionable whether any kind of a large-scale housing program would have been legally possible for the state or any authority created by it. Since the federal program, insofar as it involved the power of the Federal Government to condemn land by right of eminent domain, had already been declared unconstitutional, the whole program would have depended on a decision of the Supreme Court of the United States. No one knows how that body would have decided the issue.

After the New York decision the PWA Housing Division was confident that public housing and slum clearance were legally possible, and the division went ahead with its contemplated program. By November of 1935 fifty-one projects were authorized. This comprises the complete number of projects developed by the PWA Housing Division under the provisions of the National Industrial Recovery Act and the Emergency Relief Appropriations Act of 1935, which appropriated $450,000,000 for housing.[40]

This was the first attempt of the New Deal to solve the housing problem. This so-called "demonstration project" program had a very definite influence on future legislation. Those who were soon to draft the first real public-housing bills had the experience, the successes and the failures, of the Housing Division to guide them. They had court decisions which helped them to work out a constitutional relationship between the Federal Government and the state and local governments. But, most important of all, they had the reactions of the people. They could judge what type of program the people would support. They could see the type of program that the opponents of public housing would fight. For though it is true that the people do

---

[40] 49 Stat. 115 (1935).

TABLE 2

Federal Projects Approved 1936-1937

Location	Number of Living Units	Apartments, Flats, Row Houses	Allotment as of March 15, 1937
Atlanta, Ga.	718	Apartments and row houses	$2,968,500.00
Atlanta, Ga.	675	Flats and row houses	2,592,000.00
Atlantic City, N. J.	277	Flats and row houses	1,550,000.00
Birmingham, Ala.	544	Row houses	2,500,000.00
Boston, Mass.	1,016	Apartments and row houses	6,636,000.00
Buffalo, N. Y.	658	Apartments, flats, and row houses	4,855,000.00
Cambridge, Mass.	294	Apartments	2,500,000.00
Camden, N. J.	515	Apartments	3,176,160.50
Charleston, S. C.	212	Row houses	1,350,000.00
Chicago, Ill.	723	Apartments	5,119,000.00
Chicago, Ill.		(Land acquisition)	2,180,000.00
Chicago, Ill.	304	Apartments and row houses	1,800,000.00
Chicago, Ill.	925	Apartments, flats, and row houses	5,942,000.00
Chicago, Ill.	462	Apartments, flats, and row houses	3,038,000.00
Cincinnati, Ohio	1,039	Apartments	7,086,000.00
Cincinnati, Ohio	650	Apartments	3,384,000.00
Cincinnati, Ohio	579	Apartments, flats, and row houses	3,564,000.00
Cincinnati, Ohio	620	Apartments and row houses	3,800,000.00
Columbia, S. C.	122	Apartments, flats, and row houses	706,000.00
Dallas, Tex.	181	Apartments, flats, and row houses	1,020,000.00
Detroit, Mich.	699	Apartments, flats, and row houses	5,200,000.00
Detroit, Mich.	779	Apartments, flats, and row houses	4,500,000.00
Enid, Okla.	80	Row houses	557,100.00
Evansville, Ind.	191	Flats and row houses	1,000,000.00
Indianapolis, Ind.	748	Apartments and row houses	3,207,000.00
Jacksonville, Fla.	215	Row houses	1,000,000.00
Lackawanna, N. Y.	268	Row houses	1,500,000.00
Lexington, Ky.	286	Row houses	1,704,000.00
Louisville, Ky.	210	Row houses	1,370,000.00
Louisville, Ky.	125	Flats and row houses	758,000.00
Memphis, Tenn.	633	Flats and row houses	3,400,000.00
Memphis, Tenn.	449	Apartments and row houses	3,128,000.00
Miami, Fla.	243	Row houses	969,880.00
Milwaukee, Wis.	518	Apartments and row houses	2,600,000.00
Minneapolis, Minn.	451	Apartments, flats, and row houses	3,500,000.00
Montgomery, Ala.	100	Row houses	403,000.00
Montgomery, Ala.	156	Row houses	522,000.00
Nashville, Tenn.	314	Row houses	2,000,000.00
Nashville, Tenn.	398	Flats and row houses	1,500,000.00
New York, N. Y.	1,622	Apartments	13,569,000.00
New York, N. Y.	574	Apartments	4,219,000.00
Oklahoma City, Okla.	354	Row houses	2,000,000.00
Omaha, Nebr.	284	Flats and row houses	2,000,000.00
Philadelphia, Pa.	258	Flats and row houses	2,110,000.00
Caguas, P. R.	75	Row houses	275,000.00
San Juan, P. R.	131	Row houses	500,000.00
Schenectady, N. Y.	219	Apartments	1,500,000.00
Stamford, Conn.	146	Apartments and row houses	929,000.00
Toledo, Ohio	264	Apartments, flats, and row houses	2,000,000.00
Virgin Islands	141	Row houses	250,000.00
Washington, D. C.	274	Apartments, flats, and row houses	1,842,000.00
Washington, D. C.		(Land acquisition)	58,432.20
Wayne, Pa.	50	Flats and row houses	344,000.00
51 projects and 2 sites	21,769		$136,182,072.70

Source: Adapted from Ickes, "Report on Activities of Housing Division"; in *Hearings on S. 1685*, pp. 26-27.

not make the laws, still it is equally true that no law can be enacted which does not have the support of the people. The law might be enacted, but it would never be observed and it would be necessary to repeal or radically change it. The history of the Eighteenth Amendment and the Volstead Act gives ample proof of this statement. It is necessary, then, to study the organization of pressure groups in favor of public housing, and it is necessary to see how the public demand for some kind of a public-housing program was built up and lined up behind a specific bill. This is an important part of the legislative process, and to neglect it or underestimate it is to misunderstand the real legislative process as it works in the United States.

CHAPTER III

Pressure Groups and
Public Demand for Housing

During the years from 1922 to 1932 the interest in some kind of a solution to the housing shortage that developed out of the government experiment in housing during World War I all but died out. Only in the state of New York, under the leadership of Governor Smith, was there any practical program in operation. This was a private limited-dividend program. Popular magazines like the *Saturday Evening Post* and *Collier's* did not carry any articles or editorials on housing during this period. Even professional organizations with a direct interest in the solution of the housing problem neglected to consider the subject at their annual meetings or conventions. The National Conference of Social Work, whose leaders were pioneers in the field of housing, did not discuss a public-housing program from 1924 to 1933. The National Conference of Catholic Charities did not put the question of public housing on its programs until 1934. The National Conference of Jewish Social Service did not include a discussion of public housing at any of its meetings.

The American Federation of Labor, which was first in the fight for a real public-housing program during the period of World War I, lost its interest in housing during the period from 1922 to 1934. During these years no report on housing was made by the Executive Council, and no resolution calling for public-housing legislation was presented by the membership.

The number of articles listed under any subject in the *Reader's Guide to Periodical Literature* is a good indication of public interest in the subject. During the period from 1919 to 1921 there were ninety-seven articles listed under "Housing in the United States," and twenty-six of these articles were concerned *pro* and *con* with government participation in a public-housing program. The listings for the period from 1922 to 1924 show that the number of articles under "Housing in the United States" had dropped to twenty-five, and only one article is concerned with government participation in a housing program. Most of the articles were concerned with housing and the economy or with housing and social conditions. For the period from 1925 to 1928 the *Reader's Guide* lists under "Housing in the United States" twenty-eight articles, and only five of these articles are concerned with government participation in a public-housing program.

During the period from January of 1929 to June of 1932 the number of articles increased. Under the listing "Housing in the United States" there were forty-five articles; under the listing "Housing Legislation" there were three articles, and under the listing "Housing Projects" there were nineteen articles. An examination of the articles makes it evident that the New York housing law was responsible for this increase of public interest in the subject.

In the next period, from July of 1932 to June of 1935, the *Reader's Guide* lists 16 articles under the general subject "Housing"; under the title "Housing Legislation" there are listed 36 articles, and under the title "Housing in the United States" there are listed 118 articles. The number of popular magazines and "opinion" magazines of general interest that carried articles on housing was very large. The *Saturday Evening Post, Collier's,* the *Ladies Home Journal,* the *Commonweal,* the *Christian Century*, the *Nation*, the *New Republic*, and *Business Week* all carried articles on a public-housing program. This manifests a tremendous increase of public interest in housing. The stagnation in the building industry caused by the depression and the attempt to stimulate business, especially in the building and construction trades, by means of the federal housing program accounts mainly for this increase of public interest. Some of this interest must be credited to an educational program sponsored by the professional housers in the pressure groups. Most of the articles published during this period were written by these experts.

Some socially conscious and civic-minded individuals interested in the housing program began to organize in 1932. There was no over-all plan for organization. In fact, there was a lack of communication and coordination between the various groups. There was one thing, however, that they all had in common. It was the conviction that the housing provisions of the NIRA were inadequate; and that, as they were later administered, they were dangerous to an effective and permanent program of public housing. These leaders knew that PWA housing was a temporary "pump-priming" operation to get the building trades back to work. They wanted a permanent program of public housing founded on the policy that it was the function of the Federal Government to directly solve the housing problem.

Roosevelt's primary concern with the PWA program was to put men and materials to work, to relieve unemployment. There was no over-all plan for attacking the housing problem with a long-range permanent program. Limited-dividend housing programs had not provided dwelling units at low rents for the workers in the lowest income brackets—the group that needed decent housing worst of all; the programs had not been intended to serve the lowest income group. The direct program of government construction and operation, which did not have a plan to keep rents at around $6.00 per room per month, was subject to the same criticism as the limited-dividend housing plan. This was the dangerous part of the PWA program: the people living in the slums never got the chance to move into better housing. These mistakes made it more difficult to get public support for a real, permanent, and long-range low-rent housing program. There was also the danger of an adverse court decision declaring unconstitutional certain operations of the PWA program. This possibility made the professional housers shudder with fear. If the PWA housing program were declared unconstitutional, they would have no chance of inducing the Congress to consider a permanent long-range program of public housing and slum clearance. This danger proved to be so great that Mr. Ickes instructed his legal staff to withdraw the appeal they had filed with the Supreme Court in the Louisville case.[1] The pendency of the TVA case was also an important determinant of Ickes' decision to withdraw the appeal.

The group of "housers" in New York was the first to organize, and this was to be expected because of the existing program in that state. Two social workers, Mrs. Mary Simkhovitch and Helen Alfred, and two legal advisers to the New York State Board of Housing, Ira Robbins and Louis Pink, were primarily responsible for organizing this new group in 1931. They organized the small but active group of people in the New York area interested in public housing. They called their organization the Public Housing Conference (PHC). The next year membership was widened to take in leaders in Washington and elsewhere, and they then incorporated themselves under the title the National Public Housing Conference (NPHC). This organization was a real pressure group. The aim of the organization was to build up enough support among organizations and individuals so that Congress would be forced to consider the proposals for a long-range permanent housing program. The NPHC had all

---

[1] Statement of David Krooth (personal interview).

the elements that an effective pressure group should have. The president of the organization, Mrs. Mary K. Simkhovitch, was a woman who had made her reputation in social work. She was universally respected and she had the confidence and friendship of Mrs. Franklin D. Roosevelt, Mr. Harold Ickes, Senator Wagner, and other government officials. The NPHC counted among its members authorities in the field of housing such as Mrs. Edith Elmer Wood. The religious, racial, national, and political groups were represented by such leaders as Rabbi Edward L. Israel, Bishop Francis McConnell, Father John O'Grady, Harry W. Laidier, and Judge Charles Poletti. Influential writers, such as L. D. Lasker of *Survey* and Irving Brant of the *St. Louis Star-Times*, were officers of the organization.

The secretary of the organization was a woman of great energy. Her name was Miss Helen Alfred. She was impulsive, and lacked a delicate sense of politics; but she was a capable speaker and a good writer who was completely dedicated to the cause of public housing.[2]

The first accomplishment of this group was to have included in the National Industrial Recovery Act a provision for housing to be constructed as part of the public-works program. Earlier the group had unsuccessfully attempted to have some such provisions written into the Federal Relief and Reconstruction Act of 1932. As was mentioned in the preceding chapter, Mrs. Simkhovitch and Father O'Grady contacted Senator Wagner to give him this provision. They also spoke to General Hugh S. Johnson for the purpose of gaining his support. The main objective of the group in getting such provisions written in the NIRA was to bring the question of public housing to the public's attention. Their real plan was a long-range program.[3]

---

[2] Material concerning the NPHC, unless otherwise stated, was gathered from the files of the National Public Housing Conference, Washington.

[3] Newsletter of July 13, 1934, National Public Housing Conference, New York.

The program that NPHC was trying to sell to the people was summarized on its letterhead: *To Promote Slum Clearance and Low Rent Housing through an Established Federal-Local Service.* The group did not immediately work out its plan in precise detail. Education and a build-up of public interest were its first objective. The general plan called for a permanent long-range program of housing and slum clearance: the Federal Government, under the administration of Mr. Ickes and his housing division, would supply money for loans and subsidies, and the local government would construct and manage the projects. The financial details of the program, however, were not very fully and clearly worked out. The group supported Mr. Ickes and his program, and in turn Mr. Ickes gave very valuable support to the NPHC.[4]

In Chicago, in November of 1933, the National Association of Housing Officials (NAHO) was organized. This was not a pressure group, but rather it was planned as a governmental service organization. Its aim was to help local, state, and national housing officials in developing adequate programs for low-cost housing and slum clearance in the United States. In the first issue of its bulletin the organization officially stated its purpose as follows:

> The rapid establishment of housing agencies is encouraging, but unfortunately the body of information and experience in this country on which the newly appointed officials can draw is very small and limited mainly to the largest cities. The major immediate purpose of the N.A.H.O. is to offset as far as possible this lack of experience by facilitating the exchange of ideas and information among housing officials and other interested persons, by advising on local studies and surveys so that they will produce the most

---

[4] It is to be noted that Ickes did not give complete and unqualified support to the NPHC. In a letter to the NPHC, which was released for publication in the newspapers, Mr. Ickes stated that he did not favor a permanent housing agency (*New York Times*, September 26, 1934).

usable results, by bringing about a clearer understanding of problems and methods among local state and national officials and by
drawing upon European experience to the extent that it is applicable to American conditions and problems.[5]

The one person most responsible for the organization of this
group was Mr. Ernest J. Bohn, a member of the City Council of
Cleveland, who sponsored the first detailed study of a slum area
and who was responsible for the quick passage by the Ohio
legislature of the limited-dividend housing law in 1932 and the
nation's first public-housing law of 1933. Ernest J. Bohn was a
leader of great energy, a Republican state and local official who
was possessed of a shrewd political sense and great personal
integrity, so it was natural that he should be elected the first
president of NAHO. Charles Ascher, on loan from the Public
Administration Clearing House, was appointed the first executive director, but Coleman Woodbury took over the job in
August of 1934.[6] Woodbury, having been a member of the technical staff of the President's Conference on Home Building and
Home Ownership, was a specialist in the economics of housing,
and he was later to serve as a technical adviser to those who
were drafting the Wagner housing bill. The other officers of the
organization represented governmental agencies concerned with

---

[5] News release, *National Association of Housing Officials, Bulletin No. 1,* December
1933. A statement of the purpose of the organization printed on the back
cover of their publications; see *A Housing Program for the United States*
(Chicago: National Association of Housing Officials, 1934). Charles Ascher
in a speech before the Washington Conference on Public Housing of the
NPHC on January 28, 1934 made the following statement about the organization of NAHO: "It has established its secretariat in the same building as those
of similar associations of public officials—mayors, city managers, welfare
workers, legislators, finance officers, etc.,—all of which are dedicated to the
improvement of scientific standards in the fields." Reference is here made to
the Public Administration Clearing House which is located at 1313 East
Sixtieth Street, Chicago. See also Charles S. Ascher, "Housing Officials
Organize National Group," *Public Management* 15:372, December 1933.

[6] News release, *National Association of Housing Officials, Bulletin No. 14,* July 6,
1934.

housing. Alfred K. Stern, chairman of the Illinois State Board of Housing, was vice-president. Serving on the Executive Committee were Miles L. Colean, director of the Technical Department of the Federal Housing Administration; Bertram E. Giesecke of the Board of Directors of the Texas Rural Communities; George E. Gove, secretary of the New York State Board of Housing; Horatio B. Hackett, director of housing of the Federal Emergency Administration of Public Works; and Langdon Post, chairman of the New York City Housing Authority.

The third major group interested in housing legislation was the Labor Housing Conference (LHC). As was mentioned earlier, this organization was the outgrowth of the job of public relations and information service connected with the construction of the Carl Mackley Houses by the American Federation of Hosiery Workers.[7] The organization was formally set up in the spring of 1934 at a meeting of the Pennsylvania State Federation of Labor. The group also had the active cooperation of the labor unions in the nearby cities of New Jersey, especially Camden. Its purpose was to organize and promote a powerful, vocal, and intelligent demand for housing for the workers and to assist union groups in the formulation of their requirements. When the organization of such a conference was approved by the State Federation, it was necessary for John Edelman and John Phillips, the prime movers for the conference, to obtain a competent director. Oscar Stonorov suggested to John Edelman that he obtain the services of Miss Catherine Bauer, who had just returned from a tour of the various housing projects in Europe and who had established herself as a critical writer and researcher in the field of architecture and housing. She had at that time just completed the writing of her work on housing, *Modern Housing*.[8]

---

[7] Statement of John Edelman (personal interview).
[8] Statements of John Edelman and Catherine Bauer (personal interviews).

Miss Bauer agreed to accept the position of director of the conference. She was not able to move into Philadelphia until the summer; but once in charge of the conference, she devoted herself completely to the task of organizing the workers for the campaign for a public-housing bill. She happened to be, among other things, a young woman of boundless energy, a good writer, and a convincing speaker. She was a "social reformer," and within a few months she had already organized a series of local housing conferences that were to form the nucleus of a housing movement within the AFL that would bring that powerful organization to a position of complete support for a public-housing law.

The officers of the conference were James L. McDevitt, president of the Building Trades of Philadelphia, chairman; Charles Hollopeter, president of the Central Labor Union of Camden, New Jersey, vice-chairman; Norman Blumberg, secretary of the Building Trades of Philadelphia, treasurer; and John Edelman, American Federation of Hosiery Workers, secretary.[9]

The Labor Housing Conference had not worked out all the details of the particular program that it would propose for legislation. Catherine Bauer had accumulated a great amount of factual knowledge and experience in housing problems and programs, but at this early date she and the conference were more interested in making plans for educating workers and in building up a public demand for a program than they were with writing out the specific financial and administrative details of that program.

While the National Public Housing Conference and the Labor Housing Conference were organizing their resources to act as a lobby in support of a federal public-housing program, there were four existing and well-organized lobbies with a vested

---

[9] *Labor Housing Conference,* brochure. Philadelphia: Labor Housing Conference of Philadelphia, n. d.

interest in any kind of a housing program.[10] These organizations now turned their attention to the possibility that a federal public-housing law would be enacted and to the effects of its enactment as they foresaw them. They were the National Association of Real Estate Boards, the United States Building and Loan League, the National Retail Lumber Dealers Association, and the Chamber of Commerce of the United States.

The National Association of Real Estate Boards, through the office of their executive vice-president, Herbert U. Nelson, had followed closely the activities of the Federal Government in the field of housing. Attention was already called to the position of the NAREB in the discussion of the constitutionality of the New York rent laws. NAREB had for some years been cooperating with the Federal Government in the development of government loan agencies. The Federal Home Loan Bank Act of 1932, which was created to stabilize long-term mortgage credit by the establishment of a reserve system for it like that given by the Federal Reserve System to short-term commercial credit, was sponsored by NAREB. The association also cooperated in the preparation of the bill that was enacted as the Home Owners' Loan Act of 1933. In 1934 the association cooperated in the preparation of the bill which created the Federal Housing Administration. Mr. Herbert Nelson was active in the campaign to enact these three laws. He knew his way around Washington, and he had the confidence of influential members of Congress such as Mr. Steagall, chairman of the House Committee on Banking and Currency.[11]

---

[10] Mary E. Dillon in an article on politics makes a distinction between a *pressure group* and a lobby. According to her distinction the National Public Housing Conference would be considered a pressure group, while the NAREB would be considered as a lobby because its organization was permanent and its sole function was to look after the interests of the group it represented. See Mary Earhart Dillon, "Pressure Groups," *American Political Science Review* 36:471, June 1942.

[11] Statement of Herbert U. Nelson (personal interview).

The United States Building and Loan League was represented in Washington by Mr. Morton Bodfish, executive vice-
president of the league. Bodfish was one of the brilliant young
economists who had served on the staff of the President's Conference on Home Building and Home Ownership. He had been
actively associated with the economics of housing as a college
professor and as a research expert and author. He was appointed
a member of the original Federal Home Loan Bank Board for
1932-1933. For ideological and economic reasons the league
would oppose many provisions of a federal housing program.
Bodfish was a well-known figure around Capitol Hill, and he
was on friendly terms with Chairman Henry Steagall of the
House Banking and Currency Committee. He had appeared before his committee, as well as the Senate Committee on Banking
and Currency, on many occasions. He had been active in the
preparation of the HOLC Act in 1933, and he had also cooperated in the preparation of the National Housing Act.[12]

The National Retail Lumber Dealers Association had as
their Washington representative Mr. Frank Carnahan. Carnahan
was an active and capable lobbyist. His association was opposed
to the program because building materials other than lumber
(for example, steel window frames and concrete, brick, and
masonry construction) were to be used in the construction of
the housing units in the program aided by the Federal Government. Carnahan's part in working toward a limitation of the
program and his stimulation of the small builders to develop
a low-cost single dwelling unit as a result of the threat of a
federal program will receive attention later on in the course
of this study.[13]

Mr. E. Stuart Fitzpatrick, who for many years had been
Washington representative for the Construction and Civic De-

[12] Statement of Morton Bodfish (personal interview).
[13] Statement of Ernest J. Bohn (personal interview).

velopment Department of the Chamber of Commerce of the United States, was watching with interest the movement for a federal public-housing program. At this early date the Chamber of Commerce had not come out in opposition to the PWA Housing Division, which was considered an emergency measure and which was stimulating the construction industry and the building trades. On the principle that housing was a local problem and should be solved at the local level the Chamber of Commerce would oppose any permanent long-range, low-rent housing program sponsored by the Federal Government.[14]

These men did not coordinate their efforts during the early part of the campaign,[15] but they were all agreed in this: public housing was a dangerous socialistic experiment which threatened free enterprise and the traditional American principles of government; public housing also threatened the continued prosperity of the enterprise that each of them represented. They started their strategy of opposition during 1933 by sending letters to the White House and to other influential legislators, including Senator Wagner. They demanded that the government get out of the housing business and stay out.[16]

These organizations and certain influential citizens who personally knew President Roosevelt, such as Dwight Hoopingarner, a contractor in New York City, and Maurice Deutsch, an architect in New York City, wrote to the president to ask him to call housing conferences throughout the United States. They were convinced that, if private enterprise organized its resources, it would be able to solve the housing problem. They did not believe that things were so bad as the public-housing pressure groups made them out to be. In addition to the letters

---

[14] Statement of E. Stuart Fitzpatrick (personal interview).

[15] See "Housing Campaign." *Business Week*, No. 251, June 23, 1934, p. 7.

[16] See Roosevelt Papers, O.F. 63, Franklin D. Roosevelt Library, Hyde Park and Senator Robert F. Wagner, Sr., Papers, Housing—1934, Georgetown University, Washington.

requesting the president to call the housing conference, these groups and individuals demanded that the president put a stop to Mr. Ickes' PWA housing program. These letters were sent through the regular White House channels: from the president's secretary to Mr. Ickes, for his consideration and perhaps for an answer prepared by Ickes which the president would sign, and then into the files.[17]

With this line-up of the forces for and against public housing, the complexity of the first phase of the legislative process appears. The White House and the legislators must be convinced that the "public" demanded a certain program to be enacted and effected by law. Attention here has been given to pressure groups and recognized lobbies. All of their activities were within the law, or at least not prohibited by the law. No evidence was uncovered in any of the thousands of documents examined, nor was any evidence given in the numerous interviews with persons directly concerned with the legislation, to prove that any unethical or illegal means had been used to influence this legislation one way or the other. There was genuine pressure brought to bear by both sides upon legislators, as will be seen later; but it was a pressure that was within the bounds of the democratic legislative process.

Now attention must be turned to some of the specific activities of these organizations. As was just stated, these groups were not coordinated, and thus the story of their activities is somewhat disjointed.

The National Public Housing Conference, as an affirmed pressure group, launched an educational program that brought housing to the front as the number-one problem to be solved by the administration. Speakers and writers representing the NPHC appealed to any group that would give them an audience. They

---

[17] This procedure is very easy to trace in the Roosevelt Papers, O.F. 63, where the letters with their memoranda are clipped together.

were quick to point out to each group—to public-health officers, to social workers, to laborers, to businessmen, to nurses, to architects, to teachers—that a long-range public-housing program would go far toward solving their particular problem.

In the June 7, 1933 issue of the *New Republic*, Miss Alfred answered a critic of public housing. Miss Alfred directed her attention to the laborer in "Labor's Stake in Public Housing," in the October 1934 issue of the *American Federationist*. The "Challenge of the Slums" was the topic of her appeal in *Hygeia* for February 1935. "Housing for Health" was the argument that Miss Alfred made in *Public Health Nursing* for February 1935. The *Journal of Home Economics* carried her explanation of "Federal-Local Low-Rent Program" in the issue of March 1935. The support of rural voters was not neglected by Miss Alfred when she appealed to them in her article on "Rural Housing" in the May 1935 issue of *Social Forces*. In addition to these and other articles Miss Alfred made periodic speaking and conference tours throughout the country. As an example, during the month from March 12 to April 11, 1934 Miss Alfred visited ten cities in eight states.

Mrs. Edith Elmer Wood published a series of more authoritative articles on the housing problem: "Obsolete Housing Revealed by the 1930 Census" (*American City*, January 1933); "Housing in the 1930 Census" (*Survey*, February 1933); "Economics of the Slums" (*Current History*, November 1933); "What Makes Bad Housing Bad?" (*Scholastic*, May 12, 1934); "National Housing Program and the Home Economist" (*Journal of Home Economics*, June 1934); "Housing—Public and/or Private" (*Survey Graphic*, January 1935). Besides these and other articles Mrs. Wood wrote a booklet, *Slums and Blighted Areas in U. S.*, published in 1935 as Bulletin No. 1 by the PWA Housing Division. This booklet was widely distributed by the PWA Housing Division. It was twice reprinted, in 1936 and 1938.

Catholic groups were educated by such articles as Father O'Grady's "New Deal in Housing" in the *Commonweal* for July 21, 1933. Protestant groups were likewise educated by the *Christian Century's* "New Deal Reaches Housing" in the issue of November 8, 1935. A hundred other articles appeared in various special group and technical magazines. There was not a group in the country that did not know of public housing. And if anyone did not belong to an interest group of some kind, the *Ladies Home Journal* in May and June of 1934 and *Collier's* in June 10, 1933 and February 3, 1934 told them of the new public-housing programs.

During the time that the NPHC was doing a job of educating groups such as public-health officials, nurses, social workers, and teachers, the NAHO was engaged, in accordance with the purpose of the organization, in solving various problems involved in the housing problem for the benefit of professional and technical groups.

Charles S. Ascher, the first executive director of NAHO, published articles in the *National Municipal Review* and *Public Management*. Coleman Woodbury, who succeeded Ascher, wrote articles for *Public Management* and the *Journal of Public Utilities and Land Economics*. Elizabeth Longan, an assistant to Coleman Woodbury, also wrote for *Public Management*.

Trade and professional journals, such as the *American City* and the *Architectural Record*, carried articles, new items, and editorial comment on housing in practically every issue of 1933, 1934, and 1935. Much of this material was inspired by the work that NAHO was doing.

The Labor Housing Conference did not attempt to flood magazines and journals with articles to make their purposes and intentions known to the public. Miss Bauer did write some articles for various magazines, such as "Slums Aren't Necessary" for the *American Mercury* of March 1934 and "Slum Clearance or Housing" for the December 27, 1933 issue of the

Nation. Most of her time, however, was spent in writing letters and reports to labor unions throughout the country to educate them in the facts of public housing.[18] Miss Bauer also went on some speaking tours. In 1934 Charney Vladeck of the *Jewish Daily Forward* donated $600 to the struggling Labor Housing Conference so that Catherine Bauer could make a trip around the country in the interest of public housing.[19]

In the fall of 1933 a national conference on slum clearance was held in Cleveland. Mr. Bohn was the principal organizer of this conference, which helped to point up the problem and get it before the people.[20]

Housing had been a neglected subject at the various conferences of social welfare organizations; but beginning in 1933 these powerful groups became acquainted with the proposed long-range program, and, in particular, what it would mean to them and their work. At the sixtieth session of the National Conference of Social Work, held in Detroit in 1933, delegates from all over the country heard William W. Biddle of the School of Applied Social Sciences of Western Reserve University outline

---

[18] Statement of Catherine Bauer (personal letter). This procedure is also evident from an inspection of the files of the Labor Housing Conference, American Federation of Labor, Washington.

[19] This grant was given to Miss Bauer through the good offices of Alfred K. Stern, then a member of the Illinois State Board of Housing. Vladeck was instrumental in getting a labor housing conference started in New York. He was close to the needle trades unions, a member of the New York City Housing Authority and also a friend of Mayor La Guardia. John Carroll of Boston organized a labor housing conference in Massachusetts. It was these two housing conferences that would help to swing the AFL in favor of public housing at the 1935 convention. Miss Bauer made three separate tours, one into New England, one into the Middle West, and a third into the Deep South. A regular procedure of the tour was to schedule a speech before a central trades council or a building trades council meeting, during which Miss Bauer would develop the arguments in favor of federal legislation. As a result of this procedure some seventy local housing conferences were established by April of 1936 (statement of Catherine Bauer, personal letter).

[20] "Cleveland City Council Calls National Conference on Slum Clearance." *Public Management* 15:252, August 1933.

the "Social Aspects of Large-Scale Housing." Professor Biddle told these social workers:

> The pressure of our thinking on this problem can be made effective as at no other period in our history. We can further the desideratum of economic and social planning by beginning to convince our communities and the nation that large-scale housing is a broadly social function, to fit into broad community and regional plans, to be managed from the point of view of general social welfare.[21]

The National Conference of Catholic Charities at its annual meeting in Cincinnati in 1934 had a series of three talks on public housing. Ernest J. Bohn, president of NAHO, spoke to the group on the subject "Why Government Housing?" Stanley M. Rowe of Cincinnati took as his subject "Government Housing Program." Father Edward Roberts Moore, a pioneer in housing from New York City, discussed the problem "Planning for Public Housing."[22]

At each succeeding meeting of these national conferences the subject of public housing was given serious consideration.

A most important job of education and persuasion was carried out by the Labor Housing Conference in bringing around the American Federation of Labor to active support of a long-range and permanent government housing program. As will now be outlined, after an early interest in public housing during the years from 1914 to 1921, the American Federation of Labor had drifted over to a position which was opposed to government-aided housing programs.

This shift needs some explanation. The American Federation of Labor is made up of international unions composed of crafts-

---

[21] William W. Biddle, "Social Aspects of Large-Scale Housing"; in *Proceedings of the National Conference of Social Work at the Sixtieth Annual Session*, p. 429. Chicago: The University of Chicago Press, 1933.

[22] *Proceedings of the National Conference of Catholic Charities*, pp. 272-74, 274-79, 279-86. Washington: The Catholic University of America Press, 1934.

men who are solid citizens and who are not ready to go over-
board for any and every social program that comes along. Many
of the leaders and members of the unions felt that this housing
program was some sort of a socialistic scheme which would set
up communistic communities. They did not want to have any
part in such programs. The building-trades groups were fearful
that the government would gain some kind of monopoly control
over construction, and they were against any such government
control. For these reasons, because the program was so new and
its financial provisions confusing, and because the federation
was slow to commit itself to a government program, the AFL
did not support publicly and go on record as favoring these new
efforts at a government-aided program, more especially that
part of the program which called for direct construction by
the government.[23]

The policy of the federation was expressed in various editorials in the official journal of the AFL, the *American Federationist,* during 1932. In the January issue, while commenting
on the President's Conference on Home Building and Home
Ownership, the federation stated that it was in favor of any
plan to provide better housing for the family, "which is the
unit of society."[24] In November this position was made more
clear and precise.

> None of the foreign schemes seems to be applicable to the
> different standard of living in America. Government responsibility
> has always seemed counter to our ideals of individual initiative
> and rights, while in most European countries the State is the insti-
> tution through which social activities are carried on.[25]

In December the amount of government responsibility is discussed more in detail.

---

[23] Statement of James McDevitt (personal interview).
[24] *American Federationist* 39:20, January 1932.
[25] *Ibid.,* 39:1249, November 1932.

Since the American working man revolts against direct government intervention in providing his home, the government can encourage him only by loans or tax exemptions. So far very little
has been done in these directions. Many individuals have taken an
interest in the houses built for the man of moderate income, but
the individual can accomplish little without the cooperation of
government and private and public corporations. It is time that
everyone should take an interest in the housing conditions of the
American worker and try to improve them as much as other countries have improved theirs in the last few years.[26]

The AFL had reference to the limited-dividend housing
when it spoke of houses being built for those of moderate income. The federation was also opposed to the Garden City
projects which were being built at this time. These projects were
located at some distance from the city. The rent in these projects
was lower than in the city because they were built on cheaper
land, but their distance from the place of work was objectionable to the federation.[27] In these criticisms of the Garden City
projects and the limited-dividend projects there is an indication
that the AFL would ultimately be forced to support some
government aid or subsidy. It wanted decent housing for the
worker—and that was a position from which it could not retreat.
Every type of project put up thus far without this government
subsidy was objectionable to the AFL. It seemed that the only
thing left was to modify its position on individual initiative.

No one can tell how long it would have taken the leadership
of the AFL to arrive logically at the position of government
aid. The Labor Housing Conference did not wait for pure logic
to work this change on the leadership. John Edelman and James

---

[26] *Ibid.*, 39:1389, December 1932.
[27] The objection to the Garden City type of construction was twofold. One was the
distance of the dwellings from the place of work of the union member. The
other, and this was an important objection, was the fact that these projects
were constructed with relief labor and not with union labor at union wages
and under union conditions (statement of Catherine Bauer, personal letter).

McDevitt went to the 1934 convention in San Francisco. There they tried to convince the leadership of the necessity of supporting a program of government aid. They made a few converts among the leadership.[28] Mr. M. J. McDonough of the Building Trades Department was won over to the side of public housing, and he introduced a resolution to put the federation on record in favor of government-aided housing. The resolution read:

> WHEREAS, Housing stands out as a great present need of the work-people of the United States; and
>
> WHEREAS, It appears that private investment is not attracted to low cost housing; and
>
> WHEREAS, It is evident, that the only source of funds and activity which will provide the shelter that wage workers need is the United States Government; therefore be it
>
> Resolved, That this program shall be planned on a long range basis of at least five years ahead to clear slums and to provide low-cost housing that will rent at $4 to $6 a room per month; and furthermore be it
>
> Resolved, That the President of the United States be requested to take such executive action as is necessary to put into use immediately any funds now available for this purpose to the end that publicly built housing may be spread over the whole United States which will rent at low enough sums to afford the shelter required by all the people of the country; and be it
>
> Resolved, That the Congress of the United States is urged to enact any necessary legislation to carry forward such a housing program.[29]

The committee on resolutions recommended that the resolution be referred to the Executive Council with instructions to study existing legislation and the operation of agencies under such legislation. The committee further recommended that the Executive Council introduce and support any additional legisla-

[28] Statements of Catherine Bauer and John Edelman (personal interviews).
[29] *Report of Proceedings of the Fifty-fourth Annual Convention of the American Federation of Labor*, p. 414. Washington: Judd and Detweiler, 1934.

tion which their investigations indicated as necessary to bring about a nationwide building revival. This report of the committee was adopted unanimously.[30] So it was that the federation did not accept the resolution.

Catherine Bauer and John Edelman also drafted another resolution, this one much more radical in its provisions, and had John A. Phillips of the Pennsylvania State Federation of Labor present it to the convention.[31] The provisions of this resolution called for the uniting of all housing agencies under one permanent department of housing and public welfare. This department would have cabinet rank. Five hundred million dollars was to be immediately allocated for long-term housing and slum clearance by a congressional appropriation. The cost of the program was to be kept at a minimum; government loans were to bear a very small interest plus an administrative charge; and where necessary the government should take a loss on the project to keep the rents at a level the wage earner could afford. Groups of workers and consumers should be recognized as "responsible public bodies" and trustees for the government housing program. A bona-fide labor representative was to be included on every housing authority. Government should put up demonstration projects in every industrial center in the country. Company-owned houses and mill villages were to be ended. The convention should create a national labor-housing board. Housing and its relation to economics and social security should be kept before the federal authorities. Federal funds should not be spent for high-cost land, and legislation should be passed enabling the government to condemn land needed for housing. All government-aided housing must be built by labor working at union rates and under union conditions.[32]

---

[30] *Ibid.*
[31] Statements of John Edelman and Catherine Bauer (personal interviews).
[32] *Report of the Fifty-fourth Convention of AFL,* p. 580.

In reporting on this resolution the committee wanted it understood that it approved of public housing, but it stated that the resolution covered too many subjects. It sent it to the Executive Council for consideration, and advised the council to continue its efforts to bring about a far-reaching program.[33]

The Labor Housing Conference did not get its resolutions adopted by the convention, but it did stir up some thinking and discussion about a program. The Labor Housing Conference was satisfied with its first efforts. It had shaken the conservative portion of the building trades and some other leaders in the federation. With another year of work they were confident that they would be able to get the federation to support the program and expand the Labor Housing Conference into a national organization with the backing of the federation. This was a very important skirmish in the battle for public housing.

Another very important development in the campaign took place a few weeks later in the city of Baltimore. The NAHO conducted its educational tour of the eastern half of the United States during August and September. Three European housing experts, Sir Raymond Unwin and Miss Alice Samuel of England and Mr. Ernst Kahn of Frankfurt, had arrived in this country in August. Mr. Ernest J. Bohn, president of NAHO, who was responsible for the program, and Mr. Henry Wright, the distinguished architect and housing planner, accompanied them on the tour. Their objective was to make an accurate and expert survey of the housing problem in the United States and to acquaint persons throughout the country who were professionally interested in housing with some of the technical problems and possible solutions.

In fourteen cities this group personally surveyed problems and conditions: New York, Washington, Boston, Cleveland, Detroit, Chicago, Milwaukee, St. Louis, New Orleans, Atlanta,

---

[33] *Ibid.*, p. 581.

Knoxville, Cincinnati, Pittsburgh, and Philadelphia. During the tour they were able to meet with officials and citizens of some twenty-six cities who were interested in housing and slum clearance to discuss their housing problems.[34]

The results of this tour of investigation and study were incorporated in a report drafted by the European experts and their American companions. A summary of the report was drafted and a meeting was called for October in Baltimore. This meeting was a milestone in the history of housing in the United States. Never before had there been such a detailed and comprehensive survey conducted by experts, nor had the results of any survey ever been subjected to such pinpoint criticism and discussion by such a large group of experts representing every phase of housing in the United States. Seventy-five experts were invited to the meeting. The list is a roster of leading housers and planners and other interested individuals and representatives of groups supporting public housing:[35]

> Frederick L. Ackerman, technical director, New York City Housing Authority
> Carol Aronovici, director, Housing Research Bureau, New York City
> Charles S. Ascher, secretary, Public Administration Clearing House
> Tracy B. Augur, planner, TVA staff, Knoxville
> Frank Bane, director, American Public Welfare Association
> Harland Bartholomew, city planner, St. Louis
> Miss Catherine Bauer, executive director, Labor Housing Conference
> Charles B. Bennett, city planning engineer, Milwaukee

---

[34] Coleman Woodbury, "Introduction"; in *A Housing Program for the United States*, p. 3.

[35] Mr. Lawrence Veiller, a pioneer in campaigning for the National Housing Association, which was devoted to a study of standards of safety and sanitation and planning for housing, did not join in the public-housing movement. There were some few others who were interested in city planning and zoning who also did not give active support to the movement.

Paul V. Betters, executive director, United States Conference of Mayors

Alfred Bettman, president, National Conference on City Planning

Frederick Bigger, chairman, City Planning Commission, Pittsburgh

Walter H. Blucher, member, City Housing Commission, Detroit

Ernest J. Bohn, president, National Association of Housing Officials

Louis Brownlow, director, Public Administration Clearing House

Harold S. Buttenheim, editor, the *American City*

Ralph K. Chase, chief counsel, PWA Housing Division

Carl H. Chatters, executive director, Municipal Finance Officers Association

A. R. Clas, assistant director, PWA Housing Division

Miles L. Colean, director, Technical Division, Federal Housing Administration

G. Frank Cordner, architect, Detroit

Jacob L. Crane, Jr., president, American City Planning Institute

M. C. Downs, director, City Planning Commission, Cincinnati

Earle S. Draper, planner, TVA staff, Knoxville

John W. Edelman, Pennsylvania State Planning Board

Herbert Emmerich, Farm Credit Administration

John M. Gaus, professor of political science, University of Wisconsin

Bertram E. Giesecke, Texas Rural Communities, Inc.

Benjamin Glassberg, superintendent, Department of Out-Door Relief, Milwaukee County

Abraham Goldfeld, chairman, Housing Committee, American Association of Social Workers

George Gove, secretary, New York State Board of Housing

Ernest Grunsfeld, AIA, Chicago

Horatio B. Hackett, director, PWA Housing Division

Jefferson M. Hamilton, administrative assistant, PWA Housing Division

Edmond H. Hoben, economic analyst, PWA Housing Division

John Ihlder, executive officer, District of Columbia Alley Dwelling Authority

Ernst Kahn, former director, Housing Department, Frankfurt, Germany

A. E. Kazan, president, Amalgamated Housing Corporation, New York City

Eugene H. Klaber, AIA, Chicago

Robert D. Kohn, FAIA, New York

Miss Loula D. Lasker, associate editor, the *Survey*

Miss Elizabeth Longan, assistant director, National Association of Housing Officials

Charles Dana Loomis, Maryland Emergency Housing and Park Commission

Miss May Lumsden, New York City Housing Authority

Bleecker Marquette, executive secretary, Better Housing League, Cincinnati

Albert Mayer, architect, New York City

John H. Millar, publisher of *Millar's Housing Letter*, Chicago

Robert B. Mitchell, acting chief, Branch of Initiation and Recommendation, PWA Housing Division

Bernard J. Newman, managing director, Philadelphia Housing Association

John Nolen, president, International Federation for Housing and Town Planning

Reverend John O'Grady, secretary, National Conference of Catholic Charities

Robert M. Paige, secretary, Governmental Research Association.

William Stanley Parker, chairman, Advisory Committee on Housing, Boston City Planning Board

Horace W. Peaslee, chief economic analyst, PWA Housing Division

Clarence Arthur Perry, Russell Sage Foundation

Langdon W. Post, chairman, New York City Housing Authority

Clarence Ridley, executive director, International City Managers Association

Ira S. Robbins, counsel, New York State Board of Housing

Miss Alice J. Samuel, manager, Housing Estates, Liverpool, England

L. Segoe, planning consultant, National Resources Board

Albert C. Shire, engineer, New York City

Mrs. Mary K. Simkhovitch, president, NPHC, New York City

Donald Slesinger, associate dean, Division of Social Sciences, University of Chicago

Lawrence V. Smith, secretary, Delaware State Board of Housing

Alfred K. Stern, chairman, Illinois State Housing Board

Donald C. Stone, executive director, American Society of Municipal Engineers

O. G. Stonorov, architect, Philadelphia

Sidney T. Strickland, chairman, Massachusetts State Board of Housing

Robert R. Taylor, manager, Michigan Boulevard Garden Apartments, Chicago

Henry W. Toll, executive director, American Legislators Association

Joseph P. Tufts, executive director, Pittsburgh Housing Association

Allan A. Twichell, TVA, Knoxville

Sir Raymond Unwin, chief, Technical Division, British Ministry of Health

H. P. Vermilya, Federal Housing Administration

Bernard F. Voell, PWA Housing Division

Stephen F. Voorhees, chairman, Construction Code Authority

John O. Walker, manager, Radburn Association, New Jersey

Roland A. Wank, architect, Knoxville

Mrs. Edith Elmer Wood, member, New Jersey State Housing Authority

Miss Elizabeth Wood, executive director, Metropolitan Housing Council, Chicago

Coleman Woodbury, executive director, National Association of Housing Officials

Henry Wright, FAIA, New York City

This was the first time that all these groups and interests had ever met together. It was very important for the success of the program that the Washington officials should have met with the representatives of the three organizations. This meeting also provided the first opportunity for the three big groups—NAHO, NPHC, and the Labor Housing Conference—to map out a working agreement and to exchange their ideas with respect to government participation in a housing program. Although the groups still remained independent, there were less friction and more communication with one another after this meeting.

As far as all of the groups were concerned, this meeting helped to clarify ideas and consolidate support for the program. There would still remain stubborn individual opinions about specific proposals that would not be compromised, but this was inevitable in such a large group.[36] Mr. Louis Brownlow was named chairman of the meetings because of his position as director of the Public Administration Clearing House and because of his experience in private large-scale housing at Radburn, New Jersey—"the city for the motor age." He urged a complete and frank discussion of all parts of the report by all those present.[37]

The results of these four days of discussion were published as *A Housing Program for the United States*. This report was approved in principle by all those listed. It is certain that, if one or another of the participants had written the report, he would have made a change here or there and placed more emphasis on this section rather than that; but all examined the report as it was published and were in substantial agreement with it.

The report was divided into six sections: General Considerations; Functions and Relations of Public Housing Agencies; Financial Policy; Type of Developments, Location and Design; Housing Management; Housing in City Building.[38]

The first division stated that there was no question about the housing shortage, or the reality of the slums with their danger to health and morals and their economic waste. Workers could not afford to pay an economic rent and induce private industry to build decent housing for them; hence the responsibility for securing an adequate supply of housing for these workers should be recognized as a governmental responsibility. Public

---

[36] *A Housing Program for the United States.*
[37] Statement of Ernest J. Bohn (personal letter).
[38] Loula D. Lasker, "Heading Up the Housing Program." *Survey* 70:348, November 1934.

credit and, when necessary, a public subsidy should be used to secure the needed dwellings.

In time of industrial depression low-cost housing provides one of the most effective and least costly types of work relief. The fact that housing in the United States in 1935 must be approached as an emergency measure and also as a permanent program was brought out in the discussion. Hence any program must take both of these factors into consideration. And while discussing a program, all those in attendance were agreed that time was important. A program must be worked out immediately. Housing was losing favor because of the indefiniteness of the present government program. The provision of good housing and slum clearance could be the best type of relief work.

The second division is concerned with the respective functions and relations of public-housing agencies. It was recognized by the conference that a successful program depended on a local sense of responsibility and local interest. Federal and state authorities have important functions concerned with financing the program and providing the necessary legal powers to the authorities on the local level, but it is the local agency that has the most direct responsibility with regard to construction and general management.

The federal agency, according to the report and the conference, should be a permanent one with adequate powers and sufficient independence to perform its functions. The state agency should be modeled after the federal agency, and it should stimulate, coordinate, and regulate local authorities.

It was pointed out in the discussions that there must be provisions in state legislation for great variation in the local authority. Such variation will not hinder the program so long as conditions of responsibility, independence, and integrity are properly secured, and the agency is required to work in the public interest for low-cost housing and not for the making of profits beyond the prescribed rate of return on capital. Local agencies would be subject to state and federal control as regards their operation and finances.

A warning was given by the members of the conference that, while decentralization was necessary, it could not be a reality until the program was under way and local support had been developed and established.

The section concerned with financial policy was general in its proposals. It was recognized that a sound financial policy was of the first importance. Every effort should be made to reduce the cost of construction of the dwellings. Planning and management of the units should be so efficient that there would be no losses from high vacancies, repairs, or rapid obsolescence. These measures and a long period of amortization with a low rate of interest would bring rents into the range of the income of the lowest income group. When all of these provisions failed to bring the rents to the level that the worker could afford, then a subsidy by the government could be given. This subsidy would be either a capital grant to offset high initial cost of construction or an annual grant to balance the deficit between the rent collected and the total operational costs. A subsidy should be revised as costs changed and should be given only as long as necessary. All these suggestions must be subject to adjustment to suit differing conditions.

It was urged that limited-dividend corporations be encouraged. It was suggested that the loan be greater than the usual 80 per cent of the capital. Better methods should be worked out to distribute the risk on the equity of the corporation. It was brought out in this discussion that slum clearance was essentially a different problem from that of providing low-cost housing to catch up with the shortage. Some method should be worked out economically to take care of the loss involved in demolishing buildings for slum clearance. Sir Raymond Unwin pointed out that the British plan was to pay the owner for the land but to give no compensation to the owner for the dilapidated and condemned building. The group was inclined to agree that this would be the best solution for the United States.

The fourth division was concerned with site planning, zoning, and the relation of the project to the over-all plan of the city. The question of suburban sites and satellite location, as well as construction on slum-clearance sites, was considered. Local conditions would have to be decisive in determining this question. Various problems of construction were considered: type of construction, layout of site, standards, community facilities, and so forth. It was urged by the experts that housing be so constructed that it would keep its value during the entire period of amortization. The right technical treatment for securing good living conditions, pleasing appearance, reasonable amenity, and adequate community provisions should be the prevailing factor in determining the character of the project.

Housing management was the fifth topic for discussion. It was here that the European experts stressed the necessity of good management when the buildings were ready for occupancy. The problem of selection of tenants and collection of rents received special consideration. Miss Samuel explained the work of the woman housing manager who makes a career of housing management.

The last division was concerned with housing as it relates to all the other problems in a city. The interdependence of housing with all other civic problems was discussed, and it was suggested that a continuing scientific study be made by all levels of government of all those factors that are related to the housing problem: the number and size of families; tendencies to migration; the number, condition, wastage, and demolition of buildings; and so forth. Such information should be made available to private enterprise, together with definite programs developed by public agencies.

Such was the program of housing for the United States. It was the first long-range and carefully considered program to be formulated in the United States. A copy of the program, together with a letter from Mr. Bohn, was sent to President Roosevelt. Later a revised copy of the program was sent with a covering letter by Coleman Woodbury.[39]

Previously to sending the written report Sir Raymond Unwin, Lady Unwin, John Ihlder, Mrs. Roosevelt, and Ernest J. Bohn visited President Roosevelt in the White House on the second day of the conference. The president was informed of the proceedings of the conference currently in session and was given an oral report of the six-week study made throughout the United States. According to Mr. Bohn the president was impressed with this report.[40] This meeting had been suggested to Mrs. Roosevelt by John Ihlder. Mrs. Roosevelt agreed to the advisability of such a meeting, and the arrangements were made with her aid through the proper diplomatic channels: the United States Department of State and the British Embassy.[41]

Attention must now be turned to the campaign that the groups in opposition to a federal public-housing program were conducting. Each of these groups was in process of developing substitute programs that it could propose as a better solution to the housing problem.

The National Association of Real Estate Boards was attempting clearly to formulate its position on housing relative to government aid. The principles that the association was following at that time were set forth by a special committee on government loans and housing. It was recommended:

> 1. That the association advise the Federal Government and our members throughout the country that we do not believe that limited dividend tax exempt, state supervised, multi-family housing corporations constitute a sound solution to the problems of slum

[39] Bohn to Roosevelt, November 1934, and Woodbury to Roosevelt, November 1934, Roosevelt Papers, O.F. 63.
[40] Statement of Ernest J. Bohn (personal letter).
[41] Office memorandum, October 1934, Roosevelt Papers, P.P.F. 4684.

clearance and housing development, and that, therefore, we wish to discourage government loans and subsidies and tax exemptions to such projects.

2. We take this position because a thorough analysis of these types of projects clearly shows that if such projects are carried out on any business basis at all they will be of no benefit to the poorer classes of people for which they are intended, but can merely benefit a restricted group in a higher income class. To provide for these poorer classes of people these projects must be practically a total gift from the Federal Government and we do not believe that the Federal Government should extend housing facilities to small groups of poorer persons in a limited number of cities. Where housing conditions for the poorer classes may be notably unsatisfactory, whatever relief can be given to such conditions should be provided by private or local philanthropy at the points where these conditions prevail.

The association was also determined to work out some kind of a plan for neighborhood reconstruction to prevent the development of slums and blighted areas.[42]

During 1934 the association had worked for the passage of the National Housing Act,[43] which was finally approved on June 27, 1934.

The membership of the United States Building and Loan League had been alerted to the possibility of a federal public-housing bill by Morton Bodfish. He told the membership in his annual report, published in the *Building and Loan Annals*, that the move in the direction of government housing will carry on

---

[42] Minutes, Board of Director's Meeting, November 18, 1932, NAREB Office, Chicago.

[43] 48 Stat. 1246 (1934). Sec. 207, "Low-Cost Housing Insurance," was the only section concerned with public housing. The National Association of Real Estate Boards and the National Retail Lumber Dealers Association were supporting and advising Congress on this legislation. See "Housing Campaign," *Business Week*, No. 251, June 23, 1934, p. 7; "Recovery Housing," *Business Week*, No. 241, April 14, 1934, p. 7; "Housing Progress," *Business Week*, No. 242, April 21, 1934, p. 10; "Real Estate Starts Back," *Business Week*, No. 245, May 12, 1934, p. 12.

until it was clearly demonstrated that the housing supply could be better provided with building and loan funds and private enterprise than by government regulations, finance, or subsidy. Bodfish favored a plan of garden cities with individual family homes built on vacant land.[44]

Mr. Frank Carnahan, the alert lobbyist for the National Retail Lumber Dealers Association, was active during the fall of 1934. He wrote to the president to protest an expanded PWA housing program.[45] The lumber dealers' organization did not have a substitute program for public housing worked out in detail. The organization favored a more wide and effective use of the National Housing Act which had been approved in the summer of 1934.

The Chamber of Commerce of the United States had not yet actively entered into the campaign to prevent a federal public-housing law. Mr. E. Stuart Fitzpatrick did not believe that there was the possibility of such a law's being enacted during that Congress, and the membership of the Chamber had not expressed itself definitely on the subject of a public-housing program. Some of the members in the construction trades favored an emergency program to stimulate the industry; the philosophy of the Chamber of Commerce, however, could not justify the activity of the national government in a field which was considered to be of primary concern to the local government.[46]

In addition to the activity of organized lobbies for and against a federal public-housing program, certain individual citizens wrote letters to the White House and to Senator Wagner and other members of Congress. One of the most important letters sent to the president came from an old friend of Mr. Roosevelt, Mr. Joseph Day.[47] The president was much impressed

---

[44] *Building and Loan Annals,* 1934, pp. 638-39.
[45] Carnahan to Roosevelt, November 24, 1934, Roosevelt Papers, O.F. 63.
[46] Statement of E. Stuart Fitzpatrick (personal interview).
[47] Day to Roosevelt, November 23, 1934, Roosevelt Papers, P.P.F. 476.

with "Joe" Day's letter and gave it his personal consideration. Day had objected that the land used for public housing and slum clearance was taken from the tax rolls. He also expressed his view that, if people were in the slums, it was their own fault. He argued that it was not the Federal Government's, or any government's, business to provide housing.

Franklin Roosevelt wrote an answer to his friend "Joe" in which he set out some of his ideas on government and housing. It was evident that Roosevelt was going to do something about the problem, but his plan of action was not yet specific. He was open to suggestions. In this frame of mind he wrote an important letter, the last two paragraphs of which were as follows:

> Here, however, is one phase of urban housing that I should like to have your slant on. Let us suppose for the sake of example that there are ten thousand families in a given city whose earning power is so low that they can afford to spend say ten dollars a month for the item of rent in their budget. What are we going to do with them? Are we going to compel them to live under slum conditions, let us say in one room, for which they pay ten dollars a month? Has society as a whole no obligation to these people? Or is society as a whole going to say we are licked by that problem? Private capital cannot afford to do anything about it and, therefore, these ten thousand families must continue to live in one room for each family.
>
> You quote one President. Another President said "We are faced with a condition and not a theory." I wish you would give me a solution.[48]

A solution was presented to the president in December in a proposal for privately owned and operated housing projects. The plan was drawn up by Mr. Harold Riegelman and Mr. Peter Grimm. With a memo dated December 10 the president sent it to Ickes for his consideration.[49]

---

[48] Roosevelt to Day, November 26, 1934, Roosevelt Papers, P.P.F. 476.
[49] Roosevelt to Ickes, December 10, 1934, Roosevelt Papers, O.F. 63.

Housing was on the president's mind during November and December. He had been receiving numerous letters and suggestions. He had had an interview with Sir Raymond Unwin, the British authority on housing. By December 3, 1934 the president had decided that he must take some action on the housing question. He dictated a memo to his assistant, Marvin H. McIntyre: "When I return to Washington arrange a conference with Ickes, Hopkins and Post." The subject of the conference was to be Mr. Day's objection to the program on the grounds that the land was taken from the tax rolls.[50]

Roosevelt was also conditioning the thinking of his advisers. A copy of a report on the slums in Cincinnati had come into his office. It was written by the author of "Children of the Shadows," and it dealt with slum children and a portrayal of existing conditions. F.D.R., as the president was accustomed to signing his memoranda, sent a copy of the report to Jesse Jones, chairman of the RFC, with the suggestion that he might read it. He also suggested: "You might show it to some of our more confirmed conservatives."[51] He also sent a copy of the same report to Secretary Ickes with the memo: "For you to read and pass along to Harry Hopkins."[52]

There was not complete peace and harmony in the president's official family. There were arguments over the control of the housing program within the Federal Government. Administrator Ickes and James A. Moffett, administrator of the Federal Housing Administration, had an open clash over the housing question and a $2,000,000,000 public-works program.[53] Mr.

---

[50] Roosevelt to McIntyre, December 3, 1934, Roosevelt Papers, O.F. 63.
[51] Roosevelt to Jones, December 8, 1934, Roosevelt Papers, O.F. 63. This "report," as it is called in the memo, is not in the files. "Children of the Shadows" was written by Paul de Kruif and published in the *Ladies Home Journal* for March 1935. It seems that this report was a prepublication copy of the article.
[52] Roosevelt to Ickes, December 8, 1934, Roosevelt Papers, O.F. 63.
[53] *New York Herald Tribune*, November 23, 1934.

Ickes was also the target of sharp criticism by the New York Chamber of Commerce and the furniture dealers. Both of these powerful organizations sent letters to the White House protesting against Mr. Ickes' housing plans.[54]

But an incident occurred in January of 1935 that was to indicate which side the president would choose in this battle over Mr. Ickes and his housing plans. The National Public Housing Conference was holding its annual meeting in late January. At the beginning of the month Mrs. Mary Simkhovitch and Helen Alfred wrote to the president asking him to send the conference a message on housing to be read at the annual meeting. The letter was given to Steve Early, who was to take care of the business. Early sent a copy of the request to the Federal Housing Administration (which was representing the government agencies concerned with loans, mortgages, insurance, and so forth) and to Mr. Ickes, asking them for their comments. The FHA replied that the president should not give any statement to the NPHC. Mr. Ickes, who had always been supported by Mrs. Simkhovitch and Miss Alfred, replied that the president should give the statement to the NPHC. Early sent these contradictory answers to the president with a memo dated January 9, stating that the president must decide the matter.[55]

The president decided to send a statement to the conference. It was read to the members at the opening session on January 24. It was written in general terms, but it did praise the work of the conference in behalf of slum clearance and low-cost housing. The president gave some indication that more government aid would be given.[56]

---

[54] Letters written during December 1934, Roosevelt Papers, O.F. 63.

[55] Early to Roosevelt, January 9, 1935, Roosevelt Papers, O.F. 63. The original letter from NPHC and the various memos are clipped together with the Early memo.

[56] *Public Housing Progress* 1:1, February 15, 1935; "Housing Conference in Washington, D.C.," *Monthly Labor Review* 38:624, March 1934.

So it was that the first phase of the legislative process was completed. By January of 1935 the question of public housing had been brought into national prominence. Pressure groups and interest groups and lobbies had been lined up for and against government participation in a long-range program. Programs, plans, and proposals were being worked out by both sides. This was the situation just prior to the introduction of Senator Wagner's first housing bill.

CHAPTER IV

The Wagner Bill
and the Ellenbogen Bill

Several important meetings were held during January of 1935 by the policy committee of the National Public Housing Conference, at which it was decided to draft a bill for a long-range public-housing program. Mrs. Simkhovitch, Helen Alfred, Louis Pink, and Ira Robbins were the key members of this committee. It was Ira Robbins who drafted the bill. He was the legal counsel for the New York State Board of Housing and had done some legislative drafting for the state. Mrs. Simkhovitch and Helen Alfred, as well as Louis Pink, had suggestions to offer concerning provisions in the bill. Helen Alfred and Mrs. Simkhovitch were especially interested in putting the administration of the program under the supervision of Mr. Ickes and the Department of the Interior.[1]

Mrs. Simkhovitch and Ira Robbins had attended the Baltimore conference some weeks before, and the discussions that had been held there were still fresh in their memory. They also had the benefit of the final report, *A Housing Program for the United States,* to guide them.

The first draft of the bill was completed by the end of January. Mrs. Simkhovitch and Helen Alfred approached Senator

---

[1] Statement of Ira Robbins (personal interview).

88

Robert Wagner of New York and asked him to sponsor the legislation in the United States Congress. Senator Wagner agreed to introduce the bill.[2]

The choice of Senator Robert Wagner was a natural one. In 1935 the senator was at the peak of his career. He was the spokesman in the Senate for many aspects of the New Deal. He was ranking member of the powerful Senate Committee on Banking and Currency. He was a close friend and confidant of the president. In addition to the powerful position that the senator had in Congress, he was personally sympathetic toward this housing legislation. Robert Wagner grew up in the slums of New York. As a boy he lived in the tenements at Lexington Avenue and One-hundred-and-fourth Street.[3]

The personal experience that Wagner had had of the disease and crime and injustice of the slums influenced his political thinking. When he was elected as a member of the State Assembly, he introduced various bills during 1907 and 1908 for the benefit of the slum dwellers. Later, when he went to the Senate of the state of New York in 1909, he introduced legislation during every session to better the conditions of the people in the tenements. His coworkers in this campaign were Al Smith, Frances Perkins, and a young lawyer named Franklin D. Roosevelt.[4] As a justice of the Supreme Court of the State of

---

[2] Alfred to Roosevelt, February 1, 1935, Roosevelt Papers, O.F. 63.

[3] Thomas Byrne, *The Social Philosophy of Senator Robert F. Wagner*, Chap. 1. Unpublished dissertation. Georgetown University, 1951.

[4] These laws were concerned primarily with standards of safety and sanitation, but they manifested the sincere interest of Wagner in the whole problem of housing. Some of these laws were: "An Act To Amend the Labor Law in Relation to the Housing of Men," New York Assembly, 1907, INT. No. 806, PR. No. 871; "An Act Amending Tenement House Law Generally," New York Senate, 1912, INT. No. 617, PR. No. 1086, Chap. 454; "An Act in Relation to the Housing of People in Cities of a Second Class," New York Senate, 1913, INT. No. 1748, PR. No. 2277, Chap. 774. Consult also an informative article, "In Washington," by Arthur Krock, in the *New York Times* for April 14, 1936.

New York he ruled in favor of the "rent laws," and his opinion manifested a political philosophy sympathetic to the people in the slums.[5]

Since coming to the United States Senate, Wagner had introduced and fought for most of the legislation that became the New Deal. The Wagner labor law, social security, industrial recovery, were all part of the legislative program of Senator Wagner. The National Public Housing Conference knew the practical realities of the legislative process. Any senator can introduce a bill; but if the bill is of any importance, involves an appropriation of money, and will bring out strong opposition, only a senator with seniority and energy and authority can ever hope to get it passed in Congress.

After the two important steps of drafting the bill and obtaining a powerful senator to sponsor it had been completed, Miss Alfred did one of those strange, impolitic, and impulsive things that often caused friction in the NPHC. She wrote a letter to the president, under date of February 1, 1935, telling him that the NPHC had drafted a housing bill and had obtained the promise of Senator Wagner to sponsor it in the Congress.[6] Once Senator Wagner had agreed to sponsor the legislation, the management of the various phases of the legislative process were his responsibility. Miss Alfred had gone out of bounds in her enthusiasm for the bill. There was little enthusiasm for the letter and the bill when they arrived at the White House. The letter and the draft of the bill were filed away, and no official notice was taken of them.

During the month of February, Mrs. Simkhovitch and Miss Alfred approached Mrs. Roosevelt and asked her help in getting the bill passed. Mrs. Roosevelt's interest in housing and slum clearance was well known. She had actively cooperated with the

---

[5] *Supra*, Chap. 1.
[6] Alfred to Roosevelt, February 1, 1935, Roosevelt Papers, O.F. 63.

Alley Dwelling Authority in attempting to clean up the slums of the Capitol. One of her favorite occupations was to go out with Mrs. Morgenthau as a companion to Greenbelt, one of the Resettlement Administration projects outside of Washington, to watch the progress of the work.[7] Mrs. Roosevelt told Mrs. Simkhovitch and Miss Alfred to delay the introduction of the legislation until after the president secured from Congress the appropriation for the work-relief bill.[8]

So Mrs. Simkhovitch and Miss Alfred watched the activities of Congress and waited until they were assured that the president would get his appropriation. During the first week of March, Miss Alfred was convinced that the president would get his appropriation, and wrote to Mrs. Roosevelt to tell her that the NPHC was going to ask Senator Wagner to introduce the bill at an early date. Miss Alfred stated that there were at work forces hostile to public housing and that as a consequence this early introduction was necessary. A copy of the second draft of the bill was enclosed in this communication. Mrs. Roosevelt turned over the letter and the draft of the bill to the White House office.[9]

The second draft of the bill differed from the first in one minor and one major respect. The minor change involved the addition of one sentence to the title of the bill—"and to further industrial recovery through the employment of labor and materials." This argument for public housing had not been played up or sufficiently emphasized in the first draft of the bill. The major change concerned the appropriation for the housing program. The first draft called for an immediate appropriation of $5,000,000,000 and another $1,000,000,000 to be appropriated to the Housing Division in each of the next five years. The

---

[7] Statement of John Taylor Egan, architect at Greenbelt and former commissioner (1948-1953) of Public Housing Administration (personal interview).

[8] Alfred to Mrs. Roosevelt, March 1, 1935, Roosevelt Papers, O.F. 63.

[9] *Ibid.*

second draft changed the total appropriation from $5,000,000,-
000 to $800,000,000, and did not stipulate that there should be
any further appropriation.[10]

Mrs. Simkhovitch and Miss Alfred came down to Washington in the middle of March. They went to Senator Wagner's
office and presented him with the bill. The bill was turned over
to Leon Keyserling, Senator Wagner's legislative assistant. Mr.
Keyserling made only one technical change in the text prepared
by Ira Robbins. He changed the date on which the provisions of
the bill would be scheduled to go into effect from June 30, 1935
to June 15, 1935.[11]

Senator Wagner had no intention of pushing this bill
through Congress during that session. He was occupied with
other bills which were consuming a great deal of his time and
attention, principally the social-security bill and the labor-
relations bill.[12] The leaders of the NPHC were well aware of
this, but they also knew that the only way to get national publicity and national support was to have the bill in Congress and
before a committee.

On March 26, 1935, shortly after the routine business of the
day was completed, Senator Wagner was recognized and made
the following speech:

> Mr. President, I introduce a bill, and although it involves an
> appropriation, nevertheless, because it deals with the subject of
> housing, I am going to ask that it be referred to the Committee on
> Education and Labor. It involves a subject which that committee
> has studied and is still studying. After that committee shall have
> completed its consideration of the bill, I shall ask that it be re-
> ferred to the Committee on Appropriations.

---

[10] These two drafts of the bill are in Roosevelt Papers, O.F. 63 (Box 3).

[11] Statement of Leon Keyserling (personal interview).

[12] Statement of Leon Keyserling (personal interview). Wagner, however, did
deliver some speeches in favor of the housing bill, one of them being a
radio address over NBC on April 13, 1935. This radio address, "Labor's Stake
in World Trade," is printed in *Vital Speeches* 1:512-13, May 6, 1935.

The *Congressional Record* then states:

> There being no objection, the bill (S. 2392) to promote public health, safety, and welfare by providing for the elimination of insanitary and dangerous housing conditions, to relieve congested areas, to aid in the construction and supervision of low-rental dwelling accommodations, and to further national recovery through the employment of labor and materials, was read twice by its title and referred to the Committee on Education and Labor.[13]

Wagner was using some of the strategy that made him such a successful legislator. The Committee on Appropriations was a more conservative committee than the Committee on Education and Labor. Besides, the Committee on Appropriations had just given a large appropriation to the president for the work-relief bill which provided $450,000,000 for housing construction by the PWA Housing Division,[14] and so this committee would be inclined to let the bill die. The Committee on Education and Labor had a number of so-called New Dealers in its membership, and it would be much more interested in holding hearings and making a favorable report. Senators Hugo Black of Alabama and James Murray of Montana, together with Robert La Follette of Wisconsin, could be counted on to fight for public housing. Senator David I. Walsh of Massachusetts was chairman of the committee. He was not a New Dealer, but he would support legislation which he thought would benefit the workers.

The assignment of a bill to a committee is one of the most important actions in the legislative process. As will be seen in a later chapter, a committee chairman or a few members of a committee can prevent a bill from reaching the floor of the house. Since a bill such as this housing bill comprehended a number of provisions, it would not be absolutely determined to the jurisdiction of one committee; and if it could be steered into

---

[13] *Congressional Record*, March 26, 1935, p. 4419.
[14] 49 Stat. 48 (1935).

a sympathetic committee, the chances of its passage would be greatly improved. The advantage of having Senator Wagner sponsor the legislation was very evident in this instance, where he requested, and John N. Garner, president of the Senate, followed his request, that the bill go to a sympathetic committee where it would be given immediate consideration.

The NPHC also asked one of the representatives to sponsor a companion bill in the House of Representatives. Their choice was Reuben T. Wood of Missouri, who was actively associated with the AFL in Missouri and a member of the Committee on Labor. It was their hope that the bill would be assigned to the House Committee on Labor, which was considered a "liberal" committee. Mr. Wood, however, did not have the influence that Mr. Wagner exercised. Bills are introduced in the House by placing them in a receptacle called the "hopper" on the clerk's desk. They are referred by the speaker, in routine cases by the parliamentarian acting for the speaker, to the appropriate committee. The notice of introduction is then printed in the *Record* on the next day.[15] Mr. Wood's bill is listed with the others that had been introduced on the same day and is given its number:

> Under clause 3 of rule XXII, public bills and resolutions were introduced and severally referred as follows: [Wood's bill was the twenty-second bill for that day] H. R. 6998 to promote the public health, safety, and welfare [same as in Wagner bill] . . . , to the Committee on Ways and Means.[16]

So, instead of being referred to the Committee on Labor, the bill ended up in the Committee on Ways and Means, which had jurisdiction over revenue measures and subjects relating to the Treasury. In the opinion of the parliamentarian, and in the absence of any effective encouragement of the speaker by the

------

[15] Rule 22, Clause 3; in *Rules of the House of Representatives,* edited by Lewis Deschler, p. 432. Washington: Government Printing Office, 1949.
[16] *Congressional Record,* March 25, 1935, p. 4408.

NPHC or Congressman Wood to assign it to the Committee on Labor, the bill went to a committee which was much less sympathetic to the measure than would have been the Committee on Labor.[17] The failure to convince Speaker Joseph W. Byrns that the really important features of the bill were the labor and industrial recovery provisions was a bad mistake. This was so because, as will soon be seen, the next housing bill was sent to the ultraconservative Committee on Banking and Currency. This referral of bills to appropriate committees illustrates two important operations in the legislative process: the important and controlling position of the speaker of the House and the equally important and controlling position of the committee chairman. Much more will be said in the following chapters about the position of the committee chairman and the powers enjoyed by him. It should here be noted that the assignment by the speaker, or his parliamentarian, is of extreme importance in the legislative process.[18]

It is to be noted that Representative Wood introduced the bill under his own name. This indicated that he was fully in accord with the policy of the bill and that he was willing to take credit for the hoped-for good effects of the bill. There is provision in the rule of the House of Representatives to indicate that the bill being introduced is introduced "by request." This qualifying phrase can be used when the representative may not be willing to take responsibility for the bill. An example of the introduction of a bill by request can be found at the same period that Representative Wood introduced the housing bill. The fol-

---

[17] See the remarks of Paul Douglas concerning the assignment of the Social Security Bill to the Committee on Ways and Means during this same session in *Social Security in the United States*, p. 85 (New York: Whittlesey House, 1936).

[18] See the remarks of Stephen Kemp Bailey concerning the referral of bills to committees in *Congress Makes a Law*, p. 151 (New York: Columbia University Press, 1950).

lowing bill, as we learn from the *Congressional Record* was introduced by Mr. Celler of New York on April 10, 1935:

> H. R. 7396 Mr. Celler [by request], A bill to encourage inventive genius by amending income-tax laws with respect to incomes of inventors; to Committee on Ways and Means.[19]

The strategy of introducing the same bill in both houses of Congress has advantages and disadvantages. There is no necessity because of rule or statute for introducing the same bill in the two chambers. When this is done, however, the sponsors hope that the bill will in both cases be referred to sympathetic committees and that both committees will hold hearings and report the bill favorably to the House without any major changes. This procedure saves time, but has disadvantages. The first chamber may receive the bill and act favorably upon it, while in the other chamber the committee may give an unfavorable verdict. In this case, when the bill comes to the second chamber from the first, the first chamber will not be interested in taking any action upon it because its own committee has already given an adverse decision. When the bill is introduced in only one chamber, it comes with no prejudices and it comes with the recommendations of the other chamber.

The National Public Housing Conference was satisfied with its initial efforts, and in its news magazine *Public Housing Progress* it was stated editorially:

> . . . this permanent plan involves no departure from methods already in use. These methods were evolved under Harold L. Ickes

---

[19] *Congressional Record*, April 10, 1935, p. 5393. This procedure is provided for by Sec. 4 of Rule 22 of the House of Representatives. While there is nothing in the Senate rules so stating, a bill, resolution, petition, or memorial may be introduced "by request" with these words entered in the *Journal* and in the *Record*. See *Precedents, Decisions on Points of Order with Phraseology in the United States Senate from the First to the Sixty-second Congress Inclusive, 1789 to 1913*, compiled by Henry H. Gilfry, p. 228 (Washington: Government Printing Office, 1914).

as Public Works Administrator, and as a natural consequence, the permanent Federal Housing Division will remain under his supervision as Secretary of the Interior.[20]

Coleman Woodbury made the following comment about the bill in the bulletin for NAHO:

> I understand that this bill was introduced chiefly as a result of efforts of the N.P.H.C., and other bills for permanent housing agencies are now being prepared by other groups. I will keep you informed of late developments on this or any similar measure.[21]

While the New York group was pushing to get its version of the public-housing program introduced in Congress, the Philadelphia group of the Labor Housing Conference was also considering the provisions of a bill for a long-range housing program. Edelman, Stonorov, and Catherine Bauer had been at the Baltimore conference. One Sunday morning in March these three, together with Bill Jeanes, met at Edelman's home. They discussed various aspects of the housing program and formulated some definite policies. They would show their approval of the statements of the Baltimore conference on the housing shortage and its effect on social, health, and labor problems.[22] Being labor people, they put emphasis on unemployment and the necessity of stimulating the building trades. They knew that more liberal financial schemes were necessary. Their experience with the Juniata Park Housing Corporation impressed this fact upon them. Provision should also be made for union wages and working conditions on the projects. PWA relief workers had been in competition with union workers. These ideas and some others found in the resolutions of McDonough and Phillips at the AFL convention in 1934 were discussed by the group.[23]

---

[20] *Public Housing Progress* 1:1, April 15, 1935.
[21] *National Association of Housing Officials, Bulletin No. 43*, April 4, 1935.
[22] Statements of John Edelman and Catherine Bauer (personal interviews).
[23] *Supra*, Chap. 3.

After working up their program, they had to decide on a legislator to sponsor it in Congress. There was not much discussion about the man they wanted. He was Representative Henry Ellenbogen. He was the representative from Pittsburgh, he had a liberal voting record, and John Edelman had met him on a number of occasions. So Edelman went to Washington to talk with Ellenbogen.[24] Ellenbogen was already considering a housing bill. For two years he had been working to perfect the HOLC. He had written a number of amendments to the original act. Now he was ready to do something for the millions who did not even own a home they could mortgage.[25]

When asked by the author how and why he became interested in housing legislation, Judge Ellenbogen (he has been a judge in the courts in Pittsburgh since his retirement from the House in 1937) pointed to a picture on the wall. There were three autographed pictures on the wall: those of President Franklin Roosevelt, of Justice Hugo Black, and of a priest. "That priest," he said, "is Father James R. Cox, and he was responsible for my active interest in housing." Father Cox was pastor of old Saint Patrick's in Pittsburgh at Seventeenth and Liberty. That was his official title. Unofficially, he was known to everyone as the "Mayor of Shanty Town." In the midst of the depression thousands came to him to be fed and clothed. Father Cox did this until he went deep into debt, but he could not house the thousands of unemployed. Some he put into his old school building, but hundreds lived in packing-box shanties in the vacant lots around his church. Here was a vivid argument for public housing. Not content with this argument, Father Cox gathered the unemployed into the University of Pittsburgh stadium in the dark days of 1932 to show the administration by this mass demonstration the necessity of doing something. When

---

[24] Statement of John Edelman (personal interview).
[25] Statement of Henry Ellenbogen (personal interview).

this failed, he led twenty thousand unemployed to the Capitol. After their demonstration, which was not successful in bringing action, he led his "army" back to Pittsburgh.[26]

This dangerous condition in Pittsburgh and the example and encouragement of Father Cox inspired Representative Ellenbogen to do something practical and effective to relieve the situation while he was a member of Congress.[27]

Ellenbogen was ready to discuss the plans of the Labor Housing Conference. Edelman, Catherine Bauer, and James McDevitt told the representative what they thought should be included in the bill. Ellenbogen decided to draft a new bill. The NPHC bill that Senator Wagner introduced was defective in many respects. The financial scheme was too vague. The administrative provisions of the bill which placed everything under the control of Mr. Ickes were not satisfactory to the Labor Housing Conference. They argued that the program of the PWA Housing Division had made many mistakes and many enemies. It would be better to have a new and independent administration that would not be burdened with the past record of the PWA Housing Division.[28]

The new bill of Representative Ellenbogen was introduced on April 10, 1935. There is the same type of notice in the *Congressional Record* as there was for Representative Wood's bill:

> Under clause 3 of rule XXII, public bills and resolutions were introduced and severally referred as follows:
>
> H. R. 7399 to establish the United States Housing Authority, to provide modern, large scale housing for families of low income,

---

[26] Statement of Henry Ellenbogen (personal interview). This "army" of Father Cox is not to be confused with the "bonus army" which camped in Washington and was eventually evicted by the Army. Father Cox arrived in Washington before the "bonus army" and led his unemployed back to Pittsburgh before the others arrived.

[27] Statement of Henry Ellenbogen (personal interview).

[28] Statements of Henry Ellenbogen, John Edelman, and Catherine Bauer (personal interviews).

to provide employment in the building and allied trades, to stimulate and stabilize the building industry, to increase consuming
power, to further national recovery, and to promote the public
health, safety, morals, and welfare, to the Committee on Banking
and Currency.[29]

There was a real tactical error on the part of the Labor
Housing Conference and Representative Ellenbogen in not ex-
erting enough pressure to convince Speaker Byrns that the bill
should go to the Committee on Labor rather than to the Committee on Banking and Currency. There was sufficient notice in
the title of the bill that its purpose and its subject matter were
more concerned with labor and unemployment and low income
families of laborers than with banking and currency. The referral of the bill to this particular committee and the attitude
of the chairman of the committee killed the bill in 1935 and
1936 and almost killed it in 1937. Once this committee took
jurisdiction over the bill—a public-housing bill—it was practically impossible to have it referred to another committee.

An examination of the provisions of the two bills shows the
different emphasis of the two groups and demonstrates the experience and ability of Representative Ellenbogen as a legislative draftsman. The first Wagner bill, drafted by Ira Robbins,
was done in the style of Wagner's NIRA.[30] The style of Ellenbogen's bill is that of the HOLC Act,[31] with which he was so
familiar. It should be noted that, aside from two minor provisions, legislators are given complete freedom in the drafting
of bills. There is a statutory provision that each bill shall have
a descriptive title.[32] This should be so accurate that when a leg-

---

[29] *Congressional Record*, April 10, 1935, p. 5393.

[30] 48 Stat. 90 (1933).

[31] 48 Stat. 64 (1933).

[32] Chester Lloyd Jones, *Statute Law Making in the United States*, p. 66 (Boston:
F. W. Faxon Company, 1923). Also see Asher C. Hinds, *Hinds' Precedents
of the House of Representatives of the United States*, Vol. 4, Sec. 3367,
pp. 288-89 (Washington: Government Printing Office, 1907).

islator reads it, he knows of all the major provisions that are contained in the bill. Abuse in this matter in bills other than appropriation bills is quite possible.[33] Another statute requires that each bill must have an enacting clause which is written out in the beginning of the bill.[34]

A comparison of these two bills[35] with the report of the Baltimore conference, *A Housing Program for the United States,*

---

[33] Jones, *Statute Law Making*, p. 67.

[34] *Ibid.*, p. 82. A comparison of the provisions of H. R. 7399 and S. 2392 is to be found in Appendix I.

[35] All bills introduced in Congress and amendments offered to them on the floor of the House are preserved in the Legislative Reference Service of the Congressional Library. It is to be noted that S. 2392 was introduced on *March 13 (calendar day, March 26, 1935).* This brings up the difference between the "legislative day" and the "calendar day." A "legislative day" is reckoned as that day which starts after an adjournment and continues until the next adjournment. In the Senate it happens that a "recess" will be taken from day to day rather than an adjournment. The reason for this tactic is that the recess keeps alive the unfinished business that was being transacted during the daily legislative session of the house when it is appropriate to call a break in the proceedings. An adjournment would mean that the legislative session of that day was finished, although there was unfinished business that would be taken up in the regular order of business at the next session. But with a recess there is no need to follow the regular daily order of business when the time for the recess is finished and the house reconvenes.

The following statement is found in the *Record* for March 13, 1935.

"Mr. Glass. As in legislative session, I move that the Senate take a recess until 12 o'clock noon tomorrow.

"The motion was agreed to: and (at 5 o'clock and 8 minutes P.M.) the Senate took a recess until tomorrow, Thursday, March 14, 1935, at 12 o'clock meridian" (*Congressional Record,* March 13, 1935, p. 3542).

The Senate went into legislative session at the end of each day, although immediately before the motion to recess the Senate had been in executive session (that part of the day during which presidential appointments or treaties are passed upon by the Senate) from March 13, 1935 until April 8, 1935. This was the period when President Roosevelt's work-relief program was being considered by the Senate. At the end of the session on April 8, 1935, after congressional leaders agreed to give priority to the unfinished business of a part of the work-relief program, Senator McKellar made the motion: "Mr. President, I move the Senate adjourn" (*Congressional Record,* April 8, 1935, p. 5245). So on April 8, 1935 (that was the date on the ordinary calendar) the legislative day of March 13, 1935 was concluded. All legislation introduced between March 13 and April 8, 1935, such as Wagner's

will show that many of the provisions and sections follow closely the report. This is not surprising, as the groups behind both of the bills were in attendance at the conference.

Section 1 in both bills was quite similar. In the Ellenbogen bill there was more emphasis on the relief of unemployment and on new building for families of low income; and a federal authority was contemplated. These ideas show the influence of advice that had been received from the labor group. In the Wagner bill there was more emphasis on unsanitary housing, slum clearance, and local government participation. These were the ideas of the NPHC.

In the section concerned with definitions, Section 2 in the Ellenbogen bill and Section 9 in the Wagner bill, there was a great difference. Ellenbogen's bill was much more detailed and provided for limited-dividend and nonprofit housing agencies. These were ideas that Catherine Bauer had developed. The Baltimore report (Section iii, 5) contemplates loans to limited-dividend corporations, but the plan is not developed.

In the section concerned with the administration of the housing authority there was a marked difference. The Ellenbogen bill provided for an independent authority administered by a three-member board. The Wagner bill provided for a single director. The Ellenbogen bill allowed the employees to be selected without regard for civil-service regulations, while the Wagner bill stated that appointments were to be made in accordance with civil-service laws and the classification act of 1923. The Ellenbogen bill spelled out in detail the organization of the au-

---

bill S. 2392, was considered as of the legislative day of March 13, 1935. On the calendar day of April 9, 1935 was begun the legislative day of April 9, 1935.

The House of Representatives, which operates on a more rigid schedule of business provided for by a number of different calendars, normally adjourns from day to day. Thus in the House the legislative day and the calendar day will coincide (*Hinds' Precedents*, Vol. 5, Secs. 6738-39, pp. 878-79).

thority, while the Wagner bill merely outlined it. The Baltimore conference report merely stated that the authority should have "sufficient independence" (Section 7).

The financial scheme of the Wagner bill was very simple. It called for an appropriation of $800,000,000. The Ellenbogen bill provided for a stock issue of $1,000,000, a bond issue not to exceed $1,000,000,000, and a $1,000,000 allotment from the Treasury. All the details of the scheme are worked out in Sections 4 and 5. The Baltimore conference report did not elaborate any specific financial scheme.

In outlining the powers and duties of the authority Ellenbogen placed more emphasis on direct construction (Section 6 (a), (b), (d), (e)). Wagner's bill looked to local bodies (Section 3, A (a), (b)). This difference in emphasis is attributable to the different backgrounds of the NPHC and the LHC. In making loans and grants to public-housing agencies both bills allowed for a grant of 30 per cent of the combined cost of labor and materials. The Baltimore conference report had recommended a grant of more than 20 per cent. The Ellenbogen bill was more liberal in the interest rates for which it provided. This bill also allowed a loan of 100 per cent to all housing agencies except limited-dividend.

The Housing Division was completely absorbed by the new authority in both plans. The Wagner bill, which contemplated local activity, made the necessary provision for demonstration projects in any area where no responsible local agency existed to do the job. Both bills provided for a research and planning section. This was recommended in Division VI, Number 5, of the Baltimore report.

The Ellenbogen bill had a section (Section 8) which guaranteed the prevailing rate of wages. It also provided for a priority for those projects which were already planned and ready to go and where land costs were low. Both of these provisions can be found in the Phillips resolution that Bauer and Edelman prepared for the 1934 AFL convention.[36] The Wagner bill also gave priority to those projects that were already planned and that were ready for construction.

The Ellenbogen bill then had sections which were concerned with the annual report of the authority and with penalties for those who acted illegally. These sections made a complete bill ready for enactment.

The Baltimore conference spoke of a subsidy. There is no mention of any subsidy in the Wagner bill, but in the Ellenbogen bill there was a provision which was in effect a subsidy. It provided for a change in the interest rate ranging from zero to the cost of the money to the government plus 1 per cent and it further provided that the interest rate could vary from time to time on the same project as well as in different projects.

In view of the fact that these bills followed the recommendations of the NAHO Baltimore conference, it is interesting to note the NAHO reaction. The reaction of NAHO to these bills was expressed in its bulletin for April 29, 1935.

> I wish to make clear that N.A.H.O. has taken no position either on this measure or on the bill introduced by Senator Wagner. Both bills, however, are indications of a growing realization that the assistance of low-cost housing eventually should be recognized as a permanent activity.[37]

The reason for this neutrality was that NAHO as a service organization was enjoying tax exemption. It could not engage in politics.

It was June 4, 1935 before David I. Walsh, senator from Massachusetts and chairman of the Senate Committee on Education and Labor, held hearings on the Wagner bill. The witnesses who were asked to testify on behalf of the bill had been care-

---

[36] *Supra*, Chap. 3.
[37] Comment of Coleman Woodbury, executive director, *National Association of Housing Officials, Bulletin No. 47*, April 29, 1935.

fully selected by Leon Keyserling with the help of the representatives from the NPHC.

Walsh allowed Wagner considerable freedom in setting the
pattern of the hearings. He allowed Wagner the first two days
in which to present the witnesses who would support the bill. On
the third and fourth days Walsh provided for the testimony of
those opposed to the bill and those representatives of organizations who wished to present substitute plans.[38]

When the hearings opened on Tuesday morning, June 4,
1935, Chairman Walsh and Senators Black and Thomas of Utah
were present. This was an attendance record of three members
in a total membership of twelve committee members. On the
other three days of the hearings only two members were present.
La Follette was present with Walsh on June 5 and 6, and
Donahey was present with Walsh on June 7.[39] More will be said
about the attendance of members at committee meetings in the
discussion of the Senate hearings of 1936 in Chapter 7 of
this study.

Senator Wagner was the first witness called by Chairman
Walsh. Wagner asked to be excused from testifying for the
present, and asked the committee to hear the testimony of Mrs.
Mary Simkhovitch at this time.[40] After Mrs. Simkhovitch had
explained the necessity for the legislation in terms of solving
the social problem, two witnesses from the United States Public
Health Service were called to testify on the relationship between
poor housing and poor health conditions. Dr. Joseph Mountain
spoke for Surgeon-General Cumming, who was unable to attend
this particular hearing. Rollo Britten, senior statistician of the
USPHS, presented to the committee the data that had been col-

---

[38] *Hearings before Senate Committee on Education and Labor on S. 2392 (Slum
[sic] and Low-Rent Public Housing)*, 74th Cong., 1st Sess. (1935). Washington: Government Printing Office, 1935.

[39] *Ibid.*, pp. 1, 29, 83, 141.

[40] *Ibid.*, p. 4.

lected by his staff relating to the relationship of poor housing and poor public-health conditions.[41]

The next witness was Ellis Searles, who appeared as the representative of Mr. John L. Lewis, president of the United Mine Workers.[42] The favorable testimony of Searles was followed by statements presented by Rabbi Edward Israel and by Reginal Johnson of the National Urban League, an organization made up of social workers among the Negroes. The testimony of these two representatives indicated the attitude of two important pressure groups.[43]

These witnesses were followed by representatives of people who were forced to live in the slums of New York City: John Volpe, of the East Side Public Housing Conference; and Mrs. Ida Harris, Rosa Beleteri, and Sheba Ziprin, of the Lower East Side Housing Conference. This group described vividly the horrible conditions of housing quarters in the areas in which they were particularly interested. They also mentioned that there were present in the committee room thirty-seven more persons from the Lower East Side Housing Conference.[44]

Mr. J. W. Williams, president of the Building Trades Department of the American Federation of Labor, was the final witness to be heard on the first day of the hearings.[45]

On Wednesday, June 5, 1935, testimony was taken from the housing experts. Langdon Post, of the New York City Housing Authority, made a lengthy and detailed statement concerning the results of the New York program and the necessity of further government aid to solve the housing problem.[46]

Horatio Hackett, director of the PWA Housing Division, presented to the committee the nationwide statistics that were gathered by the Housing Division together with the results of

---

41 *Ibid.*, pp. 7-8.
42 *Ibid.*, p. 10.
43 *Ibid.*, pp. 13, 16.

44 *Ibid.*, pp. 19-26.
45 *Ibid.*, p. 27.
46 *Ibid.*, pp. 29-47.

the practical experience of the PWA Housing Division program. Herbert Berman, director of the legal division of the PWA, accompanied Mr. Hackett and answered technical difficulties that the committee brought forward concerning the program.[47] This practice of an important witness bringing an expert technical adviser to a committee hearing is not uncommon.

Mrs. Edith Elmer Wood gave the committee the benefit of her long years of research in the field of housing in a statement in support of the bill.[48] Milton Lowenthal, of the Housing Study Guild, a research organization located in New York, gave the committee a statement in favor of the bill, and supplemented his remarks with a set of charts that filled twenty-one pages of the printed record.[49]

At the end of the testimony on Wednesday, a letter from Madame Frances Perkins was included in the record. She regretted that she was unable to attend because of the pressure of her duties, and asked the committee to consider a provision to be incorporated in the bill which would guarantee to the workers on the housing projects the prevailing rate of wages. She also asked that this new program be separated from any kind of a "relief-work" project. These two suggestions of Madame Perkins were in line with the policy of the AFL.[50]

Further testimony was taken from housing experts on Thursday, June 6. Miss Catherine Bauer, of the LHC, was called to give her statement. It was expected by the supporters of the bill that Miss Bauer would give testimony favorable to Senator Wagner's bill, but Miss Bauer praised the Ellenbogen bill and criticized many features of the Wagner bill.[51]

Mr. Ickes followed Catherine Bauer as a witness, and stated that it was satisfactory to him to have the new housing agency

[47] *Ibid.*, p. 48.
[48] *Ibid.*, p. 53.
[49] *Ibid.*, pp. 56-81.
[50] *Ibid.*, p. 82.
[51] *Ibid.*, pp. 83-92.

created by this bill located in his Department of the Interior. He objected, however, to the local control of the program that was outlined in the bill. Ickes thought that the program should be controlled from the central office in Washington.[52]

This statement clearly drew the line of battle between the followers of Ickes, who wanted a centralized agency, and the followers of Ellenbogen and the Labor Housing Conference, who wanted an independent agency in Washington which would supervise a decentralized program. It is true that the NPHC called for a program with local control, but by its constant insistence that Mr. Ickes be given jurisdiction of the program and the agency it was weakening the local-control provision of the bill. The one person in the NPHC most responsible for this inconsistency was Miss Helen Alfred. There were other officers of the organization who did not share her views, but they would not be able to control her writings in *Public Housing Progress* and they could not relieve her of her position as policy maker for the organization without the risk of impeding the progress of the entire organization.

Father John O'Grady, executive secretary of the National Conference of Catholic Charities and an officer of the NPHC, appeared before the committee after Ickes had concluded his testimony. Father O'Grady told the committee that government should foster the program of public housing, but he added that it should be decentralized.[53] He thus went on record as being opposed to the centralized control advocated by Mr. Ickes.

Mayor La Guardia and Helen Alfred testified in favor of the bill on the same morning. Ira Robbins made a very brief statement and then asked that the NAHO report, *A Housing Program for the United States*, be included in the record as a part of his testimony.[54]

---

[52] *Ibid.*, p. 92.
[53] *Ibid.*, p. 95.

[54] *Ibid.*, pp. 97, 102, 108.

John Edelman was called to testify after Ira Robbins, and provided another surprise for the supporters of the bill when he presented an unfavorable report on the Wagner bill. He started his statement with an apologetic remark to Senator Wagner, who was present at all the hearings, that he did not wish to criticize Senator Wagner's work but that, in the case of this bill, he thought it necessary. Wagner interrupted him to say: "You go on and do it [criticize the bill]. I favor constructive criticism, you know." Edelman then testified that the Ellenbogen bill was a better bill. He filed with the committee as a part of his testimony an analysis of the two bills made by the American Institute of Architects under the direction of Arthur C. Holden of New York, in which the Ellenbogen bill was shown to be superior to the Wagner bill. Edelman also suggested that provision be made in a public-housing bill for the construction of projects on vacant land rather than on slum sites.[55]

After Edelman had finished his testimony Walsh called the recognized opponents of the bill. Jacob O. Pedersen, of the Bronx Taxpayers Association, testified that the bill put the government in competition with private enterprise. He also testified that the provisions of the bill were unconstitutional. He presented to the committee Irving Isaacs, legal counsel for the Bronx Taxpayers Association, who developed a legal argument for the benefit of the committee to demonstrate that the measure was unconstitutional. Charles Eidt, of the Real Estate Owners Association of Manhattan, testified against the bill as fostering competition unfair to the real-estate owners. He suggested that old buildings should be rehabilitated. With this last statement the hearings were concluded for that day.[56]

The last day of the hearings was Friday, June 7, 1935, and on this day Chairman Walsh called a variety of witnesses who

[55] *Ibid.*, p. 123.
[56] *Ibid.*, pp. 130, 134, 139.

did not fit into either of the major groups supporting or opposing the bill. Benjamin Marsh, of the People's Lobby of
Washington, said that appropriations called for in the present
bill were unfair to the taxpayers. He suggested an alternate plan
of financing the program.[57]

Edgar Chambless, of Roadtown Foundation (a foundation
that Chambless had organized in New York to promote his ideas
for solving the housing problem), was the next witness. He explained his idea for city planning and housing construction.
"Your land is a constant," he stated, "and the more speed you
get, the more neighbors and fewer community institutions, and
the more land." This idea was explained further, in response
to questions by Senator Donahey, to mean that America should
build *out* instead of *up*. "There should be a line of improved
cities through the country, with coordination of agriculture,
commerce, communications, and the home."[58]

Testimony such as that of Chambless is not uncommon at a
committee hearing. If time is available, a committee will take
the testimony of individuals with new and revolutionary ideas
about methods of solving present problems.

Robert Sentmen appeared before the committee in behalf of
the Federation of Architects, Engineers, Chemists and Technicians. He asked that provision be made in the bill so that these
technical specialists would be specifically mentioned as covered
by the prevailing wage contracts.[59] This federation after much
negotiation, as will be seen in the development of the history
of the 1937 bill, finally had its request written into the provisions of the law.

Sentmen was the last witness called to testify. Chairman
Walsh ordered the clerk to include in the record all the various
briefs and statements that had been sent to the committee. Walsh

---

[57] *Ibid.*, p. 142.
[58] *Ibid.*, pp. 150-66.

[59] *Ibid.*, p. 167.

then declared that the hearings were closed and that the committee would take the evidence under advisement.[60]

The committee failed to report the bill to the Senate. And although Senate Rule 32 provides for carrying over such legislative proposals from one session to the next, still, for all practical purposes, Wagner bill S. 2392 was killed. Although the chairman did not make a report to the Senate on the bill, Walsh ordered that the testimony taken during the hearings be printed.

The most important thing that happened as a result of the hearings was the union of the Ellenbogen and Labor Housing group with the Wagner and National Public Housing Conference group. After the hearings Edelman and Bauer met Senator Wagner and Leon Keyserling and discussed their objections to the bill. Miss Bauer impressed Keyserling and Wagner, and they asked her to give them further information and advice.[61] This was the beginning of a working agreement between Catherine Bauer and Senator Wagner's office that was to have a direct influence on housing legislation.

After the hearings were completed Ellenbogen decided that the best thing to do to get a housing bill that would be passed by Congress would be to draft a compromise bill. The main compromise was to place the administration of the program under Mr. Ickes and the Department of the Interior. This change would assure the support of Mr. Ickes, of Senator Wagner, and of the National Public Housing Conference.[62]

Ellenbogen's second draft was introduced on June 25, 1935.[63] It was given the number H. R. 8666. It was referred to the Committee on Banking and Currency. In the first section he

---

[60] *Ibid.*, p. 169. The briefs and letters filed with the committee filled the remaining pages (pp. 170-226) of the printed *Hearings on S. 2392.*

[61] Statement of Catherine Bauer (personal interview).

[62] Statement of Henry Ellenbogen (personal interview).

[63] *Congressional Record*, June 25, 1935, p. 10127.

put added emphasis on slum clearance and stated that the United States Housing Authority was to be established in the Department of the Interior.

In the second section he added a definition of "slums":

> . . . an area in which predominate dwellings that either because of dilapidation, obsolescence, overcrowding, arrangement or design, lack of ventilation, light or sanitary facilities, or a combination of these factors, are detrimental to the safety, health, morals and comfort of the inhabitants thereof.

Also added was a definition of families of low income:

> . . . those families who, in good as well as in bad times, cannot afford to pay enough to induce the ordinary and usual channels of private enterprise to build adequate, safe and sanitary housing for their use.

Section 3 (b) was changed to read:

> Management of the authority shall be vested in a board of directors consisting of three members. The Secretary of the Interior shall be one of the members ex officio. The other members shall be appointed by the Secretary of the Interior.

There were other minor changes in language, and certain additions to clarify the provisions of the bill and avoid legal difficulties; but the only real change was that concerned with the administration.

Ellenbogen was recognized by the speaker on July 8, 1935 for the purpose of extending his remarks in the *Record*. The speech he had hoped to give was thus printed in the *Record*. He started this speech with an explanation of the fact that for over two years he had been working on housing legislation. He recalled his amendments to the HOLC legislation in order to save mortgages on homes. Now he was turning his attention to the fight for low-cost housing for people of low income.

Everyone, he said, recognized the need for housing; hence the United States must have a long-term program that looked to the future. In proof of the need for a program looking to the future, Ellenbogen gave statistics showing the increase in population, which argued for the need of an ever-increasing number of dwelling units. He went on to say that, considering all the factors of housing, rebuilding, vacancies, and new building, the United States would need 14,064,000 homes in the next ten years to meet decent standards of housing. For this last statement he quoted Catherine Bauer as the expert authority on housing needs. Only 5,000,000 of these homes could be built by ordinary channels of private industry, so Mr. Ellenbogen concluded that 9,000,000 of them would have to be built with government aid.

The argument that there were advantages in putting unemployed skilled workers back at jobs was stressed by Ellenbogen, then the argument that bad housing and slums breed crime and disease. Ellenbogen went on to demonstrate that the majority of families in the United States have low incomes. "Even during the peak year of 1929," he stated, "42 per cent of the families had incomes of less than $1,500 a year." That meant that they could not afford more than $25.00 a month for rent. Only with government aid could the problem be solved. He concluded with an explanation of the major provisions of the bill.[64]

Despite a personal and eloquent plea of Representative Ellenbogen to Chairman Steagall, the House Committee on Banking and Currency took no action on the bill.[65] Mr. Steagall of Alabama was not interested in the bill, and so he killed it.

---

[64] *Ibid.*, July 8, 1935, p. 10768. Because of the order of business in the House, which is strictly followed, Mr. Ellenbogen did not get an opportunity to deliver a speech on the day that he introduced his bill in the House. Finally, on July 8, he decided that because of the pressure of business he would not have any opportunity to deliver his speech. Hence on this day he asked for unanimous consent to extend his remarks in the *Record*. Thus it happened that this speech, as happens with many others printed in the *Congressional Record*, was never delivered on the floor of the House.

[65] Statement of Henry Ellenbogen (personal letter).

The House Committee on Ways and Means also failed to take any action on the House companion bill to Senator Wagner's bill that Representative Wood had introduced.

So when Congress adjourned on August 26, 1935, the House had taken no action on the two bills that had been introduced, and the Senate Committee on Education and Labor had held hearings but had failed to report out of committee the bill that Senator Wagner had introduced. With the adjournment of Congress, for all practical purposes, these bills died. It would be necessary to reintroduce housing legislation at the next session of Congress.

CHAPTER V

Pressure Groups
and the 1936 Campaign

During the summer and autumn of 1935 a series of events occurred that was so to influence the campaign for public housing that at the beginning of the next session of Congress there would be a three-cornered battle for control of public-housing legislation.

After Representative Ellenbogen introduced his second bill on June 25, 1935, he sent a letter to Senator Wagner requesting a conference with him to discuss the provisions of the new draft of the bill.[1] Ellenbogen was sufficiently independent to write his own bill and to introduce it without Wagner's help, but he was also vitally interested in getting a housing bill passed by Congress and for this purpose he needed the advice and support of the senator.

Ellenbogen and Senator Wagner's legislative assistant, Leon Keyserling, who was managing the housing legislation for Wagner, had several conferences; but as the adjournment of Congress was imminent, the serious work of drafting a bill that would be jointly sponsored by Wagner and Ellenbogen was postponed until the first of the year.[2]

---

[1] Ellenbogen to Wagner, June 25, 1935, Wagner Papers, Pending Legislation—1935.
[2] Statement of Henry Ellenbogen (personal interview).

Meanwhile the policy committee of the NPHC had several meetings to revise its bill. On August 20, 1935 it announced that a revised draft of the bill was ready.[3] By this time, however, NPHC had lost control of the drafting of the legislation. Wagner had now joined forces with Ellenbogen and had shown his preference for the latter's bill. He was not interested in introducing the revised bill of the NPHC.

The NPHC as a pressure group had accomplished the first step of the work. It had drafted and obtained congressional sponsorship for its legislation. It could not consider itself slighted if the legislator who assumed responsibility for sponsorship took over control of the revision and drafting of the bill. The chief job of the NPHC was still before it. It was to build up public support for the legislation to insure its passage by Congress. This the NPHC did by sponsoring luncheons and dinners and meetings, all with speeches and publicity in favor of the legislation. During the last months of 1935 NPHC did not miss an opportunity for organizing any kind of demonstration that would get public housing in the news and before the public. New members were recruited and the conference was publishing its news bulletin, *Public Housing Progress,* which brought to the members of NPHC and friends of public housing the news of latest developments.[4]

Some individual labor leaders supported the bill at the hearings, but the American Federation of Labor as a national organization had not come out in support of the measure. The members of the AFL who gave favorable testimony were officials of the Building Trades Department who had been influenced and convinced by the members of the Labor Housing Conference at the 1934 convention in San Francisco. And now in October

---

[3] Open letter of NPHC, August 20, 1935, NPHC File, 1935.
[4] See *Public Housing Progress,* August 15, 1935 (Vol. 1) to December 15, 1935 (Vol. 2).

of 1935 the Labor Housing Conference was ready to complete
its work at the convention to be held in Atlantic City.[5]

At this convention Catherine Bauer, James McDevitt, and
John Edelman arranged to have the advice and support of
Ernest J. Bohn and Warren J. Vinton, the research director of
the Resettlement Administration. During the first week of the
convention the Labor Housing Conference leaders arranged to
present a labor housing forum for the information and inspiration of the delegates. Announcement to all the delegates of the
first meeting of the forum was made at the end of the general
session on the morning of October 9, 1935. James L. McDevitt
was chosen to preside at the meeting, and Catherine Bauer was
the secretary. The list of sponsors of the forum included the
leaders of the labor housing conference from Pennsylvania and
New Jersey; and in addition to these veterans, the group had
been successful in obtaining the active support of George Meany
of the New York State Federation and John Carroll of the
Massachusetts State Federation. The two leaders of two of
the most powerful organizations in the AFL, together with
some other men from their own states and a few from other
large cities, made up the impressive list of sponsors.[6] This
list of influential sponsors was an indication that the convention would be forced to give favorable consideration to public-
housing resolutions.

Ernest J. Bohn and Warren Vinton, who were present at the
forum as experts on technical housing problems, were very
helpful to the conference in convincing the leadership of the
federation of the advisability and necessity of supporting a
government-aided public-housing program.

---

[5] Information about this convention was obtained from Catherine Bauer, John
Edelman, James McDevitt, Ernest J. Bohn, and Warren Vinton (personal
interviews).

[6] *Report of Proceedings of the Fifty-fifth Annual Convention of the American
Federation of Labor*, p. 315. Washington: Judd and Detweiler, 1935.

Three resolutions were presented at this convention in favor
of public housing. In the report of the Committee on Resolutions
the first resolution to be considered was presented by J. W.
Williams of the Building Trades Department. He had testified
in favor of public housing at the Senate committee hearings.

> *Resolution No. 116: Slum Clearance and Low Rent Housing
> Program . . .*
>
> WHEREAS, The Building Trades Department of the American
> Federation of Labor has given very careful consideration to the
> question of the unemployment situation with a view of being help-
> ful in providing steady employment to all those engaged in building
> and construction thereby eliminating the necessity of supplying
> relief for those who have been forced to accept relief; and
>
> WHEREAS, The Building Trades Department of the American
> Federation of Labor has reviewed the efforts of the Federal Housing
> Administration, The National Public Housing Conference, and the
> Labor Housing Conference in their endeavor to correct the unem-
> ployment situation and in Convention adopted this resolution and
> calls upon the American Federation of Labor to endorse the action
> of the Building Trades Department: therefore be it
>
> *Resolved,* That the American Federation of Labor go on record
> as being in sympathy with the Slum Clearance and Low Rent
> Housing Program which has for its purpose provisions that will
> furnish employment to those engaged in the building and construc-
> tion industry.[7]

This resolution was adopted unanimously by the convention.
It placed the American Federation of Labor on record as officially in favor of a slum-clearance program. This resolution
manifested the strong influence of the NPHC with its emphasis
on slum clearance.

The next resolution reported by the committee was presented
by Frank Hughes of the Pennsylvania State Federation of Labor. This resolution was very much like the one that Catherine
Bauer and Edelman had prepared with Phillips the year before.

---

[7] *Ibid.,* p. 612.

This year, however, the resolution was not presented to incite discussion, for the labor housing conference was interested in winning the approval of the convention. The resolution omitted such controversial provisions as the establishment of a new Cabinet office and a very large appropriation. It did put the federation on record in favor of a permanent long-range program. It stipulated the necessity of union laborers working at union rate of wages. It also contained a clause providing for union and consumer representation on housing authorities and priority for projects when the authorities had plans and were ready to build. But the important provision, as far as effective support of the legislation was concerned, was contained in the last section, which stated:

> *Resolution No. 119: Housing Projects . . .*
>
> *Resolved,* That the American Federation of Labor, in convention assembled, authorize the appointment of a committee to aid, direct and collaborate with the Labor Housing Conference or other suitable agency in providing information, promoting legislation, developing projects, and protecting the interests of labor and consumers in the housing movement.[8]

The committee reported its approval of the resolution and recommended its adoption. It was accordingly unanimously adopted by the convention.

The third resolution on public housing was presented by Charles Hollopeter of New Jersey, vice-chairman of the labor-housing conference. This resolution was almost identical with the resolution of Hughes, but it added two practical provisions not contained in the Hughes resolution.

> *Resolution No. 98: Public Housing . . .*
>
> *Resolved,* That local Labor Housing Committees should be set up, to take the lead in developing an active public demand for housing, to initiate suitable projects, and to represent, protect and

---

[8] *Ibid.,* p. 613.

promote the interests of labor and consumers in the location, design, construction and management of public housing projects: . . .

Resolved, That the American Federation of Labor, in convention assembled, authorize the appointment of a committee to aid, direct and collaborate with the Labor Housing Conference or other suitable agency in providing information, promoting legislation, developing projects, and protecting the interests of labor and consumers in the housing movement.[9]

This resolution with its two very practical provisions was also unanimously adopted by the convention.

The adoption of the program outlined in these resolutions made the American Federation of Labor the largest and most important pressure group in the fight for public housing. The federation had the largest and best-organized membership of any group in the United States, and it had influence with the Roosevelt administration. With the active support of the AFL, the promoters of a public-housing program were now certain of a victory for their bill.

The persons in the American Federation of Labor responsible for making effective the pressure exercised by the organization were the members of the Labor Housing Conference and the Labor Housing Committee. After the convention was over, the headquarters of the Labor Housing Conference were moved from Philadelphia to Washington, and both the staff and the budget were increased by the AFL. Boris Shishkin, an economist, was brought into the conference to collaborate with Catherine Bauer. The Housing Committee of the AFL was appointed by the Executive Council at its 1936 January meeting. It was composed of Harry C. Bates, president of the Bricklayers, Masons and Plasterers' International Union and a vice-president of the AFL; John Coefield, president of the Plumbers and Steam Fitters United Association and a vice-president of the AFL; and

---

[9] *Ibid.*, p. 614.

M. J. Colleran, president of the Operative Plasterers International Organization.[10]

This committee worked with the Labor Housing Conference in the development of a legislative program for public housing. Actually all the technical work connected with the drafting of a legislative program was done by Catherine Bauer. Boris Shishkin presented the position of the AFL to various legislators and congressional committees. The Labor Housing Committee gave advice and approval to the conference and represented the AFL at the White House and spoke to members of Congress in the name of the federation.

The housing program drafted by the Housing Committee provided for federal loans and subsidies to local agencies for the construction of safe and sanitary housing for families of low income. This federal assistance was also designed to encourage slum clearance and to provide a wide base for a revival of durable goods and reemployment. It was recommended that an independent agency should be appointed to administer the program. Funds were to be provided through the sale of bonds. Safeguards to guarantee union labor to work at union rates and under union conditions were to be written into the bill.[11] This program was then transmitted to the delegates of the nineteen building-trades organizations at a meeting in February of 1936 for their consideration. It received their final approval by the twenty-fifth of February.[12]

In addition to the convention of the American Federation of Labor there were convened during this time other conferences and conventions concerned with housing. None of them were of the same importance with regard to the Wagner housing bill as

---

[10] "Report of the Executive Committee"; in *Report of Proceedings of the Fifty-sixth Annual Convention of the American Federation of Labor,* p. 177. Washington: Judd and Detweiler, 1936.

[11] *Ibid.,* p. 178.

[12] *Ibid.*

was the AFL convention, but they did have something to contribute to the housing program.

Immediately before the AFL convention the National Conference on Labor Legislation held its meeting in Asheville, North Carolina, on October 4 and 5. This conference had previously appointed a housing committee under the chairmanship of John Ihlder to investigate and report on housing programs and legislation.[13] The committee report favored a program of government-aided public housing. It did not specify a particular program, but its support of the policy of public-housing legislation was helpful to the Labor Housing Conference in convincing wavering delegates at the AFL convention.

Immediately after the AFL convention there was convened the joint National Conference on Housing in Washington (October 16, 17, and 18). Again Ernest J. Bohn was the prime mover of the conference. Frederic A. Delano, chairman of the Central Housing Committee, was chairman of the conference. The organization committee, under the direction of Ernest J. Bohn, was composed of Miss Helen Atwater, secretary of the American Home Economics Association; John Ihlder, of the Alley Dwelling Authority; Harlean James, of the American Civic Association; Leifus Magnusson, director of the International Labor Organization; John Nolen, president of the International Federation of Housing and Town Planning; Samuel Rotensky, executive secretary of the Housing Study Guild; Mrs. Mary K. Simkhovitch; and Alfred K. Stern, of the Illinois State Board of Housing.[14] The immediate result of this meeting was a consolidation of support for the public-housing program.

The president received a great deal of advice during the last half of 1935. Most of the many plans that arrived in the White House office were filed away without any consideration.

---

[13] *Report of the Fifty-fifth Convention of AFL*, p. 217.
[14] *National Association of Housing Officials, Bulletin No. 69*, September 25, 1935.

But there were a few that received personal and serious consideration by the president. This usually resulted from the fact that the author of the plan had a reputation as an expert. One such plan was presented by Sol A. Rosenblatt. His plan impressed the president. It provided for a government loan to limited-dividend corporations of 90 per cent of the cost of the project at an interest of $2\frac{1}{2}$ per cent. The president thought the plan had some merit and sent it to Jesse Jones with a memorandum in which he asked him to talk it over with the secretary of the interior and inform the president about a reply.[15] So many of the departments and agencies of the executive branch were becoming involved in housing affairs that the president sent a memorandum to the National Resources Board early in 1935 in which he asked it to investigate the possibility of coordinating all housing activities. The Central Housing Committee evolved out of the activity initiated by this memorandum.[16]

The National Resources Board appointed a special committee to investigate the situation to which the president had referred. On May 27, 1935 this committee made its *Report of the Committee on Coordination of the Housing Activities of the Federal Government.* This report covered the steps already taken on the initiative of the various staff groups of the government agencies. The report also recommended to the president that he appoint a central committee. By a memorandum dated June 29, 1935 the president approved the organization of the Central Housing Committee. On August 29, 1935 there were two conferences at the White House of the heads of important housing agencies. Present at the meetings were A. R. Clas, director of the Housing Division of PWA; John Fahey, of HOLC; Peter Grimm, special assistant to Secretary of the Treasury Henry Morgenthau; James A. Moffett, of the Federal

---

[15] Memorandum of Roosevelt to Jones, August 6, 1935, Roosevelt Papers, O.F. 63.
[16] Delano to Roosevelt, January 30, 1936, Roosevelt Papers, O.F. 2694.

Housing Administration; Stewart McDonald, of the Federal Housing Administration; and Rexford G. Tugwell, of the Resettlement Administration.

After these two meetings the president issued another memorandum authorizing the continuance of the committee and its work. He also granted the committee $10,000 to pay for a secretariat. The Bureau of the Budget, however, refused to authorize the grant of $10,000, so the secretariat was made up of a staff contributed by the participating agencies.

The full membership of the Central Committee (as of January 30, 1936) was made up of the following agencies and representatives: Frederic A. Delano, chairman; Peter Grimm, of the Treasury, assistant to the chairman; N. Max Dunning, of the Treasury; W. I. Meyers and Herbert Emmerich, of the Farm Credit Administration; John H. Fahey and Ormond E. Loomis, of the Federal Home Loan Bank Board; Stewart McDonald and Miles Colean, of the Federal Housing Administration; Lyle T. Alverson and C. H. Coter, of the National Emergency Council; Horatio B. Hackett and A. R. Clas, of the Housing Division of PWA; Earl B. Schwulst and John W. Slacks, of the Reconstruction Finance Corporation; and Rexford G. Tugwell and John Lansill, of the Resettlement Administration. Horace W. Peaslee, of the Housing Division of PWA, was secretary of the committee and Don K. Price, of the National Resources Board, was the personal assistant to the chairman.[17]

This committee began to work out plans for a long-range housing program. This program would naturally emphasize government loans and mortgage insurance because the membership of the committee was taken almost entirely from agencies involved in such programs. The first publication of the committee

---

[17] Frederic A. Delano, "The Central Housing Committee, A Report to the President of the Housing Activities of the Federal Government," Roosevelt Papers, O.F. 2694.

was a large booklet filled with charts and diagrams and statistics entitled *Present Activities and Organization of Federal Housing Agencies.* This was a confidential publication of limited circulation that was dated January 1936.

Of more importance than this booklet was the *Report of the Central Housing Committee,* dated January 30, 1936. This was a confidential typewritten report of Chairman Frederic A. Delano to the president. In it he asked that the president give a definite signed authorization to the committee covering its organization and procedure. The committee had been operating up to that time on a temporary basis. Chairman Delano was asking that it be put on a permanent basis. This report also had some recommendations about a permanent housing program. It emphasized the necessity of loans and mortgage insurance and the role of private enterprise. The report also criticized the work of the Housing Division of PWA as competitive to other government programs and as resulting in these other programs becoming stalled and ineffective.[18]

The report was delivered to the White House by Don Price on January 31, 1936. It was to be kept confidential and to be released only after the president's approval. But there was a leak in the administration. Delano suggested that it might have been J. M. Daiger, special assistant to the Federal Reserve Board, who let out the information. The *New York Times* carried an article on the report and some of its contents on January 31, 1936. As a result of this story a number of telephone calls, telegrams, and letters were sent to Washington by persons professionally interested in the housing program asking for an explanation of the confusing story in the *New York Times.* Mary Simkhovitch sent a telegram to the White House that very day asking the president to make a statement clarifying the

---

[18] Report of Delano to Roosevelt on Central Housing Committee, January 30, 1936, Roosevelt Papers, O.F. 1972.

story.[19] Finally, on February 7, 1936 Delano telephoned the White House and asked if the White House had released the report. The White House told him that the president had not authorized the release of the report. Delano then asked if the president would authorize the release. The White House office made a telephone call to Delano one hour later to inform him that the president said that no publicity was to be given to the report at this time.[20]

The president could not give his approval to the report of the Central Housing Committee because of the simple, hard fact that such approval and release would give it an official character, thus indicating to all those interested in housing that this particular plan was the one he favored. Because of the president's commitments to Senator Wagner, to Secretary Ickes, and to the National Public Housing Conference and because of the position of the American Federation of Labor on housing, any such move would have been impolitic. In addition to this very strong argument against approval of the Central Housing Committee report, there was also the fact that the president had not made up his mind about any particular housing plan.

Ben Grey, a housing adviser to the president, was given the task of evaluating the various plans that had been submitted to the White House, and in a letter to the president dated January 30, 1936 he presented the president with an unfavorable report on all the plans he had considered as possibilities.[21] The most important of these plans were submitted by Allie Freed and Alexander Sachs and Marriner Eccles.

The Sachs-Eccles plan was modeled in great part on the English system, with a number of modifications to meet the circumstances peculiar to the United States. It contained provi-

---

[19] Telegram of Simkhovitch to Roosevelt, January 31, 1936, Roosevelt Papers, O.F. 63.

[20] White House office memoranda, February 7, 1936, Roosevelt Papers, O.F. 1972.

[21] Grey to Roosevelt, January 30, 1936, Roosevelt Papers, O.F. 63.

sions for loans with contingent liability and an interest subsidy. It was worked out so that there would be no government inter- ference with private enterprise.[22]

Allie Freed, who was chairman of the Committee for Eco- nomic Recovery, a committee which Mr. Freed himself organ- ized, outlined in his plan the job of the Federal Government in solving the housing problem. The government was to aid and promote home building by private enterprise. This government aid and promotion was to take the form of a proper flow of mortgage credit to finance the product of the building industry. Finally, the Federal Government would develop, in cooperation with state and local governments, noncompetitive projects for the benefit of the lowest income groups which could not be served by private enterprise.[23]

The "Washington Merry-Go-Round" for February 12, 1936 carried the story that President Roosevelt favored the plan of Mr. Allie S. Freed. It also stated that Mrs. F. D. Roosevelt was in favor of making Freed head of the new government housing agency. This statement was incorrect, as were many of the other statements that were made during this period by Washington correspondents in reference to the housing bills being advocated by individuals or by groups.

The president also considered a memorandum, which was unsigned, which provided for the participation of the Depart- ment of Commerce in increasing the supply of housing units. The Department of Commerce would be responsible for organ- izing private industry into an efficient team to end the housing

---

[22] *Ibid.*
[23] *Ibid.* Also consult Allie S. Freed, "Home Building—The Nation's Hope," *Savings and Loans Journal of the American Savings and Loan Institute* 11:3-8, April 1936. Allie S. Freed also filed with the Senate Committee on Education and Labor a long brief in which he outlined his ideas on housing. See *Hearings before Senate Committee on Education and Labor on S. 4424,* 74th Cong., 2d Sess. (1936), pp. 299-308 (Washington: Government Printing Office, 1936).

shortage. All the activities of loans, and so forth, would be channeled through the Central Housing Committee.[24]

One plan that aroused the president's interest was outlined in the report which was submitted by Charles G. Meyer, delegate of the FHA to the International Housing and Town Planning Conference in London during July of 1935, wherein he recommended a system of insuring the existing home mortgages by the Federal Housing Administration.[25]

After studying various and sundry plans of mortgage insurance the president jotted down a personal memorandum about a second mortgage:

> 2nd Mortgage by Gov. 6$
> Credit diff. between the 6
> and what Gov. pays (3%) to
> the owner to amortize
> his 2nd Mtg.[26]

Later he received a memorandum from John Fahey of HOLC on a second-mortgage plan. Fahey pointed out that housing needs could be filled by employing private funds in the main and using government funds only as an aid. Provision of a second mortgage would help to finance the housing needs within the existing framework of the HOLC.[27]

Fahey continued his memorandum by stating that, given the opportunity to make a small down payment of 10 or 15 per cent and regular monthly amortization and interest payments at the equivalent of normal rent or less, American families would be in the market for homes, with consequent beneficial results to the entire country.

---

[24] Memorandum to the president (unsigned), February 26, 1936, Roosevelt Papers, O.F. 1972.

[25] Meyer to Roosevelt, January 15, 1936, Roosevelt Papers, O.F. 1614.

[26] Personal memorandum of Roosevelt, February 26, 1936, Roosevelt Papers, O.F. 1972.

[27] Fahey to Roosevelt, April 18, 1936, Roosevelt Papers, P.S.F.—Housing, 1936.

This plan impressed the president so much that he requested that it be placed in the "President's Secretary's File" and kept in his office.[28] As will be seen later, during the housing conferences of February and March of 1936 the president was constantly bringing up this second-mortgage plan and asking his advisers to work it out in specific provisions. Congressman Ellenbogen, who had a number of conferences with the president at this time, said that it was the president's idea that each family should have its own little home. He was opposed to families' living in large multi-unit dwelling projects.[29] It was a most difficult job for the public-housing supporters—one that required a period of almost two years—to convince the president that there was no disagreement about his plan as an ideal but that, as a plan to be put into operation that very year, it was not practical. The "public housers" claimed that the families in the lowest income groups could not afford to carry a mortgage and that, even if they could, there would not be enough private capital to supply the tremendous demand; nor would the private builders be willing to put up a decent house meeting minimum standards at a price between $2,000 and $4,000.

There were other practical difficulties connected with the second-mortgage plan. The workers did not want to move into the country, where the cheap vacant land was to be found, and the AFL had already manifested its disapproval of the "garden cities." Moreover, the city politicians did not want their "votes" to move out of their district. Roosevelt finally decided that these practical considerations outweighed the arguments in favor of his plan. But this change of mind was not to take place until the early part of 1937.

The procedure of individuals and agencies presenting plans directly to the president demonstrated that the Central Housing

---

28 It was noted on the folder: "Kept in President's Office at his own request."
29 Statement of Henry Ellenbogen (personal interview).

Committee was not functioning as the clearing house for housing activities that it was intended to be. In the scramble for control of the government housing program each agency was attempting to preserve its own existence.

When the *New York Times* carried its news story, on January 31, 1936, about the Central Housing Committee report, Mayor La Guardia telephoned to the Housing Division of PWA to ask for an explanation of the existing status of public housing. New York City and PWA had entered into negotiations concerning a number of projects, and the mayor wanted to know what was the status of the program. A. R. Clas, director of the Housing Division, spoke with the mayor over the telephone about the matter and then wrote him a letter explaining more fully the status and future possibilities of the public-housing program. In this letter he explained that the Housing Division was in favor of government aid to municipalities for projects that were well planned (inferring that those in New York City were so planned). He further stated that the PWA always pleaded its case in the meetings of the Central Housing Committee. He refuted the charge that the PWA Housing Division was wrecking the program of other agencies, pointing out that PWA Housing Division was concerned only with the low income group which could not be served by assistance from any other government agency. Clas then stated that the Housing Division of PWA was drafting a bill for a permanent housing program at the request of Senator Wagner. He enclosed with the letter the latest draft of the bill.[30]

This last statement of Clas brings out the alliance between Wagner and Ickes. This alliance was one of necessity, and dated from December of 1935.

On September 24, 1935 the *New York Times* reported that President Roosevelt had cut back government spending, and

---

[30] Clas to La Guardia (copy), February 3, 1936, Vinton Papers.

thus funds for housing construction by the Federal Government were stopped. During October some funds from those appropriated for housing construction by the Emergency Relief Appropriation Act of 1935[31] were transferred to the FERA to be used for relief work. Both of these transfers of funds were effected without an official executive order. Ickes thought that Hopkins was more responsible for this transfer than was the president, because of this absence of an executive order and because the money went into the agency of which Hopkins was the administrator;[32] but it did not matter to those affected by the cutback whether Hopkins or Roosevelt was the prime mover. Roosevelt must take the responsibility for the action. The White House was flooded with messages of protest. Senators and representatives and Democratic party leaders sent telegrams and letters to the president to tell him he was making a bad mistake by this action. He was going back on his promises, they reminded him; and he was in danger of losing votes in the big states, especially New York.[33] The *Public Housing Progress* for October 15, 1935 reported that 18,000 telegrams were sent to the White House in protest over the end of housing construction. The NPHC was behind this protest demonstration.

The president was so upset by this public reaction that before he left Washington for a vacation at Warm Springs,

---

[31] 49 Stat. 48 (1935).

[32] The confusion about the responsibility for the cutback of funds for housing construction is caused by the lack of promulgation of any official order, such as an executive order, and by the various newspaper reports of the cutback. Three reports in the *New York Times* are concerned with this incident: September 24, 1935, December 20, 1935, and January 31, 1936. In none of these reports is the incident explained accurately or authoritatively. Ickes' remarks are given in the article in the issue of December 20, 1935. There are a number of executive orders issued at this time to authorize the transfer of funds from one agency to another, but there is no executive order to authorize this particular transfer. See Lord, *Presidential Executive Orders.*

[33] Various letters to Roosevelt, October and November 1935, Roosevelt Papers, O.F. 63.

Georgia, he dictated a memorandum to Senator Wagner. He told him that when he got back to Washington from his vacation and when he (Wagner) was back in Washington, "I should much like to have a talk with you in regard to the more permanent aspects of slum-clearance and low-cost housing."[34] A copy of this memorandum was sent to Mrs. Roosevelt because of her activity in behalf of Mrs. Simkhovitch and the NPHC message urging the adoption of a federal public-housing bill.[35]

Even at Warm Springs the president did not get away from the pressure for a public-housing bill. Miss Alfred sent to him at Warm Springs a petition adopted at an abolish-the-slums luncheon held in New York's Hotel Commodore on December 3, 1935.[36] When the president had returned from Warm Springs and was preparing his message to Congress, Mrs. Simkhovitch sent him a long telegram requesting that he include in that message the importance of a government subsidy to insure "low-rent housing initiated and carried forth by local authorities."[37]

The PWA Housing Division had been working on drafts of a housing bill during the autumn. These drafts were really amendments to the National Housing Act. They provided for more liberal insurance and especially for loans and insurance for multi-unit dwelling structures.[38]

Then in December of 1935 the PWA Housing Division adopted a new tactic. After the PWA funds were diverted to the Relief Administration, the Housing Division realized that any effective housing program would have to be divorced from relief consideration. At the same time the division had become convinced by its legal difficulties that responsibility for the program

[34] Roosevelt to Wagner, October 28, 1935, Roosevelt Papers, O.F. 63.
[35] Copy of Roosevelt to Wagner to Mrs. Roosevelt, October 28, 1935, Roosevelt Papers, O.F. 63.
[36] Alfred to Roosevelt, December 3, 1935, Roosevelt Papers, O.F. 63.
[37] Simkhovitch to Roosevelt, December 31, 1935, Roosevelt Papers, O.F. 63.
[38] Copies of these drafts are to be found in the Vinton Papers.

must be put on the local authorities and municipal bodies. On the nineteenth of December, Administrator Ickes made a statement in which he said that he would aid Senator Wagner and that he would throw the support of the Department of the Interior to Wagner's bill because it solved the two problems that had crippled the program of the Housing Division.[39] In acknowledgment of this support Senator Wagner asked Secretary Ickes to have his staff draft some provisions to be included in the housing bill.

Senator Wagner found himself in a very difficult position because of his action in accepting the aid of Secretary Ickes. He knew that Ickes and his supporters in the National Public Housing Conference wanted the administration in the Department of the Interior. Wagner also knew that it was essential for the successful passage of the legislation to cooperate with the American Federation of Labor. This group, under the guidance of Catherine Bauer and Boris Shishkin, were stubborn in their demand that the housing program be administered by an independent agency. The working out of this conflict of interests is one of the most interesting parts of the story of the housing bill.

With the social-security law[40] passed during the last session of Congress (August 14, 1935), Wagner was able to devote his time and energy to the building up of public support for his housing bill. The activity of Wagner during this period is typical of the role of a legislator in the intricacies of the modern legislative process. As stated before, Wagner had turned over all the technical work of drafting the housing bill to his legislative assistant Leon Keyserling. He had told Representative Ellenbogen to work out the provisions of the bill with Keyserling.[41] At this same time Wagner told Ickes to send to his office

---

[39] *New York Times,* December 20, 1935.
[40] 49 Stat. 531 (1935).
[41] Statement of Henry Ellenbogen (personal interview).

any suggestions that he might wish to make. Catherine Bauer, Warren J. Vinton, and others were giving technical assistance to Keyserling. Keyserling's office in the Senate Office Building thus became the clearing house for housing information and a headquarters for the technical experts who were attempting to develop broad statements of policy and spell them out in specific legislative proposals.

Senator Wagner, except for daily conferences with Keyserling and occasional conferences with other housing experts, had almost no part in this work. His was the job of selling public housing to the voters, getting presidential support, and guiding the bill through the senatorial legislative channels. This is all that can be expected of a legislator in this day and age, when legislative drafting involves technical and specialized knowledge for every different legislative proposal. It is noteworthy that Senator Wagner did not use the legislative counseling services available at that time.[42] He preferred to draft the legislation in his own office.

On October 27, 1935 Wagner delivered a radio address on housing needs.[43] He made another address on the same subject before the National Public Housing Conference at its Washington meeting on December 3, 1935. The title of his speech was "Housing, A National Program." In it Wagner outlines his philosophy of public housing.

> To state this development in another way, we are passing from an age when the worthy individual could help himself to an era when we must rely more and more upon cooperative action. No

---

[42] The Office of the Legislative Counsel was organized in 1919 in order to assist the committees, and if possible the members, of Congress with the technicalities of the drafting of bills. It has done some excellent work with its limited staff. Wagner, however, preferred to get his information from the departments of the executive branch of the government. See Frederic P. Lee, "The Office of the Legislative Counsel," *Columbia Law Review* 29:381, April 1929.

[43] *New York Times*, October 28, 1935.

longer is it easy for a man to build his own home, to go prospecting in the West, or to rise rapidly in industry. Society has become more stratified. There is, of course, no reason why we should abandon hope or cut short our efforts to raise wage standards, or lose our objective in giving dignity to all occupations. But we need to realize fundamentally that individual action must be supplemented by a well-planned and coordinated housing program for the people of the country. . . .

The object of public housing, in a nutshell, is not to invade the field of home building for the middle class or the well-to-do which has been the only profitable area for private enterprise in the past. Nor is it even to exclude private enterprise from major participation in a low-cost housing program. It is merely to supplement what private industry will do, by subsidies which will make up the difference between what the poor can afford to pay and what is necessary to assure decent living quarters. . . .

The subsidy idea, like schools and parks, hospitals and public libraries, embodies the principle that the distribution of our national income has not been entirely just, and that the interests of all the people require that the Government play its part in promoting improvement. . . .

The bill that I introduced at the last session of Congress, and that I believe will be pushed to a successful conclusion when Congress meets again, is built around this principle. While the subsidy must be Federal, the initiation, the supervision, and the major part of the home building program must be left to the localities. This is desirable not only from the administrative point of view, but because homes are part of the fabric of community life. They express sectional and regional habits and ideals. They must reflect spontaneous impulses of the people themselves.[44]

On January 30, 1936 the senator made an important address before the New York Building Congress, a powerful organization whose support or opposition could definitely affect the entire fate of the bill under consideration. Before this group Wagner emphasized the relationship between the provision of low-rent housing and business recovery.

---

[44] Collected Papers of Wagner, Vol. 7, Sec. 3, No. 13.

It is a grievous mistake to entertain fears that a low-rent program would encroach upon private industry. In the first place, it would by very definition be confined to that section of the population which individual enterprise alone cannot serve. Its tenants would be limited to those whose incomes would not permit them to seek similar quarters elsewhere. Secondly, the strict decentralization of administration among the various localities would guarantee that all activity would be carried on in close contact with the general business needs of the community, and would be quickly responsive to them.

In fact, a low-rent program would give a decided impetus to private industry. It would create purchasing power by swelling the volume of employment. It would increase the demand for raw and fabricated materials that business produces. It would open up an area for some investment by private capital. It would tone up the residential standards of every element of the population.

But the real benefits of a low-rent housing program must be gauged in broader terms. The disease and crime that are generated in slum areas produce an appalling social waste. They multiply the costs of fire and police protection, of hospitals, reformatories, and prisons. They pyramid taxation and decrease industrial efficiency. They undermine the strength of free institutions. All these evils would be mitigated by the removal of the slums. The British have found, in a low-rent housing program, the most concrete reinforcement for political democracy and individual enterprise in a troubled and unsettled world.

There is no business group that will not bend every effort toward giving all the youth of America a chance—a chance to breathe fresh air, to play in safe places, to be free from the threatening influences of sordid home surroundings.[45]

The press reports of this speech were so slanted that some of those interested in a public-housing program got the impression that Senator Wagner had changed his views. Miss Harriet Townsend, of the Women's City Club of New York, writing on February 7 for the membership, asked Senator Wagner to ex-

---

[45] *Ibid.,* Vol. 7, Sec. 3, No. 14.

plain his change of view. Wagner, in a letter dated the eighth of February, replied:

> I can understand how one might believe that I had changed my views on Low Rent Housing if one were guided simply by certain newspaper accounts that have appeared in recent weeks. For example, the *New York Times* story of January 31st, the day following my talk before the Building Congress in New York, said that I had made an "about face" on Housing, and that my views reflected the withdrawal of the Administration from the support of a genuine Low Rent Housing Program.
>
> I do not know where this story originated. It did not originate with any one in authority. It evidently came from those seeking to block Low Rent Housing by the same tactics that have been directed against other progressive legislation. No one, even if a trained newspaper reporter, could read my talk before the Building Congress, and wring from it the tortured construction of the *Times* article.[46]

This was the first of many misinterpretations of Senator Wagner's housing policy and the provisions of his bill that were to appear in the press.

These speeches demonstrate that Wagner's heart was in his work. He was deeply convinced of the necessity of public housing and sincerely concerned with his housing bill, which he hoped would relieve the distress of those now living in the slums which were once the home of Robert F. Wagner. Wagner was one legislator who was very careful in the preparation of his speeches. The speeches were drafted by Keyserling; but if a speech failed to express exactly what the senator wanted to say, it was discarded and Keyserling was given specific instructions about what to emphasize in the rewrite. Many a speech was discarded and rewritten many times before the senator accepted it as the exact expression of his policy.[47]

---

[46] *Ibid.*, Vol. 7, Sec. 4, No. 11.

[47] Statement of Minna Ruppert, personal secretary to Wagner during his terms as senator (personal interview).

When the Seventy-fourth Congress convened, the major groups of which we have spoken were fighting to get control of the housing legislation and were scrambling to get the favor and approval of the president for their specific programs. The American Federation of Labor was well organized, it had excellent technical advisers in the housing field, and it had influence in Congress and at the White House. The Central Housing Committee was split with dissension because the member agencies were competing with one another to control the whole program. The third group was a combination of pressure groups, the most important ones being the National Public Housing Conference and the Housing Division of Secretary Ickes. This group had among its members many influential friends of the president from the state of New York. All three of these groups were attempting to win the support of the president and of Senator Wagner, who was the acknowledged congressional leader in the field of housing.

The organizations opposed to a federal public-housing program, which was now seriously proposed in the Wagner bill, were organizing their efforts to prevent the enactment of the Wagner bill. Among the best-organized and most influential of these organizations was the National Association of Real Estate Boards, which was opposed to a federal public-housing program on both ideological and economic grounds. Mr. Walter S. Schmidt, of Cincinnati, at that time president of NAREB, prepared a report to be submitted to the Board of Directors at the annual meeting in 1935. It is a clear statement of the position of NAREB on the subject of federal housing. It said in part:

> One of the distinguishing marks of our American civilization is a widespread ownership of land which is the bulwark of a democratic form of government. It was to obtain such a stake in land that the founders and early settlers of our country were motivated to endure the hardships involved in building this civilization. Wise federal action should tend to protect and stimulate private ownership. The necessities of the emergency should not cause government

to take such action as will discourage ownership by setting up competition which individuals cannot meet, or by making tenement occupancy so attractive that the urge to buy one's own home will be diminished. . . .

Housing should remain a matter of private enterprise and private ownership. It is contrary to the genius of the American people and the ideals they have established that government become landlord to its citizens. This is not true of countries in which certain classes of people have been submerged for generations, and in which it is practically impossible for members of great sections of population ever to come into possession of their own homes. Sound conclusions, therefore, cannot be based on policies followed abroad. Very serious repercussions to our national life will follow if government continues its policy of direct action in becoming landlord to masses of its people, and the same can be said of its becoming the holder of mortgages on the homes of its citizens. The ultimate result will be that we will find government supporting the citizen instead of the citizen supporting Government. . . .

There is sound logic in the continuance of the practice under which those who have initiative and the will to save acquire better living facilities and yield their former quarters at modest rents to the group below. The movement might well be accelerated by Federal help. A means to this end might be supplied by the following plan: that arrangements be made with mortgage lending institutions whereby loans up to eighty or eighty-five per cent of value will be granted, that the federal government advance twenty-five or thirty per cent of the total mortgage at an interest rate of two or three per cent with the provision that a major portion of the differential in interest rate would apply to amortize the Government's advance.[48]

The National Association of Real Estate Boards also developed "The Neighborhood Improvement Act—A Suggested State Statute for the Protection and Improvement of Neighborhoods through Action of Property Owners."

---

[48] Walter S. Schmidt, "Report Concerning Certain Federal and Private Activities in the Field of Real Estate and Housing," made to the Board of Director of NAREB, Detroit, May 30, 1935, NAREB Files, Chicago.

The association held its annual meeting for 1935 in Atlantic City during the last week of October. A resolution adopted at this meeting was directed against a federal public-housing program such as provided for in the Wagner bill. The members of the real-estate groups also asked the president for some kind of representation in the deliberations of the government concerning housing. As a result of this pressure Peter Grimm, a former president of the Real Estate Board of New York and a man with much experience in civic affairs, was appointed a special adviser on housing legislation to the secretary of the treasury and to the president. Mr. Joseph Day, the real-estate manager for the Roosevelt family and a personal friend of the president, wrote a letter to the president to congratulate him on his choice of so able and experienced a man as Peter Grimm. This appointment of Grimm, and the strength of the NAREB, would definitely block the immediate passage of a public-housing program.[49]

The United States Building and Loan League, under the leadership of Morton Bodfish, was waiting for developments to take place with respect to the Wagner bill. Bodfish was a friend of Coleman Woodbury of NAHO, and he was corresponding with him and suggesting certain changes in and amendments to the bill.[50]

In November 1935 the National Retail Lumber Dealers Association held its annual meeting. A resolution was passed by the association protesting the government's activities in the construction of housing. This resolution was sent to the president by Frank Carnahan.[51]

Action with reference to the Wagner bill and a federal public-housing program in general was taken by the Chamber of Commerce of the United States with the organization of a

---

[49] Day to Roosevelt, October 1935, Roosevelt Papers, P.P.F. 476.
[50] Bodfish to Woodbury, 1935, National Association of Housing Officials, Housing Bill—1937, Chicago.
[51] Carnahan to Roosevelt, November 26, 1935, Roosevelt Papers, O.F. 63.

housing committee in November of 1935. Mr. E. Stuart Fitzpatrick, who for many years had represented in Washington the
Construction and Civic Development Department of the Chamber of Commerce, was the secretary of this newly formed committee. Mr. Samuel F. Clabaugh, an insurance executive from
Birmingham, Alabama, was chairman of the committee. The
other members of the committee were representatives of various
business enterprises concerned with housing. At the first meeting, held on November 9, 1935 at the Muehlebach Hotel in
Kansas City, Missouri, Chairman Clabaugh explained that the
purpose of the committee was first, as indicated in its charter, to
examine the Federal Government's activities in the housing field
from the viewpoint of which were helpful and which were competing with private enterprise, and second, as suggested by Mr.
Sibley's letter of invitation, to make such recommendations to
private capital as would encourage the revival of residential
construction, broaden its market, and eliminate past mistakes.

The secretary of the committee was requested to prepare a
draft of a report, including tentative recommendations agreed
upon at this meeting, for discussion at the next meeting of the
committee, which was scheduled for December 7, 1935 in Washington. At the December meeting Clabaugh told the committee
members that its report must be positive and constructive in
tone as well as in content. The draft of the report was discussed.
The local character of housing activities was emphasized, and
also the importance of not attempting or appearing to favor
attempts to force artificially a residential construction boom in
order to relieve unemployment. Re-employment of a permanent
character was the desired objective, and this could be accomplished only through the orderly expansion of economic activities, including house building.

Mr. Herbert U. Nelson was there as a guest and presented
to the committee the plan of the NAREB for neighborhood protective and improvement districts.

The next meeting of the committee was set for January 11, 1936. This was an important meeting in terms of setting a policy to be followed by the Chamber of Commerce during the 1936 campaign for a public-housing law. Present at the meeting were John C. Taylor, vice-president, J. C. Nicholes Investment Company of Kansas City, Missouri; Harland Bartholomew, city planner from St. Louis, Missouri; Henry I. Harriman, of the New England Power Company of Boston, Massachusetts; Charles F. Lewis, of the Buhl Foundation; L. A. McLean, of the Southern Trust Company of Louisville, Kentucky; John H. Zink, of the Heat and Power Corporation of Baltimore, Maryland; Robert L. Davison, director of housing research, John B. Pierce Foundation; M. J. Cleary, president, Northwestern Life Insurance Company of Milwaukee, Wisconsin; I. Friedlander, president, Gibraltar Savings and Building Association of Houston, Texas; I. N. Tate, president, Weyerhaeuser Sales Company of St. Paul, Minnesota; Ross F. Tucker, professor of building construction, Department of Civil and Sanitary Engineering, Massachusetts Institute of Technology; and Stephen F. Voorhees, of Voorhees, Gaelin, and Walker of New York City. In addition to these committee members the following guests were present: Morton Bodfish, of the United States Building and Loan League; Herbert U. Nelson, of the National Association of Real Estate Boards; A. G. Dietz, of the Massachusetts Institute of Technology; Lawrence Mehren, assistant secretary, Construction League of the United States; and A. P. Greensfelder, president, Fruin-Colnon Construction Company of St. Louis, Missouri. Mr. Clabaugh, chairman of the committee, and Mr. Fitzpatrick, secretary, supervised the committee proceedings. A set of principles for the guidance of government and private enterprise in solving the housing problem were formulated:

> 1. The problem of housing for poor families who cannot afford an economic rent for accommodations should be clearly distinguished from the problem of housing for families that are self-

supporting. Provision of housing for the latter properly belongs to individual initiative and private enterprise and the former to private philanthropy and to public authority.

2. The rehabilitation and gradual rebuilding of the older and neglected areas in cities, called blighted districts and slums, is a local problem for community planning.

3. Small house construction, which in the future as in the past will constitute the major volume of residential building, should be encouraged by removing unnecessary and speculative costs in the financing of the purchase of a home and by providing the mortgage investor with reasonable security.

4. The customary market for small house construction, namely, houses which sell in the general bracket beginning with $5,000, can be most extended by a reduction of costs, which will make possible the building of well designed houses of good standards both as to construction and location which will sell at prices, including the land, coming in the bracket under $5,000. This is a problem for industry.

5. Technical and economic and market research with reference to housing relatively neglected until the last few years should be encouraged.

6. The construction of residences and the improvement of housing conditions, while of national interest, are inherently a localized activity and problem and should be so recognized.

These principles were submitted to the board of the Chamber of Commerce at its meeting on January 30. These principles served as guide lines for the Chamber of Commerce during the campaign of 1936.[52]

---

[52] Minutes of the Housing Committee, Chamber of Commerce of the United States, E. Stuart Fitzpatrick Files, Washington.

CHAPTER VI

The Wagner-Ellenbogen Bill
of 1936

Senator Robert F. Wagner's housing bill was not introduced at the beginning of the second session of the Seventy-fourth Congress. The president had hopes of bringing together all the diverse groups interested in housing, so that one bill sponsored by the administration could be introduced. This bill would then, it was hoped, have sufficiently strong and widespread support to pass during that session of Congress.

The word had gotten around Capitol Hill that the president would call several conferences to iron out the details of the housing bill. Congressmen interested in housing legislation and its political consequences made every effort to identify themselves with the program. Representative Maury Maverick of Texas wrote to President Roosevelt in mid-January to tell him of his interest in housing and to ask the president to include him in the housing conferences.[1] Representatives Alfred Beiter[2] of New York and Martin J. Kennedy[3] of New York demonstrated their interest in the subject by taking Wagner's bill of the pre-

---

[1] Maverick to Roosevelt, January 15, 1936, Roosevelt Papers, O.F. 63.
[2] *Congressional Record*, January 20, 1936, p. 770. Beiter delivered a speech in behalf of his bill a week later; the text is given in the *Congressional Record*, January 27, 1936, p. 1078.
[3] *Ibid.*, January 22, 1936, p. 889.

vious session (S. 2392) and introducing it in the House under their own names.

There is no rule which prohibits one congressman from taking a bill introduced earlier by another congressman and introducing it, with or without amendments, under his own name. In fact, this is quite a common practice because of the rule of the House of Representatives which prohibits joint sponsorship of bills.[4] Thus, if a congressman wishes to put himself on record as completely and wholeheartedly in support of a particular bill, he must either reintroduce the bill under his own name or sign a statement as a cosponsor.[5] In the case of the housing bill the tactic of reintroducing the earlier Wagner bill was the one employed by the congressmen.

The president had by this time made up his mind about the legislators with whom he would consult on the housing problem. They were Representative Henry Ellenbogen and Senator Robert Wagner. These were the two members of Congress, and the sponsors of legislation for the citizens' groups, who were to work out some kind of a compromise bill with the key members of the Central Housing Committee. The president informed Ellenbogen that he would call him for these conferences. Ellenbogen then wrote to the president on February 4 to ask his leave to bring expert technical advisers with him to the conferences. He submitted the names of Ernest J. Bohn, Catherine Bauer, and Mrs. Edith Elmer Wood.[6] Wagner conferred frequently with Ellenbogen between February 4 and February 20. The object of these meetings was to work out the differences between the two bills which these leaders had respectively introduced at the last session.

---

[4] Clarence Cannon, *Cannon's Precedents of the House of Representatives of the United States*, Vol. 7, Sec. 1029, pp. 145-46. Washington: Government Printing Office, 1935.

[5] See the example cited by Bailey in *Congress Makes a Law*, p. 153.

[6] Ellenbogen to Roosevelt, February 4, 1936, Roosevelt Papers, O.F. 63.

Thus when Wagner attended the special White House housing conference on February 27 the housing plan that he had in mind was a combination of the ideas of Ellenbogen and the ideas he had received from the PWA Housing Division. The members of the president's special housing committee present at this meeting were Peter Grimm, John Fahey, Stewart McDonald, A. Clas, M. Eccles, Jesse Jones, and Wagner.[7]

In accordance with the president's practice at meetings such as this, he talked with the committee for a few minutes about the necessity of a good and economically sound housing program that would get enough support to pass in Congress. Then he told the committee members to retire to the Cabinet room and work out their differences.[8]

After the meeting that day, which ended without any effective compromise on the part of the representatives of the government financial agencies involved, Wagner decided that he would try to work out a compromise bill and present it to the committee. As only A. Clas of the PWA Housing Division had any enthusiasm for Wagner's plan, Wagner asked him to have the PWA draw up a draft of a housing bill that would be modeled on the Ellenbogen bill (H. R. 8666), but one that would also take into consideration the plans of the representatives of the other financial agencies on the president's special committee. Wagner could not be satisfied with anything that was merely an amendment to the National Housing Act, as had been the previous drafts of the PWA. Wagner was personally convinced of the merits of the Ellenbogen plan, and in addition to that he was well aware of the fact that the AFL had adopted a housing program which was quite similar to Ellenbogen's plan. Wagner would not consider going into the fight for a public-housing bill without the support of the AFL.

---

[7] Private Notes on the Housing Bill of 1936, by Warren Vinton, Vinton Papers.
[8] Statement of Leon Keyserling (personal interview).

The PWA representatives drew up a memorandum after the meeting in which they outlined all the available methods of financing a housing program. They finally decided that they would use a combination of all methods of financing: the sale of bonds by the Housing Authority, loans from the RFC, and moneys transferred from the appropriations authorized for the Housing Division of PWA. They were working on the principle that adequate funds could not be obtained from tax money or from general borrowing by the government and that it would be necessary to utilize private sources as much as possible. One other important principle, an essential one in Wagner's policy, was that some kind of government subsidy was necessary, so that rents could be kept at a level which the lowest income families could afford.[9]

With these principles to guide them, the members of the PWA legal division set to work to draft their bill. The bill produced was numbered in their code as P. W. 51147. It displayed four significant differences from Ellenbogen's H. R. 8666. The financial arrangements were quite different. It provided for a subsidy and made the subsidy a part of the policy of the bill. It provided for the termination of the housing program on June 30, 1941. It was called by short title "The Slum Clearance Act."[10]

This draft bill opened with a statement of policy not unlike that in the Ellenbogen draft, except that it was shorter. The section on administration in P. W. 51147 was the same as in H. R. 8666. In the financial section both bills provided for a stock issue of $1,000,000. P. W. 51147 provided for loans from the RFC not to exceed $100,000,000; H. R. 8666 had no provision for loans from the RFC. P. W. 51147 made provision for a bond issue of $100,000,000; H. R. 8666 had no provision

---

[9] PWA memorandum, February 27, 1937 (mimeographed), Vinton Papers.
[10] P. W. 51147 (mimeographed), Vinton Papers.

for loans from the RFC. P. W. 51147 made provision for a bond issue of $100,000,000 as opposed to the provision of H. R. 8666 for a bond issue of $1,000,000,000. The bonds of the Authority to be issued under the provision of P. W. 51147 were to mature in forty-five years, those of the Authority under provisions of H. R. 8666 were to mature in sixty years. In both bills these securities were exempt from all taxation, except surtaxes and estate, inheritance, and gift taxes.

The Authority and all its capital, income, and property, both real and personal, were exempt from all taxation under the provisions of P. W. 51147. By the provisions of H. R. 8666 property owned by the Authority was not to be exempt from state and local taxation unless state law specifically provided for such exemption.

The provisions for making loans to housing agencies were somewhat different in P. W. 51147 from those of H. R. 8666. The P. W. 51147 bill provided for loans up to 100 per cent of the cost of the project. Interest was to be at a rate not less than the average paid by the United States on other bonded indebtedness at the time of the loan. Amortization was to be completed in a period of fifty years. No loans were to be made after June 30, 1941. H. R. 8666 provided for loans up to 100 per cent of the cost of the project, at an interest range from zero to "not more than the cost of the money to the Authority plus one per centum."

This sliding interest rate was the subsidy that H. R. 8666 provided. But P. W. 51147 was much more detailed in treating of a subsidy. The principle of the subsidy and the specific provisions for a subsidy were detailed in Sections 30, 31, and 32. This subsidy was to make up the difference between gross rents determined on the basis of what low income families could pay and the aggregate gross charges due to the government. The Authority was to determine the amount of the subsidy each year. But the subsidy was limited, so that in no case could it exceed 3.5 per cent of the original cost of the project, nor could it exceed the rate of interest and charges due to the government. These annual contributions were to diminish each year, and they were to cease after fifty years. No new contract was to be made for annual contributions after June 30, 1941.

P. W. 51147 also stated that in lieu of local taxes the Authority could make a grant to the local government for services rendered to the project, provided that this service charge was not more than 5 per cent of the gross rents of the project, or not more than the taxes that would be levied on the project by the local government.

The bill also had sections similar to those of the Ellenbogen bill H. R. 8666 which provided for the Authority to engage in housing research, study, and so forth. The staff of the Authority could be assembled without regard to civil-service laws. The Authority could acquire quarters, materials, and so forth. Housing construction contracts should provide for the prevailing rate of wages for laborers on the project. P. W. 51147 provided for a performance bond for contractors which was not included in H. R. 8666. P. W. 51147 provided for the fulfillment of certain conditions in the locality before loans were to be made to the local agency. These conditions were the same as those of H. R. 8666 except that P. W. 51147 also stipulated that there should be "existing unemployment in the locality."

The section in both bills concerned with definitions of terms used was quite similar. The short title of P. W. 51147 was to be "The Slum Clearance Act." H. R. 8666 was known as "A Public Housing Act."

Wagner received this draft bill on March 3, 1936. The date on the mimeographed copy of the bill was March 4, 1936. The senator phoned the White House on that day and told Marvin McIntyre's secretary, Roberta Barrows, that he was sending to the president on the next day (March 4, 1936) a copy of a housing bill. He also informed her that she was to tell McIntyre that on the following Monday (March 9), he was coming to the White House with William Green, president of the AFL, and the Housing Committee of the AFL, Bates, Coefield, and Colleran, to see the president. Mr. McIntyre was to phone Bates and tell him of the time set for the meeting.[11]

The AFL had sent the president its housing program on February 26,[12] and its leaders wanted to talk over the housing problem with the president. The Democratic party leaders considered such a conference as this of great political importance; so to make certain that it was successful, James Farley, the national chairman of the party, sent a letter to Marvin McIntyre advising him to make sure that the AFL Housing Committee got in to see the president. He also advised "Mac" to check with Senator Wagner about the members of this committee.[13]

The alert Frank Carnahan of the lumber dealers also heard about the pending conference of the president with the AFL Housing Committee. On March 6 he wrote to the president to ask him to see a committee of businessmen in regard to the housing problem.[14] Carnahan was writing to the president almost every day during the month of February.[15]

Herbert Nelson of the NAREB was also in contact with the White House. On February 24 he wrote a letter to Marvin McIntyre to tell him that private enterprise was being badly hindered and confused by all the government regulations about building. He declared that, if private enterprise were only left free of government restrictions, it would be able to solve the housing shortage.[16]

----

[11] Memorandum of Barrows to McIntyre, March 3, 1936, Roosevelt Papers, O.F. 63.
[12] AFL Housing Committee to Roosevelt, February 26, 1936, Roosevelt Papers, O.F. 63.
[13] Farley to McIntyre, February 29, 1936, Roosevelt Papers, O.F. 63.
[14] Carnahan to Roosevelt, March 6, 1936, Roosevelt Papers, O.F. 63.
[15] Carnahan to Roosevelt, February 1936, Roosevelt Papers, O.F. 63.
[16] Nelson to McIntyre, February 24, 1936, Roosevelt Papers, O.F. 63.

Catherine Bauer had been alerted to the fact that the PWA Housing Division was acting as chief adviser to Senator Wagner by her friend Charney Vladeck of the New York City Housing Authority. He informed her of the bill that PWA was preparing for Wagner.[17] Catherine Bauer obtained a copy of the March draft of P. W. 51147 as soon as it was circulated. The Labor Housing Conference, which was in effect Catherine Bauer and Boris Shishkin, wrote a confidential memorandum to Senator Wagner under date of March 6 in which they criticized very strongly the provisions of the bill.[18]

Their general observation about the bill was that it was a weak and timid bill in which so many compromises had already been made that, if any changes were made during the legislative process, it would be totally unworkable. They criticized the fact that it was a temporary program to end on June 30, 1941. They criticized the lack of guarantee that the annual grants provided for in the bill would be continued after June 30, 1941.

The Labor Housing Conference was opposed to any bill that was so drafted as to be a slum-clearance program rather than a housing program which would increase the number of housing units available. A slum-clearance program had connected with it the serious problem of relocation of occupants which could slow down the construction of new dwellings.

The financial provisions of the bill were criticized as involving too much dependence on the RFC. The Authority should be able to finance itself by a bond issue, and the upper limit of the funds of the Authority should be nearer a billion dollars rather than the $100,000,000 provided for in P. W. 51147. The Authority should make capital grants as well as annual grants, and these grants should be on an *absolutely contractual* basis.

---

[17] Vladeck to Bauer, February 18, 1936, Vinton Papers.
[18] Confidential memorandum of the Labor Housing Conference to Wagner, March 6, 1936, Wagner Papers, Housing Bill—1936.

An independent board of five members should administer the Authority. In urging this provision the Labor Housing Conference intended no criticism of Mr. Ickes. It was a conviction of the LHC that only an independent board could do the job. LHC suggested, and hoped, that Mr. Ickes might be one of the members of the board, but the president should select the director. The board should include one member who represented labor and one member who represented the consumer. The Authority should recognize cooperatives and other bona-fide consumer groups as housing agencies, and it should be able to deal directly with them without the necessity of going through local or state government.

The memorandum finished with the strong statement that the LHC could not support this PWA bill. The view was expressed that, because of the several unsatisfactory provisions of the bill, it would be better to get another appropriation for the Housing Division of PWA and thus carry on for another year, rather than to accept this bill as a permanent housing program and enact it as a law.

Wagner received this memorandum a couple of days before he was to see the president in company with the Housing Committee of the AFL. The Housing Committee of the AFL had been briefed for this meeting by the Labor Housing Conference, and they voiced their disapproval of P. W. 51147. So after this meeting Wagner was doubtful about his strategy of working out some kind of a compromise bill that would represent the thinking of all groups of the housing problem. He began to feel that he would have to work with one group of organizations that was influential enough to insure the passage of the bill in Congress.

Wagner's bill, P. W. 51147, which he sent to the White House for the president's suggestions, was sent by the president to Marvin McIntyre on March 9 with a memorandum that he send the bill to "Morgenthau's committee" for a one-page digest of "What this bill does."[19] The bill was given to Mr. Peter Grimm, who was Morgenthau's chief adviser on housing at the time. The bill was returned with a criticism on March 12. Peter Grimm was strongly opposed to new building for families of low income. He favored only government participation in a slum-clearance program.[20]

There was another meeting of the president's committee on housing on March 12. Present at this meeting were Mr. Grimm; Mr. Delano; Mr. Fahey; Mr. West, under-secretary of the interior; Mr. J. M. Daiger, special assistant to the Federal Reserve Board; Mr. Lyle Alverson of the National Emergency Council; and Senator Wagner. The discussion at the meeting concerned government participation in second-mortgage financing. This was the plan that had made a strong impression on the president.[21] There was no agreement among the members of the committee about this plan. A number of the members were opposed to it. Alverson sent a memorandum to the president in which he stated his opposition to the plan. Another meeting of the committee was held on March 16 concerning details of the second-mortgage plan.[22]

Wagner made up his mind after these meetings that he would never make progress in the right direction if he attempted to work out a bill to everyone's satisfaction with this committee. So the senator decided to work out a bill with the housing crusaders and the professional housers—the Labor Housing Conference, the National Public Housing Conference, and the experts from the National Association of Housing Officials. On

---

[19] Memorandum of Roosevelt to McIntyre, March 9, 1936, Roosevelt Papers, O.F. 1972.

[20] Memorandum of Gaston of Treasury to McIntyre, March 12, 1936, Roosevelt Papers, O.F. 1972.

[21] Memorandum for the president (unsigned), March 12, 1936, Roosevelt Papers, O.F. 1972.

[22] Daiger to McIntyre, March 17, 1936, Roosevelt Papers, O.F. 63.

March 15 Warren J. Vinton and Leon Keyserling had had a meeting to discuss certain aspects of the problem and to work out some details for the housing bill.[23] Keyserling then set to work to combine in one bill the acceptable provisions of the Ellenbogen draft H. R. 8666, P. W. 51147, and the March 6 confidential memorandum of the Labor Housing Conference.

Before this draft was ready on March 20, a series of events occurred which were of importance in regard to the housing program. On March 13 Mr. Langdon Post, chairman of the New York City Housing Authority and a friend of the president, wrote a frank and confidential memorandum to the president concerning the housing situation. Post wrote this memorandum at the suggestion of McIntyre after discussing the housing situation with him. He told the president that it was necessary for him to get some housing legislation passed in this session of Congress. He warned that it would be dangerous to go into the presidential campaign with a negative record on housing. He told the president that he could not accomplish a low-rent housing and slum-clearance program through government credit alone. It was mathematically impossible to do it, Post stated. He maintained that he had figures and statistics based upon European and American experiences to prove this point. He also made the request that the president take into his conferences some professional public-housing people who had a knowledge of the problem of public housing and who were sympathetic to the program. These statements were in effect a criticism of the president's "housing advisers."[24]

On March 19 the American Federation of Labor sent out an open letter "to individuals and organizations interested in a National Housing Program." This letter gave a summary of the results of the meeting of the AFL Housing Committee with the

---

[23] Private Notes on the Housing Bill of 1936, by Warren Vinton, Vinton Papers.
[24] Post to Roosevelt, March 13, 1936, Roosevelt Papers, O.F. 63.

president on March 9.[25] The letter, signed by Bates, Coefield, and Colleran of the Housing Committee of the AFL, said:

> The President recently stated that one of the causes for delay in formulating an Administration housing policy is the disagreement among his advisors and the proponents of housing as to the best plan to follow. *If you are in agreement with any or all of our program, this is the moment to write or wire both the President and Senator Wagner and your own Senators and Congressmen.*
>
> In this session of Congress, the most important matter is not the amount of the appropriation. But the establishment of a permanent housing agency, with adequate powers, is absolutely essential to the future of the housing movement in this country.

Telegrams and letters poured into the White House as a result of this letter. Most of these messages urged the passage of a housing bill, but a few of the messages (from businessmen who would be affected by the legislation) urged a delay during which the problem could be studied more fully.[26] Meanwhile, on March 17, Mr. Peter Grimm wrote a letter of resignation to the president. He was resigning because he had completed his study of the housing problem. He had submitted his report and he felt that the work assigned him was finished; there were also urgent demands on his time from his private business, which needed his attention; and so he asked the president to give him leave to return to New York. His resignation was to affect all three positions he held: that of assistant director of the National Emergency Council, that of vice-chairman of the Central Housing Committee, and that of assistant to the secretary of the treasury.[27] The president in accepting his resignation thanked him for his fine work.[28]

---

25 AFL Housing Committee to Roosevelt, March 19, 1936, Roosevelt Papers, O.F. 63.
26 Roosevelt Papers, O.F. 63.
27 Grimm to Roosevelt, March 17, 1936, Roosevelt Papers, O.F. 1972.
28 Roosevelt to Grimm, March 19, 1936, Roosevelt Papers, O.F. 1972.

The report that Grimm submitted with his resignation was the subject of quite a bit of discussion. Grimm stated in his report that he was against building any new housing for the families in the low income group. He considered the real solution to be the building of housing for middle income families, then the lower income families could move into the housing vacated by the middle income group. He recommended that the low-rent housing program of the Federal Government be discontinued, except the slum-clearance projects. His main recommendations concerned the reorganization of the governmental financial agencies.[29]

Grimm wanted his report to be made public. If this were done, he would then be the recognized "presidential housing adviser." There were also a number of others, especially those on the Central Housing Committee, who wanted the report released. The president refused to release the report, and so the housers could only guess what its contents were, although they knew pretty well just what Grimm's ideas on housing were.[30]

After Grimm left, J. M. Daiger took over as liaison officer for the president's special committee on housing. On the day that Grimm was leaving Washington, Daiger wrote to McIntyre about the future work of the committee and the next meeting, which would be held on April 1.[31] But as Wagner had decided to draft his own bill and go along without the members of that committee, who could not come to any agreement, the future meetings of this committee had no direct bearing on housing

---

[29] Report of Grimm to Roosevelt, March 19, 1936, Roosevelt Papers, O.F. 1972. The technical work in the drafting of this report was done by Lucius Wilmerding, an assistant to the secretary of the treasury (statement of Lucius Wilmerding, personal interview).

[30] Alverson sent a telegram to McIntyre asking him to get the president to release the Grimm report for the meeting of the special committee on housing to be held the next day (Alverson to McIntyre, March 31, 1936, Roosevelt Papers, O.F. 63).

[31] Daiger to McIntyre, March 17, 1936, Roosevelt Papers, O.F. 63.

legislation. For all practical purposes this special committee on housing ceased to function as an effective instrument for determining housing policy when Senator Wagner decided to draft his own bill and when Peter Grimm resigned.

The first draft of Wagner's new bill was ready on March 20. It was drafted by Keyserling, then typed and sent to some of the experts for their suggestions. This bill was fundamentally the Ellenbogen draft H. R. 8666, but incorporated a few of the features of P. W. 51147 and the suggestions contained in the confidential memorandum of the Labor Housing Conference. Some grammatical changes were made in this draft and it was sent to the Government Printing Office and a confidential committee print was run off.

The use of confidential committee prints is a practice that has grown up over the years. Major bills that are being drafted by or with the aid of a congressional committee, or a major bill that has already been once introduced and referred to committee, will be so printed. This print is a working copy of the draft for the use of the members of the congressional committee, or the special advisers, or the Legislative Reference Service, or a committee of experts, whichever the particular legislator is employing. By this practice many errors and mistakes are worked out of the draft before it becomes public. The bill when introduced thus makes a better impression on the Congress and on the interested groups.[32]

Senator Wagner had the bill printed for the use of a special committee of experts which was called to meet in Washington on March 24 by Ernest J. Bohn, president of the National Asso-

---

[32] Statements of various members of the staff of the Legislative Reference Service and of William Hallahan, clerk of the House Committee on Banking and Currency (personal interviews). Mr. Hallahan, who is one of the highly respected and competent career men in the Federal Government service, was recently appointed by the president and confirmed by the Senate as a director of the Home Loan Bank Board.

ciation of Housing Officials. This committee print was dated
March 23. It was to be kept *strictly confidential* because Wagner
and his advisers did not want the opponents of the bill, especially those in the Central Housing Committee, to have an opportunity of fighting the bill even before it was introduced.[33]

Ernest J. Bohn was chairman of the meeting. Those in at-
tendance were Warren J. Vinton as secretary, Leon Keyserling,
Catherine Bauer, Mrs. Edith Elmer Wood, Ira Robbins, Mrs.
Mary Simkhovitch, Helen Alfred, Coleman Woodbury, Herbert
A. Berman of PWA, Langdon Post of the New York City Hous-
ing Authority, Charles Abrams, George Gove of the New York
State Board of Housing, and Bleecker Marquette of the Civic
Better Housing League. A. R. Clas and Horatio Hackett were
present for the first few hours of the meeting.[34]

The committee examined and criticized the bill section by
section. Charles Abrams, legal counsel for the New York City
Housing Authority, thought that the title might be changed a bit
to render it more legal and constitutional. He was to send his
suggestions directly to Mr. Keyserling. In the first section
and throughout the bill the adjective "comfortable" should be
changed to "adequate" so that the phrase would read "to provide adequate, safe, and sanitary housing."

Concerning the power of the Authority, it was suggested
that the Authority in Washington be allowed to charter local
federal housing authorities. This was a provision of the Ellenbogen bill that had not been included in the draft. The Labor
Housing Conference was in favor of such an arrangement, but
the NPHC was opposed to it.

Catherine Bauer suggested that provision should be made
for loans to bona-fide consumer organizations that would be

---

[33] Private Notes on the Housing Bill of 1936, by Warren Vinton, Vinton Papers.
[34] Memorandum of the Bohn Committee Meeting on the Wagner Housing Bill,
   March 24, 1936, by Warren Vinton, Vinton Papers.

public-housing societies. The vote on this suggestion was seven to five in favor of loans to strict cooperatives that would operate as limited-dividend corporations. The vote was eight to four in favor of loans to societies whose sole purpose was the provision of homes for their own members. These societies would operate on a lease from the Authority.

During the discussion of interest rates Warren Vinton told the group that he had been in contact with the Treasury Department experts concerning this matter. He cautioned that care must be taken to set forth a precise definition of the term "going rate." He suggested that they use the average rate, published in the *Federal Reserve Bulletin*, on federal bonds callable in not less than eight years.

With regard to the administration of the Authority, Mr. Berman, Mr. Clas, and Mr. Hackett expressed the wish of Secretary Ickes that the Authority be kept within the Department of the Interior. The draft provided for an independent board of five members, one member to be the secretary of the interior. This was the suggestion set forth in the confidential memorandum of the Labor Housing Conference. The majority of those at the meeting were in favor of the provision as written. In view of the fact that there were political and other considerations outside the purview of the committee, it was voted unanimously (Miss Alfred demurring) that this decision should be left to Senator Wagner and Representative Ellenbogen.

The question of taking over the employees of the Housing Division of PWA was discussed, and it was agreed that the board should be free to take only those it desired to retain. Mr. Berman suggested that those who were retained by the new board should receive civil-service status.

The financial provisions were the subject of much discussion. Mr. Clas thought that the provisions of the bill called for a "staggering" amount of money. The consensus was that the bill should ask for as much money as Senator Wagner and Representative Ellenbogen thought wise. It was, however, suggested and agreed upon that the initial appropriation from the Treasury should be boosted from $26,000,000 to $51,000,000 to avoid the implication that little could be done in the way of housing construction during the first year of the program.

The question of complete tax exemption of the income of the Authority was brought up in the discussion. It was decided by the committee that this question involved a policy decision and should be left to the discretion of Senator Wagner and Representative Ellenbogen.

On the question of insurance of obligations of the local housing agencies there was no consensus of opinion, but it was agreed upon by the committee that provisions should be inserted into the bill giving local government legal jurisdiction over the demonstration projects put up and owned by the Federal Government. It was also suggested that as a matter of policy preferences for loans and grants would be given to localities that made an effort to extend financial aid to low-cost housing.

As was to be expected, the provision of a subsidy to the local projects, so that the rents would be kept at a level that the families of low income could afford, brought much discussion. The "deficit-annual-contribution" plan was the very simple plan provided for in P. W. 51147. The Ellenbogen bill H. R. 8666 had made an attempt to help the local projects by providing a sliding interest rate from zero to the cost of the money to the Authority plus 1 per cent. The plan in P. W. 51147 was prefaced with the policy statement that a subsidy would be provided for the specific purpose of keeping the rents at a low level. The mechanics of this subsidy were to be worked out by the Authority, and each year a definite contribution would be given to help make up the deficit between total rents collected and the total charges to be paid out. Limits to this contribution were set out in the bill. The money was to come from any source whence the Authority could get it.

It was agreed by those present (Mr. Berman receded from his previous position) that the fixed and annual contributions based upon an "annuity" was preferable to this "so-called deficit annual contribution." It was also agreed that these provisions for the subsidy were to be embodied in a *contract* rather than an *agreement*. No attempt was made at the meeting to work out the language and details of this annuity plan. That would be done later by Keyserling.[35]

Keyserling was present at the meeting, and he also received a copy of the report of the meeting from Vinton.[36] With these specific suggestions he set to work to revise the draft. The title was reworded so that it was more concise and clear. The term "Public Housing Authority" was changed to "United States Housing Authority." The term "comfortable" was changed to "decent" in the phrase "decent, sanitary, and safe" housing. The term "public-housing society" was substituted for "non-profit housing agency" in the section of definitions. "Limited-profit housing agency" was also substituted for "limited-dividend housing agency" in the same section. Both of these changes were revisions in line with the suggestions of Miss Bauer at the special committee meeting.

The term "going federal rate" was added in the section of definitions. This was Mr. Vinton's proposal at the meeting, though the definition was not precisely as he had suggested.

In Section 4 (d) there was the addition of a provision for civil-service status for employees taken over by the new Authority. This was in line with Mr. Berman's suggestion.

In Section 5 subdivisions (f) and (g) were included, which provided for free use of the mails and tax exemption for the Authority. These two provisions were in Ellenbogen's H. R. 8666 and had been overlooked in the revision.

---

35 *Ibid.*
36 Vinton to Keyserling, March 24, 1936, Vinton Papers.

In Section 11, which was concerned with provision for demonstration projects, two sections were added to the text which made it necessary for the Authority to respect the decisions of the local government with regard to the development and lease of such projects.

In Section 12 there was included a provision (g), stating that local government had civil and criminal jurisdiction on federal demonstration projects. This was in accord with another of the suggestions of the committee.

In Section 14 there were included a number of provisions concerned with foreclosures on the projects and the resulting relationships between the new third party who foreclosed and the Authority. It was pointed out at the meeting that these should be clearly stated, so that private capital would not hesitate to purchase the bonds.

The financial provisions of the bill were left unchanged, except that the initial appropriation was raised from $26,000,-000 to $51,000,000 as recommended by the committee. The number of years in which loans from the RFC might be repaid was raised from forty-five to sixty.

The section concerned with grants and loans was completely revised. The total amount of the grant remained the same; it was not to exceed 45 per cent of the total cost of the project. The system of annual contributions was based on an "annuity" plan which Vinton had discussed at the meeting.

The so-called "deficit annual contribution" was replaced with a fixed and uniform annuity contribution. The annuity plan was thus spelled out in the revision:

> Each such annual contribution shall be equal to the amount of the annual payment which such balance [the balance of the total value of the grant, which was not to exceed 45 per cent of the total cost and could be paid in whole or in part, and in this case only a part was paid out initially] would yield over such fixed period of years [the maximum number of years was 60] in an annuity com-

puted at the going-rate of interest at the time such grant is made. The Authority shall embody the provisions for such annual contributions in a contract.

The amortization period on loans was raised from fifty to sixty years. The remainder of the draft, which was concerned with labor standards and penalties, remained unchanged.[37]

This revised draft was then sent to the Government Printing Office and came back printed as Confidential Committee Print, March 31, 1936. Wagner and Ellenbogen discussed the provisions of this new revision, and their only changes concerned the financial provisions of the bill. They decided to trim down the total amount of money to be appropriated to a sum less than was appropriated for housing under the NIRA. This was a wise move psychologically because it gave the legislators a chance to tell the Congress that the amount was smaller than they had already appropriated for housing under NIRA. They also set a smaller limit to the total value of notes and bonds to be issued by the Authority. The drafts of March 23 and 31 provided for an appropriation of $100,000,000 for the fiscal year of 1937, and $100,000,000 for each of the years 1938, 1939, 1940, and 1941. The revision called for an appropriation of $75,000,000 for the fiscal year of 1938, and $100,000,000 for the years 1939 and 1940.

The total amount of notes and bonds to be issued was reduced from $1,000,000,000 to be issued over an indefinite period of time to a limit of $100,000,000 for the fiscal year of 1937 and $150,000,000 for each of the fiscal years of 1938 and 1939. The maturity period on the bonds was raised from forty-five years to sixty years. The interest rate was kept at 4 per cent.[38]

---

[37] Copies of the committee prints of March 23 and March 31 are in the Wagner Papers.

[38] See copy of S. 4424 in Appendix II.

So, with this final draft agreed upon, the bill was sent to the printer, and Wagner and Ellenbogen prepared to introduce the bill in the Senate and the House on April 3, 1936. The Senate number for the bill was S. 4424, and it was automatically referred to the Committee on Education and Labor, which had taken jurisdiction over the bill introduced in the last session.[39] Ellenbogen's bill, when it was introduced in the House, was numbered H. R. 12164 and was again referred to the Committee on Banking and Currency.[40]

At this session both Ellenbogen and Wagner were well aware of the hostility of Chairman Steagall to the housing bill; but as the bill had been referred to the Banking and Currency Committee during the previous session, there was nothing they could do to have it assigned to another committee. If the committee refused to act on the bill, there was a possible remedy in the use of the "discharge rule." This rule is of comparatively recent origin, having been adopted June 17, 1910. It was revised on December 8, 1931 and amended January 3, 1935. It is a difficult procedure to employ because, by a ruling given the very month that Ellenbogen introduced his bill (April 15, 1936), Speaker Byrns interpreted the phrase "a majority of the total membership of the House" to mean 218 members. No signatures by proxy are allowed on the discharge motion. Hence if a discharge motion could be passed, a bill must have such strong support that it would be foolish for the committee to use any delaying tactics in reporting it to the House.[41] Rather than attempt this difficult procedure of waiting for a period of thirty days and then getting signatures for the discharge motion from 218 members of the House, the proponents of the bill made an

---

[39] *Congressional Record*, April 3, 1936, p. 4889.

[40] *Ibid.*, p. 4950.

[41] A complete explanation of the motion to discharge committees is given in *Cannon's Precedents*, Vol. 7, Secs. 1007-14, pp. 120-29. Rule 22, Sec. 2, of the Rules of the Senate provides for a motion to discharge a committee.

appeal to the president to have the bill reported out, as will be seen in subsequent chapters.[42]

Senator Wagner was recognized by Vice-President Garner, and he introduced his bill with an accompanying speech.[43] It is well to note the place of such speeches in the legislative process. When a legislator speaks in the Senate, he is more often speaking to the press gallery and through them to the nation than he is to his colleagues. The hope is that this tactic will build up the public support that is necessary to move the legislators to favorable action. Wagner's speech on this morning was for the benefit both of his colleagues and the nation.

He began his speech by saying that this program he was sponsoring was the next step in the recovery drive, both to make further progress and to consolidate what had already been gained. He continued his speech by mentioning how the New Deal had brought about business recovery. But the current problem of unemployment could be finally solved only by the proper stimulation of the construction industry through a government-aided housing program.

Then Wagner went on to his favorite argument. He recounted how bad housing breeds crime and disease. While he was in the middle of this part of his speech he was interrupted by Senator Walsh, chairman of the Committee on Education and Labor, who wanted to ask the senator a series of questions. And in this series of questions Walsh stated his position on the housing question very clearly.

> MR. WALSH. I hope the Senator will point out that whatever efforts have been made in the construction of housing by the Federal Government have not in any way met the problem of slum-clearance.
>
> MR. WAGNER. Exactly.

---

[42] See Chaps. 8 and 12.
[43] *Congressional Record*, April 3, 1936, p. 4889.

MR. WALSH. The houses which have been constructed in New York, Cleveland, and Boston and elsewhere are really in competition with private property and are available for tenements only by the so-called middle-class workers or people in comfortable circumstances.[44]

By the means of the questions Walsh, who was chairman of the Committee on Education and Labor, was telling the Senate, his constituents in Boston, and the public exactly where he stood on the question. It also happened, because of Wagner's fast action in the introduction of the bill, that Walsh had not seen the bill before its introduction that morning and that he did not know its specific provisions.

Wagner, continuing his speech, noted that in a period of depression the average man may start feeding and clothing himself as soon as he regains his job, but that he cannot do much about improving his housing conditions until he has built up a surplus over a period of sustained prosperity. A public-housing program, Wagner was arguing, would sustain the prosperity of the nation and keep the laboring man in decent, safe, and sanitary housing until he had a surplus large enough to provide his own housing.

Wagner then stated that there were some 18,000,000 families in the United States in 1936 (60 per cent of the nation) whose income was less that $1,500 a year and who could afford to pay out of their income a rent of only $5.00 per month per room. Only public housing with a government subsidy could provide housing at that low level of rent.

The other provisions of the bill were briefly explained by the senator. In speaking of the financial provisions of the bill he emphasized the fact that the total amount of money provided for in this bill was less than the original amount provided for in the NIRA.

---

[44] *Ibid.*, p. 4890.

As Wagner was ending his speech Senator Duncan V. Fletcher, of Florida, asked him a question.

> MR. FLETCHER. I understand that the President appointed a board or commission to look into the problem of housing, and I would like to ask the Senator whether he has had contact with them.
>
> MR. WAGNER. I have. I might say to the Senator that I have had a number of conferences, covering a period of three months, with the different public agencies, and also with outside groups of public-spirited citizens and with individuals, all of whom are interested in this subject, which I regard as the most significant confronting the country today. Their views are not all embodied in the proposed legislation, nor is the bill in complete accord with all their views. As now drafted the bill is solely my own responsibility.
>
> MR. FLETCHER. May I ask the Senator whether the proposition is that the Federal Government will take second mortgages on these properties and private enterprise will furnish capital for first-mortgage security?
>
> MR. WAGNER. No; that has been proposed with reference to encouraging the building of small homes—homes worth five or six thousand dollars. . . . What I propose deals only with providing homes for the very low income group.[45]

At the same time that Wagner was making his speech in the Senate, Representative Ellenbogen was speaking in favor of the bill in the House. As the House is a much larger legislative body, it is not so easy to obtain the floor and make a speech as it is in the Senate. The House operates on a set calendar, and the business of the day is strictly adhered to by the party leaders and the speaker; but by the use of various parliamentary devices a representative may obtain the floor for a short speech, and if he has the favor of the speaker, he will be allowed to deliver his speech. This was the situation when Ellenbogen introduced the bill on April 3. He merely placed the bill in the "hopper" on the clerk's desk. He did not have the same opportunity as Senator Wagner personally and verbally to introduce it.

---

[45] *Ibid.*, p. 4892.

After the opening prayer[46] and usual preliminary business, the House resolved itself into the Committee of the Whole House on the State of the Union for the consideration of some special bills. Representative Byron Harlan of Ohio was in the chair.

The clerk read the title of the bill (H. R. 12098—an appropriation bill). The clerk, proceeding with the reading of the bill, read as follows: "Envoy Extraordinary and Minister Plenipotentiary to the Netherlands, $12,000."

> MR. ELLENBOGEN. Mr. Chairman, I move to strike out the last word. Mr. Chairman, I want to address the house on the provisions of a very important piece of legislation which is being introduced today by Mr. Wagner in the Senate and by myself in the House.[47]

Ellenbogen then made a short speech in which he mentioned that this piece of legislation was the culmination of a great deal of study, consultation, and experimentation. He emphasized the fact that it was a nonpartisan piece of legislation. To prove this last point he pointed out that it was during the Hoover administration that the necessity of taking public action to solve the housing shortage was recognized. The President's Conference on Home Building and Home Ownership had re-

---

[46] The rules of both houses provide for a chaplain who daily opens the session with a prayer. A permanent chaplain is appointed by each house, but on occasion other clergymen are invited to offer the prayer.

"The House met at 12 o'clock noon. Father Timothy L. McDonnell, S.J., of the University of San Francisco, San Francisco, California, offered the following prayer: 'Let us pray: O God, our Creator, who endowed us with life and liberty and decreed that our pursuit of happiness should be aided by the help of Your grace and through the guidance of law, grant to our Representatives the wisdom and prudence necessary to enact the laws we need to attain the common good in this time of trial; and grant us Your grace that we may know You and love You and serve You in this life and be happy with You forever in the next. Amen'" (*Congressional Record*, May 28, 1953, p. 5772). See also *ibid.*, May 6, 1953, p. 4570.

[47] *Ibid.*, April 3, 1936, p. 4923. The parliamentary device that Mr. Ellenbogen employed is known as a *pro-forma* amendment. See *Hinds' Precedents*, Vol. 5, Secs. 5778, 5222, pp. 394, 128, and *Cannon's Precedents*, Vol. 8, Sec. 2560, p. 270.

ported that housing was too expensive for two thirds of the population and that the breakdown in construction and financing of homes was not a temporary or emergency situation and therefore required more than emergency measures for its solution.

He further emphasized the part to be played by local government and local housing authorities in this program. Concerning the financial provisions of the bill, Ellenbogen stressed the fact that they were carefully worked out so that no money would be wasted in the program. The money would go directly into the construction of homes. HOLC funds went into refinancing; they did not produce new homes. These funds will not be for relief or other emergency measures which bring no future return and add nothing to the wealth of the country. "The money spent under the United States Housing bill," Ellenbogen said, "will build monuments which fifty years hence will still give concrete evidence that the Congress of 1936 was an enlightened and forward-looking body."

He then attempted to take the force out of the arguments of the opposition by mentioning that there would be opposition to the bill and that, since the bill had such widespread nonpartisan support, such opposition would come from "the small handful who for their own selfish reasons are opposed to any truly constructive activity."[48]

Behind the two questions that Senator Fletcher asked Senator Wagner was the fact that Wagner's introduction of the bill took the Congress by surprise. Wagner was sponsoring his own bill and not an administration bill. Actually the president was away in Florida[49] on a vacation when Wagner drafted the bill and he was still in the South the day it was introduced. The president and his advisers in the Treasury Department and other government financial agencies did not have an opportunity to

---

[48] *Congressional Record*, April 3, 1936, p. 4924.
[49] *New York Times*, April 5, 1936.

study the bill before its introduction. Wagner had not sent the committee prints of S. 4424 to the White House as he had done with P. W. 51147.

The first report about the bill in the *New York Times*—date line, Washington, April 3—missed the meaning of Wagner's answer to Fletcher. This report stated that the bill "evolved" from the conferences that were held at the president's direction. The report expressed mild surprise that the bill had been introduced because the president had given some the impression that a housing program was "in abeyance" for this session of Congress. But in its report the next day—date line, Washington, April 4—the *New York Times* had had an opportunity to consult with agencies interested in housing, and it reported that these government financial agencies saw in this bill a "challenge." They declared, in a statement which they made to the newspaper, that they still had the intention of presenting a bill of their own.

Senator Walsh gave the bill a high priority on the calendar of business of the Committee on Education and Labor. He planned to hold hearings before the end of the month. In his official capacity as chairman of the committee he sent a letter and a copy of the bill to the president, and he told him that the committee would be pleased to receive his views and any recommendations he might desire to make to the committee.[50]

The president told his secretary, Marguerite Le Hand, to send a memorandum to "Mac" (Marvin McIntyre), who was to tell Walsh that the president was not replying to his letter in writing, but that he expected to have a housing conference within a few days and hoped that Walsh would come. McIntyre telephoned the message to Walsh on April 15.[51]

---

[50] Walsh to Roosevelt, April 10, 1936, Roosevelt Papers, O.F. 63.
[51] Memorandum of Le Hand to McIntyre, April 14, 1936, Roosevelt Papers, O.F. 63.

The conferences which the president called in order to work out a housing program, the submission of bills by legislators to the president for his inspection before their introduction, the transmission of bills before committees to the president for his views and recommendations, are all evidence of the important and decisive role that the president plays in the legislative process. This aspect of the legislative process will be discussed in detail in later chapters. It is sufficient at this point of the study to bear it in mind.

CHAPTER VII

Senate Committee Hearing
and Floor Debate

Senator Walsh decided to begin the hearings on the Wagner housing bill, S. 4424, on April 20, 1936. As soon as this decision became known the various groups interested in the passage or defeat of the measure started to work. The National Association of Housing Officials thus stated its position on the issue in its bulletin:

> In conformity with its established policy, the Association has taken no stand for or against this bill. My personal opinion, however, is that it is the most comprehensive and intelligent measure yet put forward in congress for dealing with the problems of low-rent housing.
>
> I am happy to say that its framers called upon N.A.H.O. officers and consultants for advice and counsel in the technical aspects of the measure. These advisers, however, consistently took the position that in matters of broad policy affecting existing administrative setup, the authors of the bill alone were responsible for decisions.[1]

Although this was the official position of the NAHO, there was nothing to prohibit individual members of the organization from taking positive action in support of the measure, acting in

---

[1] Coleman Woodbury, *National Association of Housing Officials, Bulletin No. 84,* April 3, 1936.

their capacity as individual citizens or as members of other organizations. Ernest J. Bohn, who was president of NAHO, was also the chairman of the housing committee of the council of the city of Cleveland. He was most active in securing support for the Wagner housing bill. He sent to all municipal governments a copy of the resolution endorsing the measure he introduced in the Cleveland council, which unanimously adopted it. He urged all municipalities actively to support the measure. He was also working with the leaders of the various religious groups to get their support for the measure. Father E. Roberts Moore, of New York City, and Father John O'Grady, of the National Catholic Charities, were contacted by Bohn in an effort to get Catholic support. Bohn also contacted Abraham Goldfeld, chairman of the housing committee of the National Conference of Social Work, and asked him to secure the support of Jewish organizations. Bohn was also working with some Protestant leaders, in particular with Reverend Worth Tippy, secretary of the Federal Council of Churches of Christ in America.[2]

In order to provide a central office where all the groups interested in housing could apply for information and publicity materials, Bohn arranged for the opening in Washington of a housing-legislation information office. He acquired a room on the third floor of the building at 730 Jackson Place, N.W. Bohn placed John Millar, a publicist from Chicago who had been issuing a housing letter for two years, in charge of the office. Bohn then asked various organizations and individuals to make a contribution toward the expenses of the office. During the period from April 15 to July 1, 1936 the office mailed out thousands of copies of the bill, speeches, press releases, and a newsletter written by John Millar. Bohn received a total of only $1,492 in individual contributions for the expenses of the office.

---

[2] Bohn's letters and memoranda, April 1936, National Association of Housing Officials, Ernest Bohn File—1936.

The total expenses for the campaign came to $2,106.01, so Bohn had to make up that deficit by collecting special contributions.[3] John Millar was released as director of the office after the campaign ended, primarily because of his suddenly developing unsympathetic attitude toward the Wagner bill which he manifested in various of his newsletters, especially one that was dated May 5, 1936.[4]

While Bohn was busy with his work Catherine Bauer was organizing the local housing committees of the American Federation of Labor. By the time the hearings began on April 20, 1936 there were seventy of these organizations in operation in cities throughout the United States. These local conferences tried to develop local support and enthusiasm for the Wagner bill. They received their information and publicity material from the Labor Housing Conference in Washington.[5]

The National Public Housing Conference was working with various groups in New York City and the surrounding area. They were urging all organizations to send briefs, resolutions, and petitions to congressmen, senators, and the president.[6]

As the time for the start of the hearings on S. 4424 approached and those opposing the measure did not publicly state their opposition or announce to Chairman Walsh that they wished to appear before the committee, some supporters of the bill were taken by surprise.[7] They did not know that the big lobbies were working quietly within the framework of their own organizations. They were also unaware of the fact that the government financial agencies concerned with loans and mortgages

---

[3] Bohn's letters and memoranda, April to July 1936, National Association of Housing Officials, Ernest Bohn File—1936.

[4] Memorandum of Bohn, July 1936, National Association of Housing Officials, Ernest Bohn File—1936.

[5] Statement of Catherine Bauer (personal letter).

[6] *Public Housing Progress*, Vol. 2, April 15, 1936 and May 15, 1936.

[7] Arthur Krock, "In Washington." *New York Times*, April 14, 1936.

were trying to work out a substitute measure to the Wagner bill to be presented to the committee. On April 19 there was a meeting in the office of Jesse Jones on the principles involved in planning this substitute measure. Stewart McDonald of FHA and John Fahey of HOLC were at the meeting.[8] Marriner Eccles was out of the city at the time, but it was known that he would be sympathetic to any compromise plan that this group could work out.[9] The meeting proved unsuccessful, however, and no alternate plan was presented to oppose the Wagner bill. Fahey later supported the Wagner bill at the committee hearings.

Walsh, as chairman of the committee, had the power to determine the manner in which the hearings would be conducted; but he allowed Wagner, as sponsor of the bill, to select a panel of witnesses to appear in support of the bill. Walsh, too, would select his own special witnesses. The chairman also wrote to experts in the government agencies to ask them for an analysis of the bill. It was recounted at the end of the last chapter that Walsh wrote to the president for his views and recommendations. Gerald Reilly, solicitor of the Labor Department,[10] Secretary Ickes, of the Department of the Interior and administrator of Public Works,[11] and Marriner Eccles, of the Federal Reserve Board and economic adviser to the president,[12] were important experts upon whom Walsh called for a written analysis and criticism. Walsh invited Madame Perkins, secretary of labor,[13] John Fahey, of the Home Owners Loan Corporation,[14] and Peter Grimm, former housing adviser to Secretary Morgenthau, to appear before the committee as expert witnesses.[15]

---

[8] *Ibid.*, April 19, 1935.
[9] Eccles to Walsh, May 1, 1936; letter published in *Hearings on S. 4424*, p. 283.
[10] Reilly to Walsh, April 22, 1936; letter published in *ibid.*, p. 11.
[11] Ickes to Walsh, April 20, 1936; letter published in *ibid.*, p. 25.
[12] Eccles to Walsh, May 1, 1936; letter published in *ibid.*, p. 283.
[13] Testimony of Frances Perkins; in *ibid.*, p. 61.
[14] Testimony of John Fahey; in *ibid.*, p. 125.
[15] Testimony of Peter Grimm; in *ibid.*, p. 191.

Walsh, as chairman of the committee, had the right to determine which representatives of the various groups that wrote to him and asked for time to give testimony before the committee would be allowed to appear. Walsh allowed certain representatives, such as Benjamin Marsh of the People's Lobby, to testify, but he appointed them for a time at the end of the hearings after his witnesses and Wagner's witnesses had been able to create the impression they wished.[16]

Wagner's panel was selected with great care by Keyserling with the aid of advisers such as Ernest J. Bohn, Catherine Bauer, and Mary Simkhovitch. It was decided that Wagner himself would start the testimony with a statement of general policy.[17] He would be followed by Secretary Ickes. It was known that Ickes would object to the administrative provisions of the bill, but there was nothing that could be done about that. Everyone concerned, including Mr. Ickes himself, wanted him to testify. Aside from a criticism of the administrative provisions of the bill, Ickes' testimony would be favorable and would carry a great deal of authority.[18]

The American Federation of Labor was given a prominent place in the testimony. Harry Bates and Michael Colleran, of the housing committee, would testify on the necessity of stimulating the building and construction industry and on the need of a long-range program.[19] William Green would impress on the committee the fact that the AFL considered this bill as "must" legislation. The great number of unemployed demanded it, Green testified.[20]

Langdon Post of the New York City Housing Authority would be presented as an expert. He would testify on the actual

---

16 Testimony of Benjamin Marsh; in *ibid.*, p. 255.
17 Testimony of Robert F. Wagner; in *ibid.*, p. 13.
18 Testimony of Harold Ickes; in *ibid.*, p. 19.
19 Testimonies of Harry Bates and Michael Colleran; in *ibid.*, pp. 41, 175.
20 Testimony of William Green; in *ibid.*, p. 76.

operation of housing projects. He was given the task of trying to impress on Walsh that this public housing was really for people in the low income group. Post was so successful in this approach that his testimony was extended and carried over to the next day. Post was also to answer the objection that the real-estate group brought up, to the effect that the people make the slums by their sloppy habits of living.[21]

Ernest J. Bohn was given the task of explaining the cost of the slums to the municipalities in terms of dollars and cents. It is to be remembered that it was under his inspiration that Father Robert Navin undertook the first scientific study of the cost of the slums. Bohn, a member of Cleveland's city council, was also to explain the role of the municipal government in the program.[22] To emphasize this important aspect of the program, and also to forestall any objection about "centralization of the program in Washington," the mayor of Louisville and the mayor of Philadelphia were also brought in as witnesses.[23]

Monsignor John A. Ryan, well-known Catholic author on social questions, told the committee that, when no private agencies could do the job, the government had a moral obligation to clear the slums and take care of the health and safety of the slum dwellers.[24] Dr. Worth Tippy, of the Federal Council of Churches, appeared as a witness in favor of the bill, emphasizing in his testimony the beneficial social effects that would result from this legislation.[25] Rabbi Edward Israel, of the Conference of American Rabbis, pointed out that the slums break down the morals and health of the slum dwellers.[26]

---

[21] Testimony of Langdon Post; in *ibid.*, pp. 51, 57.

[22] Testimony of Ernest J. Bohn; in *ibid.*, p. 67.

[23] Testimonies of Honorable Neville Miller, mayor of Louisville, and Honorable S. Davis Wilson, mayor of Philadelphia; in *ibid.*, pp. 97, 103.

[24] Testimony of Monsignor John A. Ryan; in *ibid.*, p. 89.

[25] Testimony of Dr. Worth Tippy; in *ibid.*, p. 95.

[26] Testimony of Rabbi Edward Israel; in *ibid.*, p. 123.

To prove that the financial provisions of the bill were sound, the Wagner group had arranged for a representative of Blythe and Company of New York, Mr. James Couffer, to assure the committee that private investment would be interested in the bonds of the Authority.[27]

All the opponents of the bill had argued in their public statements that the bill made for government competition with private industry. In order to answer this argument Louis Horowitz, formerly president of one of the largest construction companies in the United States, was asked to testify before the committee. He emphasized the point that Wagner had often made in his speeches, that this bill provided for construction of dwelling units for people in the lowest income groups who could not be served by private enterprise.[28]

The technical experts were also worked into the lineup of witnesses. Edith Elmer Wood, Miss Bauer, and Coleman Woodbury testified on various technical aspects of the program.[29]

Nathan Straus was called to testify as one who had had actual experience with all the phases of the limited-dividend corporation. He had furnished the land and capital equity for the Hillside Homes in New York. The project was in operation at the time Mr. Straus was called to testify.[30]

These were the principal witnesses who, together with others, like Mrs. Simkhovitch, presented to the committee a united front of solid arguments in favor of the bill.

Chairman David I. Walsh's witnesses did not present the testimony that the opponents of the bill expected they would. Madame Perkins favored a bill that provided for slum clearance

---

[27] Testimony of James Couffer; in *ibid.*, p. 109.

[28] Testimony of Louis Horowitz, former president of Thompson-Starrett Company; in *ibid.*, p. 204.

[29] Testimonies of Edith Elmer Wood, Catherine Bauer, and Coleman Woodbury; in *ibid.*, pp. 209, 183, 235.

[30] Testimony of Nathan Straus; in *ibid.*, p. 158.

and the construction of housing units equivalent to the number of slum units demolished.[31] This was Walsh's idea of the program. Peter Grimm was against the bill and government participation in a construction program. This testimony was expected. But the testimony of John Fahey of HOLC in favor of the bill was unexpected. He stated that he saw no conflict between the provisions of this bill and the program of loans and mortgages carried on by the other agencies of the government.[32] This was a victory for the Wagner group and the first breech in the wall of opposition within the administration.

During the course of the hearings a report from the Federal Housing Administration was published which caused much comment. The FHA report stated that a home could be built for $1,200. The opponents of the bill used this report to prove that it was unnecessary for the government to enter the housing field. The public-housing groups said that it was impossible to build a home for so little. These statements *pro* and *con* were made before Chairman Walsh, and he decided to summon a representative of FHA to testify before the committee. So on Saturday, April 25, 1936 the last scheduled day of the hearings, Miles L. Colean, technical director of the FHA, appeared before the committee to explain the statement about the $1,200 house. Under questioning by Walsh, Colean qualified somewhat the meaning of the statement. The price of $1,200 did not include the land cost. "In order to get the results we have planned here, it would take labor of great skill to do it, labor that knew how to handle materials without waste, labor that was competent to work efficiently." Colean also stated that $1,200 was the lowest bid offered. Other contractors bid $1,500 on the same plans.[33]

---

[31] Testimony of Frances Perkins; in *ibid.*, p. 61.
[32] Testimony of John Fahey; in *ibid.*, p. 125. The common opinion concerning the anticipated hostile testimony of Fahey is expressed in the *New York Times*, April 5, 1936.
[33] Testimony of Miles L. Colean; in *Hearings on S. 4424*, p. 243.

When the testimony was finished on Saturday, April 25, the opposition decided that it would be necessary to give some testimony in opposition to the bill. Walsh was therefore asked to give the opposition a day. He decided on Wednesday, April 29. In addition to the requests that he received, Walsh also sent out a request to certain authorities on housing. He sent a telegram to Lawrence Veiller, the veteran in the fight for housing legislation which set up standards of health and safety. Veiller replied to Walsh in a letter of May 2 that he was in Albany on business on the twenty-ninth and could not come to the hearings on that day. He could not delegate anyone to appear in his place. He wanted to appear himself and state his opposition to the Wagner bill. He asked Walsh to give him a special day to testify.[34] Walsh did not give Veiller his day. After he heard the testimony on the twenty-ninth he was satisfied that everyone had had sufficient opportunity to testify.

In the testimony given in favor of the bill Dr. John A. Ryan, who was a recognized authority on social problems and a supporter of President Roosevelt's New Deal, discussed a very fundamental principle of political science. "Does the Federal Government have the right to engage in a public housing program?" was a very basic question. Ryan's answer was that the Federal Government does have the right when certain conditions are present. He worked from the statement of the principle found in the encyclical letter of Pope Leo XIII *On the Condition of Labor:* "Whenever the general welfare of any particular class suffers or is threatened with injury which can in no other way be met or averted, it is the duty of the public authority to intervene." As is clear from the statement of the principle, it is to be applied after it has been established by the existing facts that a condition is such that only the government can remedy the

---

[34] Bohn memorandum on this letter, May 1936, National Association of Housing Officials, Ernest Bohn File—1936.

situation. It is a prudential judgment that demands the intervention of the government. Ryan recognized this important factor when he stated that the basic solution to the problem would be to give the worker higher wages so that he could provide his own housing. This, Ryan maintained, would not be possible under existing conditions.

> If all the wage earners of the land had steady employment at decent wages, America would have no serious housing problem. Whatever problem then existed could be taken care of by the Federal Housing Administration.
>
> Whenever employers cannot or will not pay wages sufficient to provide the workers with decent housing it is the duty of the State to compel employers to pay adequate wages. An important first step toward this was taken by the Federal Government under the National Recovery Administration. Unfortunately that beneficent measure was destroyed by the decision of the Supreme Court in the *Schechter case.* As a consequence, the method of providing the workers with decent housing through the payment of decent wages will apparently have to wait upon an amendment to the Federal Constitution.
>
> That will take considerable time. In the meantime, the housing problem is immediate, urgent, and acute. Therefore, the right of millions to adequate housing has become a right against the State to provide such housing.[35]

Members of the opposition to the Wagner bill did not see the facts the same way that Monsignor Ryan saw them, and they sincerely believed that the problem could be solved by other agencies than the Federal Government. Mr. Nelson, executive vice-president of NAREB, denied that there was an acute housing shortage, as was suggested by the proponents of the bill. The determination of the actual shortage of housing, however, was a very difficult problem, as Mr. Nelson was to admit during his testimony.

---

[35] Testimony of Monsignor John A. Ryan; in *Hearings on S. 4424,* p. 90.

SENATOR DAVIS. My own observations are that there are so many of these houses, so many of these buildings in the business sections of the country that ought to have been razed years ago.

MR. NELSON. Well, I can present the facts as I have them and the facts show that there are some 400,000 urban dwelling units, both in single family dwellings and in multiple dwellings, standing vacant today, and those are of every possible type, inexpensive, medium-priced, and expensive. Now, that is the fact.

When some people speak of a housing shortage very often they mean a shortage of a certain type of dwelling which they regard as desirable, and it usually depends on who is speaking as to what kind of an estimate you get. Architects feel a great number of houses should be destroyed and rebuilt. If you talk to a man who is responsible for a lot of mortgage investments, like the president of a savings bank, he is very apt to feel that much of the present housing is good enough to be used for a long time, just so he gets his money out of it. So it depends on whom you talk to as to what estimate you get as to how many houses we now have that should be replaced.

I am perfectly willing to say, from our observation, that there are a great many houses that should be replaced as soon as we can afford to do it.[36]

During the course of his testimony and in the material filed with the committee, Nelson pointed out other ways that could be used to increase the supply of housing without direct action by the Federal Government.

I would like to suggest to the committee that two of the principal obstacles in the way of better housing are those created by Government itself. The first one consists of an archaic set of building codes. The Federal Government has recognized this for years, and through the Department of Commerce and Bureau of Standards has sought to persuade the various cities to modernize and simplify the present building codes. The codes are so archaic and so varied in their requirements that it necessarily raises questions of construction.

---

[36] Testimony of Herbert U. Nelson; in *ibid.*, p. 310.

Another very serious obstacle in the way of good, cheap housing is our tax system. In this country, according to Prof. Paul
Studensky, of the New York City College, who has made quite a
study of the matter of housing and sheltering, real estate pays
approximately 58 percent of all the costs of government, all government, that is, local, State, and National. Canada pays the next
highest or raises the next highest proportion of public funds from
shelter, where they raise 40 percent of their public revenue in that
way. In England it drops down to 19. In France it is about 12. In
Belgium it is less than 1 percent. In the Scandinavian countries it
is about 3 percent.

THE CHAIRMAN. In your opinion the high rate of taxation and
the increased rates of taxation is a large contributor to the holding
back of the recovery in the building-trades occupations?

MR. NELSON. No question about it, Senator. If you load most
of the cost of government on shelter, necessarily shelter is going
to cost more.[37]

When Mr. Nelson finished his testimony Mr. John Mowbray,
president of Roland Park Company of Baltimore, was called
to testify. Mowbray explained how neighborhoods became
blighted. He then informed the committee of the Neighborhood
Improvement and Development Act which was being sponsored
by NAREB.[38] Mowbray stated further that the ideas of this act
had been successfully used in Baltimore.

Another important witness before the committee was Walter
S. Schmidt of Cincinnati. He explained to the committee that
many of the dwelling units that were not adequate could be
repaired. Schmidt made a statement that "it is people who make
slum areas, and not houses."[39] This was a very sensitive point
to discuss, but it was a fact that had not escaped the attention
of Ernest J. Bohn. Bohn had heard Joseph Day make the same
statement at a housing conference in New York. After the meet-

---

[37] *Ibid.*, p. 315.
[38] Testimony of John Mowbray; in *ibid.*, p. 320.
[39] Testimony of Walter S. Schmidt; in *ibid.*, p. 330.

ing Bohn wrote to Alfred of the NPHC making some comments on this statement of Day.

> It strikes me that one thing that none of us have properly answered is the question that Day raised which has to do with the way in which slum residents live. His point was, you remember, that the slum resident does not know and does not care about the surroundings in which he lives. Put him into a modern and sanitary dwelling and he will soon turn it into a place of filth and dilapidation.
>
> It seems to me that the point about this matter is that what we are all talking about is the creation of new environment rather than merely building new rooms and new houses. . . . Not only do we intend to give people open spaces, proper recreational facilities, air, sunshine, sanitation, and privacy in the new projects, but we hope to exercise the proper social control and to furnish the education and guidance . . . necessary . . . for these people who have never had a chance . . . to . . . enjoy their new surroundings.[40]

Peter Grimm had given testimony before the committee at an earlier date. As the former presidential adviser on housing matters, Mr. Grimm was invited by Chairman Walsh to appear before the committee. Mr. Grimm reviewed the housing activities of the Federal Government and made comments about the results of the various government programs. While he was opposed to most of the activities of the government in the field of housing, he did see a place for the government with respect to slum clearance. This comment was in line with Walsh's thinking about government activity, and it strengthened his convictions. While discussing the problem with Grimm, Walsh stated:

> I personally think it was never the intention of Congress to allow Federal funds to be used for the character and type of housing that apparently is undertaken. [Walsh is here referring to the PWA projects.][41]

---

[40] Bohn to Alfred, December 20, 1934, National Association of Housing Officials, Folder—NPHC.
[41] Statement of David Walsh; in *Hearings on S. 4424*, p. 192.

So far as the determination of Walsh's attitude toward the bill is concerned, the most important argument was given by Dr. Ryan. His testimony served to convince Walsh that the government did have a legitimate part to play in the solution of the housing emergency.[42]

The system of hearings before a congressional committee serves an extremely important and necessary function in the legislative process. Information, facts and figures, and arguments, social and economic and political, with respect to proposed legislation are presented to the committee. And this information eventually affects the general thinking of groups interested in the legislative problem under discussion. Even if the proposed bill fails to be passed by Congress, still there will be an improvement made by interested groups with respect to the problem under legislative scrutiny.

The next step after the public or open hearings on the bill was the closed or executive sessions of the committee. The proceedings of these meetings are kept secret. Only the members of the committee and the committee staff are present at these meetings. It is in these executive sessions that compromises are worked out. The bill is amended; the committee vote is taken; if the vote is favorable, the bill is then ready to be reported to the Senate; if the vote is unfavorable, the bill is thus killed in committee.

Walsh did not hold these executive sessions immediately after the hearings. He was waiting for the president to give him his views and recommendations. Walsh and Wagner were to meet with the president on Friday, May 8. Wagner had an engagement in New York which he considered of more importance than this meeting, and so he let Walsh go to visit the president alone. At this time Wagner was tired of going to meetings. He thought it was time for the president to come out in favor of the

---

[42] Statement of Ernest J. Bohn (personal interview).

bill.[43] The president also had a meeting with Ickes on Friday, May 8, during which they were to discuss housing. Ickes had sent the president an analysis of the Wagner bill drafted by Clas in preparation for this meeting. Ickes was attempting to get the administration of the program located in the Department of the Interior.[44]

It was impossible to know where the president stood with regard to housing at this time. During the president's press conference on May 4 he told the reporters that he approved the bill in principle and hoped that it would pass. He said, however, that he would like certain changes to be made (which he did not specify at the conference). In reply to a question he stated that he did not consider the bill to be a "must" measure.[45] On May 6 the president talked with Representative Bankhead, majority leader of the House, and told him that he wanted the bill to pass; but he would not force Congress to remain in session to enact the bill after they had enacted the relief and taxation bills. It was also reported at the time that Bankhead was actually lining up votes for the housing bill in response to a request of the president.[46]

At the press conference for May 15 the president told reporters that he was making good progress on the housing bill and that he hoped to have something over the week end on it.[47]

On May 15 Wagner got quite a shock when he heard Senator Robinson, majority leader of the Senate, outline the legislative

---

[43] Report of Bohn to Woodbury, May 13, 1936, National Association of Housing Officials, Ernest Bohn File—1936.

[44] Ickes to Roosevelt, May 6, 1936, and office memorandum for the president, May 8, 1936, Roosevelt Papers, O.F. 2694.

[45] Report of the press conference is given by Coleman Woodbury, *National Association of Housing Officials, Bulletin No. 89*, May 13, 1936.

[46] Report of Bohn to Woodbury, May 13, 1936, National Association of Housing Officials, Ernest Bohn File—1936.

[47] Press Conference No. 295, May 15, 1936, Roosevelt Papers, Transcripts of Press Conferences.

program for the remaining days of the session. "Mr. President, for the convenience of the Senators and the Press, it is deemed proper at this time to make a brief statement concerning the future proceedings in the Senate. . . ."[48] Robinson then went on to say that the Senate should act on the omnibus flood control bill, the commodity-exchange bill, the work-relief bill, and the tax bill. That was all that the president and the party wanted; after that the Senate could adjourn.

Senator McNary, the minority leader, then asked Robinson if his statement excluded any other bills from consideration. Robinson answered that it did not exclude those bills that he expected to be brought forth that day. He said that he had mentioned those special measures because it was his opinion that the country, as well as the members of both houses of Congress, expected that action would be taken on them.

Wagner then entered the discussion and told the Senate that he understood the senator (Robinson) to have left out the housing bill "which I regard as one of the most important of all bills pending before the Senate." Robinson replied:

> I think the Senator from New York has had sufficiently liberal experience in legislative matters to know that it is a physical, moral, mental and every other kind of impossibility to pass judgment on whether a measure that has not even been reported by one of the committees of the Senate shall be disposed of during this session. . . . I would not favor continuing the session beyond the 6th of June for the purpose of passing the bill to which the Senator has referred, although I recognize its importance.

Wagner replied:

> I appreciate that but I did not want it to be understood that the program was limited, and that we were foreclosed from the consideration of the housing bill.[49]

---

[48] *Congressional Record,* May 15, 1936, p. 7384.
[49] *Ibid.*

This interchange of questions and answers well illustrates the position of the majority and minority leaders in the Congress. The majority leader is in contact with the president (if the Congress and the president are of the same political party), and it is the majority leader who organizes the business with the president of the Senate or the speaker of the House so that the legislative program of the party can be enacted. The minority leader represents the opposition party and he is charged with the responsibility of looking out for the interests of the party. He enters into various compromises with the majority leader so that legislation can be enacted and so that there will not be plain obstruction on the part of the opposition.

Wagner was being rebuffed by the administration for going ahead with his housing bill on his own. Robinson, in effect, told him that the administration would not put its support behind the bill. Wagner now knew where he stood, but he was not beaten as yet. He still had great personal power, and he intended to use it. Within a ten-day period he delivered a series of three major radio addresses in favor of the housing bill. On May 14 he spoke over Station WOL and a network of stations in the middle-Atlantic states.[50] On May 21 Wagner took part in a housing rally broadcast of Station WHN.[51] Wagner, together with Holden of the New York State Housing Board and D. E. McAvoy of the Home Mortgage Advisory Board of Long Island formed a panel to discuss housing on Theodore Granik's Forum of the Air program. This was on Sunday night, May 24.[52]

While those in favor of housing were attempting to build up support for the bill, the National Retail Lumber Dealers Association[53] and the Chamber of Commerce of the United

---

[50] Collected Papers of Wagner, Vol. 7, Sec. 4, No. 15.

[51] Ibid.

[52] Ibid.

[53] Typical of the letters that Carnahan sent to members of Congress is the letter published in the Congressional Record, June 15, 1936, p. 9350.

States circulated statements against the bill. The position of the Chamber of Commerce was that the building industry should provide new homes for people in the middle income bracket, and then the people living in substandard and slum dwellings could move into the houses vacated by those of the middle income group who moved into new homes.[54] These statements of the NRLDA and the Chamber of Commerce were not seen by as many people as were the statements published by the Housing Legislation Information Office, but they were sent to the senators and representatives. This is a good example of the difference in operation between a pressure group which works on the widest possible base of public opinion and a lobby which carries on its operations within its own organization, allied organizations, and the Congress.

All during the month of May the professional housers in the various groups were waiting anxiously for the report of the Committee on Education and Labor. When this report did not appear by the last week of May, some of the people interested began to condemn Chairman Walsh for the delay. Bohn, who was in Washington at this time, reported that it was not Walsh's fault that the report was not made. Wagner and the president were to blame for the delay. Walsh said that he would get out the report when the president and Wagner asked him to do so. La Follette told Bohn that this was a true picture of what was going on.[55]

The party conventions were to be held in June, and so on May 29 Roosevelt called a special meeting of the "liberals" in the Senate to plan strategy. Wagner and Minton were there, as also were La Follette and Norris. When the question of the plat-

---

[54] See résumé of this statement in *Hearings before House Committee on Banking and Currency on H. R. 5033 and S. 1685*, 75th Cong., 1st Sess. (1937), p. 249 (Washington: Government Printing Office, 1937).

[55] Report of Bohn to Woodbury, June 1, 1936, National Association of Housing Officials, Ernest Bohn File—1936.

form came up for discussion, Wagner was given the opportunity he was waiting for to use his personal power in favor of his housing bill. He told the president and the group that he did not have any time to work on the platform because he was too busy getting support for his housing bill. This was Wagner's answer to the president's refusal to put the bill on his "must" list of legislation.

This threat of Wagner got some action. The president said he would go along with Wagner if Wagner would agree to some restrictive amendments. Wagner, knowing that it was an amended bill he must accept or no bill at all, went along with the president.[56]

The next morning a meeting was called. It was attended by Walsh and Daiger, who was taking Grimm's place as administration housing adviser, by Wagner, and by Keyserling. At this meeting Daiger attempted to take over the proceedings on the basis of his position as presidential adviser. Wagner told him that he had seen the president the night before and that the plans that the president discussed were not the plans that he (Daiger) was presenting. After this statement by Wagner, Walsh was ready to go along with Wagner. They worked out some of the restrictive amendments that the president and Walsh wanted to see incorporated in the bill, and they outlined a report.[57] Walsh then called an executive session of the committee on June 2, at which session the committee voted unanimously to accept the amendments and to report the bill out with a recommendation to the Senate that it be passed. On Wednesday, June 3, Walsh reported S. 4424 with amendments.[58] It was placed on the calendar under Number 2270.

---

[56] *Ibid.*

[57] *Ibid.*

[58] Senate Committee on Education and Labor, *To Create a United States Housing Authority*, S. Rept. No. 2160, to accompany S. 4424, 74th Cong., 2d Sess. (1936). Washington: Government Printing Office, 1936.

The major changes in the bill were made to restrict the amount of money to be spent and to make sure that the public-housing units would be occupied by people who were living in the slums because of their low income. Thus the provision for loans to "limited-profit housing agencies" was struck out. The sum of money to be appropriated for the first year of housing operations was cut from $51,000,000 to $10,000,000. The provisions for the Reconstruction Finance Corporation to participate in the program by loan and by purchase of Housing Authority bonds was also struck out. The total amount of obligations to be issued by the Authority was cut by $50,000,000 and the time period in which to issue the obligations was shortened by one year, from July 1, 1939 to July 1, 1938.[59]

Certain other minor changes were written into the bill. The Authority was to place its employees under the provisions of civil-service regulations. This was done as a result of the insistence of the United States Civil Service Commission, the National League of Women Voters, and the Civil Service Reform League. All these organizations sent briefs to Walsh asking for the inclusion of this provision.[60]

The provision which appointed the secretary of the interior as an *ex-officio* member of the Board of the Housing Authority was also struck out of the bill.[61]

Wagner, however, knew that he could not wait for the bill to be called off the calendar. He then got Robinson to put the bill on the agenda as soon as the Senate convened after the recess for the Republican national convention. The Senate had taken a recess after the daily session of June 8 until June 15.

During the recess Ellenbogen and Wagner had a conference on the strategy to be used in an attempt to get the bill passed

---

[59] S. 4424 (Rept. No. 2160), June 1, 1936, pp. 30-31. (The date listed here, June 1, is the legislative day. The calendar day was June 3, 1936.)

[60] These letters are published in *Hearings on S. 4424*, pp. 258, 259, and 273.

[61] S. 4424 (Rept. No. 2160), June 1, 1936, p. 8.

in the few days that remained. The only hope of getting any action in the House was to have the committee report the bill, but Steagall was deaf to all Ellenbogen's pleas for the hearings.[62] The president would have to intervene to get action in the House.

As far as the Senate debate was concerned, Ellenbogen advised Wagner to stress the fact that the program was to be decentralized. Ellenbogen told him of the fear throughout the country of an "octopus" located in Washington. If the building and the management of the housing units was carried out on the local level, there would be more support for the bill.

When the Senate reconvened on June 15, Mr. King, after the usual preliminary business, made a parliamentary inquiry about the order of business. He said:

> I understand the able Senator from New York had given notice of his intention to proceed to the consideration of the housing bill at the termination of the morning hour, and it was understood that the motion would be made. I may be in error.
>
> MR. VANDENBERG [who was then trying to get the floor to do some business]. How was an understanding like that arrived at?[63]

The presiding officer in the chair did not explain to Vandenberg; he merely told him to continue with his business, as he had the floor at that time.

As soon as Vandenberg completed his speech and his bill, which was to give retirement benefits to members of the FBI, was acted upon, Wagner was recognized. He was managing the

---

[62] Statement of Henry Ellenbogen (personal interview).

[63] *Congressional Record*, June 15, 1936, p. 9342. The "morning hour" is the assigned time for the conduct of the routine daily business of the Senate according to Rule 7 (Morning Business) of the *Standing Rules of the Senate (Senate Manual Containing the Standing Rules, Orders, Laws, and Resolutions Affecting the Business of the United States Senate, Jefferson's Manual, Declaration of Independence, Articles of Confederation, Constitution of the United States, Etc.* [S. Doc. No. 10, 83d Cong., 1st Sess., 1953]. Washington: Government Printing Office, 1953).

bill because Walsh, the chairman of the committee who should manage the debate, was absent at a conference meeting. Wagner gave a short speech in which he distinguished the housing operations under the PWA and the housing operations that would be conducted under the provisions of this bill. He emphasized the "local responsibility" in this bill. He read sections from the report where the bill was highly praised and told the Senate that it was passed by an unanimous vote in committee.[64]

Wagner then went on to say that in his entire career he never handled any legislation that had had such universal support as this present bill. He remarked that he had some days previously put into the record the long list of organizations supporting the bill.[65] He then briefly outlined the provisions of the bill. He took special care to emphasize that there was no competition with private industry in the operation of this program.

After this presentation of the bill Wagner was interrupted for questions and the actual debate on the bill was begun. Senator James Couzens of Michigan asked Wagner for a legal definition of a family. He mentioned that he could find no such definition in the bill. Wagner replied: "It means at least a man and a wife, I suppose. I thought it was pretty well established what a family is." Couzens continued that he did not wish to be technical but that he could not find a definition and thought there should be one. Wagner explained a little more in detail about a family, but he did not satisfy Couzens. The senator from Michigan told Wagner:

> I can visualize a family consisting of a widowed mother and her children living together and having a substantial income. . . . Are the incomes . . . of the mother and her children, and perhaps the income of a third generation to be combined in arriving at what is a low income family?[66]

---

[64] *Congressional Record*, June 15, 1936, p. 9344.
[65] *Ibid.*, May 26, 1936, p. 7893.
[66] *Ibid.*, June 15, 1936, p. 9345.

Wagner replied that all incomes would be combined in arriving at the definition of a low income family. He then thanked the senator from Michigan for his question, which helped to clarify a point that had not been raised before. He was happy to have the question raised at this time so that there could be no legal difficulty or misunderstanding in regard to what was intended.

Wagner then went back to his speech to give proof that there would be no competition with private industry in the operation of the program. He appealed to the testimony of Mr. Horowitz made before the committee wherein he stressed the fact.[67]

The senator from New York then made use of the argument that was his favorite whenever he was speaking of the need for better housing.

> Do we desire to have less prisons, do we desire to have less hospitals, . . . ? Then clear the slums, enact this legislation which goes to the root of the problem and removes the cause of the difficulty.[68]

Wagner next quoted local authorities, such as the mayor of Louisville, who wanted this legislation to save tax money for the city as well as for all the other reasons.[69]

As Wagner was speaking, he could see Senator Couzens rise and attempt to get the floor. Wagner said: "I know what the Senator has in mind. He will say that we should increase wages." Couzens admitted that that was what was on his mind, and he further stated that, if this bill was passed, it would be an excuse for the employers to keep the wages low because they knew that the government would provide decent housing with a subsidy. Wagner agreed that that might be true, but went on to say that we could not wait until wages were brought up to the proper level. The problem of the slums was one that must be

---

[67] *Ibid.*
[68] *Ibid.*

[69] *Ibid.,* p. 9348.

dealt with immediately. Wagner then spoke in his own defense, saying that no one was more interested in raising the wages of workers than he was.[70]

Couzens obtained the floor again to say that if employers were not going to pay adequate wages to the underprivileged families and were going to make it necessary for the government to provide housing facilities, the obvious result would be that they would pay the cost of the program in the bill anyway. If the employers, then, did not approach this problem in a legitimate way by letting the employee have his own freedom in the selection of homes and the expenditure of money, it seemed that the Federal Government would have to take the money out of the pockets of the employers in order to provide and maintain decent homes for the employees.

After this statement of Couzens, Wagner started to explain that business would be stimulated by his housing program. Vandenberg rose from his seat in the chamber to ask Wagner a question. He read from a letter of Frank Carnahan, of the Retail Lumber Dealers, that business would be retarded by the competition of the government in the housing field.[71] Wagner's answer was that the private builders could not and would not provide housing for the people in the lowest income groups.

Senator James Pope of Idaho then asked Wagner about the effect of housing programs in foreign countries. Wagner told Pope about the results of the program in England. According to a statement of Mr. Morrison, said Wagner, the housing program was primarily responsible for postwar recovery.[72]

Vandenberg entered into discussion with Wagner as soon as the question of Pope was answered. Vandenberg asked a very embarrassing question of Wagner. He wanted to know "to what extent are the resources provided in the bill going to meet the

---

[70] *Ibid.*, p. 9346.   [72] *Ibid.*
[71] *Ibid.*, p. 9347.

sum total of the problem?" Wagner did not want to give out an estimated figure that would go into billions of dollars, especially as there was an economy drive on in Congress at that session. So he tried to parry the question by saying that the present appropriation merely scratched the surface, and that later it would have to be expanded. Vandenberg was not satisfied with this answer, but came right back to the sensitive question again: "Is there a figure available which indicates the sum total of the demand and need?" Wagner answered: "Yes, there is, but I would not dare mention it because the senator would be able to fight the bill as so entirely inadequate that the figure ought to be expanded." Wagner then commented that it was necessary to begin on a small scale. Vandenberg would not be satisfied; he pressed Wagner again for a total estimate of the cost of the program, saying that, once we start a program such as this, it is necessary to treat alike all the citizenship in respect to this necessity of housing. The government is then committed to a final program, and he was wondering upon what in the long run we are embarking.

Wagner again evaded the question and replied that something must be left to the future. The program was economically sound, and it was a worthy undertaking to clear the slums. Hence we must begin somewhere, and we must rely upon the housing authorities to distribute fairly the benefits of the program. Wagner ended by saying there was no reason for not beginning this worthy project.

Vandenberg replied that he was not arguing that we must not creep before we walk. He was still wondering about the total cost. To this comment Wagner said that the problem would be reduced as conditions in the country get better. With prosperous times, Wagner continued, there would be less need for the program. He then moved on to another part of his speech.[73]

---

[73] *Ibid.*, p. 9348.

He talked about the standards that were written into the bill to make sure that the objectives of the bill would be obtained when it was finally put into effect.

As Wagner was ready to finish the speech, Vandenberg was ready with another objection. The junior senator from Michigan stated that there was a provision for $450,000,000 in bonds to be issued within a three-year period, and he wanted the senator from New York to tell him if there was "any report from the Treasury Department as to the effect of this burden upon the public credit in any aspect?"

This was another very dangerous question in view of the fact that Wagner had not waited for Treasury approval, but had gone ahead on his own to introduce this bill. He simply answered: "There is not any estimate." But Vandenberg would not be satisfied. "Is there a report," he continued, "from the Treasury on the possible effect of this operation upon the fiscal policy of the government?" Wagner answered cautiously: "No, although I have consulted the Treasury Department with reference to the proposed legislation." Such an evasion did not satisfy Vandenberg. He pressed Wagner again: "Does the senator mean that the Treasury Department favors it?" What could Wagner say? Again he parried the question: "Let me say to the senator that these are loans, not grants." He then went on to stress the loan features of the financial provisions. When he finished Vandenberg was back with another question: "Does the senator think it would be an operation rather well calculated to repay the loans?" This question gave Wagner an opportunity to get out of a difficult spot. He told Vandenberg that the housing projects were well calculated to repay the loan, and that he had received assurances that private capital would be invested in these loans. Private banks would regard this as a good investment and would purchase the bonds.[74]

_____

[74] *Ibid.*

That answer seemed to satisfy Vandenberg for the time. Senator Daniel O. Hastings of Delaware then asked Wagner who would purchase the bonds. Wagner answered that the local housing authorities would guarantee the bonds and sell them to private investors. Hastings next asked for an explanation of how the local housing authorities operated.

Wagner was not able to give a very satisfactory answer to this last question. He told Hastings that there were some twenty-one existing state housing authorities, but he did not explain in any detail the legal basis or the administrative operations of the authorities.[75] This is the type of specific question that the legislator finds difficult to answer because in the drafting of the bill he has been concerned only with questions of broad policy. The drafting of details was left to his expert advisers. And there are no experts permitted on the Senate floor to advise the senators in debate.[76]

After his attempted answer Wagner tried to end the debate. He was most anxious to push the legislation to a vote on that day. "Unless some senator has some question to ask," Wagner concluded, "I think that is all I care to say. Unfortunately, my statement has been a disjointed one; but I spoke as the thoughts came to me."

Senator Vandenberg had a question for Wagner. Again he referred to the letter of the lumber dealers and asked Wagner to make a comment on the statement that there were some thirty-five different federal agencies dealing with one phase or another of housing.

In reply Wagner pointed out that there was only one federal agency which dealt with slum clearance. This subject of slum clearance is separate and distinct from the other activities

---

[75] *Ibid.*, p. 9349.

[76] Rule 33 of the *Standing Rules of the Senate* regulates admission to the floor of the Senate and no provision has been made for the admission of experts or advisers.

which deal with home loans and mortgages. Wagner again emphasized that his bill was designed to put the slum-clearance program on a permanent basis. And then he added that it was also a decentralized program.

Vandenberg then wanted to know if the demonstration projects provided for in the bill were of the same nature as the resettlement projects. Wagner answered that they were not of the same nature, and then in an apologetic way he added that he doubted whether many such projects would be undertaken, and, in addition to that fact, the section was very well guarded against any abuse. Vandenberg, seizing upon this weakness in the program, told Wagner that he did not think that any limit was placed on the number of demonstration projects. Wagner replied that the "consent of the local authorities is required," and he added that the provision for demonstration projects was a minor provision of the bill.[77]

Senator Hastings then asked a question about the selection of tenants in the housing projects. The selection of tenants, Wagner informed him, was made by the local authorities on the basis of their low income. After receiving this answer, Hastings addressed the chair and told the house that he did not understand the program and that he did not know whether there was any opposition to the bill. Moreover, he did not have an opportunity to read the report on the bill. The report of the bill covered twelve and one-third pages printed ordinary book size. Hastings then said:

> I should certainly be opposed to the matter being disposed of today. I should like to have it go over until at least tomorrow so that we can have at least an opportunity to study the speech made by the Senator from New York, all of which I have not been able to hear because I was engaged in a conference.[78]

---

[77] *Congressional Record*, June 15, 1936, p. 9349.
[78] *Ibid.*, p. 9350.

The senator from New York told the chair that he was opposed to any postponement of final action on the bill until tomorrow. He mentioned the fact that they were approaching the end of the session and stressed the fact that the bill had been on the calendar for a long time and that there had also been a detailed report on the bill. He thought it would be unfortunate to have a postponement because it would mean that the bill could not be enacted at this session of the Congress.[79]

What had actually happened was that the minority—the Republicans—had been caught off guard by the agreement that Wagner reached with the majority leader to take the bill up the day the Congress convened after the recess for the Republican convention. The Republicans had not expected the housing bill to come up that day, and they were unprepared. Wagner was attempting to push the bill through in that one afternoon, but the Republicans were not going to permit that to happen. Charles McNary, the minority leader, addressed the chair and Senator Wagner to state that, just before Mr. Hastings made his motion, he was about to move that the Senate should take a recess until two o'clock the next afternoon. He stated that he had been asked by a number of senators to make such a motion so that they would have more time to study the measure. McNary commented that this bill was an important measure and that as such it should not be considered and acted upon the same day. This is the usual request, he commented. McNary added: "I think the senator from New York would gain time by acting reasonably, as he always desires to do, and allow us to lay the pending measure aside until tomorrow, at which time everyone will be prepared to go forward in the consideration of the bill and reach a conclusion as early as possible."

Wagner replied that he would agree to this, and then asked that the time for debate be limited or that a time for the vote

[79] *Ibid.*

be set, so that the final decision could be reached the next day, since otherwise it would be impossible to have the bill passed by both houses. McNary replied that he did not think it possible to enter into such an agreement; however, from his experience he knew that the Senate would act upon the bill.[80]

This remark of McNary brings out a procedure of the Senate which is held in highest regard. It is the freedom of debate. The ordinary procedure in the House would have been for the Rules Committee to give a special rule along the lines that Wagner requested, which would limit the time of debate and set a specific time for the vote. But in the Senate no such procedure is adopted. As this group is a smaller house and debate is usually carried on more efficiently, no such rules are ordinarily necessary. Because of the rule of freedom of debate the filibuster is possible. A filibuster can be avoided by the use of the motion for cloture, which was adopted in 1917, but which is difficult to employ.[81]

---

[80] *Ibid.*

[81] The second half of Rule 22 of the *Standing Rules of the Senate* provides for cloture: "If at any time a motion signed by sixteen Senators, to bring to a close the debate upon any pending measure is presented to the Senate, the Presiding Officer shall at once state the motion to the Senate, and one hour after the Senate meets on the following calendar day but one, he shall lay the motion before the Senate and direct that the Secretary call the roll, and, upon the ascertainment that a quorum is present, the Presiding Officer shall, without debate submit to the Senate by an aye-and-nay vote the question:

" 'Is it the sense of the Senate that the debate shall be brought to a close?'

"And if that question shall be decided in the affirmative by a two-thirds vote of those voting, then said measure shall be the unfinished business to the exclusion of all other business until disposed of.

"Thereafter no Senator shall be entitled to speak in all more than one hour on the pending measure, the amendments thereto, and motions affecting the same, and it shall be the duty of the Presiding Officer to keep the time of each Senator who speaks. Except by unanimous consent, no amendment shall be in order after the vote to bring the debate to a close, unless the same has been presented and read prior to that time. No dilatory motion, or dilatory amendment, or amendment not germane shall be in order. Points

Wagner finally agreed to the minority leader's motion. He asked that there be printed in the *Record* a statement of Stewart McDonald of the FHA in which he stated that he would support the Wagner bill. There had been reports that he was opposed. Vandenberg then asked that the letter of Frank Carnahan be printed in the *Record*. Wagner's attempt to push the bill through in one day had failed.[82]

When the Senate convened the next day Wagner asked for unanimous consent that the formal reading of the bill be dispensed with and that it be read immediately for amendment. There was no objection to the motion and the clerk read the first amendment reported by the Committee on Education and Labor. It was an amendment to the definition of families of low income. The new formula stated that families of low income were those whose total income was less than six times the yearly rent. The cost of heat, light, and water, where such services were not supplied by the lessor, were to be counted as part of the rental. This amendment was agreed to unanimously without debate.[83] There was the same automatic agreement to all the other amendments up to the one concerning the financial provisions of the bill.[84]

---

of order, including questions of relevancy, and appeals from the decision of the Presiding Officer, shall be decided without debate."

This half of Rule 22 was an amendment adopted on March 8, 1917. This provision for cloture by a two-thirds vote has been used successfully on only four occasions during the period from its adoption to the end of the Eighty-fourth Congress, Second Session, July 27, 1956. The following were the four occasions when the motions were adopted: Debate on Treaty of Peace with Germany (November 15, 1919); Debate on the World Court (January 25, 1926); Debate on Establishment of National Bank Branches (February 15, 1927); Debate on Bureau of Prohibition in Treasury Department (February 28, 1927). Cloture motions were rejected on eighteen occasions during this period. Cloture motions were withdrawn or unacted upon on ten occasions during this period.

[82] *Congressional Record*, June 15, 1936, p. 9350.

[83] *Ibid.*, June 16, 1936, p. 9553.

[84] *Ibid.*, pp. 9554-57.

Mr. Vandenberg objected to the financial provisions. He wanted to limit the program to $150,000,000. He stated that the reasons for such a limitation were obvious. This was experimental legislation, yet there never was a piece of fundamental legislation concerning which the Senate had less per-capita information on which to base a decision. "I doubt whether there is any senator in the Chamber [except Wagner and Walsh] who could stand even a kindergarten examination on the bill," concluded Vandenberg.[85]

This was a bald statement of the fact that, because of the complexities of the legislative process and the volume of business the Senate is asked to act on in the closing weeks of each session, the majority of senators vote on legislation about which they have little or no expert knowledge.

The amendment of Vandenberg to limit the program to $150,000,000 was rejected.[86] All the amendments of the committee were thus adopted. McNary proposed some amendments for Mr. Hastings, who was absent at a conference meeting.[87] The first amendment was to limit the members of the board from the same political party to three of the total of five members. This amendment was agreed to.[88] The second amendment that McNary presented was to reduce the $10,000 a year salary that was to be given to the members of the board. Walsh objected to this. It was a responsible and important position, he contended, which would take all of the time of the member. A salary of $10,000 would be in line with the salaries of the directors of various bureaus. McNary then replied that the senator in charge of the bill agreed to the amendment. This is an indication of the backstage preparation that goes on before the debate on the floor. But Wagner spoke up that he was not the senator in charge of the bill. The bill as coming out of the

---

85 *Ibid.*, p. 9558.   87 *Ibid.*
86 *Ibid.*, p. 9561.   88 *Ibid.*

committee was Mr. Walsh's bill, and it was only because of Senator Walsh's necessary absence at the conference meeting that he had been managing the bill on the floor.[89]

This amendment to limit the salary was rejected.

The third amendment that McNary presented for Hastings was one which would limit the total cost of a "demonstration project" to $2,500,000. Walsh did not object to this limitation and the amendment was agreed to.[90]

Vandenberg then asked some questions about the economic foundation of the bill. His amendment had been defeated earlier, but he did not give up his attempt to limit the bill. He asked about the testimony that a certain Mr. Kruesi gave during the hearings. He quoted a few passages from the hearings wherein Kruesi criticized the financial provisions of the bill. Wagner's reply was that Mr. James Couffer of Blythe and Company, the New York investment firm, testified that the bill was financially sound. Vandenberg then repeated the objection that there had been no representation on the floor of the Senate of the opposition side of the bill. He commented that he regretted this, if there was another side. Vandenberg also stated that the hearings were nine tenths in favor of the bill. His objection in raising these questions was to inquire about some of the testimony he read in the hearings which indicated to him that it was not a noncontroversial piece of legislation by any means.

Wagner countered that the bill had been publicized for two years. More than that, he had listed the tremendous number of organizations in favor of the bill. He then proceeded to call off the list of individuals and organizations in Vandenberg's home state of Michigan.[91]

Walsh returned to the chamber from a conference meeting and entered the debate and said that Kruesi was not an im-

---

89 *Ibid.*, p. 9562.   91 *Ibid.*, p. 9563.
90 *Ibid.*

pressive witness and represented only himself. He said that Dr. Ryan (Monsignor John A. Ryan) was very complimentary of the bill in his remarks to the committee. Walsh stressed the fact that all the amendments were restrictive, in that they limited the time period of issuing bonds or limited appropriations.

Walsh suggested a further amendment that the ratio of rent to income for families of low income be cut from six times to five times. Wagner interjected the remark that that was the formula he had suggested to Walsh earlier.[92]

Couzens then asked for an amendment to cut the number of members on the board from five to three. This was an economy move. It would save total salaries, expenses, and personnel, and three could do as good a job as five. This amendment was agreed to by the house. Couzens then asked for an amendment to an earlier amendment so that the membership of the board would comprise only two members of the same political party. This was agreed to.[93]

The president *pro tempore* (Senator Key Pittman of Nevada) stated that the question was on the engrossment and third reading of the bill. This motion passed and the bill was ordered to be engrossed and was read for the third time.[94]

The president *pro tempore* then said: "The question is, shall the bill pass?"

Before there was any vote on the question Senator Walter George of Georgia asked for permission to make a brief statement. He stated that he had been working on the conference committee to draft the tax bill; that it was with great difficulty that the conferees were able to find $620,000,000 of revenue; that he did not like to see the Congress spend almost the same amount without an adequate understanding of the bill. He mentioned that slum clearance was for the cities and would not

[92] *Ibid.*
[93] *Ibid.*

[94] *Ibid.*, p. 9564.

benefit the rural areas. Furthermore, he said: "I do not accept the doctrine that the federal government has any rightful power or authority as here proposed to promote homes for the citizens of the States."[95]

Couzens and Walsh then had an exchange of remarks about tax exemption for the housing authority's property, especially as it affected the demonstration projects. But as soon as it was possible to interrupt this discussion, the president *pro tempore* once more put the question: "Shall the bill pass?" Mr. Vandenberg and Mr. McNary asked for the yeas and nays, and the yeas and nays were ordered, and the clerk proceeded to call the roll.

> MR. DAVIS [when his name was called]. I have a general pair with the junior Senator from Kentucky [Mr. Logan], I understand that if present he would vote as I am about to vote. Therefore, I feel at liberty to vote and vote "yes."
>
> MR. BARKLEY [when Mr. Logan's name was called]. I desire to announce the absence of my colleague [Mr. Logan] on important official business. If present, he would vote "yea." He is paired with the senior Senator from Pennsylvania [Mr. Davis].
>
> MR. MCNARY [when his name was called]. On this vote I have a pair with the senior Senator from New York [Mr. Copeland], who is absent. Not knowing how he would vote, I withhold my vote.

The roll call was concluded.

> MR. AUSTIN. I announce the general pair of the Senator from Maine [Mr. White] with the Senator from Indiana [Mr. Van Nuys].
>
> MR. BARKLEY [after having voted in the affirmative]. I have a general pair with the senior Senator from Delaware [Mr. Hastings]. I am authorized to say that if present he would vote "nay." I transfer my pair to the junior Senator from Ohio [Mr. Donahey] and allow my vote to stand.
>
> MR. CAREY [after having voted in the negative]. I inquire if the Senior Senator from Ohio [Mr. Buckley] has voted?

---

[95] *Ibid.*, p. 9566.

THE PRESIDENT PRO TEMPORE. The Senator from Ohio has not voted.

MR. CAREY. I have a general pair with that Senator, who if present and voting, would vote "yes." I therefore withdraw my vote.

YEAS, 42

Ashurst	Byrnes	Holt	Pope
Bachman	Capper	La Follette	Reynolds
Barbour	Caraway	Lonergan	Robinson
Barkley	Chavez	McGill	Schwellenbach
Benson	Clark	McKellar	Sheppard
Bilbo	Davis	Maloney	Thomas, Utah
Black	Duffy	Moore	Wagner
Bone	Fletcher	Murray	Walsh
Borah	Guffey	Neely	Wheeler
Brown	Hatch	Norris	
Bulow	Hayden	Pittman	

NAYS, 24

Adams	Dieterich	King	Russell
Austin	Frazier	Metcalf	Smith
Bailey	George	Murphy	Steiwer
Burke	Gerry	Nye	Townsend
Connally	Gibson	O'Mahoney	Truman
Couzens	Hale	Radcliffe	Vandenberg

NOT VOTING, 30

Bankhead	Donahey	Loftin	Overton
Buckley	Glass	Logan	Shipstead
Byrd	Gore	Long	Thomas, Okla-
Carey	Harrison	McAdoo	homa
Coolidge	Hastings	McCarran	Tydings
Copeland	Johnson	McNary	Van Nuys
Costigan	Keyes	Minton	White
Dickinson	Lewis	Norbeck	

So the bill passed.[96]

---

[96] *Ibid.*

Of those who were not voting there were only a few, like McNary and Carey, who were in the chamber. Bankhead, Harrison, Johnson, and McCarran were announced as absent because of illness. Buckley, Copeland, Lewis, McAdoo, Thomas (Oklahoma), and Tydings were absent on official business. Byrd, Coolidge, Costigan, Donahey, Glass, Gore, Minton, Overton, and Van Nuys were unavoidably detained away from the chamber. These announcements were made so that the constituents of these senators might understand the absence of their senators at the time of the vote. It was also announced that Lewis, Harrison, McAdoo, Donahey, and McCarran, if they had been present, would have voted yea. Senator Byrd, it was announced, if he had been present, would have voted nay.[97]

As can be seen from the announcements made above and from the statements made during the debate on the bill, a number of the senators were absent on official business. At the close of each session there is a log jam of legislative business. This means that members and conference committees must work during the meetings to clear the way for the essential legislation, such as appropriations and tax measures. This results in a hasty and superficial consideration of the technical provisions of important bills, such as was the case with this housing bill. There seems to be no solution to this problem, even though *Jefferson's Manual* contains the following provision:

> When a session is drawing to a close and the important bills are all brought in, the House, in order to prevent interruption by further unimportant bills, sometimes comes to a resolution that no new bill be brought in, except it be sent from the other House.[98]

This provision, however, is obsolete.

---

[97] *Ibid.*, p. 9565.
[98] *Jefferson's Manual*, Sec. 385; in Lewis Deschler, *Constitution, Jefferson's Manual, and the Rules of the House of Representatives of the United States, Eighty-third Congress* (H. Doc. No. 564, 82d Cong., 2d Sess.). Washington: Government Printing Office, 1953.

The announcement of pairs during the vote on the housing bill brings up an interesting parliamentary practice which is a part of the legislative process. The practice of pairing was a procedure in the English parliament that finally worked its way into the Congress of the United States. A pair may be defined as an agreement by one member of a legislative body with one of his colleagues, who is going to vote on the opposite side of a measure, which provides that, if either is absent, the other will refrain from voting and announce to the House that his vote would be cast for the other side. This practice makes possible the absence of a member from the meeting without the loss of a vote because he has canceled out a vote of the opposition, and provides for the name of the absent member to be registered in the list.[99]

The practice of pairing did not become common in the Senate until about 1860.[100] The Senate does not have a long list of rulings and precedents on pairs such as is to be found in the House. The basic ruling on the practice of pairs in the Senate was stated by Mr. Henry Cabot Lodge, Sr.: "The Chair is of the opinion that pairs are not recognized by the rules anywhere, and that they are only a reason for not voting."[101]

---

[99] This definition is derived from the actual practice of the pair in the United States Congress. *Hinds' Precedents*, Vol. 5, Sec. 5981, pp. 519-20, gives a history of the pair in the House. The first mention of the pair was on May 17, 1824, when Representative Dwight of Massachusetts made an agreement with a member of the opposing side of the issue who would also be absent. He asked the House to excuse him from voting on the issue because of that agreement. The House voted to excuse him.

[100] Thomas Hart Benton, *Thirty Years' View*, Vol. 2, p. 178. New York: D. Appleton Company, 1856.

[101] *Gilfry's Precedents*, p. 461.

CHAPTER VIII

The House Committee
Kills the Bill

While Wagner was using all his experience and skill in attempting to get the Senate to pass his housing bill, Representative Ellenbogen was working just as zealously, but with less success, to get the House to consider and pass the bill. The first and most important obstacle that Ellenbogen encountered was Chairman Henry Steagall of the House Committee on Banking and Currency. Ellenbogen knew that Steagall was personally opposed to the bill, and therefore Ellenbogen considered it necessary to argue that the bill was an administration measure. Once convinced of this, Steagall as a loyal administration man—and he was certainly that—would report the bill out of his committee and let the House act on it. Ellenbogen therefore tried to convince Steagall that the president wanted the bill to pass.[1]

Finally, in the middle of May, Steagall told Ellenbogen that he had been in Congress for twenty-five years, that he had been running the Committee on Banking and Currency for a long time, that no president had ever failed to tell him personally whenever he wanted a hearing or committee action, and that thus far Roosevelt had not spoken with him about the bill. And

---

[1] Statement of Henry Ellenbogen (personal interview).

Steagall added that Roosevelt was no "shrinking violet" when it came to asking for committee action on anything in which he was interested.[2]

When this word was passed around the public-housing groups, they did not know just what to do. To attempt a discharge motion in the House was too difficult a procedure, and moreover it was too dangerous because, if it failed, the bill was finished. So rather than attempt such a test of strength at this time, leading members of the housing groups decided that it would be better to attempt to talk with Steagall and Roosevelt. Bohn and Langdon Post talked with Steagall, but they did not accomplish anything. Steagall put them off with the excuse that he was waiting for the Senate to act on the bill. When they suggested to him that he could at least hold the hearings on the bill, Steagall was not convinced.[3]

After his failure to influence Steagall, Post wrote a letter on June 4 to the president. He told him that the Senate committee had reported the bill, and that Steagall would not move until the Senate had taken final action on the bill. The session was fast drawing to a close and therefore, Post told the president, time was most important. He was writing this letter to urge the president to ask Steagall to hold the hearings on the eighth or ninth

---

[2] Statement of Ernest J. Bohn (personal interview) and report of Bohn to Woodbury, May 23, 1936, National Association of Housing Officials, Ernest Bohn File—1936. An example of Roosevelt's requests to committee chairmen for action on certain legislation in which he was interested is given in a letter to Samuel E. Hill, chairman of the House Committee on Ways and Means. The letter is dated July 5, 1935 and Roosevelt wrote: "I hope your committee will not permit doubt as to constitutionality, however reasonable, to block the suggested legislation." It is quoted in an address given by Representative Bertrand Snell at the Republican national convention at Cleveland, Ohio, June 10, 1936. It is printed in the *Congressional Record*, June 15, 1936, p. 9353. Roosevelt made it a policy to contact committee chairmen in order to tell them of his desires about pending legislation. A number of such examples will be found in the Roosevelt Papers, P.P.F. 1702.

[3] Statement of Ernest J. Bohn (personal interview).

of June. Post commented that such a procedure could do no harm, and it was the only way that the bill would have a chance of being passed at that session of Congress.[4]

Roosevelt was impressed by this letter of Post and sent a memorandum to "Mac" to tell Steagall "for heaven's sake" to hold the hearings even if the House was recessing. And he concluded the message by saying that he wanted "the thing all ready to shoot." "Mac" phoned to Steagall and relayed the president's message. Steagall told "Mac" that he would hold the hearings on the eighth of June, but also stated that he wanted to talk with the president.[5]

Whether Steagall talked with Roosevelt within the days between June 5 and June 16 is not revealed by the material in the White House files. But in any event, Steagall did not hold any hearings on June 8 as he had told McIntyre that he would. No action was taken on the bill by Steagall and the committee until the time of the Senate debate on June 16. At that time Steagall called some executive sessions of the committee to clear up all the pending measures before the committee.

On June 8 Mrs. Simkhovitch sent a telegram to Mrs. Roosevelt asking her to "please help us." Mrs. Simkhovitch told Mrs. Roosevelt that the committee (the NPHC) had sent a telegram to the president asking him to put the legislation on his "preferred list" before he left Washington during the recess. It would be embarrassing to Senator Wagner and disheartening to the countrywide supporters of the bill if it failed to pass, concluded Mrs. Simkhovitch in her telegram.[6]

When Post learned that no action was taken on the bill after the president's message to Steagall, he wrote again to the president on June 17. He reminded the president that this bill was

---

[4] Post to Roosevelt, June 4, 1936, Roosevelt Papers, O.F. 63.
[5] Roosevelt to "Mac" [McIntyre], June 5, 1936, Roosevelt Papers, O.F. 63.
[6] Simkhovitch to Mrs. Roosevelt, June 8, 1936, Roosevelt Papers, O.F. 63.

important in reference to the 1936 campaign. If Congress failed to take action, Post said, the party was in danger of losing some votes in New York, Ohio, and Illinois.[7]

Roosevelt replied to Post on June 19, addressing him as "Dear Tubby," and telling him that he had done everything by "personal persuasion, etc.," to get the bill out of Steagall's committee. He told Post that the vote on the bill in the committee a few hours before was ten to seven against the bill. Roosevelt ended the letter by saying, "I still have hopes."[8]

It is well known from statements of Representative Everett Dirksen that Steagall assigned Dirksen the task of trying to work out some amendments to the bill so that it would be satisfactory to the conservative members of the committee. Dirksen attempted some thirty-eight amendments to the bill, but these were not satisfactory to the committee. The final result was that the bill was allowed to "lie on the table."[9] This failure of the committee to report the bill to the House killed the bill for that Congress because after the meeting on June 20 the Seventy-fourth Congress would be adjourned *sine die* pursuant to the House Joint Resolution Number 63.[10] The Democratic national convention was

---

[7] Post to Roosevelt, June 17, 1936, Roosevelt Papers, O.F. 63.

[8] Roosevelt to Post, June 19, 1936, Roosevelt Papers, P.P.F. 3646.

[9] Dirksen made the following statement before the House Committee on Banking and Currency at the hearings on August 4, 1937: "Mr. Chairman, I shall streamline my remarks, and not trespass unduly upon the time of the committee. I feel something like Rip van Winkle this morning, because in the third week of June of last year, we were considering the housing bill when I was a member of this committee, and I believe that the last commission that I had from you, Mr. Chairman, was to prepare some amendments to that bill, and by action of the committee we placed the bill on the table" (*House Hearings on H. R. 5033 and S. 1685,* p. 77). Dirksen made the statement to Coleman Woodbury that he had drafted thirty-eight amendments to the housing bill (Memorandum of Woodbury, November 24, 1936, National Association of Housing Officials, Housing Notes—1936).

[10] H. Con. Res. No. 63. Resolved by the House of Representatives (the Senate concurring), That the two Houses of Congress shall adjourn on Saturday, the 20th day of June, 1936, and that when they adjourn on said day they stand adjourned *sine die*. Passed June 20, 1936 (49 Stat. 2388 [1936]).

to be held in Philadelphia from June 23 to 27. A new Congress, the Seventy-fifth, would be elected in November.

Just how much "personal persuasion, etc." Roosevelt employed with Steagall is unknown, except for the message relayed by "Mac" which was not very "personal." It was the opinion of people close to the scene in Washington that Roosevelt's efforts in behalf of the bill were halfhearted.[11] Steagall had told many people that he was against the bill because he thought that it was socialistic and would bankrupt the country; however, if the "chief" wanted it he would get it out of committee.[12] And the ability of Steagall to get a bill out of committee when he wished to do so was well known. Steagall ruled his committee with an iron hand; and when he wanted action, the committee followed him.[13] It is also well known that Roosevelt was not convinced of the necessity of passing the legislation that year. He consistently refused to put the measure on his "must" list. Roosevelt realized that there was an economy drive on in Congress, and he knew that the South, generally, did not favor appropriations for a housing program. Moreover, it was an election year. So when Roosevelt the politician balanced the forces *for* the bill with those *against* the bill, he could well have decided that he would not lose any votes by failing to bring about the passage of the bill, since the supporters of the bill were indebted to him for

---

[11] *Public Housing Progress* 2:1, June 15, 1936 sharply criticized Roosevelt for his lack of support of the housing bill.

[12] Statement of Ernest J. Bohn and David Krooth (personal interviews).

[13] Herbert Emmerich, director of the Public Administration Clearing House, who held a number of important government positions connected with housing programs including that of commissioner of the United States Housing Authority, had occasion to appear before Mr. Steagall's committee on a number of occasions. He related, in a personal interview with the author, that Steagall pushed through the proceedings so mechanically that the witness got the impression that Steagall did not hear what was being said and that he cared less. Steagall appeared to be going through the motions, though his mind was already made up; and the committee members would follow that decision or suffer the consequence of losing influence in the committee.

previous New Deal legislation, but that he might lose the support of some of the financial and real-estate interests if he forced
the passage of the bill. The decision, then, to let the bill die
would appear to have been a calculated one.

The position of the president in this legislative battle was an
indeterminate one. According to the Constitution there is a separation of powers; and because of this separation of powers
between the legislative and the executive branches of the government Roosevelt could shift the blame for the failure of passage of the housing bill on to Chairman Steagall. But in reality
Roosevelt controlled the legislative process to a very large extent.[14] And only a small handful of people in Washington had
any idea of the amount of responsibility that Roosevelt should
have assumed for the failure of the bill to pass. This important
and uncontrolled position of the president in the legislative
process will be more fully explained in a later chapter. At this
point it is necessary to examine the powers and functions of the
congressional committee in the legislative process.

As mentioned in the previous chapter, legislative work must
be done in committees. This is especially true in a body as large
as the House of Representatives. No student of the legislative
process ever questioned the necessity of committees. There have
been many criticisms, however, concerning the method of select-
ing committee members and the committee chairmen.

Representatives usually attempt to obtain an appointment to
a committee which primarily controls legislation that affects
their regional or population interests. Farmers, bankers, businessmen, and labor representatives thus seek appointments to
the committees that have jurisdiction over their respective inter-

---

[14] It is to be remembered that though some New Deal legislation was declared
unconstitutional, still it had been passed by the legislature at the request of
the president. The legislature did not break with Roosevelt until he asked the
legislature to reorganize the Supreme Court so that it would be under
his control.

ests. The difficulty with such a system is that it gives the committee a slanted view of legislative proposals. Legislation should be considered in the light of the common good of the country, not in the light of the interests of a particular group.

Until the adoption by the House of Representatives of Rule 10 in 1911 (which rule was preserved in the Reorganization Act of 1946), committee members and the chairmen of committees had been appointed by the speaker of the House. Rule 10 provides for the election of committee members by the House.

It has been the practice of the House, ever since the overthrow of Speaker Cannon, for the Democratic members of the Committee on Ways and Means to select the Democratic members of the various committees, which selection is later approved by the party caucus; the Republicans select the Republican members of the various committees by means of a special Committee on Committees which is made up of one member from each state delegation of Republicans. The members of this committee have as many votes as there are members of their state delegation. These selections are later approved by the Republican conference. At the beginning of the session it is the practice for the leaders of the two parties to present a resolution that the members selected by the party machinery for committee assignments be ratified by the House. The House then votes on the resolution and gives legal form to the selections made by the party machinery.[15]

---

[15] "Rule X. Standing Committees. (a) There shall be elected by the House, at the commencement of each Congress, the following standing committees: [there follows a list of the nineteen committees, with the number of members for each, authorized by the Legislative Reorganization Act of 1946]." This rule was made effective on January 2, 1947. For a history of the selection of committees in the House of Representatives consult *Cannon's Precedents*, Vol. 8, Secs. 2171-98, pp. 1-18. The practice in the House is to elect the committee members and chairmen on a resolution by the majority leader. The following example shows the organization of committees in the Eightieth Congress. At the beginning of the meeting on January 14, 1947 the speaker

The Senate under the provisions of Rule 24 elects its committee chairmen and committee members. Party machinery has modified this rule. The Republicans at the beginning of each session hold a party conference which elects a Committee on Committees consisting of eight members. This committee then draws up a list of committee members for each of the committees. The Republican conference approves the selection, and it is then ready to be presented to the Senate for ratification. The Democrats employ a special committee of twelve members, which is a continuing committee, for the selection of its members for the various committee assignments. At the opening session of the Senate it is the practice to present both lists of committee

---

recognized the majority leader of the Republicans, Mr. Halleck. " 'Mr. Speaker, I offer a resolution (H. Res. 47), which I send to the desk.' The clerk read the resolution as follows: *Resolved,* That the following named Members be, and they are hereby, elected members of the following committees of the House of Representatives: [a list of the majority members of each committee follows. It is understood that the first-named member is the chairman]. Mr. Halleck. 'Mr. Speaker, I move the previous question.' The previous question was ordered. The resolution was agreed to. A motion to reconsider laid on the table.

"Mr. Forand, minority leader, was then recognized by the speaker. 'Mr. Speaker, I ask for this time in order to acquaint the House, particularly the Democratic Members, with the fact that the Democratic Committee on Committees has completed its work and is ready to report tomorrow. At 11:30 A.M. there will be a Caucus of the Democrats on the floor of the House [the leaders of the two parties had agreed beforehand to have a recess on this day so that this business could be attended to], and I hope that shortly thereafter we will be prepared to present our committee assignments to the House' " (*Congressional Record,* January 14, 1947, pp. 307-08).

The Democratic party held its caucus on January 15 and on the next day the minority leader was ready to make his motion. After the usual routine business the speaker announced: "The Chair recognizes the gentleman from Rhode Island [Mr. Forand]. 'Mr. Speaker, I offer a resolution (H. Res. 49), which I send to the desk.' The clerk read the resolution as follows: *Resolved,* That the following named Members be, and they are hereby, elected members of the following standing committees of the House of Representatives: [there follows a list of Democratic (minority) members of all the standing committees]. The motion was agreed to. A motion to reconsider was laid on the table" (*ibid.,* January 16, 1947, p. 371).

assignments in one resolution. The Senate then votes on the resolution and upon its adoption gives legal sanction to the selections made by the party machinery.[16]

---

[16] "Rule XXIV. Appointment of Committees. 1. In the appointment of the Standing committees, the Senate, unless otherwise ordered, shall proceed by ballot to appoint severally the chairman of each committee, and then by one ballot, the other members necessary to complete the same. A majority of the whole number of votes given shall be necessary to the choice of a chairman of a standing committee, but a plurality of votes shall select the other members thereof. All other committees shall be appointed by ballot, unless otherwise ordered, and a plurality of votes shall appoint." This rule is not adhered to strictly and it has become a custom in the Senate to elect the whole committee, including the chairman, who is the first-named member of the majority members, by a motion from the floor. The following example taken from the Eightieth Congress illustrates this practice. On January 6, 1947 Mr. White, the senior senator from Maine and the majority leader, announced that the Senate would attend a joint meeting with the House to hear the president's annual message; and he asked that after the message all return to the chamber for the morning business, "and in particular for the election of the Committees of the Senate. . . . MR. BARKLEY. 'I will say for the minority that we shall be ready to report our committee assignments, which, according to custom, are brought to the attention of the Senate simultaneously with the majority assignments, so that the committees may be complete.' . . . MR. WHITE. 'Let me add that the report of the majority will be presented by the Senator from Wyoming [Mr. Robertson], who served as chairman of the Committee on Committees which recommended the majority appointments.'" After the president's message, when the Senate was convened in its own chamber, Mr. Robertson presented the resolution for the appointment of committees. " 'I send to the Desk a resolution and ask for immediate consideration.' THE PRESIDENT PRO TEMPORE. 'The Clerk will state the resolution.' The resolution (S. Res. 18) was read as follows: The following shall constitute the standing committees of the Eightieth Congress: [a list of committee appointments followed]. MR. BARKLEY. 'I present the minority list, by direction of the Democratic Steering Committee.' Thereupon the clerk read the list of committees and the assignments thereto, as follows: [a list of committee appointments follows]. Before the vote was taken, Mr. Barkley had some remarks to make about the mathematical disproportion in certain of the committees between Republicans and Democrats. After explaining why there was this disproportion in certain of the committees, Mr. Robertson added: 'As I have said, we felt that the choice was entirely up to the Republican Party. I rest my presentation of the case on that statement.' Barkley also stated, after this exchange with Robertson on committee representation: 'Mr. President, before the vote is taken there is a slight correction to be made in the minority representation on two of the committees.' Mr. Hayden

It is generally agreed that the defect of this system is that
"special interests" are given greater consideration than the common good of the entire country, because of the practice of ap-
pointing to the committees members representing such interests.
This is a greater defect in the House than in the Senate. Once a
member gains any rank on a committee, whether it be as a majority or minority member, he remains with the committee in
the hope that changes will take place that will advance him to
the chairmanship. As the Senate is a much smaller body, and
as there are more committee assignments for each of the 96
senators than there are for the 435 representatives, there is
greater mobility among committee members in the Senate. Despite this defect the committee system has worked out well, even
if not ideally; and no one has presented a better practical
method of selection of committee members.

It is with the selection of the chairmen of committees that
certain political scientists find fault. Even in the party caucus
the principle that has been used is seniority based on the number of years of continuous service on the committee. The main
objection to this system is that length of service does not guarantee ability. Despite the fact that the special committees of the
two parties choose the committee chairmen, there is no real
party responsibility because a chairman knows that the rule of

(of Arizona) then stated that the conflict (between certain appointments to
the Public Lands committee which involved Senator Murray of Montana and
Senator Magnuson of Washington) could not be corrected on the floor and
asked that the selection of the minority members of the committees be deferred until the matter could be corrected. Because of this difficulty, which
centered around a question of seniority on the part of Senator Murray of
Montana and committee appointments he had asked for, Barkley withdrew
the names of the minority members. On January 8 Barkley presented the
revised list, which was accepted by the Senate. It is interesting to note that
Senator Murray received the appointments he claimed he was entitled to
receive on the basis of his seniority" (*Congressional Record*, January 6, 1947,
pp. 115-18, and January 8, 1947, p. 158). For a history of appointment of
committees in the Senate consult S. Doc. No. 1122, 63d Cong., 3d Sess., 1913.

seniority is so ironclad that he can flout the program of the party with impunity. Another difficulty is that many southern Democrats who are members of Congress are constantly re-elected year after year because of the one-party system of the South, thus gaining seniority and an eventual number of chairmanships of committees that is out of proportion to the number of voters in these sections of the country in comparison with the rest of the United States.

The seniority rule is well illustrated by events that took place after the election of 1936. Mr. Steagall was returned to Congress by his district, and he became automatically the chairman of the House Committee on Banking and Currency. No one would have even thought of trying to replace him. A few changes were made in the membership of the Committee on Banking and Currency; for example, Everett Dirksen moved over to the Committee on Appropriations, which is considered a more important committee. Such changes, however, take place only at the bottom of the list. Dirksen was next to last in seniority among the minority members of the Committee on Banking and Currency; and when he left that committee for the Committee on Appropriations, he found that he was next to last in seniority among the minority members of that committee also.[17]

In the Senate there is no need to change committee assignments after each election, for the Senate is a continuous body, only one third of its members standing for re-election at each

---

[17] The career of Representative Louis C. Rabaut of Michigan's Fourteenth District (which comprises a portion of the city of Detroit and two of the suburbs) affords an interesting example of how difficult it is for a congressman from a metropolitan area to acquire seniority. Mr. Rabaut was elected to each Congress since the Seventy-fourth in 1934, except the Eightieth Congress. In 1936, when changes were taking place on the Appropriations Committee, Mr. Rabaut was the nineteenth ranking Democratic member of the committee. In 1953 he was the sixteenth ranking Democratic member of the committee. Only two of the fifteen Democratic members who outrank Rabaut have served more years in Congress.

election. Some few changes, however, do take place because of the defeat, death, or retirement of former members.[18] The changes in 1936 were more numerous than usual. David I. Walsh moved from the chairmanship of the Committee on Education and Labor to the Committee on Naval Affairs. Park Trammel of Florida died, leaving a vacancy. Both the party leaders and Walsh were in agreement about Walsh's move to the Committee on Naval Affairs.[19] Hugo Black, a liberal and a New Deal supporter, was then named chairman of the Committee on Education and Labor. Black had been the fourth-ranking member of the committee before,[20] but now with the move of Walsh to Naval Affairs, the death of Park Trammel of Florida, and the fact that Copeland of New York,[21] who also outranked him in seniority, was chairman of the important Committee on Commerce, Hugo Black was eligible to become chairman of

---

[18] There is no need for a complete change of committees unless the majority changes from one party to the other. Even then, those with seniority on a committee will remain, but that party which was the majority party will have fewer committee assignments and hence they will lose a number of places on each committee. The reshuffling usually will affect only the members without seniority. The change in the Eightieth Congress is an interesting one because it had been fourteen years since the Republicans had held the control as the majority party. Consult the *Congressional Record*, January 6, 1947, pp. 115-18, for the reorganization of the Senate; and consult the *Congressional Record*, January 14, 1947, pp. 307-08, for the reorganization of the House of Representatives.

[19] Walsh had long had a strong and well-known desire to chair the Naval Affairs Committee. Many interesting facts about the life of the colorful senator from Massachusetts can be found in a recent biography by Dorothy Wayman, *David I. Walsh, Citizen-Patriot* (Milwaukee: Bruce Publishing Company, 1952).

[20] The *Official Congressional Directory* which is compiled under the direction of the Joint Committee on Printing, and published by the United States Government Printing Office, is issued each year for each session of Congress. This valuable source book gives all information about committees and seniority as well as all factual data available concerning Congress and its operations.

[21] Royal S. Copeland was a doctor of medicine. He had served as health commissioner of New York City from 1918 until his election to the Senate in 1922. The Commerce Committee had jurisdiction over certain health and safety matters concerned with interstate commerce.

the Committee on Education and Labor. He was very acceptable to the party leaders. This move was also acceptable to those
interested in public housing because they knew that Black was
favorable to the housing bill.[22]

Roland Young[23] and other political scientists, such as George
Galloway,[24] have proposed that the seniority rule be abolished
in favor of the appointment of committee chairmen by the party
caucus. Veteran members of Congress and experienced career
staff members of congressional committees do not accept the
suggestion of Young and Galloway. They claim that in practice
the seniority rule is the best working plan. They also point out
that in most cases, if an election were held to select the committee chairman, the senior member would be elected as the best
qualified to hold the position. They will admit that there are a
few notorious instances where a committee chairman has been
obstructive to the party program, but this does not happen often;
and if his position is unreasonable, a majority of the committee
members can always vote to take action on the measure.[25]

There are two arguments that can be employed against the
continued use of the rule of seniority as the determining factor
for the assignment of committee chairmanships. The first argument is concerned with the disproportionate influence exercised
in the Congress by the representatives and senators of the South
and the rural states as a result of the operation of this rule. The
second argument is concerned with the fact that the ironclad

---

[22] Black was very sympathetic to the Wagner public-housing bill as drafted in
Wagner's office, and he was ready to employ the talents of Keyserling when
the committee took action on the bill.

[23] Roland Young, *This Is Congress*, p. 111. New York: Alfred A. Knopf, 1946.

[24] George Galloway, *Congress at the Crossroads*, p. 190. New York: Thomas Y.
Crowell Company, 1946.

[25] Statements of Representative Brent Spence of Kentucky, chairman of the House
Committee on Banking and Currency, and William Hallahan, formerly clerk
of the House Committee on Banking and Currency and at present a director
of the Federal Home Loan Bank Board (personal interviews).

rule of seniority puts the chairman of a committee in an independent position in reference to party responsibility and renders him immune to effective sanctions of party discipline.
With respect to the first argument, a comparative study of
Tables 3, 4, and 5 will illustrate the preponderant control that
the "single-party South" has exercised over legislative affairs

TABLE 3

Comparison of Legislative Influence of Some Southern Rural
Representatives and Some Urban Representatives from
Other Parts of the Country

Representative	State and District	Committee Rank	Vote in 1938	
Rankin	Mississippi, District 1	Chairman of Veterans	D.	4,384
			R.	——
Rayburn	Texas, District 4	Majority Leader	D.	16,523
			R.	349
Sumners	Texas, District 5	Chairman of Judiciary	D.	10,344
			R.	508
Barden	North Carolina	Chairman of Education	D.	17,507
			R.	——
Steagall	Alabama, District 3	Chairman of Banking and Currency	D.	10,089
			R.	——
Crosser	Ohio, District 21 (Cleveland)	Second-Ranking Member of Interstate Com- merce	D.	53,180
			R.	24,249
Hennings	Missouri, District 11 (St. Louis)	No Rank	D.	63,332
			R.	38,866
Havenner	California, District 4 (San Francisco)	No Rank	D.	64,452
			R.	40,842
O'Toole	New York, District 8 (Brooklyn)	No Rank	D.	134,461
			R.	111,252
McKeough	Illinois, District 2 (Chicago)	No Rank	D.	129,620
			R.	108,483
Meyers	Pennsylvania, District 6 (Philadelphia)	No Rank	D.	62,524
			R.	59,548

Source: *Congressional Directory*, 76th Cong., 1st Sess.

TABLE 4

Chairmen of House Committees from States Not in the South,
75th Congress

Committee	Chairman	State and District	Vote in 1934	1936
District of Columbia	Norton	New Jersey, District 13	D. 73,342 R. 26,447	93,702 27,615
Expenditures in Executive Department	Cochran	Missouri, District 13	D. 60,198 R. 31,165	85,630 39,714
Education	Palmisano	Maryland, District 3	D. 27,988 R. 13,042	37,446 23,941
Insular Affairs	Kocialkowski	Illinois, District 8	D. 27,682 R. 9,671	34,452 8,945
Immigration	Dickstein	New York, District 12	D. 14,895 R. 3,092	19,280 2,136
Labor	Connery	Massachusetts, District 7	D. 62,666 R. 40,988	76,521 51,009
Post Office and Public Roads	Mead	New York, District 42	D. 49,251 R. 26,036	57,132 32,395
Rules	John O'Connor	New York, District 16	D. 22,528 R. 9,735	33,082 17,832
Irrigation	White	Idaho, District 1	D. 42,223 R. 25,969	58,941 24,959

Source: *Congressional Directory*, 75th Cong., 3d Sess.

in the House of Representatives. Table 6 illustrates the preponderant influence of the rural states in the Senate when the Republicans are in control of the Senate. This problem, however, is quite a different one from that found in the House of Representatives because in the Senate the small rural states have equal representation with the large states according to a constitutional compromise. But the balance involved in this compromise is upset as long as the House is controlled by the rural South. The control of the House by the rural areas compounds the problem of establishing a fair balance between urban and rural interests.

Though the rural control of the Senate is understandable, the southern and/or rural control of the House of Represent-

TABLE 5

Chairmen of House Committees from the South, 75th Congress

Committee	Chairman	State and District		Vote in 1934	1936
Accounts	Warren	North Carolina, District 1	D. R.	11,786 1,617	35,333 3,833
Agriculture	Jones	Texas, District 18	D. R.	23,202 ——	44,652 1,526
Appropriations	Buchanan	Texas, District 10	D. R.	19,306 ——	33,631 ——
Banking and Currency	Steagall	Alabama, District 3	D. R.	13,191 ——	22,535 ——
Civil Service	Ramspeck	Georgia, District 5	D. R.	5,206 ——	35,540 4,213
Flood Control	Whittington	Mississippi, District 3	D. R.	3,586 ——	15,688 407
Foreign Affairs	McReynolds	Tennessee, District 3	D. R.	21,559 14,387	32,065 15,096
Interstate and Foreign Commerce	Rayburn	Texas, District 4	D. R.	16,684 ——	33,355 ——
Judiciary	Sumners	Texas, District 5	D. R.	27,302 ——	43,954 5,579
Merchant Marine	Bland	Virginia, District 1	D. R.	7,637 406	20,012 4,592
Military Affairs	Hill	Alabama, District 2	D. R.	18,592 ——	32,452 ——
Naval Affairs	Vinson	Georgia, District 6	D. R.	3,067 ——	22,966 ——
Public Lands	De Rouen	Louisiana, District 7	D. R.	16,528 ——	27,563 ——
Rivers and Harbors	Mansfield	Texas, District 9	D. R.	23,257 ——	36,968 2,700
Ways and Means	Doughton	North Carolina, District 9	D. R.	44,780 32,171	60,223 32,659
Veterans	Rankin	Mississippi, District 1	D. R.	6,825 ——	19,208 391

Source: *Congressional Directory*, 75th Cong., 3d Sess.

atives cannot be justified. The South with single-party and restricted elections has utilized a corruption of the democratic
system to maintain its control, while the urban states with a

vigorous two-party political life in the metropolitan districts do not usually have representatives with long years of service and consequent seniority. This comes about because veteran urban representatives are occasionally defeated by able candidates from the rival party, and the constant campaigning for office

TABLE 6

Chairmen and Ranking Majority Members of Senate Committees, 80th Congress, 1947

Committee	Chairman and Ranking Majority Members	State	Total Number of Votes Cast in Election
Agriculture and Forestry	Capper	Kansas	497,359 (1942)
	Aiken	Vermont	123,248 (1944)
	Bushfield	South Dakota	181,649 (1942)
Appropriations	Bridges	New Hampshire	162,257 (1942)
	Gurney	South Dakota	227,257 (1944)
	Brooks	Illinois	2,973,229 (1942)
Armed Services	Gurney	South Dakota	
	Bridges	New Hampshire	
	Robertson	Wyoming	75,989 (1942)
Banking and Currency	Tobey	New Hampshire	217,057 (1944)
	Buck	Delaware	85,308 (1942)
	Capehart	Indiana	1,651,385 (1944)
District of Columbia	Buck	Delaware	
	Capper	Kansas	
	Ball	Minnesota	758,447 (1942)
Expenditures in Executive Department	Aiken	Vermont	
	Ferguson	Michigan	1,189,966 (1942)
	Hickenlooper	Iowa	1,021,681 (1944)
Finance	Millikin	Colorado	494,888 (1944)
	Taft	Ohio	2,983,219 (1944)
	Butler	Nebraska	382,958 (1946)
Foreign Relations	Vandenberg	Michigan	1,618,720 (1946)
	Capper	Kansas	
	White	Maine	167,274 (1942)
Interior and Insular Affairs	Butler	Nebraska	
	Millikin	Colorado	
	Robertson	Wyoming	
Interstate and Foreign Commerce	White	Maine	
	Tobey	New Hampshire	
	Reed	Kansas	669,191 (1944)
Judiciary	Wiley	Wisconsin	1,256,480 (1944)
	Langer	North Dakota	165,382 (1946)
	Ferguson	Michigan	

Committee	Chairman and Ranking Majority Members	State	Total Number of Votes Cast in Election
Labor and Public Welfare	Taft	Ohio	
	Aiken	Vermont	
	Ball	Minnesota	
Post Office and Civil Service	Langer	North Dakota	
	Buck	Delaware	
	Flanders	Vermont	73,340 (1946)
Public Works	Revercomb	West Virginia	463,861 (1942)
	Cooper	Kentucky	615,119 (1946)
	Cain	Washington	660,342 (1946)
Rules and Administration	Brooks	Illinois	
	Wherry	Nebraska	380,217 (1942)
	Hickenlooper	Iowa	

Source: *Congressional Directory*, 78th Cong., 2d Sess. (1944) ; 80th Cong., 2d Sess. (1948) ; 81st Cong., 2d Sess. (1950).

and the possibility of a defeat with a resultant loss of seniority has had a definite influence on the decision of a number of capable urban representatives to leave the House and stand for election to the Senate. Thus it is that a small, insignificant, and politically atrophied single-party district is the ideal type of district to insure seniority for a congressman. Certainly this is an absurd defect in the democratic system. However, it is to be noted that this disease in our body politic will not be cured by abolishing the rule of seniority. The underlying cause of this defect is to be found in the rotten-borough, single-party system of elections that has existed for generations in the South. The many examples of ranking representatives from southern districts who control the Congress by virtue of the rule of seniority is the result of this more fundamental shortcoming in our democratic system. Effective efforts on the part of the leadership of the two major parties to bring about a more vital two-party system of elections in the South and throughout the whole country would be a more radical and definite cure for this shortcoming than would be the mere abandonment of the rule of seniority. Merely to change the rule of seniority to cure this evil would be like chasing shadows.

The second argument proposed against the continued use of the rule of seniority for the assignment of committee chairmanships is concerned with the fact that this ironclad rule puts the chairman in an independent position with respect to party responsibility and renders him immune to effective sanctions of party discipline. This argument would seem to be founded on the theory that in the United States political parties should be monolithic in their structure and operation. Certain European political parties are so structured and there is evident a tight party discipline. This type of political party is necessary for a parliamentary form of government in which it is essential to locate party responsibility.

The development of political parties in the United States, however, has brought about a new organizational structure and mode of operation which has definitely contributed to the unique system of government to be found in this country. We have a government that is unique in its stability and in its progressive and orderly development. Political parties in the United States have within their membership liberals and conservatives and moderates, and thus it happens that, when there is a change of party control in the government, there always remains a definite balance of liberalism and conservatism which delays any radical changes which a new party in power may desire to make when it takes over the administration of the government. This combination of liberalism and conservatism in both parties operates as a check and balance which will guarantee stability and provide that progress will be made in an orderly and considered procedure.

Party responsibility is a desired objective; but if complete party responsibility can be purchased only at the price of molding all party policy, especially that of the legislators, in the form of the contemporary National Committee policy, then the price of this complete party responsibility is too high. The resultant cure would be worse than the existing defect. The continued existence of liberals, conservatives, and moderates in each of the two great parties can give the United States more desirable and more permanent political advantages than a monolithic responsible political party. This type of political party would require the machinery of the parliamentary form of government in order to operate with minimal efficiency. And the people of the United States have never shown any desire to adopt the parliamentary form of government.

Thus in addition to the practical argument of the legislators and career staff members for the continued use of the rule of seniority to select committee chairmen, there is a solid theoretical argument for the continued use of the rule. No one can deny that there have been abuses in the operation of committees because of this rule, but such abuses are few and infrequent when the entire committee structure of Congress is examined, and these abuses are incidental and accidental to the operation of the rule of seniority. These abuses could be corrected by the adoption of regulations for committee procedure which would eliminate patently arbitrary and obstructionist tactics.

Only so long as the rule of seniority is in force will it be possible to have conservatives as committee chairmen when the liberal group of the party have assumed control of the party.[26] This was the case when Congressman Henry B. Steagall of Alabama was chairman of the House Committee on Banking and Currency. The results of this case study demonstrate that even the obvious obstructionist policy of Mr. Steagall and his open sympathy for the position of the building-and-loan and real-estate opponents of public housing served as a challenge

---

[26] A recent battle between a powerful committee chairman and the president of the United States and the leadership of the House of Representatives was the long-continued refusal of Representative Daniel Reed of New York, chairman of the House Ways and Means Committee, to act on the president's tax bill. The details of this battle and the extraordinary measures threatened by the House leadership can be found in *Newsweek* 42:17-18, July 6, 1953.

and an incentive to the supporters of the Wagner public-housing bill to draft the best possible bill, to compromise controversial provisions of the bill, and to restudy and re-examine policy decisions. It was this process of refinement and compromise that was directly responsible for the enactment of a law which was a tremendous improvement over the first bills introduced. If there had been a monolithic party system, and if without the use of the rule of seniority the Democratic party in 1936 had been most monolithic, a very inferior public-housing bill would have been enacted into law.

Before we conclude this chapter some observations should be made about the hearings on a bill that are conducted by the various committees. These hearings serve a very important purpose in our democratic process. Each pressure group or interest group is given an opportunity to present testimony to the members of the committee which will justify a position that the bill under consideration should be passed, or passed with amendments, or killed. These hearings also afford the chairman of the committee another opportunity to exercise influence in the legislative process.

By the selection of witnesses who appear before the committee the chairman can influence committee members and the press. By prolonging the hearings the chairman can hold the bill in his committee until public opinion has developed in favor of the position the chairman has taken. The classic example of this procedure is that of Chairman Henry Cabot Lodge, Sr., who held the bills concerning the League of Nations in his committee until he judged that public opinion, which immediately after the war was favorable to the League, had become unfavorable to the entrance of the United States into the League of Nations.[27]

---

[27] George A. Finch, "The Treaty of Peace with Germany in the United States Senate," *American Journal of International Law* 14:155, January 1920.

With respect to the testimony of witnesses there are no set rules of procedure. The chairman at his discretion can set the day and the hour for a witness to present his testimony, and he can set a limit of time for each witness. Chairman Steagall, during the hearings in 1937, kept some witnesses waiting so long that they might have become discouraged and returned home without presenting their testimony. Ernest J. Bohn was kept waiting through six sessions of the hearings before he was called to testify, but Bohn was not the type to become discouraged and go back home. A long wait takes the edge off of a witness' testimony. Witnesses may not be allowed sufficient time when there is a last-minute rush to get hearings completed.

During these same hearings Mr. Kennedy, representative from New York, objected to the manner in which Chairman Steagall was conducting the hearings. Congressman Dirksen had concluded his testimony, and Chairman Steagall called Congressman Ellenbogen to testify. Before Ellenbogen started his testimony, Kennedy broke in:

> Before he goes, I would like to make an observation, and it is unfortunate that it is coming at this time, when one member has finished, but we have a great many people who have come here from different parts of the country, representing organizations, and so forth, and I think the Members of Congress have the opportunity of speaking on the floor—and this is no personal reference, but I think it is unfair to keep these witnesses sitting here while Members of Congress take up the time of the committee and, so far as I am concerned, I hope that when this gentleman finishes we will allow the witnesses to testify rather than our colleagues.[28]

Congressman Steagall gave an apologetic answer to Mr. Kennedy, but the fact of the matter was that witnesses who were to give testimony had to spend extra days in Washington before they were heard.

---

[28] *House Hearings on H. R. 5033 and S. 1685*, p. 93.

Mr. Kennedy brought up an interesting problem when he stated that congressmen could speak on the floor of the House. In actual practice it is rather difficult for a congressman to make a detailed statement about legislation under debate, because the debate usually proceeds under a rule strictly limiting the time of debate and the number and types of amendments that will be in order.[29] The majority leader or committee chairman or sponsor of the bill usually picks the representative who will be given the floor during the debate, and it often happens that some representative who might have a statement or amendment to make is prevented from making it because of the rule and the refusal of the manager of the bill to permit him the floor. For this reason members of the House of Representatives often appear before committees to express their views. Dirksen, Ellenbogen, and Beiter of New York appeared before the House committee in 1937 to express their views on the housing bill.[30] As will be seen in the pages of Chapter 14 where the House debate on the 1937 housing bill is recorded, Congressman Ellenbogen was not

---

[29] The following rule given for the consideration of the Independent Offices Appropriation Bill, 1935, is a typical example of the limitations to debate and discussion imposed on the House by the resolution.

"House Resolution 217

"Resolved, That during the consideration of H. R. 6663, a bill making appropriations for the Executive Office and sundry independent bureaus, boards, commissions, and offices, for the fiscal year ending June 30, 1935, and for other purposes, all points of order against title II or any provisions contained therein are hereby waived; and no amendments or motions to strike out shall be in order to such title except amendments or motions to strike out offered by direction of the Committee on Appropriations, and said amendments or motions shall be in order, any rule of the House to the contrary notwithstanding. Amendments shall not be in order to any other section of the bill H. R. 6663 or to any section of any general appropriation bill of the Seventy-third Congress which would be in conflict with the provisions of title II of the bill H. R. 6663 as reported to the House, except amendments offered by the Committee on Appropriations, and said amendments shall be in order, any rule to the contrary notwithstanding" (*Congressional Record,* January 11, 1934, p. 480).

[30] *House Hearings on H. R. 5033 and S. 1685,* pp. 77, 94, 260.

given an opportunity to adequately express his arguments in favor of the bill he had helped to draft.

In the Senate, where debate is not restricted and where the process of offering an amendment is easy, senators can say all they wish to say on the floor of the Senate, and hence they do not make a practice of appearing before a committee to give their views.

Attendance of members at the open meetings of the committee presents a problem for the chairman and the members themselves. In general, the attendance of legislators at these open meetings is not good. Even if a roll-call record lists a large number of members in attendance at the opening of the meeting, this record does not indicate how long the legislator was present or how many interruptions prevented his attention to the proceedings. An analysis of the roll-call records at the meetings of the Senate Committee on Education and Labor shows that at no time during the seven days of the hearings in 1936 was there a majority of the members of the committee present. The reason for poor attendance at the open sessions of the committee is not a lack of interest in the legislation, but a lack of time to do all the jobs a legislator is called upon to perform.

The record shows that certain senators, such as Borah and Copeland, did not attend any of the meetings during the two years that the bill was before the committee. Senator Borah, however, was the ranking minority member of the Committee on the Judiciary and of the Committee on Foreign Affairs, and hence his absence is understandable. Senator Copeland was the chairman of the Committee on Commerce, which had business pending before it at the time of the hearings.

Legislators of the Congress of the United States simply have too many duties to perform. Some of these duties are nonlegislative jobs, matters which their constituents want them to handle personally. Two things are necessary to correct this evil. First of all, the constituents of the legislators must realize that their senators and congressmen are *legislators,* that this is their principal duty. Too many voters consider their congressmen to be their Washington messenger boys. The second remedy to the present evil is to lighten the burden of the national legislators by reorganization of Congress and of the legislative procedure. Steps in this direction were taken with the adoption of the Legislative Reorganization Act of 1946. The Federal Tort Claims Act is a good example of a procedure that will take away from the office of the legislator much nonlegislative business. The Reorganization Act made some attempt to eliminate some of the burdens of legislative committee work; but there is still much more reorganization work to be accomplished.

CHAPTER IX

Preparations
for the Campaign of 1937

The housing plank of the Democratic platform, adopted at the national convention in Philadelphia, June 23 to 27, 1936, was drafted by Senator Wagner. The platforms of political parties are designed to appeal to voters, and a party is always cautious in what it says about issues on which there are strong differences of opinion within its own ranks. The housing plank was therefore not the type of statement on housing that Wagner would have written if he had had complete freedom in the drafting of the platform; but it was as strong a statement as was possible when it is remembered that the Democratic party had within its ranks southern delegates who were opposed to any kind of federal agency that operated within the borders of a state, and certain conservatives from all parts of the country who were opposed to public housing on general principles. Hence it was necessary for Wagner to state the program of the Democratic party in vague and weak terms.

(6) We maintain that our people are entitled to decent, adequate housing at a price they can afford. In the last three years the Federal Government, having saved more than two million homes from foreclosure, has taken the first steps in our country to provide decent housing for people of meager incomes. We believe every encouragement should be given to the building of new homes by

private enterprise; and that the Government should steadily extend its housing program toward the goal of adequate housing for those forced through economic necessities to live in unhealthy and slum conditions.[1]

During the presidential campaign of 1936 the question of public housing was never a major issue, but it was a good subject for a campaign speech to the citizens in the slum areas. A promise to these people of better housing would keep their votes in the Democratic column on election day.

On October 28, 1936 Roosevelt spoke to the voters of the East Side of New York City. He told them:

> We need action to get better city housing. Senator Wagner and I had hoped for a new law at the last session of the Congress. We who believe in better housing have not been defeated. I am confident that the next Congress will start us on our way with a sound housing policy.[2]

These voters on the East Side of New York and the great majority of voters throughout the nation voted for Roosevelt in the election of 1936. Helen Alfred was overenthusiastic when she wrote in *Public Housing Progress* that the re-election of Roosevelt indicated a mandate from the people for him to enact a public-housing law,[3] but it was generally conceded by those favoring and by those opposing a public-housing law that some kind of law would be passed by the new Congress. Wagner had a meeting with Roosevelt at the White House on November 17, during which the public-housing law was discussed.[4]

---

[1] *New York Times*, June 27, 1936.
[2] *Public Papers and Addresses of Franklin D. Roosevelt*, Vol. 5, p. 546. New York: Random House, 1938.
[3] *Public Housing Progress* 3:1, November 15, 1936.
[4] Bohn to Woodbury, November 24, 1936, National Association of Housing Officials, Ernest Bohn File—1936. It was predicted after this meeting of Wagner and Roosevelt that there might be some changes in the bill to be introduced at the next session. The maximum grant might be cut to 30 per cent of the cost of the development.

But long before this meeting, and long before election day, the various public-housing groups had begun to work for an improved housing bill to be introduced at the coming session of Congress. In July, while the results of the battle for housing were still vivid in his mind, Coleman Woodbury wrote certain memoranda and letters for the improvement of the bill. The memorandum of July 6, 1936 was an important one. Woodbury made some suggestions about the definition of families of low income. He was opposed to putting into the definition incorporated into the law the ratio of an income equal to or less than five times the yearly rental. If it must be included, however, he suggested the ratio of six rather than five. He also suggested that the cost of heat and hot water should be included in the rental. As concerned the people living in substandard housing who were to be relocated, Woodbury was against loading up the definition so that it would appear that a family of low income must inhabit a dwelling that was unsafe *and* unsanitary *and* indecent *and* overcrowded. Concerning that part of the bill which dealt with the power of the Authority to revise contracts, he felt that it must be made clear that the Authority had the right to revise all contracts with all parties engaged in the housing program.[5]

Woodbury wrote to Miss Catherine Lansing, member of the management staff of the New York City Housing Authority, asking her to try to keep out of the new draft of the housing bill the provisions of rentals as a proportion of income.[6]

While NAHO was thus attempting to perfect the technical provisions of the bill, NPHC was making preparations to build up a stronger and more widespread support for the bill. The officers of NPHC decided to bring to the United States Captain

[5] Woodbury memorandum, July 6, 1936, National Association of Housing Officials, Revision of the Housing Bill.

[6] Woodbury to Lansing, July 14, 1936, National Association of Housing Officials, Revision of the Housing Bill.

Reiss, an English expert on public housing, who would make a speaking tour of the principal cities of the country in order to increase local interest in the housing bill.[7] The usual program of publicity for housing was carried on by these organizations during the autumn and winter.

The Labor Housing Conference was at work organizing conferences on the local level. By the time the AFL convention was held in November, the LHC had organized more than seventy local conferences which were prepared to urge the AFL delegates to give full support to housing legislation.[8] The report of the Executive Council to the convention said:

> The United States Housing Bill, unchanged in any important respect except for a larger appropriation of funds and greater bond-raising powers, can and must be passed this coming winter. Senator Wagner has promised to lead the fight again. The American Federation of Labor Housing Committee and the Labor Housing Conference are already at work on detailed plans in preparation for the coming legislative session. Organized labor is determined to place the United States Housing Bill on the statute books next year.[9]

There was no need for the Labor Housing Conference to sponsor resolutions at this meeting. The leadership of the organization, as was evident from the report of the Executive Council, was solidly behind the Wagner bill. There was a faction from Chicago, however, that was disappointed because of the failure of the Wagner bill to pass on two occasions. They were in favor of placing the support of the AFL behind the Scott bill, which had been introduced by Representative Byron Scott of California during May of 1936.

This bill set up a permanent United States Housing Authority which would build 10,000,000 homes to rent at $5.00 per

---

[7] *Public Housing Progress* 3:2, December 15, 1936.
[8] Statement of Catherine Bauer (personal letter).
[9] *Report of the Fifty-sixth Convention of AFL*, p. 178.

room per month. The initial appropriation would be $1,000,-
000,000 from the moneys of the United States Treasury. Each
year thereafter the Authority would give its estimate at the start
of the year, and the appropriation would be included in the
regular budget. Under the provisions of this bill labor was
guaranteed union wages and union conditions of work.[10]

Delegate Irving Meyers of Chicago introduced a resolution
to transfer the support of the AFL from the Wagner bill to the
Scott bill.[11] Very tactfully the Committee on Resolutions referred this resolution to the incoming Executive Council. It did
not want to offend any of the friends of labor, "and it did not
want to hinder itself by a too previous commitment."[12]

Another very important convention held during autumn was
that of the United States Conference of Mayors. The annual
meeting was held during November in Washington. On November 19, 1936 Senator Wagner addressed the group. After re-
peating some of the ideas that were to be found in all his
speeches on housing (concerning the necessity of giving the
children in the slums a chance to grow up to be healthy and
respectable citizens, and the beneficial effects of the program on
the economy of the country), Wagner directed a special appeal
to the mayors. He said:

> In any discussion of proposed legislation, you as mayors will
> be interested primarily in the proper relationship between the Fed-
> eral Government, the States, and municipalities. Naturally the

---

[10] Bill introduced by Representative Byron Scott of California. "H. R. 12835. To
provide financial assistance to the States and political subdivisions thereof,
to the District of Columbia, or any Territory of the United States for the
elimination of slums, for the construction of decent, safe, and sanitary dwellings at low rental for families of low income, and for the reduction of unemployment and the stimulation of business activity, and for other purposes: to
the Committee on Ways and Means" (*Congressional Record*, May 22, 1936,
p. 7830).

[11] *Report of the Fifty-sixth Convention of AFL*, p. 599.

[12] *Ibid.*, p. 600.

Federal Government will have to undertake the major burden of the subsidy aspect; whether through outright appropriations, or lower interest rates, or both. But I am firmly convinced that in so far as possible housing should be initiated by local authorities, controlled by local authorities, and financed by local authorities. Homes are not standardized products that can be distributed from Washington like committee hearings. They are intimately tied up with the lives of our people. They involve ways of living, the preservation of local cultural values, the maintenance of long-formed regional habits. They must spring spontaneously from the impulses of the people everywhere, made manifest by local organs of government and self expression. . . .

It is at this time less important to elaborate further upon the minute provisions of prospective legislation, than to drive home to the public a full consciousness of the need for a housing program, and the tremendous benefits that would flow from a housing program. The argument may be stated to the banker or industrialist or tradesman in economic terms because many of us are engaged in various pursuits. But it can be stated to the whole population in humanitarian terms because all of us are human beings, who shrink from the horrors of the slums and who want the children of America to live and work and play in healthy surroundings, rather than in an atmosphere oppressively heavy with disease and crime. Every citizen should bend every effort toward the achievement of this great objective. But in your hands as community leaders rests the fulfillment of this obligation to a unique degree. Your presence here attests your interest, and with your cooperation we in Washington shall have no qualms about the results.[13]

Another meeting held during the autumn which considered housing legislation was the American City Planning Institute, which met in Milwaukee during October. This group was in favor of housing legislation, but it was also insistent that provision be made in the housing bill for sound city planning and for the participation of planning officials in the housing program. This group sent its request for specific recognition in the

---

[13] Collected Papers of Wagner, Vol. 7, Sec. 4, No. 16.

housing program to Coleman Woodbury of NAHO. During the discussion of the housing bill in 1936, NAHO had made efforts to have requirement for city planning included in the provisions of the bill. The city planners were particularly interested in securing places for members of their group on the boards that determined policy.[14]

The United States Building and Loan League recognized that some sort of housing legislation was certain to be enacted during the coming session of Congress; consequently it was decided to work with NAHO in an attempt to secure amendments to the bill that would make it acceptable to the League. In the report of the Public Housing Committee of the USBLL of October 16, 1936 it was stated that only in an emergency should the government provide relief in the form of shelter to some portion of the population. The permanent provision of housing to any portion of the people is not within the proper activities of the Federal Government. Local bodies, the report continued, should initiate, develop, and control all public housing. Such activities were not a matter for either state or federal government. Finally, the report stated, it is to be recognized that housing conditions in the United States are better than those existing anywhere else in the world. As a substitute measure the committee recommended that the local government extend rent relief or rent assistance rather than undertake the construction and management of housing units.[15]

Though this was the official position of the USBLL, and though these principles were considered as sound by the organization, still, because the organization saw that a Wagner hous-

---

[14] Planning Institute to Woodbury, November 19, 1936, National Association of Housing Officials, Revision of the Housing Bill.

[15] The complete report of the Housing Committee of the USBLL is printed as a supplement to the testimony that Bodfish presented to the House Committee on Banking and Currency during the hearings in 1937 (*House Hearings on H. R. 5033 and S. 1685*, pp. 223-35).

ing bill was inevitable, Morton Bodfish wrote to Woodbury of
NAHO telling him he would cooperate with him in an effort to
find some "common ground."[16]

The national realtors' convention was also held during the
autumn and went on record as opposing the Wagner bill. The
housing committee of the association, under the chairmanship
of John McC. Mowbray of Baltimore, made a four-point report
to the convention. The four points were: (1) The Federal Government should abandon all direct construction of housing and
turn over the job of constructing and operating housing units
to private industry. (2) Private enterprise can serve all the
people of the United States except a small fraction of the population. (3) For the "very lowest income group" housing can
be provided by the limited-dividend or public-utility housing
companies organized locally and eligible to receive loans and
assistance from federal agencies. (4) Local government should
undertake the clearance of slums (separated from lowest-income-
group housing) with help, if necessary, from the Federal Government, but in no case should the local government undertake
to build or operate new housing facilities.[17]

The attitude of the Chamber of Commerce of the United
States was expressed in a report similar to that of the United
States Building and Loan League.[18] In the column, "Washington
and Your Business," in *Nation's Business* (a publication of the
Chamber of Commerce of the United States), Ira E. Bennett

---

[16] Bodfish to Woodbury, December 29, 1936, National Association of Housing
Officials, USBLL.

[17] *National Real Estate and Building Journal* 37:68, December 1936.

[18] The report of the Housing Committee of the Chamber of Commerce was pub-
lished in a four-page brochure under date of May 21, 1936. Mr. Samuel
Clabaugh, chairman of this housing committee, appeared before the House
Committee on Banking and Currency during the hearings in 1937 and incor-
porated the report into his testimony (*House Hearings on H. R. 5033 and
S. 1685*, pp. 245-50). An account of the 1936 meeting of the Chamber of
Commerce of the United States was published in *Literary Digest* 121:41,
May 9, 1936.

gave the readers an account of the developments concerning the housing bills. In the May issue of 1936 he predicted that the bill would not pass during that session of Congress. He mentioned that Fahey, of HOLC, and McDonald, of FHA, had been making efforts to get a bill introduced and passed that would keep alive their own agencies. Bennett then went on to state that the real "threat" was the Wagner bill with its permanent housing subsidy. It will find strong opposition, Bennett commented, in local real-estate boards and lending agencies.[19]

In the October issue Bennett mentioned that it was only an "unexpected tax bill" made necessary by the bonus and a soil-erosion fund which forced the administration to bypass the housing bill during the last session of Congress. In 1937, he warned, there would not be a tax bill, and the chances of the passage of a housing bill would be "greatly improved."[20]

The Central Housing Committee took hope from the defeat of the Wagner bill in 1936, and decided to make another attempt to draft a bill that would be accepted by the president and thus would become the administration housing program. Mr. Delano, chairman of the committee, had a draft bill ready by September 15, 1936. Don Price, personal assistant to Delano, gave an outline of the bill to Ormond Loomis, assistant to John Fahey of HOLC. Loomis wrote to Fahey to tell him about the new activity in the Central Housing Committee and to give him the outline of the bill. Loomis mentioned that there would probably be slight revisions in the bill before it was officially distributed; the bill, however, would be substantially the same as outlined in the enclosed papers.[21]

The bill was divided into three major divisions. The first division provided for a department of research which would

19 *Nation's Business* 21:18, May 1936.
20 *Ibid.*, 21:42, October 1936.
21 Loomis to Fahey, September 15, 1936, Wagner Papers, Housing—1936.

study the housing problem and the most effective methods of solving the problem. The second division was called "Aid to Private Enterprise." There was to be educational activity and the passing along to private enterprise of the findings of the research department. There would also be financial aid along the lines of loans and mortgage insurance, which were already available in the HOLC and the FHA. It was also stated in this division that there should be community planning. The private builders would work with a master plan for the housing of the community. The third division of the bill was concerned with "Aid to Local Government." This division had three subdivisions concerned with land acquisition and control, building and financing, and administration and management.[22] This bill was never seriously considered by the president as a substitute for a Wagner housing bill.

Ickes and his PWA had not given up hope of getting control of the housing program. The legal division was at work gathering data and statistics for a new draft of a housing bill. By January of 1937, when Congress had convened, the PWA had a draft bill ready for circulation in an emergency. This draft was called: *Housing and Slum Clearance Administration in Department of Interior.* This bill did not differ substantially from P. W. 51147 of 1936. The administration of the program was left entirely with the Department of the Interior. The secretary of the interior was to appoint the director of the Housing Administration and delegate to him powers to administer the agency. Grants were to be given to housing authorities that would cover up to 45 per cent of the cost of the development. Provision was also made for annual contributions to the project to keep the rents at a level low enough for the people in the lowest income group. But in no case could the contributions exceed 45 per cent

---

[22] The outline of the bill is clipped together with the letter of Loomis to Fahey, September 15, 1936, Wagner Papers, Housing—1936.

of the cost of the development, less the amount of any grant that was given.[23]

It was well known that Ickes had instructed the legal division of PWA to prepare a housing bill. Mr. Holden, an architect from New York, wrote to E. H. Foley, Jr., then in charge of the legal division, to ask him to make provision in this bill for the participation of the city planners in the housing program.[24]

There was so much scattered activity with regard to public-housing legislation during the autumn that Langdon Post wrote to the president in November to ask him to summon all of the people interested in public housing to a meeting so that they could compromise their differences and present a united front in favor of housing when the new Congress convened.[25]

Despite all this activity on the part of the PWA, it was still well known that Senator Wagner was the man whom Roosevelt would support in the Congress. The PWA could expect its bill to receive support only if the Wagner bill was stalled in Congress. And the PWA staffers realized this, because at the time that they were drafting their own bill they were also working with Wagner's office in the preparation of his bill for the coming session of Congress. The PWA was hoping, first and foremost, to have Wagner's office draft the type of a bill that they desired. A bill which would place the administration of the pro-

---

[23] *Housing and Slum Clearance Administration in Department of Interior.* Draft of January 20, 1937 (mimeographed). A copy of this draft is preserved in the Vinton Papers.

[24] Holden to Foley, December 10, 1936. A copy of this letter was sent to Coleman Woodbury, National Association of Housing Officials, Revision of the Housing Bill. The various city planning groups had contacted Holden, who was a leader of the American Institute of Architects, and asked him to appeal to those drafting the housing bill in behalf of the planners. Mention had been made of community planning in the draft of Delano for the Central Housing Committee. Alfred Bettman of Cincinnati had written to Delano asking him to include the planners in the provisions of any bill the committee would draft.

[25] Post to Roosevelt, November 6, 1936, Roosevelt Papers, P.P.F. 3646.

gram in the Department of the Interior would be perfectly satisfactory to Ickes and to his followers.[26]

During the autumn months previous to the opening of
the new session of Congress two representatives asked Senator
Wagner for the honor of sponsoring his legislation in the
House at the coming session of Congress. Representative Maury
Maverick wrote to Keyserling to tell him that he wanted some
material on housing because he had seen Senator Wagner in
New York and talked with him about housing. As a result of
this conversation Maverick judged that the senator was going
to let him sponsor the Wagner bill in the House.[27] Maverick
also wrote directly to Senator Wagner asking him to send him
some material on housing that would be suitable for an article
that he was going to write for a national weekly.[28] Another representative who wrote to Wagner at this time was Alfred Phillips
of Stamford, Connecticut. He was mayor of Stamford before
his election to the House. He had supported housing as mayor,
and he sent a letter of support to the Committee on Education and Labor when the committee was holding hearings on
Wagner's bill, S. 4424. Now that he was a member-elect of Congress, he was interested in housing legislation. He asked the
senator for some technical information, and promised his support for Wagner's housing bill.[29] Wagner thanked both of these
representatives for their interest in his bill and sent them information and statistics about public housing, but he did not commit himself on the question of a choice between Maverick and

---

[26] The close working agreement between Senator Wagner's office and the legal
division of the PWA will be explained in detail in the next chapter of
this study.

[27] Maverick to Keyserling, October 13, 1936, Wagner Papers, Housing Suggestions—1937.

[28] Maverick to Wagner, October 13, 1936, Wagner Papers, Housing Suggestions—
1937.

[29] Phillips to Wagner, November 7, 1936 and December 7, 1936, Wagner Papers,
Housing Suggestions—1937.

Phillips to introduce his bill in the House. Representative Ellenbogen had a prior right to introduce the bill.

The letters that began to pour into Wagner's office at this
time manifest an increased interest in public housing on the part
of the ordinary citizen, as opposed to those citizens who were
members of NAHO or NPHC or LHC. Mr. Edward P. Doyle of
New York wrote to the senator to make some suggestions about
improving the housing bill.[30] Phelps Phelps, radio commentator
for Station WMAC in New York, wrote to the senator for some
information on the housing bill.[31] Wagner sent him material that
would be useful in his radio broadcasts.[32] These are samples of
the various communications that were sent to Wagner during
the month before Congress convened.

In addition to the letters that Wagner received from the ordinary citizen, he received a number of communications from
housing officials who wished to offer the senator some suggestions for improving the new draft of the bill. Mr. Miles Frisbie,
of the Municipal Housing Authority of Schenectady,[33] and
Mr. T. T. McCrosky, of the Municipal Housing Authority of
Yonkers,[34] were two officials who sent suggestions to Wagner
at this time.

Despite all this interest in the housing bill Senator Wagner
was in no great hurry to get his bill perfected in time to introduce it at the opening of the new session of Congress. Keyserling
was in contact with Woodbury at the NAHO office, with Bauer

---

[30] Wagner to Doyle, December 10, 1936, Wagner Papers, Housing Suggestions—
1937.
[31] Phelps to Wagner, December 5, 1936, Wagner Papers, Housing Suggestions—
1937.
[32] Wagner to Phelps, December 10, 1936, Wagner Papers, Housing Suggestions—
1937.
[33] Wagner to Frisbie, December 17, 1936, Wagner Papers, Housing Suggestions—
1937.
[34] Wagner to McCrosky, January 5, 1937, Wagner Papers, Housing Suggestions—
1937.

at the LHC office, with Alfred at the NPHC office, and with Vinton and Foley in the government departments in Washington, but Keyserling had not received any instructions from Wagner to have a draft prepared by January 5, 1937.

There were others, however, who were prepared to introduce Wagner's housing bill on the opening day of Congress. William Green, president of the AFL, sent a telegram to Ellenbogen asking him to introduce his housing bill on the opening day of Congress.[35] Ellenbogen took the housing bill as reported by the Senate Committee on Education and Labor and introduced it on the opening day. Ellenbogen did not have any consultation with Wagner before the introduction of the bill. This early introduction was more of a gesture to satisfy the AFL than a determined effort to have that version of the bill seriously considered by the Committee on Banking and Currency, to which it was automatically referred. Ellenbogen expected to consult with Wagner about the new draft of the bill.

Representative Boylan introduced his housing bill to provide for loans for housing construction under the supervision of the Department of the Interior. This bill was referred to the Committee on Appropriations.[36] Representative Goldsborough of the Committee on Banking and Currency introduced a bill "To create a United States Housing Authority under the direction and control of the Secretary of the Interior." This bill was the same as S. 4424 except for the section on administration.[37]

Representative Steagall also introduced a housing bill which was the same bill as Wagner's bill, S. 4424, of the previous session, with the exception that Steagall put the administration of

---

[35] Green to Ellenbogen, December 31, 1936, American Federation of Labor, National Legislative Committee, Housing File, Washington. The bill was given the number H. R. 1489 (*Congressional Record*, January 5, 1937, p. 31).

[36] Boylan's bill was given the number H. R. 1599 (*ibid.*, p. 34).

[37] Goldsborough's bill was given the number H. R. 1644 and was referred to the Committee on Banking and Currency (*ibid.*, p. 35).

the United States Housing Authority under the jurisdiction of the secretary of the interior.[38] The introduction of this bill by Steagall indicated that the chairman of the Committee on Banking and Currency had decided that there would be so much pressure on his committee during the coming sessions that a housing bill would have to be reported out to the House. Steagall therefore decided that he might as well have his name on the bill, especially as it would be his committee that would be responsible for the bill on the House side of Congress. This introduction of the bill by Steagall signified to all that he would be the representative who introduced Wagner's bill in the House when the senator had it prepared for introduction. Although Representative Ellenbogen should have been the representative honored by sponsorship of the legislation in the House, and though he should have had the honor of seeing his name associated officially with the law that was later enacted, still when the chairman of the committee decided that he wanted this honor, any other representative would have to yield.

President Roosevelt delivered his annual message to Congress on the next day, January 6, 1937. In this message he made a specific reference to the housing problem.

> There are far-reaching problems still with us for which democracy must find solutions if it is to consider itself successful.
>
> For example, many millions of Americans still live in habitations which not only fail to provide the physical benefits of modern civilization, but breed disease and impair the health of future gen-

---

[38] Steagall's bill was given the number H. R. 1544 and was referred to his Committee on Banking and Currency (*ibid.*, p. 33). It is to be noted that four bills were introduced on this first day. The total number of bills introduced on this first day of Congress, January 5, 1937 is a good indication of the excessive number of bills that are presented to Congress. There were 1,951 bills, both public and private, introduced the first day. Public bills were numbered H. R. 1 to 300 and H. R. 1480 to 1671. Private bills were numbered H. R. 301 to 1479 and H. R. 1672 to 1951. There were also a number of resolutions and joint resolutions introduced that first day (*ibid.*, pp. 22-60).

erations. The menace exists not only in the slum areas of the very large cities, but in many smaller cities as well. It exists on tens of thousands of farms, in varying degrees, in every part of the country.[39]

In these sentences the president was answering the charges of the opponents of housing within the Congress who claimed that it was legislation that would benefit only the people in New York City and a few of the other very large cities.

It was in the president's inaugural address on January 20, 1937 that he made his most-quoted statement about housing conditions in the United States. Speaking from a platform in front of the National Capitol, the voice of Franklin Delano Roosevelt carried to the thousands who stood before him and to the millions who listened to him on the radio these words:

> But here is the challenge to our democracy:—In this nation I see tens of millions of its citizens—a substantial part of its whole population—who at this very moment are denied the greater part of what the very lowest standards of today call the necessities of life. . . . I see one-third of a nation ill-housed, ill-clad, ill-nourished.[40]

Roosevelt put himself definitely on record as favoring some kind of a housing law that would relieve the distress of the "one-third of a nation ill-housed." It was now the responsibility of Senator Wagner and his staff to draft the law that would fulfill the promise of the Democratic party and the Democratic president to give better housing to the millions of Americans who needed it.

---

[39] *Ibid.*, January 6, 1937, p. 84.
[40] Franklin D. Roosevelt, "A Changed Moral Climate in America." *Vital Speeches* 3:227, February 1, 1937.

CHAPTER X

Technical Experts
Perfect the Wagner Bill

Wagner's intention, and that of his advisers, was to introduce as perfect a bill as possible in 1937. Many improvements had been made in the provisions of the various drafts of the 1936 housing bill (S. 4424), but because the groups advising Wagner realized that the bill would be weakened by congressional amendments, it was deemed essential that the draft introduced in Congress be as perfect as possible.

Keyserling in Senator Wagner's office and Warren Vinton and Coleman Woodbury worked with marked success and energy to perfect the technical aspects of the bill. Another group that worked effectively to perfect the provisions of the bill was the legal division of PWA. It was the practice of Vinton and Woodbury to interview and consult with the representatives of government agencies, such as the Farm Credit Administration, the Federal Home Loan Bank Board, the Post Office Department, and other agencies to obtain from these administrators information and advice based on their actual experiences with certain types of administration or subsidy. By following this procedure Vinton and Woodbury made certain that their proposals were practical. These experts made it a rule always to apply the tests of working success or of failure when engaged in the drafting of legislative proposals.

Woodbury spent most of his time in Chicago at the office of NAHO. As he was also working in the same building which was occupied by the Public Administration Clearing House, he had the advantage of consulting with experienced men in every phase of government operation. Especially was Woodbury fortunate in getting the advice of Louis Brownlow, the director of PACH, an acknowledged expert on public administration and governmental affairs.

The United States Building and Loan League maintained its headquarters in Chicago, and Morton Bodfish wrote frequently to Woodbury to make suggestions for amendments to the bill that would make it more acceptable to the USBLL. Bodfish suggested in a letter of January 25 that the administration of the new housing agency should be given to a nonsalaried part-time commission which would exercise an effective veto over the actions of the commissioner.[1] Woodbury replied in a letter of January 26 that he was in favor of a commission which would act in an advisory capacity, but that he would not favor giving such a commission responsibilities in connection with the administration of the project.[2]

In a letter of January 27 Bodfish suggested that the Hancock bill be accepted as the working copy of the housing bill, and then certain amendments could be made to this bill to meet with the approval of the various groups interested in housing. Bodfish informed Woodbury that the Hancock bill had been endorsed by the USBLL.[3]

---

[1] Bodfish to Woodbury, January 25, 1937, National Association of Housing Officials, USBLL.

[2] Woodbury to Bodfish, January 26, 1937, National Association of Housing Officials, USBLL.

[3] Bodfish to Woodbury, January 27, 1937, National Association of Housing Officials, USBLL. The Hancock bill was a modified form of the Wagner housing bill which was introduced in the House on January 22, 1937 by Representative Frank W. Hancock, Jr., of North Carolina. It was given the number H. R. 3487 and was assigned to the Committee on Banking and Currency, of

The National Association of Real Estate Boards also maintained headquarters in Chicago in addition to their Washington office; and Herbert Nelson, vice-president and lobbyist for this group, had some correspondence with Woodbury about the housing bill. In a letter dated January 22, Nelson suggested to Woodbury that the bill should make provisions for public-utility housing companies and associations together with the limited-dividend corporations. NAREB was in favor of the establishment of "neighborhood improvement districts" organized under state law which would benefit by public aid. These organizations would be charged with the problem of slum clearance. The NAREB was opposed to the Wagner bill because it brought the Federal Government into the housing field. NAREB was convinced that no one in the government knew how to proceed with the problem of organizing housing. The financial plan was also considered unsound by the NAREB.[4]

Woodbury sent to Warren Vinton in Washington a synopsis of his correspondence with these organizations. Since Vinton had served as secretary of the special committee of housing groups that examined the housing bill in 1936, he acted as a

which Hancock was a high-ranking member (*Congressional Record*, January 22, 1937, p. 378). Hancock sent copies of his bill, together with a letter asking for suggestions, to various people interested in the public-housing bill of Senator Wagner. Ickes replied to Hancock's letter, dated January 25, with a letter dated January 28, in which he praised the section of Hancock's bill which put the administration under the Department of the Interior; but Ickes was not favorable to sections of the bill which gave a controlling power of policy making to representatives "of the public housing, mortgage credit, and construction interests and organizations." Ickes was also opposed to the assumption by the Public Housing Agency of one third of the risk of the development and construction of the project (Ickes to Hancock, January 28, 1937, PWA Housing Division, Housing Legislation—1937, Washington). Wagner replied to Hancock's letter that he was happy to receive his bill and he was sure that it would help him in the drafting of his own measure (Wagner to Hancock, February 1, 1937, Wagner Papers, S. 1685—1937).

[4] Nelson to Woodbury, January 22, 1937, National Association of Housing Officials, NAREB.

sort of clearing house for the housing experts. Woodbury suggested to Vinton that the housing groups should be ready to make any compromise possible with the USBLL which did not affect essentials, since this was an organization that had influence in the House and in the House Committee on Banking and Currency.[5] Because of the attitude of the NAREB there was never any question of a compromise.

Woodbury also sent to Vinton the information that he had gathered from his conferences with Brownlow concerning the administration of the housing agency. It was Brownlow's suggestion that the section concerned with the city manager in the model city charter should be studied for useful ideas. Brownlow also suggested that the administration be placed under the control of a single individual. The language of the TVA Act was suggested as a good model in this connection.[6]

Vinton himself called Herbert Emmerich of the Farm Credit Administration on January 20 and asked him for his suggestions about the form of administration of the proposed agency.[7] On January 21 Vinton had a telephone conversation with Ormond Loomis, assistant to John Fahey, director of HOLC and member of the Federal Home Loan Bank Board, concerning the desirability of the proposed five-member board.[8]

Brownlow sent Vinton a letter dated January 27 in which he discussed again the advantages that would result from having a single administrator of the proposed agency. Brownlow also discussed in this letter the function of an advisory board and the advantages of the corporate form of administration for the proposed agency.[9]

---

[5] Woodbury to Vinton, January 28, 1937, Vinton Papers, Housing Bill—1937.
[6] Woodbury to Vinton, January 20 and 21, 1937, Vinton Papers, Housing Bill—1937.
[7] Notes on Housing Bill, January 20, 1937, Vinton Papers, Housing Bill—1937.
[8] Notes on Housing Bill, January 21, 1937, Vinton Papers, Housing Bill—1937.
[9] Brownlow to Vinton, January 27, 1937, Vinton Papers, Housing Bill—1937.

During the early part of February, Vinton had another series
of conferences with governmental representatives on various
technical provisions of the bill. On February 1 he consulted with
Monroe Oppenheimer, legal counsel for the Farm Security Administration and Resettlement Administration, concerning the
provisions of the PWA draft of the housing bill. They discussed
in particular the question of demonstration projects.[10] On the
same day Vinton talked with representatives of the FHA concerning regulatory agreements for loans.[11] On this same day
Vinton received a memorandum from John Ihlder concerning
the financial provisions of the housing bill. Ihlder was at this
time advising the Department of the Treasury and was sympathetic to the plans that Morgenthau favored.[12] On February 10
Vinton had a conference with Don Price, assistant to Frederic
Delano, concerning the administration of the agency. Price favored a single administrator and cautioned Vinton against the
abolishment of the agencies then operating in the housing field.[13]
This same day Vinton also had a conference with Robert L.
Davison, a research expert in Washington, about the provisions
of the bill. Davison told him he did not think that the financial
provisions of the bill were sound. He also mentioned that he had
talked with Wagner the day before (February 9) concerning the
provisions of the bill, James Roosevelt having introduced them
to each other.[14] Lucius Wilmerding, another special adviser to
Secretary Morgenthau, was also interviewed by Vinton on this
date. Wilmerding gave his general approval to the bill, and expressed the opinion that it would be passed by the Congress.
Wilmerding favored a single administrator for the agency. He
told Vinton that he thought the bill should include a provision

---

[10] Notes on Housing Bill, February 1, 1937, Vinton Papers, Housing Bill—1937.
[11] *Ibid.*
[12] *Ibid.*
[13] Notes on Housing Bill, February 10, 1937, Vinton Papers, Housing Bill—1937.
[14] *Ibid.*

for the construction of new units equivalent to the number of slum units actually demolished. He further suggested that a provision be written into the bill requiring the cities to contribute funds to the cost of the housing program. Concerning the financial provisions of the bill, Wilmerding was of the opinion that the Department of the Treasury should make the loans rather than have the agency make the loans from money raised by an independent bond issue.[15]

This list of conferences indicates the great care exercised by Vinton and Woodbury in the drafting of a single section of the bill. All the suggestions and proposals assembled by Vinton were studied and summarized by him and were then turned over to Keyserling for his consideration. As will be seen, when Keyserling sent the drafts to the printer for committee prints, he did not always follow the suggestions that he had received; but he did have an abundance of material at his fingertips when he was ready to draft the sections of the bill. Senator Wagner expected Keyserling to consult with many experts but to use his best judgment after final consultation with the senator himself.

In addition to the information that Vinton channeled into Wagner's office, Wagner was receiving technical information almost daily from the legal division of PWA. An important letter was sent to Wagner by E. H. Foley, Jr., general counsel of PWA, under date of January 8, 1937.[16] Foley stated that, since the introduction of the housing bill the year before, the Supreme Court and the Court of Appeals of the District of Columbia had handed down decisions that made it imperative to revise the wording of certain sections of the bill. Because of the adverse decisions in the Louisville case[17] and in the case of the Court of Appeals of the District of Columbia involving

---

[15] *Ibid.*

[16] Foley to Wagner, January 8, 1937, Wagner Papers, S. 1685—1937.

[17] *United States* v. *Certain Lands in City of Louisville, Jefferson County, Ky. et al.,* 78 F. (2d) 684 (1935).

projects of the Resettlement Administration,[18] it was evident that the court would not uphold the expenditure of money for housing projects as a proper application of the general-welfare clause of the Constitution. Foley therefore urged Wagner to place the emphasis on the expenditure of money for housing projects with the purpose of relieving unemployment. Foley cited a long list of cases in which the courts had upheld as valid the expenditure of money for public works in time of unemployment.

The suggestion made by Foley had to be carried out throughout the entire bill so that, whenever there was question of an expenditure of money or of loans, there would be reference to the relief of unemployment rather than to the promotion of the general welfare. Foley hastened to assure Wagner that the PWA considered the program of slum clearance and construction of housing units to be a permanent program and not merely an emergency relief measure. Unemployment, he stated, had been and would continue to be of such recurring nature as to require a permanent agency such as the proposed United States Housing Authority to bring relief from the evil.

The next important change that Foley suggested in view of the opinion of the court was the elimination of "demonstration projects" which were to be constructed directly by the Federal Government. In view of the decision involving the Resettlement Administration, Foley advised that demonstration projects be entirely eliminated.

Foley also made some suggestions regarding those sections of the bill that set up standards to which local agencies must conform in order to receive federal aid—standards concerning the preservation of the low-rent character of the project (Section 15) and standards concerning union labor and wage rates (Section 16). Foley stated that these sections were open to attack by opponents of public housing and that an adverse deci-

---

18 *Township of Franklin* v. *Tugwell*, 85 F. (2d) 208 (1936).

sion of the court was possible in cases in which federal regulations conflicted with state regulations. He cited the Butler case,[19] in which the court declared that the spending power of the government could not be used as a means of regulating matters reserved to the states.

Foley then pointed out that in the case of *Carter* v. *Carter Coal Company*[20] the separability clause of the Guffey Coal Act, which was identical with the clause used in S. 4424, was not deemed by the court a sufficient safeguard to protect the various other provisions of the act from falling when part of it was declared unconstitutional. He suggested that the separability clause be redrafted. He also suggested that the bill be divided into titles, which was a recognized style of legislative drafting, and that the provisions of the bill that were of doubtful nature be included under one title. If this were done, the other titles might be saved in the event of an adverse court decision.

A final suggestion made by Foley concerned the operation of federally controlled projects and the restoration of state jurisdiction thereof, and the payment of sums of money by the project in lieu of local taxes. Foley reminded Wagner that the George-Healy Act,[21] passed after the introduction of the bill the year before, had taken care of this matter; thus these sections were repetitious of that act and a simple reference to the act could be placed in the bill, eliminating some involved sections of the draft.

It was evident from the intense interest manifested by the PWA in their extremely careful study and redrafting of the housing bill that Ickes and his legal staff felt certain that they were working on a bill which *they* were going to administer. The PWA had its own draft of a housing bill, but it was something

---

[19] *United States* v. *Butler*, 297 U. S. 1 (1936).
[20] *Carter* v. *Carter Coal Company*, 298 U. S. 312 (1936).
[21] 49 Stat. 2025 (1936).

to use in an emergency if Wagner's bill, the recognized administration bill, got stalled in Congress. Wagner's bill was the bill that would have congressional support, and so it was wise to have it drafted as carefully as possible. Ickes knew that the majority of Wagner's supporters favored an independent agency, but he had strong support from the New York group in the NPHC and felt certain that he could get the president and Steagall to place the agency under his administration.

An indication of how carefully the PWA legal division worked on the provisions of the bill can be gathered from a study of certain of the memoranda sent to Wagner's office. Before an important memorandum was sent to Wagner's office, it was circulated within the legal division. For example, the interdepartmental memorandum of February 13 was sent from J. B. Robinson, Jr., to David L. Krooth. This memorandum was concerned with the provisions for administrative expenses such as "paper," "printing and binding," and so forth. In this memorandum Robinson pointed out the necessity of including the words "printing and binding" in the section making provision for administrative expenses because the U. S. Code, Title 31, Section 588 provided that "no appropriation other than those made specifically and solely for printing and binding shall be used for such purposes in any executive department."[22]

This exchange of memoranda was then sent to E. H. Foley, Jr., who prepared the memorandum to be sent to Senator Wagner. Under date of February 15 Foley advised Wagner that

in view of the provisions of the U. S. Code the provisions of the bill, Section 6 (a) of S. 4424, authorizing the Authority to make expenditures should be revised so that the Authority be authorized to make expenditures for the following, at the seat of Government and elsewhere: rent, law books and books of reference, periodicals,

---

[22] Robinson to Krooth, February 13, 1937, PWA Housing Division, Housing Legislation—1937.

newspapers, printing and binding, personal services, acquiring of information at meetings by its personnel, acquisition, maintenance, repair and operation of motor-propelled passenger-carrying vehicles to be used only for official purposes, and maintenance of adequate administrative agencies and offices.[23]

On February 23 Foley sent a memorandum to Keyserling regarding the use of the term "corporation sole." Foley stated that there was no legal objection to the use of "corporation sole." He mentioned that there were precedents for the creation of such a corporation, and then concluded: "The establishment of a corporation sole appears to be the most feasible means of permitting the issuance of bonds by the housing authority and at the same time providing for management and control by one person."[24]

Keyserling was not convinced by all these legal memoranda. As can be seen from a study of the drafts which he prepared in February of 1937, practically none of the suggestions he received from the legal division of PWA were incorporated into the text. It should be noted that Keyserling himself was a lawyer. Keyserling had the first draft of the 1937 housing bill ready by February 5. This first draft was prepared by Keyserling with the aid of several housing experts, in particular Warren Vinton. S. 4424 (Report No. 2160), the bill as amended by the Senate Committee on Education and Labor, was the working basis for this draft. A few of the amendments were accepted, but most of the original provisions of S. 4424 were rewritten into this draft.[25]

The section concerned with the administration of the Authority (Section 3) provided for a five-member board to admin-

---

[23] Foley to Wagner, February 15, 1937, PWA Housing Division, Housing Legislation—1937.

[24] Foley to Keyserling, February 23, 1937, PWA Housing Division, Housing Legislation—1937.

[25] Statements of Leon Keyserling and Warren Vinton (personal interviews).

ister it as an independent agency. The Department of the Interior and the secretary of the Department of the Interior were not included in the provisions of the bill. This section was substantially the same as the amended section of S. 4424 (Report No. 2160). Appointment of employees to the Authority was to be made in accordance with civil-service laws and the Classification Act of 1923. This provision (Section 4 (b)) also followed the amended version of S. 4424 (Report No. 2160). Section 4 (d), which provided for the transfer of any and all other bureaus, agencies, and so forth concerned with public housing, was written according to the amended version of S. 4424 (Report No. 2160). The provision that the local planning board should be consulted before local housing projects were constructed (Section 14 (7)) was the Senate amendment of S. 4424 (Report No. 2160), and this provision was in answer to the repeated requests of the planning associations. The amendment to the section on labor standards (Section 16 (6)), which required contractors engaged on housing projects to list all their subcontractors and file a payroll list and account with the Department of Labor, was retained in this new draft. One other important change, concerned with the financial provisions of the bill, which had been made by the Senate committee in 1936, was retained in this redraft. It was the elimination of the RFC from participation in the financial plan (Section 20).[26]

Some new provisions were included in the redraft. The total authorized bonded indebtedness of the Authority was increased. Originally this provision called for a bonded indebtedness of $550,000,000 within the period from 1936 to 1939. The Senate committee cut this limit to $450,000,000 over the period from 1936 to 1938. The new version (Section 20 (a)) called for a bonded indebtedness not to exceed one billion dollars during

---

[26] Confidential Committee Print No. 1, February 5, 1937 is preserved in the Vinton Papers.

the period to end "on or after July 1, 1940." The appropriations to the new Authority in this redraft (Section 18) were limited to $51,000,000 for the fiscal year ending June 30, 1938. No other appropriations were specified in this draft.

The separability clause was modified (in accordance with Foley's suggestion, and this is the only section that was revised in accordance with his suggestions and memoranda) so as to offset the danger of an adverse court decision rendering the entire act unconstitutional.

The most important and fundamental change in the bill was the new provision for annual contributions. Vinton had for some time been impressed with the advantages of meeting the cost of subsidizing low-rent housing on a pay-as-you-go basis, with a contribution from the Federal Government each year to meet necessary deficits incurred in the operation of projects. He had also been impressed with the political advantages of such a plan in that it would not require the very large initial appropriations involved in a capital-grant plan. After several evenings of discussion with Keyserling, the two agreed to call in Coleman Woodbury and Langdon Post for further discussion. At a joint meeting the next evening that carried into the early hours of the morning, it was decided that the advantages of the annual contributions system were so great as to warrant its inclusion in the new draft. The only question raised at the discussion was as to whether the Congress could and would authorize the payment of annual contributions over a long period of years. The next day Vinton checked with Herbert Emmerich and other government officials and found precedent for such assumption of long-term obligations by the Congress.[27] The new section was as follows:

> Sec. 9. (a) The Authority may make grants and loans to public-housing agencies to assist the development, acquisition, or administration of low-rent-housing projects by such agencies.

---

[27] Statement of Warren Vinton (personal interview).

(b) The grant for any such project shall be paid in the form of fixed and uniform annual contributions, over a fixed period not exceeding sixty years. The Authority shall embody the provisions for such grant in a contract of grant guaranteeing such fixed and uniform annual contributions over such fixed period. Such annual contributions as are contracted for shall be strictly limited to the amounts and the period necessary, in the determination of the Authority, to assure the low-rent character of the housing project involved: *Provided,* That the fixed contribution payable annually under any such contract of grant shall not exceed a sum equal to one percentum plus the going federal rate of interest (at the time such contract of grant is made) upon the development or acquisition cost of such project.

(c) All payments of annual contributions pursuant to this section shall be made out of any funds available to the Authority when such payments are due, except that its capital and its funds obtained through the issuance of obligations pursuant to section 20 (including repayments or other realizations of the principal of loans made out of such capital and funds) shall not be available for payment of such annual contributions.

(d) In any one fiscal year the Authority shall not enter into contracts of grant which provide for annual contributions aggregating more than $10,000,000 per year exclusive of any annual contributions payable under contracts of grant made by it in prior fiscal years. The faith of the United States is solemnly pledged to the payment of all annual contributions contracted for pursuant to this section, and there is hereby authorized to be appropriated in each fiscal year, out of any money in the Treasury not otherwise appropriated, the amounts necessary to provide for such payments.

(e) The loans for any low-rent-housing project pursuant to this section shall bear interest at such rate not less than the going Federal rate at the time the loan is made, to be secured in such manner, and be repaid within such period, not exceeding sixty years, as may be deemed advisable by the Authority. The total of such loans outstanding for any such project shall not exceed the development or acquisition cost of such project, less the total amounts outstanding on loans made by third parties, senior to the loans of the Authority, and secured by such project or payable from the revenues thereof.

This draft of the bill was printed as Confidential Committee Print No. 1 and dated February 5, 1937. Wagner sent copies of this draft to the White House for the suggestions and recommendations of the president. The president handed over the copies of the bill to his administrative assistant, his son, Colonel James Roosevelt, and told him to send copies to John Fahey of the Home Owners Loan Corporation; to the secretary of the Department of the Treasury, Morgenthau; to Stewart McDonald of the Federal Housing Administration; to Frederic Delano of the National Resources Board; and to Secretary Ickes. Under date of February 9 James Roosevelt sent copies of the bill to these advisers, together with a memorandum in which he told them that the president would appreciate receiving their comments on this latest draft of Senator Wagner's bill. By February 12 James Roosevelt had received their comments. On this same day James Roosevelt sent to the president a copy of the bill, a copy of the memorandum he had sent to the advisers who had been named by the president, and the comments that the advisers had sent to him.[28]

On February 19 the president sent the folder of reports back to James Roosevelt, telling him to show them to Senator Wagner. The president mentioned that he did not think that the senator would want copies of the various reports, as they constituted "horseback opinions"; however, they would give him some idea of the first reaction to his housing bill. The president further suggested that the next step to be taken was an informal conference between himself and Senator Wagner and the five advisers asked to report on the bill, and anyone else whom Senator Wagner would like to have present.[29] James Roosevelt sent this information to Senator Wagner in a letter dated February 19.[30]

---

[28] White House office memoranda, Roosevelt Papers, O.F. 63.

[29] Quoted in full in memorandum of J. Roosevelt to McIntyre, February 19, 1937, Roosevelt Papers, O.F. 63.

[30] J. Roosevelt to Wagner, February 19, 1937, Roosevelt Papers, O.F. 63.

He also told Wagner to call McIntyre and arrange the time for the conference.[31]

While all this activity was going on in the White House office, Keyserling was busy at work on a second draft of the bill to be printed for a special committee meeting of representatives of the various housing groups. This second draft was printed on February 17 and was titled Confidential Committee Print No. 2. A few important changes were made in this second draft. The administration of the Authority was vested in a three-member board rather than in a five-member board (Section 3 (b)). Appointments to the new agency were to be made without regard to the civil-service laws and the Classification Act of 1923 (Section 4 (b)). Employees were not to be automatically transferred from the existing housing agencies to the new agency (Section 4 (d)). There was also included a new section (Section 27) which was a further clarification and explanation of the separability provisions of the Act.[32]

With the exception of the last addition, which was concerned with the separability provisions, these other changes were not new provisions. The sections on civil-service status and transfer of employees had been included in earlier drafts of S. 4424, and the change to a three-member board from a five-member board was an administrative proposal that had already been discussed at length by Keyserling, Vinton, Woodbury, and a number of their associates.

This special meeting for which Confidential Committee Print No. 2 had been printed had been planned in early February by Ernest J. Bohn. On February 10 Woodbury sent a telegram to Vinton asking him to send a list of names of representatives of housing groups that he thought should be invited to participate

---

[31] Memorandum of J. Roosevelt to McIntyre, February 19, 1937, Roosevelt Papers, O.F. 63.

[32] Confidential Committee Print No. 2, February 17, 1937 is preserved in the Vinton Papers.

in the proposed meeting. The letters of invitation were mailed on February 12. The list of those invited included representatives of all the housing groups and government agencies engaged in public-housing activities. The meeting was scheduled for two days, and was to be held in Washington. Ernest J. Bohn was again named chairman of the meeting and Warren Vinton was named secretary.[33]

Before the meeting was called to order on Thursday morning, February 18, Post, Keyserling, and Vinton talked with Wagner about strategy for the coming campaign. The important topics in this discussion concerned a definite effort to find specific means of reducing the rents in the projects and the abandonment of any guarantee of capital grants to the local authorities. It was also decided that it would be necessary to form a conference of representatives of all of the groups interested in public housing for the purpose of presenting a united front to the country and also for the purpose of consulting with the president. It was suggested that the conference be made up of some thirty-five members. There was also some talk at this meeting about working out a compromise with the representatives of FHA, so that this agency would push for the enactment of the bill. No agreement, however, was reached at this meeting on this last point.[34]

The special meeting to discuss the new draft of the housing bill was called to order on Thursday morning, February 18, by Ernest J. Bohn. Those present at the meeting, in addition to Bohn and Vinton, were Mrs. Edith Elmer Wood; Bleecker Marquette, of the Cincinnati Housing League; C. F. Palmer, manager of Techwood Homes, a PWA housing project in Atlanta; Herbert Emmerich, of the Farm Credit Administra-

---

[33] Office memoranda, February 1937, National Association of Housing Officials, Housing Bill—1937.

[34] Notes on Housing Bill, February 18, 1937, Vinton Papers, Housing Bill—1937.

tion; John Ihlder, of the Alley Dwelling Authority; George Gove, of the New York State Housing Board; Major John O. Walker, of the Resettlement Administration; Don Price, representing Frederic A. Delano; H. A. Gray, of the PWA Housing Division; Catherine Bauer; Coleman Woodbury; Langdon Post; Ira Robbins; Helen Alfred; Charles Abrams, counsel for the New York City Housing Authority; Edward H. Foley, Jr.; Horatio Hackett, of the PWA; Dr. Will Alexander, of the Resettlement Administration; Monroe Oppenheimer, counsel for FSA and RA; Dorothy Schoell, secretary of the Housing Legislation Information Office; Walter Blucher, executive director of American Society of Planning Officials; and Leon Keyserling. Alfred Bettman of the American City Planning Institute was invited but could not attend. An invitation was also extended to Mrs. Simkhovitch, but she too found it impossible to attend the meeting.[35]

On the major points under discussion during these two days of meetings the group split into two blocs. The PWA representatives and some of their supporters in the NPHC, such as Helen Alfred, voted regularly for one type of program, while the remaining representatives joined together to support an opposite position. On the question of whether capital grants or annual contributions was the better plan to keep rents at a low level for the benefit of the people in the lowest income group, the PWA bloc was in favor of capital grants, while the other bloc favored the annual contribution plan as the better plan. The PWA group was opposed to the provision in the bill for demonstration projects, but the other group favored their inclusion in the program. The PWA group was in favor of civil-service status and the transfer of the employees in its housing division to the new agency; the other group opposed them on this question. The PWA group wanted a small appropriation written into the pro-

---

[35] *Ibid.*

visions of the bill, while the opposing bloc wanted a large appropriation written into the provisions of the bill.[36]

The administration of the Authority was a very delicate question, as it was known from the meeting held in 1936 that Ickes and his supporters would not compromise on this question. Helen Alfred brought up the question of placing the administration of the new agency under the jurisdiction of Secretary Ickes and the Department of the Interior. The group was hopelessly split on this question. Ickes had the advantage of strong support from the NPHC, but he was faced with just as strong opposition from the LHC.[37]

There was also some discussion of the definition of a family of low income. The question of setting up a mathematical ratio of five to one between income and rent was discussed but no decision was reached by the conference. At the close of the meeting Bohn made an effort to unite all of the representatives of the various groups to work wholeheartedly for the enactment of the bill at the present session of Congress.[38]

Keyserling was present at this meeting, and he and Vinton discussed the results of the two days of discussion. Keyserling did not think that any significant change should be made in Confidential Committee Print No. 2 of February 17, 1937 as a result of these discussions. A few changes in style were made and a few "provided" clauses were added to this draft, but that was the extent of the revision.

The same day that Keyserling and Vinton were discussing the results of the special meeting, James Roosevelt sent the reports of the president's housing advisers to Senator Wagner. McIntyre also attempted to talk with Wagner on the telephone about the date for a conference that the president thought was

[36] Notes on Housing Bill, February 18 and 19, 1937, Vinton Papers, Housing Bill—1937.

[37] Notes on Housing Bill, February 18, 1937, Vinton Papers, Housing Bill—1937.

[38] Notes on Housing Bill, February 19, 1937, Vinton Papers, Housing Bill—1937.

necessary.[39] Wagner, however, who was not feeling well at this time, had left Washington for a long week end of rest (this week end included Washington's birthday on Monday, February 22), so McIntyre was not able to make any arrangements. The president told his administrative assistant, James Roosevelt, that he wanted to have Wagner and the other administrative housing advisers discuss the new draft of the bill and work out a compromise to their disagreements. Wagner had had enough of these conferences. He knew that he could never work out a satisfactory compromise with certain of the advisers, especially the secretary of the Department of the Treasury, Morgenthau.[40]

Thus it was that Wagner, without any previous consultation with the president or with his group of advisers, decided to introduce his bill in the Senate. As has been stated, Keyserling did not consider any major changes necessary in the Confidential Committee Print No. 2 of February 17, so with a few minor changes in style Keyserling sent the draft of the 1937 housing bill to the printer. It was to be introduced on February 24. Midway in the proceedings of the Senate on February 24 Wagner was recognized by the president of the Senate and announced that he was introducing an important bill concerned with public housing. He requested, and his request was granted, that the text of the bill and a short explanation of the major provisions of the bill be printed in the *Record*. Wagner did not deliver a speech on his bill at this time. The bill was numbered S. 1685 and sent to the Committee on Education and Labor.[41]

In addition to the fact that Senator Wagner was introducing the bill before the administration was ready to introduce it, there were other circumstances present at this time that affected his introduction of the housing bill.

---

[39] Office memorandum, February 19, 1937, Roosevelt Papers, O.F. 63.
[40] Statements of Warren Vinton and Catherine Bauer (personal interviews).
[41] *Congressional Record*, February 24, 1937, pp. 1521-25.

President Roosevelt had sent his very controversial request for a reorganization of the federal judiciary to the Senate on February 5.[42] This attempt to change the setup of the Supreme Court brought out all the latent hostility in Congress against the president. Wagner, as the senatorial spokesman for the president, was in a very difficult position. He came under suspicion by his colleagues as an accomplice to this plot. Wagner did not come out definitely against the plan, and he did not give it his open approval. He was attempting to take a neutral position until he could see which way public opinion was turning. The press, however, in writing up the story of the president's plan to change the Supreme Court, made it appear that Wagner would support the plan. And unfortunately for Wagner, there were some reports that even mentioned Wagner as one of the men who would be appointed to the Supreme Court. It was stated that this would be the crowning achievement of Wagner's long career as a public official, since he was not eligible for the office of president because he was born in Germany.[43] All this talk and speculation put Senator Wagner in a position where his congressional colleagues would be disaffected toward him and would be disinclined to support any legislation that he happened to be sponsoring.

Wagner also got himself involved in another controversial issue just at the time that he introduced his housing bill. In a Lincoln Day address, delivered on February 12, 1937, Wagner spoke of the necessity of an antilynching bill.[44] He promised his constituents, many of whom were Negroes, that he would support such a bill in the Senate. At the same time that he introduced his housing bill, Wagner introduced in the Senate, together with Senator Van Nuys of Indiana, the antilynching

---

[42] *Ibid.*, February 5, 1937, pp. 877-79.
[43] *New York World-Telegram*, February 5, 6, and 12, 1937.
[44] *New York Times*, February 13, 1937.

bill that Representative Gavagan had introduced in the House.[45] This move incited the animosity of the southern Democrats against Wagner. So it was that at the time that he introduced his housing bill there was more personal animosity toward Wagner on the part of a large number of senators and others than there had been at any other time in his long career.

The president seemed to take no official notice of the introduction of the housing bill. He told his administrative assistant, James Roosevelt, on February 25 (the day after the bill was introduced) to phone Wagner and tell him that he was holding a conference on housing at the White House on Tuesday, March 2. Fahey, Morgenthau, McDonald, Delano, and Ickes were to be there, and Wagner was also to be present. The president wanted Wagner to know that he could bring along with him any expert advisers he desired to have present.[46] James Roosevelt delivered this message to Wagner's office, and the next day Minna Ruppert, Wagner's secretary, phoned to McIntyre's office to tell him that the senator would be present at the meeting on March 2, and that he was bringing along with him as advisers Coleman Woodbury, Catherine Bauer, and Leon Keyserling.[47]

On February 26, Roosevelt held a press conference during which he was asked a question about the housing bill by Richard Saunders, a free-lance Washington correspondent with NAHO as one of his clients. The president answered Saunders' question about the bill introduced the day before in the Senate by saying that he and his advisers were still conferring about the housing

---

[45] *Congressional Record*, February 25, 1937, p. 1585. This bill was not introduced with a speech of any kind. It was listed as S. 1709 and sent to the Committee on the Judiciary. It was the same bill that Representative Joseph A. Gavagan, of New York, introduced on January 5. It was numbered H. R. 1507, and sent to the Committee on the Judiciary (*ibid.*, January 5, 1937, p. 32).

[46] Memorandum of J. Roosevelt to McIntyre, February 25, 1937, Roosevelt Papers, O.F. 63.

[47] Memorandum of Roberta Barrows to McIntyre, February 26, 1937, Roosevelt Papers, O.F. 63. Barrows was private secretary to McIntyre.

bill. Saunders picked up the information that Ickes and Morgenthau were worried about certain provisions of the bill and that they were anxious to have the president get Wagner to make certain changes in the bill to make it more harmonious with their ideas.[48]

As Representative Steagall had manifested his interest in the housing bill by introducing Wagner's draft of S. 4424 on the opening day of the Seventy-fifth Congress, it was necessary for Wagner to ask him to sponsor the 1937 draft of the bill. Wagner and his housing advisers were not enthusiastic about Steagall's sponsorship of the bill; but as he was chairman of the committee that had jurisdiction of the bill, they hoped that he would be more favorably disposed toward the bill now that he had his name associated with it. When Keyserling had the final draft ready for the printer he sent a copy of the bill to Steagall, so that he might introduce it in the House the same day that Wagner introduced it in the Senate.[49] Wagner seemed to have more support for his bill in the House Committee on Banking and Currency at this session of Congress; but he had more opposition from two members of the president's official family, Secretary Morgenthau and Secretary Ickes.

Despite the extreme care that had been exercised in drafting every detail of the Wagner bill, S. 1685, these two Cabinet members were not satisfied with the provisions that affected the departments under their jurisdiction. Secretary Morgenthau did not approve of the financial plan that Vinton and Keyserling had labored over to make as sound and as effective as possible. Administrator Ickes of PWA did not approve of the provisions concerning the administration of the new agency and the transfer of the existing PWA Housing Division projects and per-

---

[48] Saunders to Woodbury, February 26, 1937, National Association of Housing Officials, Housing Bill—1937.

[49] *Congressional Record*, February 24, 1937, p. 1578. The bill was listed as H. R. 5033 and sent to the Committee on Banking and Currency.

sonnel. The fight that these two powerful figures in the New Deal made to amend these provisions of the bill is an interesting example of pressure politics within the executive departments of the government. It also demonstrates how opposition to a certain legislative proposal will force the supporters of that proposal to make revisions and compromises until it is satisfactory to all concerned. These pressures are an essential part of the democratic legislative process.

CHAPTER XI

Pressure Politics

Duning the battle for control of the public-housing program in 1936, the Department of the Treasury had made various objections to the financial provisions of the Wagner bill, and representatives of the department had attempted to gain control of the financial program of the housing bill. Peter Grimm, who served as Morgenthau's adviser, criticized the financial provisions of the bill in a report which he submitted to the president before his resignation.[1] The Department of the Treasury, however, judged that the housing bill would not be passed during the session in 1936, and consequently made no serious effort to amend the bill or substitute an alternative plan.

But at the opening of the Seventy-fifth Congress in 1937 the Department of the Treasury, as well as everyone else interested in the housing problem, knew that some kind of a housing bill would be enacted during that session. This certainty that some kind of housing bill would be passed made it necessary for the Department of the Treasury to have an alternate plan or amendments prepared and ready to present to the congressional committees or the White House at the critical juncture in the legislative process. Henry Morgenthau, as secretary of the Department of the Treasury, was interested in any bill that in-

---

[1] Grimm's report was summarized in Chap. 6, pp. 156-57.

volved expenditures of money from the United States Treasury. Morgenthau was also of the opinion that he should have something to say about any legislation that made provision for the expenditure of money. Morgenthau held to the economic theory that the money for appropriations should be gathered from tax money; he did not favor bond issues by government agencies, nor did he demonstrate any enthusiasm for a plan which committed the government to certain payments of money over a long period of years.[2]

Morgenthau found in the veteran housing expert John Ihlder a man with experience and prestige among the housing experts who would support his position. Ihlder was willing to work with the Department of the Treasury, and he drafted a housing bill for the department which placed under the jurisdiction of the secretary of the Department of the Treasury the administration of all the financial provisions of the bill. This draft of Ihlder's was circulated among a select group of housing experts in January of 1937. The section of the bill concerned with the financial provisions was the only one drafted in detail; the remaining sections of the bill were outlined along the lines of the Wagner bill.[3] Such a bill was adequate, however, for the purposes foreseen by Morgenthau. It would be presented to a congressional committee, such as the House Committee on Banking and Currency, to be used as the basis of a bill that the committee would draft in the event of a deadlock on the Wagner bill.

The president asked Morgenthau for his comments on the first draft of the Wagner bill (Confidential Committee Print

---

[2] Morgenthau's economic theory is deduced from his statements made during the various housing conferences held during 1937. These statements are outlined in the pages of this chapter. The *New York Post* in an editorial on March 8, 1937 stated that Morgenthau's economic theory came from "reactionary" advisers like Dr. Sprague. Whether or not this charge is justified is beyond the scope of this study.

[3] A copy of this draft is preserved in the Vinton Papers.

No. 1, February 5, 1937).[4] Morgenthau's comments on this bill were the same as those he made during the White House conference on the housing bill convened on March 2 after the introduction of the bill by Senator Wagner. This conference was called by the president in the hope that the members of his official family interested in housing could reach some kind of unity and agreement on a housing policy to be adopted by the Federal Government. After a short talk to the group of advisers summoned to the meeting, the president sent them to the Cabinet room with the order to iron out their differences and present him with a housing bill that all would support. Present at this meeting in the Cabinet room were Secretary Morgenthau, Secretary Ickes, John Fahey, Frederic Delano, Stewart McDonald, and Senator Wagner. Each of the advisers was free to bring with him a technical adviser on housing. Wagner brought with him Catherine Bauer, Coleman Woodbury, and Leon Keyserling. Morgenthau's principal adviser was Daniel Bell, acting director of the budget.[5] There were other technical experts there, but they did not play an important part in the proceedings of the two-hour meeting that day. When the meeting was adjourned there was still no unity among the advisers of the president; in fact, there was even greater dissension among the group when they left the Cabinet room than when they had convened earlier that day.

Leon Keyserling, who did most of the talking for Senator Wagner at this meeting, and Morgenthau and Bell had a long discussion over the financial provisions of the bill. Morgenthau favored taxation rather than a bond issue as a means of raising the money necessary for the program. Morgenthau also favored

---

[4] J. Roosevelt to Wagner, February 19, 1937, Roosevelt Papers, O.F. 63.

[5] *New York Times*, March 3, 1937. Warren Vinton was given a detailed summary of what occurred during this meeting by Coleman Woodbury. Vinton wrote this summary in his Notes on Housing Bill, White House Conference, March 2, 1937 (Vinton Papers, Housing Bill—1937).

an outright capital grant rather than a plan of fixed annual contributions to local housing authorities as an aid to keep rents at
a level low enough for the workers in the lowest income group.
While Morgenthau was making these objections to the housing
bill, he protested to those present that he favored public-housing
legislation. In fact, Morgenthau said that he thought the government was spending too much money on roads in the public-
works program—money that could be spent for the construction
of housing units. Morgenthau then went on to advocate the establishment of a procurement department which would buy tremendous quantities of materials at wholesale prices. This
procurement department would then build the housing for the
local authorities. Morgenthau was definitely in favor of a housing program, but it was not the kind of program outlined in
Senator Wagner's bill. Morgenthau objected that such a program would cost the government too much money.[6]

Wagner had heard Morgenthau talk so much about the
money that the housing program would cost Morgenthau's department that he finally tried to inject a little humor into a
rather tense session by telling Morgenthau: "Henry, forget
about your money for a moment and try to understand the provisions of my bill."[7] But there was not enough humor in the
Cabinet room that afternoon to relieve the tension that built up
during the argument over the financial provisions of the bill.

Keyserling argued strongly against the objections brought
up by Morgenthau and Bell and in favor of the plan for fixed
annual contributions to the local authorities over a long period
of time for the purpose of keeping the rents at a low level.
Keyserling sincerely believed that this plan best achieved the
desired end. Annual contributions spread the cost of the pro-

---

[6] Notes on Housing Bill, White House Conference, March 2, 1937, Vinton Papers,
    Housing Bill—1937.
[7] Statement of Catherine Bauer (personal interview).

gram over a long period of time, thus lessening the burden on the taxpayer and making it possible to induce Congress to appropriate the necessary money. Keyserling, Bauer, and Woodbury argued for the political impossibility of persuading Congress, during that one session or any other session, to appropriate the millions of dollars necessary to operate an effective public-housing program. Morgenthau was asking for a political impossibility, they argued, when he wanted to pay for the whole program during one year with one appropriation from tax money. In addition to this point, Keyserling argued that the system of annual contributions gave the Federal Government a continuing control over the local program, thus insuring that the low-rent character of the projects would be preserved.

Morgenthau and Bell were equally sincere and vehement in their objection to the plan of annual contributions. Morgenthau's position was that capital grants are cheaper in the long run, that there is no bookkeeping cost, and that the initial appropriation is smaller than the aggregate appropriations made over the years under the annual contribution plan. And Morgenthau admitted that he was in favor of a smaller appropriation for housing than were Keyserling, Bauer, and the other advisers of Wagner. Morgenthau disagreed with these advisers of Wagner concerning the magnitude of the problem.[8]

The day after this conference Keyserling felt that he might have been too vehement in his argument with Morgenthau and Bell, so he wrote a letter to Morgenthau to explain his actions of the previous day. He hastened to assure the secretary that his vehemence came from his personal conviction of the merits of the plan. He asked Morgenthau to call on him at any time for further information about the bill and its provisions.[9] Although

---

[8] Notes on Housing Bill, White House Conference, March 2, 1937, Vinton Papers, Housing Bill—1937.
[9] Keyserling to Morgenthau, March 3, 1937, Wagner Papers, Chronological File.

Keyserling felt no animus toward Morgenthau as a result of this meeting, certain staff members of the Department of the Treasury angered both him and the other housing experts. This anger was the result of the false and misleading information about the financial provisions of the bill which was given to the press by staff members of the Department of the Treasury and published in an article in the *New York Times* on March 3, 1937. This article gave details of the special White House conference and then stated that the Department of the Treasury objected to the bill because it would cost the government one billion dollars plus the sum of all the money appropriated over the years for the annual contributions.[10]

It was the judgment of the people sympathetic to the housing bill that there was a deliberate confusion by staff members of the Department of the Treasury between a loan of money and a grant-of-aid, and this confusion was spread by the opponents of the bill. No mention was made in these press releases of the fact that the one billion dollars was money raised by a bond issue and that it was to be repaid with interest. But in all of the charges that were made by the housing experts at this time, no charge was made against Mr. Henry Morgenthau personally. Keyserling, Bauer, Helen Alfred, and the others claimed that the confusion was the work of staff members of the department.

This misinformation circulated in the papers and the consequent opposition to the housing bill was considered serious enough by Mr. Nathan Straus to justify a special trip to Washington. The object of this trip was to set up a meeting between Senator Wagner's staff and the staff of the Department of the Treasury. Straus was a friend of the president, of Wagner, and of Morgenthau, so he was the right man to make an effort to bring peace to the factions fighting over the housing bill. On the morning of March 5 he had a conference with Morgenthau

---

[10] Keyserling to Straus, March 6, 1937, Wagner Papers, S. 1685—1937.

and arranged for a meeting for that afternoon between Keyserling and the staff of the Department of the Treasury concerned
with the housing bill. Straus and Keyserling then had lunch
together and planned the strategy for the afternoon session.
William McReynolds, administrative assistant to Secretary Morgenthau, had the meeting arranged when Straus and Keyserling
returned to the Department of the Treasury that afternoon. The
discussions centered around the annual grants, loans, and appropriations. Straus sat by and let Keyserling do most of the talking. Keyserling explained in detail the provisions of Senator
Wagner's bill and answered questions about the technical matters of the bill. After the meeting was concluded both Straus
and Keyserling felt satisfied that they had made some progress
in reaching an agreement and a fuller understanding of the
financial provisions of the bill on the part of the staff members
of the Department of the Treasury.[11]

It was decided to have another meeting on Monday, March
8. The Department of the Treasury invited to this meeting
Captain Richard Reiss, a housing expert from England whom
the NPHC had brought to this country for a lecture tour to build
up interest and support for the housing bill. Keyserling heard
beforehand that Reiss had been invited, and he attempted to
discuss various aspects of the financial provisions of the bill
with him before the meeting with the staff of the Department of
the Treasury; but he was unable to locate Reiss before the meeting. The difficulty that Keyserling had foreseen occurred at the
meeting. Reiss, when asked by the staff of the Department of
the Treasury for his opinion of the financial provisions of the
bill, candidly told the group what he thought of these provisions, criticizing certain aspects of the system of annual
contributions. This was just the answer that the staff of the Department of the Treasury had anticipated that Reiss would

---

[11] Straus to Wagner, March 8, 1937, Wagner Papers, S. 1685—1937.

make. It could be used as a good argument by the opponents of the financial plan of the bill. Keyserling was consequently forced again to defend the financial plan of the bill, and he and Reiss were drawn into an argument.[12]

After this meeting there was an exchange of letters between Reiss and Keyserling, in which each one assured the other that his motive for saying what he did during the meeting was the hope of helping to draft and to pass a good, sound housing bill. Keyserling told Reiss that he was forced to argue with him on that occasion because there were present at the meeting men who would use Reiss's words as an argument against the bill; that if he had been able to talk with Reiss before the meeting, he would have told him that there would be present at the meeting men who were not sympathetic to the bill and who would not take Reiss's criticism as constructive, but rather would use it against the bill.[13]

The news of this incident spread throughout the ranks of the public-housing pressure groups. It soon threatened to cause dissension at a critical time for the passage of the bill. Finally Mrs. Simkhovitch wrote to Senator Wagner to tell him that the NPHC did not clear the written statement of Captain Reiss and his testimony before the Department of the Treasury with his office because it was given by Reiss as an individual housing expert and not as a representative of the NPHC. Mrs. Simkhovitch expressed concern in her letter because she had heard that

---

[12] Keyserling to Reiss, March 10, 1937, Wagner Papers, S. 1685—1937. Keyserling had learned from experience that experts from another country, although sincere, projected their localized experience without full appraisal of American conditions. Keyserling also found in discussion with Reiss that he favored the annual contribution system which Keyserling championed, and that the system had proved most successful in England. Reiss's comments at the meeting referred to technical details, but some of the Treasury staff were prone to exaggerate his criticism (statement of Leon Keyserling, personal interview).

[13] Keyserling to Reiss, March 10, 1937, Wagner Papers, S. 1685—1937.

Keyserling was disturbed by the incident. She wanted to assure Wagner that Captain Reiss had done much to help the cause of public housing in the United States.[14] In reply Wagner wrote to Mrs. Simkhovitch on April 5 to assure her that no harm had been done by the incident. This letter closed an episode which for a time threatened to cause a break in the ranks of the public-housing pressure groups.[15]

During the month of April there was very little activity in Washington with regard to the housing bill, and some of the leaders in the movement were worried about the delay. Finally in the middle of April two days of hearings were held before the Senate Committee on Education and Labor. During these hearings no representative of the Department of the Treasury appeared as a witness to advocate amendments to the bill.

On Saturday morning, May 1, Keyserling attended another meeting of the Department of the Treasury called by the staff of the department. The meeting was not a profitable one so far as Keyserling was concerned.[16] He found the staff no more sympathetic to the financial provisions of the bill at this time than they were at the meetings in March. The high hopes of understanding and agreement between the Wagner group and the staff of the Department of the Treasury that Straus had expressed after the March meeting proved to be ill-founded. The Department of the Treasury was now preparing to draft a bill that would supplant the Wagner bill; but representatives of Wagner's groups, the PWA Housing Division, and the Department of the Treasury continued to have meetings to discuss the housing bill. One important meeting was held at Morgenthau's home on a Sunday afternoon in May. At this meeting the PWA Housing Division representatives and Senator Wagner's representatives

---

[14] Simkhovitch to Wagner, March 30, 1937, Wagner Papers, S. 1685—1937.
[15] Wagner to Simkhovitch, April 5, 1937, Wagner Papers, S. 1685—1937.
[16] Keyserling to Alfred, May 5, 1937, Wagner Papers, S. 1685—1937.

attempted to demonstrate to Morgenthau that if he wanted a housing program, as he claimed he did, it would cost the government money. Morgenthau was still unconvinced, and the meeting ended in failure.[17]

Morgenthau then conferred with the president concerning the type of housing program and financial plan that he had discussed at the White House meeting on March 2. As a result Morgenthau received presidential permission to draft an appropriate bill and to invite a selected group of local housing officials to meetings at the Department of the Treasury to discuss it. Meanwhile Warren Vinton had heard that Morgenthau had secured the permission of the president to present a substitute bill to the local housing officials. Vinton, through mutual friends, arranged an interview with Mrs. Roosevelt. Mrs. Roosevelt was leaving for the South on the evening of May 23. Senator Barkley and a few other Democratic party officials were accompanying her on the trip. Vinton boarded the train at Washington and talked with Mrs. Roosevelt in her drawing room. During this meeting Vinton explained to Mrs. Roosevelt the need of a subsidy plan to reduce the rents to a level which the lowest income group could pay. Mrs. Roosevelt asked about the English plan of subsidies and Vinton explained this plan to her and answered her other questions on this subject. Mrs. Roosevelt then asked about the transfer of the existing government agencies engaged in public-housing programs. Vinton explained that the agencies engaged in public-housing programs would be transferred to the new Authority. The two such agencies were the Resettlement Administration and the PWA Housing Division. Vinton told her that the agencies engaged in making loans and insuring mortgages would remain outside the new Authority, these agencies being the FHA and the HOLC. When Mrs. Roosevelt brought up the question of construction of housing projects by a federal

---

[17] Statement of David Krooth (personal interview).

procurement department with great wholesale buying power, Vinton told her of the need for a decentralized program. This was an answer which Mrs. Roosevelt could appreciate. The next question that Mrs. Roosevelt brought up was concerned with the agencies handling the actual construction under the Wagner program. Vinton explained that the construction would be done by private construction companies under contract with an existing state or local housing authority. Mrs. Roosevelt manifested to Vinton a keen appreciation of the problems involved in a public-housing program and a good grasp of the program as he explained it to her. The first lady then promised that she would talk to Morgenthau about his bill and the difficulties connected with it. She also promised Vinton she would get him to lunch at the White House with the president. Vinton took dinner with Mrs. Roosevelt and Barkley and then left the train at Charlottes-ville, Virginia, to return to Washington.[18]

Vinton did not get an opportunity to talk with Mrs. Roosevelt to enlist her aid soon enough. On Monday morning, May 24, the Department of the Treasury began a three-day series of meetings with representatives of the local housing authorities for the purpose of discussing the new housing bill drafted by the Department of the Treasury. Representing the department at these meetings were William McReynolds, Daiger, Patterson, Ihlder, and members of the legal staff of the department. Invited and present as representatives of the local housing authorities were Bleecker Marquette of Cincinnati, Miles Frisbie of Schenectady, Charles Abrams of New York, John Carroll of Boston, Nathan Straus of New York, and Ernest J. Bohn of Cleveland. During the three-day period the staff of the Department of the Treasury explained to these officials the main features of its new

---

[18] Vinton wrote a report of this meeting immediately after his return to Washington. It is to be found in his personal Notes on Housing Bill, May 23, 1937 (Vinton Papers, Housing Bill—1937). Vinton added to his notes that Mrs. Roosevelt did talk with Morgenthau. But Vinton did not see the president.

bill. The bill provided that the Housing Division of PWA should become a permanent agency. The financial plan called for grants up to 60 per cent of the cost of the development of the project, but as a condition of such a grant the project would have to be exempted from all state and local taxes and the locality would have to acquire the land and construct and operate the project.

There was also provision for a loan of 40 per cent of the cost of the development, which loan was to be amortized over a period of sixty years at a rate of interest of not less than 3 per cent. It was explained to the group that the plan would operate in the following manner. Assuming that a project cost $1,000,000, the Federal Housing Agency could purchase 1,000 bonds of $1,000 each from the local housing authority. It could then make the 60-per-cent grant by canceling $10,000 of these bonds in each year of the sixty-year amortization period, in addition to canceling the current interest coupons from time to time on the remainder of $600,000 of bonds evidencing the proposed grant. The Federal Government could agree to make such annual cancellations only so long as the public-housing Authority would maintain the low-rent character of the project. There was to be no provision for cancellation of principal and interest on the actual 40-per-cent loan on the project, which would have to be repaid with interest.

The bill also provided that these federal projects could be built by a federal procurement department and sold or leased to local housing authorities. Congress would provide appropriations over a three-year period so there could be a definite program between the federal agency and the local authority. It was further prescribed that the local authority secure from the federal housing administration a guarantee for the loan of 40 per cent which the local authority might receive from the federal agency. There was also the question of the employment of relief labor by the federal procurement department in the construction of these projects.

The local housing officials at this meeting were not impressed with the new plan. Their objections were listed under five headings. (1) The 40-per-cent loan required too much private financing. (2) The plan called for too much tax exemption (contrary to many state constitutions) and failed to take into consideration the contributions given by the localities to the projects in the form of municipal services. (3) The requirement of relief labor and building by a procurement department would raise the cost of construction with a consequent raise in the rents that would have to be charged the tenants. (4) Rents would be too high in the projects because the necessity of private financing of 40 per cent of the cost would require sinking funds, reserves, second mortgages, and so forth. (5) The requirement of contributions from localities would necessitate amendments in state and local laws and would require several years.[19]

The housing officials informed the housing advisers of the Department of the Treasury that they could not accept the new plan. The housing officials invited to this meeting had been supporters of Senator Wagner from the very beginning, and it was ill-advised on the part of the staff of the Department of the Treasury to attempt the conversion of these officials to their new ideas. While the meeting was still in progress these housing officials alerted their local authorities to the danger of this new plan of the Department of the Treasury. Thus it was that, even before the meetings were concluded, thousands of telegrams were sent to the president and to senators and to representatives protesting against the amendments to the Wagner bill proposed by the Department of the Treasury.[20]

---

[19] Vinton was given a detailed report of this meeting by Bohn, which report Vinton wrote in his personal Notes on Housing Bill, Treasury Meetings, May 24, 1937 (Vinton Papers, Housing Bill—1937).

[20] Some of these telegrams were filed by the White House office (Roosevelt Papers, O.F. 63). A large number of the telegrams to Senator Wagner are filed in the Wagner Papers, S. 1685—1937.

William Hushings, secretary of the National Legislative Committee of the American Federation of Labor, presented to Senator Black, new chairman of Committee on Education and Labor since Walsh moved to chairmanship of Committee on Naval Affairs, a formal protest by the AFL to these amendments and to the delay in taking action on the Wagner bill. Senator Black presented this protest to the president. The thousands of telegrams and the personal protests made by the AFL and other powerful pressure groups brought quick action. On May 27, the day after the meetings were concluded, McReynolds told Frisbie that the plan of the Department of the Treasury had been abandoned. This, however, was an unofficial announcement.

On June 1 Wagner and Keyserling went to see Morgenthau and several of his advisers concerning the housing bill. In the course of the discussion of the proposed amendments by the Department of the Treasury, Morgenthau told Wagner that the plan he presented to the housing officials was the idea of the president. He also admitted that he had received advice from the PWA group in drafting the new plan.[21] On June 3 Wagner called a meeting of selected housing officials to discuss the events that had occurred during the past two weeks. Present in Wagner's office for this meeting were Alfred Stern of the Illinois State Housing Board, Carroll of Boston, Anthony Rathnaw of Detroit, Frisbie of Schenectady, Evans Clark of the NPHC, and Bohn of the NAHO. All those who were present assured Wagner that they would have nothing to do with the new plan. They told him of their opposition to placing the administration of the new Authority in the Department of the Interior. They urged Wagner to go to President Roosevelt and fight for his bill, and they further encouraged him to remain firm and to refuse to accept any compromise.[22]

---

[21] Notes on Housing Bill, June 1, 1937, Vinton Papers, Housing Bill—1937.
[22] Notes on Housing Bill, June 3, 1937, Vinton Papers, Housing Bill—1937.

Wagner was unexpectedly called to the White House for a luncheon meeting the next day. Catherine Bauer prepared a statement for him on the situation of the housing bill and the attitude of the pressure groups supporting it. Bauer, Woodbury, and Vinton waited in the senator's office for his return from the White House. After Wagner had returned and talked with Keyserling, Keyserling told the group that the president had agreed to accept a plan of annual contributions and he had specified that the sum for annual contributions would be $20,000,000 a year. The president had further authorized Wagner to tell Morgenthau that he had so decided. This information was immediately sent to Morgenthau at the Department of the Treasury. Three days later, on June 7, Morgenthau made a telephone call to Wagner to tell him that he had received word from the president that he (Morgenthau) had been replaced by Charles West in the position of special housing adviser to the president.[23]

This replacement of Morgenthau by Charles West as special housing adviser ended the attempts of the Department of the Treasury to gain control of the Federal Government's housing program. Wagner and the groups supporting him had won this battle, but the victory merely meant that another battle was in the offing. The appointment of Charles West, under-secretary of the Department of the Interior, was an ill omen to Wagner and his friends who were engaged in a struggle with Secretary Ickes for the control of the administration of the housing program. Much has already been said of the attempts of Ickes to retain control of the administration of the housing program, especially in the previous chapter, which described the attempts of the legal division of PWA to write the type of bill they wanted to administer. It is now necessary to examine in greater detail this struggle between Wagner and Ickes.

---

[23] Notes on Housing Bill, June 4, 1937, Vinton Papers, Housing Bill—1937.

Immediately after the introduction of the bill, the legal division of PWA made a careful analysis of the draft. As E. H. Foley, Jr., stated in the beginning of a memorandum to Keyserling: "These suggestions will supplement those which have already been previously called to your attention."[24] Following this was a list of the amendments desired by the PWA legal division. First, the demonstration projects should be eliminated from the provisions of the bill. Second, the powers of the United States Housing Authority should be vested in one person, and (pending the reorganization of the executive departments) the Authority should be placed in the Department of the Interior. Third, express provision should be made in the bill for the transfer of PWA housing projects and personnel to the new Authority. It was said above that these changes were *desired* by the legal division of the PWA; but it might have been more correct to say that these changes were declared by the legal division of PWA to be required by law. The memorandum was certainly not written in the style or form of a petition. This observation was true of the other memoranda sent from the PWA office.

There was no open clash between Wagner and Ickes, or between their advisers, at the White House conference on March 2. Ickes and his advisers were too shrewd to become involved in an open fight with Wagner or his advisers. The advice of the PWA legal division to Ickes was that he should appeal directly to the president or to the members of the Senate and House committees having jurisdiction over the bill if Wagner would not make the changes in the bill demanded by the PWA legal division. Ickes and his group allowed Wagner to go his way and gather all the support he could for his bill. Meanwhile Ickes and his advisers in the PWA, particularly Foley and Krooth, continued to work with various members of Congress in an effort

---

[24] Foley to Keyserling, February 26, 1937, PWA Housing Division, Housing Legislation—1937.

to gain support for their amendments to the bill. Ebert M. Burlew, administrative assistant to Ickes, wrote a letter in the name of the administrator to Daniel Bell, acting director of the budget, to ask him if the financial provisions of the Wagner housing bill fitted into the president's budget.[25] This was the procedure required by executive order before a federal agency could take a position on legislation or speak for the executive branch in the hearings before the Senate Committee on Education and Labor. Senator Black, chairman of the committee, had written to Ickes on March 5 to ask him to send to the committee his views on the Wagner bill, S. 1685. Ickes replied to this request with a long memorandum[26] in which he asked the committee to make the same amendments requested by Foley of Keyserling in the memorandum of February 26. All these changes were designed to place the administration of the Authority under the jurisdiction of Ickes, or to make it easy to carry out the program without legal problems such as would arise if the provision for demonstration projects was permitted to remain in the bill.

Representatives of the PWA Housing Division had appeared before the Senate Committee on Education and Labor in June of 1935 and in April of 1936 to testify on the merits of the Wagner public-housing bills. On both of these occasions certain of the members of the committee, in particular Senator Walsh, asked a number of questions which the PWA Housing Division representatives could not answer immediately. Hence it was that the PWA Housing Division and its legal staff made careful and elaborate preparations for the hearings in 1937. The PWA Housing Division wished to make as good an impression as possible, because they hoped to convince the senators that Mr. Ickes

---

[25] Burlew to Bell, March 15, 1937, PWA Housing Division, Housing Legislation—1937.
[26] Ickes to Black, March 16, 1937, PWA Housing Division, Housing Legislation—1937.

and the PWA staff should be given jurisdiction over the housing authority to be set up under the Wagner bill. Foley and Krooth of the legal staff and Gray of the Housing Division drafted detailed reports on all the activities of the PWA Housing Division.[27] They also prepared amendments to the Wagner bill bringing it into conformity with the type of program they sought. On March 20 Krooth, for Administrator Ickes, sent a memorandum to Keyserling concerning the latest amendments to the Wagner bill: "We thought you might find it helpful to have our latest draft of the changes we have previously suggested in the Wagner Housing Bill, S. 1685. Enclosed is a copy of the bill with riders and interlineations embodying drafts to these amendments."[28] Krooth also mentioned in this memorandum that he would like to discuss the proposed amendments with Keyserling before the committee hearings commenced. On April 9 Senator Black sent another request to Ickes asking for more information about the bill.[29] Black wanted Ickes to prepare a statement of the differences between S. 4424 of 1936 and S. 1685 of 1937, to be used by the committee during the hearings which would begin on April 14.

On the first day of the hearings Mr. Howard A. Gray, director of the Housing Division of PWA, represented Mr. Ickes and the PWA. He presented a very detailed statement on the housing problem in the United States and on the efforts and accomplishments of the PWA Housing Division to remedy it. He told the committee that the Wagner bill would continue these efforts and bring them to completion. The amendments which the PWA staff had prepared for the purpose of placing the administration of

---

[27] PWA interoffice memoranda for March 10, 20, 23, 1937, PWA Housing Division, Housing Legislation—1937.

[28] Krooth to Keyserling, March 20, 1937, PWA Housing Division, Housing Legislation—1937.

[29] Black to Ickes, April 9, 1937, PWA Housing Division, Housing Legislation—1937.

the new Authority under the jurisdiction of the Department of the Interior, together with amendments eliminating the demonstration projects and providing for the transfer of PWA housing projects and personnel to the new Authority, were submitted to the committee.[30] Gray also presented to the committee a number of charts, reports, graphs, and statistical tables. This material covered pages 19 to 75 of the printed hearings and gives the most complete history of the PWA Housing Division anywhere available.

When the hearings were completed the PWA legal division was convinced that Keyserling would not agree to eliminate from the bill the provisions for the demonstration projects. Foley and his associates in the legal division were sure that these projects, which involved direct construction by the Federal Government, would mean more test cases in the courts and, perhaps, an adverse court decision that might make the whole public-housing program unconstitutional. The legal division of the PWA was determined to eliminate this provision. Foley knew that Keyserling had great respect for the opinion of Jerome Frank, a lawyer working for one of the government agencies in the Department of the Interior, so Frank was briefed on the problem and asked to write a letter to Keyserling suggesting that he eliminate the provision for demonstration projects from the bill. Under date of April 19 Frank wrote this letter to Keyserling. Keyserling replied in a letter dated April 23 that he was happy to receive Frank's letter, but that under no circumstances could he eliminate the demonstration projects. Keyserling was sure that they were within the proper exercise of power of the Federal Government to promote the general welfare, health, and safety. Keyserling admitted that there was a risk involved, but he considered such a risk so essential to the commencement of a public-housing program in many areas that

---

[30] Testimony of Howard A. Gray; in *Hearings on S. 1685*, pp. 8-19.

it must be taken.[31] Further, Keyserling had by now been working hard and long to analyze the various provisions, and he did not like the custom of calling in people who were busy with other things just because of their general prestige.

Between April 15, when the Senate committee hearings were adjourned subject to the call of the chairman, and May 11, when the Senate committee held one more day of public hearings on the Wagner bill, there was very little activity "on the Hill" with regard to the housing bill. This was the period during which the public "housers" began to worry about the prospects of getting the bill passed at that session of Congress. The officers of NAHO feared that the bill would get caught in the legislative log-jam at the end of this session as it had in the previous session. Ernest J. Bohn and Woodbury of NAHO, Catherine Bauer of LHC, and Langdon Post of New York tried to get some action out of the Congress.[32]

On May 12 the legal division of the PWA met with Keyserling for a conference on the revision of the financial sections of the bill in the light of the testimony given during the hearings concluded the day before.[33] The result of this conference was a new version of the financial provisions of the bill.

> Sec. 9 (a) The Authority may make loans to public-housing agencies to assist the development, acquisition, or administration of low-rent-housing or slum clearance projects by such agencies. The total of such loans outstanding on any one project shall not exceed the development or acquisition cost of such project, less the total amounts outstanding on loans made by third parties, senior to or

---

31 Keyserling to Frank (copy), April 23, 1937, PWA Housing Division, Housing Legislation—1937.

32 These public-housing experts were attempting to convince Representative Steagall that he should hold hearings on the bill before his House Committee on Banking and Currency. Post wrote to the president to urge him to get some action (Post to Roosevelt, May 8, 1937, Roosevelt Papers, O.F. 63).

33 Memorandum of meeting at Senator Walsh's office, May 12, 1937, PWA Housing Division, Housing Legislation—1937.

of equal rank with the loans of the Authority, and secured by such project or payable from the revenues thereof. Such loans shall bear interest at such rate not less than the going Federal rate at the time the loan is made, be secured in such manner, and be repaid within such period not exceeding sixty years, as may be deemed advisable by the Authority.

(b) The Authority may make loans to limited-profit housing agencies to assist the development, acquisition, or administration of low-rent-housing projects by such agencies: *Provided:* That not more than $25,000,000 shall be loaned in any one fiscal year. The total of such loans outstanding on any one project shall not exceed 85 per centum of the development or acquisition cost of such project, less the total amounts outstanding on loans made by third parties, senior to or of equal rank with the loans of the Authority, and secured by such project or payable from the revenues thereof. Such loans shall bear interest at such rate not less than the going Federal rate at the time the loan is made, be secured in such manner, and be repaid within such period not exceeding 60 years, as may be deemed advisable by the Authority.

Sec. 10 (a) The Authority may make grants to public housing agencies to assist in achieving and maintaining the low rent character of their housing projects. The grant for any such project shall be paid in the form of fixed and uniform annual contributions, over a fixed period not exceeding 60 years. The Authority shall embody the provisions for such grant in a contract of grant guaranteeing such fixed and uniform annual contributions over such fixed period.

(b) Annual contributions shall be strictly limited to the amounts and the periods necessary, in the determination of the Authority, to assure the low-rent character of the housing project involved. Toward this end the Authority may prescribe regulations fixing the maximum contributions available under different circumstances, giving consideration to cost, location, size, rent-paying ability of prospective tenants and periods of assistance needed to achieve and maintain low rentals. Such regulations may provide for rates of contribution based upon development, acquisition or administration cost, number of dwelling units, number of persons housed, or other appropriate factors: *Provided:* That the fixed contribution payable annually under any contract of grant shall in no case exceed a sum equal to the annual yield at the going Federal rate of interest (at the time such contract of grant is made) plus one per centum upon the development or acquisition cost of the low-rent-housing project involved.

(c) All payments of annual contributions pursuant to this section shall be made out of any funds available to the Authority when such payments are due, except that its capital and its funds obtained through the issuance of obligations pursuant to section 20 (including repayments or other realizations of the principal of loans made out of such capital and funds) shall not be available for the payment of such annual contributions.

(d) The Authority is authorized on or after the date of the enactment of this act to enter into contracts of grants which provide for annual contributions aggregating not more than $6,000,000 per annum, on or after July 1, 1938, to enter into additional such contracts which provide for annual contributions aggregating not more than $7,500,000 per annum, and on or after July 1, 1939 to enter into additional such contracts which provide for annual contributions aggregating not more than $7,500,000 per annum. Without further authorization from Congress, no new contracts of grant beyond those herein authorized shall be entered into by the Authority. The faith of the United States is solemnly pledged to the payment of all annual contributions contracted for pursuant to this section, and there is hereby authorized to be appropriated in each fiscal year, out of any money in the Treasury not otherwise appropriated, the amounts necessary to provide for such payments.[34]

The above revision, which Keyserling checked with Vinton after the PWA meeting, divided into two sections the material that was before included in a single section. The more detailed and precise provisions regarding loans were put in one section, Section 9 (a) and (b). The revised provisions for the annual contributions were put in a separate section, Section 10 (a), (b), (c), and (d) in the new drafts of the bill. Between May 11 and June 8, when Confidential Committee Print No. 1 of the bill was printed, two other preliminary drafts of the bill were prepared by Keyserling and Vinton. The only other major

---

[34] Confidential Committee Print No. 1, June 8, 1937, *S. 1685*. A copy of this print is preserved in the Vinton Papers.

change in these new drafts concerned the administration of the Authority, which was maintained as an independent agency administered by a single administrator appointed by the president and a board of four members who would determine policy. The administrator in this new plan would be charged with the management and routine business of the Authority. One other change, providing for appointment to the Authority subject to civil-service laws and the Classification Act of 1923, was also made in these prints.[35]

After the completion of the hearings before the Senate committee, May 11, 1937, Ickes took occasion to send a letter to the president in which he offered for the consideration of the president "some suggestions regarding the administrative agency to be employed in carrying on any low-cost housing program that may be authorized at this session of Congress."[36] The suggestion was the same one that Ickes had made to the president so often in both written memoranda and in personal conferences: the new agency should be placed in the Department of the Interior under the supervision of Secretary Ickes. Ickes based his appeal on the need for unification of agencies charged with the same type of program. Ickes sent the same type of memorandum to the chairmen of the Senate and House committees having jurisdiction over the housing bill.

About this same time, on May 15, 1937, Ickes received the public support of the NPHC for his proposal that the new agency be located in the Department of the Interior. *Public Housing Progress*, published by the NPHC, carried a lead article in the issue of May 15 which advocated that the agency should be placed under the jurisdiction of Secretary Ickes. To those outside the NPHC it appeared that this was the official position

---

[35] These drafts of the bill were made on May 11, May 21, and June 7, and are preserved in the Vinton Papers.

[36] Ickes to Roosevelt, May 17, 1937, PWA Housing Division, Housing Legislation—1937.

of the organization on this very controversial issue; but there was only a small group within the NPHC, led by Helen Alfred and Mrs. Mary Simkhovitch, which controlled the publication of *Public Housing Progress,* and it was this group which supported Ickes in the battle. Another group, made up for the most part of men actually engaged in housing activities, such as Ira Robbins, definitely opposed any such amendment to the Wagner bill. This group was angry and disturbed by Helen Alfred's commitment of the NPHC by her article. Its members protested to the members of the other organizations interested in the housing bill that they did not share the views of Miss Alfred.[37] The organization was split with dissension over this issue. Whether Secretary Ickes asked Miss Alfred to publish this statement is not known. It is likely that Miss Alfred acted on her own initiative; her support of Ickes was constant and active.

Secretary Ickes, however, did make an attempt to silence his opposition. He made a personal call to President William Green of the American Federation of Labor to ask him to call Miss Catherine Bauer "off the Hill."[38] If Green had followed Ickes' suggestion—which he refused to do—the secretary would have destroyed one of the chief obstacles to his plan to gain control of the housing program. The Labor Housing Conference, under the direction of Catherine Bauer and Boris Shishkin, was the strongest advocate of an independent agency to administer the new housing program.

Senator Wagner called a meeting in his office for June 8 to which he invited Frisbie, Bohn, and Vinton as representatives of the groups supporting his bill, and Foley, Gray, and Krooth as representatives of the PWA staff who were seeking amendments. Charles West, the newly appointed housing adviser to the president, was also invited to the meeting. Confidential Com-

---

[37] Statement of Ira Robbins (personal interview).
[38] Statement of Catherine Bauer (personal letter).

mittee Print No. 1, June 8, 1937, had been prepared for this meeting. An attempt was made to come to an agreement on as many provisions of the housing bill as possible because the Senate committee was ready to go into executive session to amend it and report it out to the Senate. On two of the key provisions of the bill Wagner could not obtain the unqualified support of the PWA group. First, the PWA group stated that they were unable, on behalf of the executive branch, to give an unqualified endorsement to the plan for annual contributions, even though Krooth had worked with Keyserling in the drafting of the new version which was incorporated in the committee print under discussion. Second, the PWA group would not consider any compromise on the administrative provisions of the bill. When the meeting was completed it was evident to Wagner's group that Charles West, the president's housing adviser and also under-secretary of the interior, would give his support to the PWA group.[39]

After this meeting Wagner arranged a conference with the president at the White House. The subject of this conference was the financial provisions of the bill. The president was still in favor of a capital grant, the type that Morgenthau had always advocated, so Wagner agreed to incorporate a provision for capital grants as an alternate system of aid. The bill was revised by Keyserling and Vinton on June 18 so as to incorporate this alternate method of aid, which became Section 11 of the bill. This draft was printed on June 21 and was titled Confidential Committee Print No. 2. When the draft returned from the printer on that day, Keyserling and Vinton decided to revise this new section on capital grants. After a revision was agreed upon, the bill was again sent to the printer and returned the next day as Confidential Committee Print No. 3, June 22, 1937. This draft was given to the members of the Senate Committee on Education

---

[39] Notes on Housing Bill, June 8, 1937, Vinton Papers, Housing Bill—1937.

and Labor on June 25, 1937, to be used in their executive sessions on the bill. Keyserling worked closely with Senator Black at this time. After discovering that the committee members were going to demand still further changes in the bill, Keyserling made another draft of the bill limiting annual contributions to a twenty-year period and adding provision in one section of the bill (Section 14 concerned with standards) for slum clearance, which revision was an attempt to satisfy Senator Walsh. He sent the bill to the printer and it was returned as Confidential Committee Print No. 4, June 30, 1937. This was the print that was officially considered by the committee and used as a basis for the bill as reported to the Senate with amendments.[40]

During this phase of the legislative process it appeared that Wagner's group would win this long battle. First of all, Keyserling was used as a special adviser by Senator Black, chairman of the committee, and it was Keyserling who wrote up the report that accompanied the bill.[41] The provision for demonstration projects remained in the bill. Also the committee voted unanimously to create an independent agency to administer the new housing program. Senator Walsh, former chairman of the committee and still a powerful and respected member, was insistent that the agency be independent of any control by Ickes or the PWA Housing Division group. Thus it appeared when the bill was reported to the Senate on July 24 that Wagner and his pressure groups had won.

Between July 24 and August 3, however, Secretary Ickes and his advisers were busy building up support for their amendments. Ickes' plan was to convince the president of the necessity of his amendments, and then get some of his friends and sup-

---

[40] The information contained in this paragraph is taken from the notes which Warren Vinton wrote on the front page of the various drafts of the bill. This extreme care and attention to every detail makes the Vinton Papers a valuable and reliable source of material.

[41] Statement of Leon Keyserling (personal interview).

porters in the Senate to present his amendments from the floor during the debate. While Ickes was busy working out his strategy, Nathan Straus came down to Washington and discovered that Ickes had already gotten his amendment accepted by the White House advisers to the president. Straus then made a visit to the White House in hopes of seeing the president and convincing him that the amendment was ill-advised. The president was not available, so Straus wrote the president a memorandum, on White House stationery, telling him that he should study the amendment and its effect on the housing movement thoroughly. He also mentioned that Wagner had shown signs of weakening under the pressure of certain unnamed people who sought to have him accept the amendment.[42]

The people putting the pressure on Senator Wagner were Charles West of the Department of the Interior, White House aides such as Tommy Corcoran, and public housers such as Mrs. Mary Simkhovitch. Wagner called the White House on August 4 and talked with McIntyre. He told him that he had received from Charles West a proposed amendment to the housing bill which in effect made the Authority a subordinate branch of the Department of the Interior. Wagner told McIntyre that he thought that Tommy Corcoran drew up the amendment, and he wanted to make sure that the president was thoroughly familiar with it. If the president, realizing the far-reaching effects it would have on the bill, approved it, Wagner stated that he would accept it, although personally he disapproved of it entirely. Wagner also warned McIntyre that he was fearful of the result of trying to put it in. McIntyre concluded a memorandum to the president on this subject with the note that Senator Wagner wanted to talk with him on the telephone as soon as he came in.[43]

---

[42] Straus to Roosevelt, August 3, 1937, Roosevelt Papers, O.F. 63.
[43] McIntyre to Roosevelt, August 4, 1937, Roosevelt Papers, O.F. 63.

The president called Wagner on the telephone and talked with him about the proposed amendment. There is no record of this conversation,[44] but from subsequent events in the Senate it appeared that the president told Wagner that it would not be necessary for him personally to back the amendment. Wagner could let the debate go on, and see which way the vote was going to go. Then he could vote against the proposed amendment to keep the support of the groups which opposed the amendment. That afternoon, August 4, Roosevelt had a conference with Senator Barkley concerning the strategy to be used during the debate on the reorganization of the Supreme Court and the housing bill, the two controversial issues then being debated in the Senate.

Meanwhile Ickes was busy building up support for his amendment among the leaders in the public-housing movement. The most important group that Ickes wished to bring over to his side was the American Federation of Labor, so Ickes made a personal appeal to President William Green of the AFL. Ickes told Green that the amendment was necessary, and that the president was in favor of the amendment. When Green understood that the president wanted the amendment he decided to support it.[45] Thus it was that Ickes gained the support of the most powerful group in the public-housing movement.

On August 4, before the amendment concerning the administration of the new Authority was debated, Ickes won another battle in his fight for the type of housing program he wanted. Senator King of Utah proposed an amendment that the demonstration projects be eliminated from the provisions of the bill. In support of his position he quoted a statement from Secretary Ickes which was printed in the *Record*. There was no debate on

---

[44] Roosevelt penciled the notation "handled over the telephone" on the memorandum (August 4, 1937) given him by McIntyre and returned it to "Mac."

[45] Ickes to Green, August 9, 1937, and Green to Ickes, August 13, 1937, American Federation of Labor, National Legislative Committee, Housing Bill—1937.

this amendment, and it was agreed to without opposition.[46] Thus it was that with one quick move at the critical moment in the debate Ickes defeated Senator Wagner and a group of the public housers on this controversial issue. It should be said that those public housers who believed in a locally administered housing program were never for "demonstration projects," but accepted them for the sake of unity, and unity among all public-housing groups was most important at this time.

It was on August 5 that Senator Marvel M. Logan of Kentucky, who had been chosen by Ickes and the administration to present the amendment, was recognized in the course of the debate on the housing bill. He presented his brief amendment: "In the committee amendment on page 38, line 7 [Section 3 (a)], after the word 'created,' it is proposed to insert a comma and the following words: in the Department of the Interior and under the general supervision of the Secretary thereof."[47] The amended section then would read: "There is hereby created, in the Department of the Interior and under the general supervision of the Secretary thereof, a body corporate of perpetual duration to be known as the United States Housing Authority, which shall be an agency and instrumentality of the United States."

This amendment touched off a rather heated debate that concerned not only the relative merits of an independent agency and an agency subordinate to an existing agency, but also the personal record of Mr. Ickes as the administrator of the PWA Housing Division. First a technical difficulty was raised by Senator Burke of Nebraska. He contended that it might be necessary to make changes throughout the entire bill where the question of administration was discussed. Senator Logan replied:

> It would be possible that there are some places in the bill that would have to be changed, but I say to the Senator from Nebraska

---

[46] *Congressional Record*, August 4, 1937, p. 8179.
[47] *Ibid.*, August 5, 1937, p. 8282.

that I discussed this matter with some persons from the Interior Department, and I was advised that it would not be necessary to make other changes in the bill at the present time.[48]

Senator Tydings entered the debate when it was argued by Logan in support of the amendment that there should be a unification of the housing activities of the Federal Government and that, as the PWA Housing Division had already been charged with the operation of public housing, it should rightly be allowed to continue and perfect its work under the new bill. Tydings was of the opinion that all the housing activities of the Federal Government should be coordinated under the Federal Housing Administration.[49]

Senator Clark of Missouri objected to the logic of Senator Logan's argument. He was opposed to the amendment, he said; and his statement in explanation of his position brought out the fact that in this whole discussion there was question, not only of a department, but also of a personality.

> Technically there is no connection on earth between the Interior Department and the Public Works Administration. It seems to me that what the Senator is doing now is to take advantage of the dual operation of Secretary Ickes, and undertaking to put into the Interior Department something that never has been there.[50]

Senator O'Mahoney entered the debate in favor of the Logan amendment and argued that reorganization demanded that the Congress refrain from creating new independent agencies. Senator Barkley made a short speech in favor of the amendment. Senator Walsh was opposed to the amendment, and in his argument against the amendment he cited the ineffective job that had been done by Administrator Ickes' PWA Housing Division. Walsh also mentioned the fact that there was a unanimous vote in the Senate committee against such an amendment.[51]

---

48 *Ibid.*
49 *Ibid.*, p. 8285.

50 *Ibid.*, p. 8284.
51 *Ibid.*, p. 8286.

As the time for an adjournment drew near, Wagner entered the debate to say that the amendment came before the Senate as something new and unexpected. He suggested that there should be some delay before taking a vote on the question. Senator Barkley then took the floor and said that he was about to move for a recess until the next day as Senator Wagner rose to speak. He then told the senators that the debate of the previous days on the housing bill and the reorganization of the judiciary had slowed up the legislative schedule. Unless some action was taken quickly on the housing bill, it would be necessary to have night sessions in order to complete the legislative program before final adjournment.[52]

When the Senate reconvened the next morning after the recess, there was some further discussion on the merits of the Logan amendment, and it was then put to a vote. The yeas and the nays were asked for and were so ordered. By the small margin of three votes the Logan amendment was passed 40 to 37, with eighteen members not voting.[53]

Ickes had won his battle in the Senate. He now turned his attention to winning support in the House. At this time the House Committee on Banking and Currency was holding hearings on the housing bill. Ickes himself appeared before Steagall's committee and asked that the committee adopt the amendment placing the agency under the jurisdiction of the Department of the Interior.[54] Representative Beiter of New York also appeared before the committee and asked that the House committee adopt the same amendment which he was told the Senate had just adopted. Beiter was answered vigorously by Representative Frank W. Hancock, who declared that Beiter appeared to be advocating this amendment because of a personal friendship

---

[52] *Ibid.*, p. 8288.
[53] *Ibid.*, August 6, 1937, p. 8357.
[54] Testimony of Harold Ickes; in *House Hearings on H. R. 5033 and S. 1685*, p. 154.

with Ickes rather than because of the intrinsic merits that the amendment itself possessed.[55]

While the House committee was in executive session Ickes sent a letter to Steagall and to the other members of the committee asking them to adopt the Logan amendment, together with certain other amendments that he thought necessary for a successful housing program.[56] Ickes' suggestion was accepted by Steagall. In addition to accepting the amendments offered by Ickes, Steagall asked Ickes to send him one of his staff to help him prepare the report to accompany the bill. Ickes sent David Krooth to the House committee, and Krooth together with the clerk of the committee prepared the report. Krooth also was Steagall's adviser when the House managers met with the Senate managers in a conference committee.[57] Ickes was the winner in this battle. When the final operations of the legislative process were being worked out, Ickes was definitely in control of the housing policy.

There were a few die-hards among the public-housing pressure groups who wanted to have the whole bill thrown out because Ickes had gained control of the policy; but it was the opinion of Woodbury, Bohn, Vinton, and the other leaders of the movement that it would be better to accept the administration of Ickes and fight for a good financial plan to carry out the program rather than to give up entirely on the bill. This was the advice that prevailed.[58]

An interesting conclusion to this story is the fact that after Ickes had worked so hard to get the Authority placed in the Department of the Interior, he was not successful in convincing the president that he should appoint the man he wanted to be

---

[55] Testimony of Representative Alfred F. Beiter; in *ibid.*, p. 263.
[56] Ickes to Steagall, August 10, 1937, PWA Housing Division, Housing Legislation—1937.
[57] Statement of David Krooth (personal interview).
[58] Statements of Ernest J. Bohn and Warren Vinton (personal interviews).

administrator. After much strife among the leaders of the various public-housing pressure groups, it was decided that Senator Wagner should propose the name of Nathan Straus to the president to be appointed the first administrator of the United States Public Housing Authority. Roosevelt sided with Wagner on this appointment. Straus and Ickes could not get along with each other, so it worked out that Straus administered the Authority almost as if it were an independent agency. Ickes would have nothing to do with it after Straus took over as administrator.[59]

---

[59] Statements of Ernest J. Bohn and Warren Vinton (personal interviews).

CHAPTER XII

Pressure-Group Activity
and Senate Action

Appeals to all those interested in the public-housing bill were numerous as the time for Senate hearings drew near. The following is typical:

> Demand that your congressman support immediate initiation of further emergency projects by the Housing Division, that he pass adequate legislation as the basis for a long-range program of low rent housing. Swamp him with letters, telegrams, phone calls. *Remember: The wheel that squeaks the loudest gets the grease.*[1]

During the months that followed the introduction of the bill, the members of NPHC were constantly urging the Congress to take action on the housing bill. Helen Alfred and Mrs. Mary Simkhovitch made a number of visits to Washington to talk with congressmen and urge them to enact the Wagner bill. They were also active in the movement to have the new Authority placed in the Department of the Interior under the jurisdiction of Secretary Ickes.

The Labor Housing Conference worked within the organization of the various labor unions to make sure that the labor groups presented to Congress and the White House an intelligent, united, and powerful voice in favor of Senator Wagner's

---

[1] *Public Housing Progress* 3:1, February 15, 1937.

housing bill. Catherine Bauer and Boris Shishkin were almost daily "on the Hill" in an effort to convince various legislators of the necessity of the housing bill. Catherine Bauer was especially effective in convincing people of the necessity of a sound housing program. Secretary Ickes recognized her as such a powerful opponent to his plan for locating the administration of the new authority in the Department of the Interior that he asked President Green to silence her.[2]

The American Federation of Labor, under the direction of the National Legislative Committee, held periodical meetings with selected members of the Congress. At these meetings the federation explained to the members of Congress the necessity of certain legislative proposals. The Wagner housing bill was discussed at these meetings. At one of the meetings in the spring a senator from a rural area told the group that he was not interested in housing, since the benefits of the bill were restricted to a couple of the big cities. Frank statements such as this one enabled the leaders in the public-housing movement to prepare a defense against the objections to the bill.[3]

In addition to the difference of opinion concerning the administration of the new housing authority, there was another basic difference of opinion that split the NPHC and the LHC. This difference of opinion was concerned with the type of program that was to be carried out by the Authority. The NPHC favored a slum-clearance program, while the LHC wanted to place emphasis on the construction of new dwellings to relieve the housing shortage. These two groups were never able to reach a compromise on these questions. It was feared by some in the public-housing movement that this difference of opinion would hurt the chances of passage of the Wagner bill. Through the

---

[2] Statement of Catherine Bauer (personal letter). See also this study, Chap. 11, p. 301.

[3] Memorandum of Bohn, May 18, 1937, National Association of Housing Officials, Housing Bill—1937.

efforts of Ernest J. Bohn and because of the threat of a new
organization which would take over the control of the housing
movement, the LHC and the NPHC joined with the Housing
Legislation Information Office to share a common office and to
present a united front to the Congress and the White House. It
was not until May of 1937, however, that this harmony move
took place.

Meanwhile a new group of housing officials was organized
by Langdon Post. The movement for a new organization began
in December of 1936. At that time Post told Bohn that he was
interested in organizing a housing-officials group affiliated with
the United States Conference of Mayors, whose executive director was Paul Betters. Post was interested in utilizing the effective
organization of the conference of mayors in the interests of the
housing bill. Bohn, however, wished to keep the office independent of but utilizing the help of the conference of mayors, to
take steps to have it utilize the help of the conference, and to
have it serviced by all the groups interested in the public-housing
bill. Post wrote to Bohn again in January to sound him out on
the plan.[4] Post told Bohn that Catherine Bauer was interested in
the type of organization that he had planned. Bohn replied that
he was still of the opinion that the office should be set up independently. He realized that certain of the people in the housing
movement had been dissatisfied with the selection of the director
the year before; and so to forestall any break in the ranks of
those supporting the movement he admitted that his choice of
John Millar of Chicago, whose interest in public housing had
waned, was a poor one. Bohn was certain, however, that he and
the other housing advocates had learned a great deal from the
operation of the office the year before. He was now ready to
open an independent office under the direction of an efficient

---

[4] Post to Bohn, January 7, 1937, National Association of Housing Officials, Ernest
Bohn File—1937.

young woman who was entirely in sympathy with the public-housing movement and who would work closely with him and with the other leaders in the movement.

Miss Dorothy Schoell was chosen to be the director of the housing-legislation office. She was ready to start her work at the beginning of February. Bohn arranged for offices in the Duryea Building on Connecticut Avenue at L Street in Washington. He wrote to a number of leaders interested in the housing movement to ask them for contributions to defray the expenses of the office. Bohn then wrote to Wagner on February 5, 1937 saying that the Housing Legislation Information Office was open and ready to work for the enactment of his bill.[5]

Even after Bohn had opened the office Post continued to plan a new organization. What he first conceived as an information office grew in time to become an administrative and service organization. Post felt that the NAHO had never exerted enough pressure on the Congress in favor of housing legislation. NAHO replied to these charges:

> As you all know, NAHO is not and never has been a pressure agency to influence legislative policy. We are directly and deeply concerned with all the various phases of official housing administration from planning to rent collecting and from financial aid and direction to outright construction.[6]

Post thought that there was a place for an organization that would coordinate all the work of the local housing authorities and that would act as representative of the local housing authorities in their negotiations with the new federal Authority to be created under the Wagner bill.

Bohn, Vinton, Catherine Bauer, and the other housing experts wanted a united effort and a united front for the enactment

---

[5] Bohn to Wagner, February 5, 1937, Wagner Papers, S. 1685—1937.

[6] Statement of Coleman Woodbury, executive director, *National Association of Housing Officials, Bulletin No. 111*, May 3, 1937.

of the law. They judged that it was necessary to fight for the enactment of the law before they planned an organization that would operate after the law was enacted. This new Federation of Housing Authorities envisioned by Post acted as a catalyst in the establishment of a joint office by the major pressure groups pushing for the enactment of the Wagner bill. During the first week of May the Housing Legislation Information Office, the Labor Housing Conference, and the National Public Housing Conference opened a joint office in the Hay-Adams House.

Post went ahead with his plans, and on April 20, 1937 he called a meeting of representatives of the local and state housing authorities. The meeting was held in the offices of the Conference of Mayors at 730 Jackson Place, Washington. Post told the group that their first task was to work for the enactment of the Wagner bill, but that the organization, in addition to this emergency purpose, had a permanent position in the housing field. It would furnish a common medium through which state and local public-housing agencies might give effective expression to their views and purposes in the field of public housing. The organization would deal directly with the new federal Authority in the name of the state and local authorities. Any attempt to deal individually with the United States Housing Authority, he believed, would foredoom the program to failure. The organization was not intended to supplant the NAHO; rather it would supplement the work of this organization. The title of the new organization would be the American Federation of Housing Authorities. Officers of the organization were to be chosen as representatives of various housing authorities and not as individuals. Langdon Post was elected president and Miles Frisbie was elected secretary-treasurer. Four vice-presidents were to be elected, representing the Massachusetts State Board of Housing, the Memphis Housing Authority, the Chicago Housing Authority, and the District of Columbia Alley Dwelling Authority. Nine directors were also to be chosen as representatives of the housing authorities in New Jersey, Detroit, Syracuse, Schenectady, Cleveland, Cincinnati, Yonkers, and Boston.[7]

This organization worked effectively in putting pressure on the White House and the House Banking and Currency Committee during the critical period when it appeared that the Wagner bill would be crippled by excessive limitations. The AFHA, however, never operated as an administrative and service organization. Soon after the passage of the Wagner bill the organization broke up, and thus the only threat to the NAHO through the setting up of a duplicating organization came to an unsuccessful end.

The National Association of Housing Officials, as a service organization, took no part in the pressure politics of the housing campaign. Director Coleman Woodbury and President Ernest J. Bohn represented the organization and gave expert testimony to the congressional committees, but that was as far as the NAHO organization entered into the campaign.[8] Members of NAHO, however, acting in their capacity as individuals, played a very important part in the pressure politics of the housing campaign. Ernest J. Bohn wrote to Wagner to tell him that he was attempting to convince the Construction League of the United States that the housing bill was for the benefit of the construction industry and that opposition to the bill on their part was unwarranted.[9] The Construction League had opposed the bill in 1936. Bohn received a reply from Mr. Stanley Parker, newly elected president of the league. Parker told Bohn that he could not speak for the league, but that he personally was favorable to the bill and would speak for it at the meeting of the executive

[7] American Federation of Housing Authorities, Statement No. 27, August 21, 1937, American Federation of Housing Authorities, Washington.

[8] Coleman Woodbury regularly stated in the bulletin published by the National Association of Housing Officials that the organization took no official stand on pending legislation.

[9] Bohn to Wagner, February 13, 1937, Wagner Papers, S. 1685—1937.

board. Bohn forwarded this letter to Wagner under date of March 5, 1937.[10] Bohn was also kept busy on Capitol Hill. As a Republican he attempted to build up support for the bill among Republican members of Congress. Senator Vandenberg was one senator with whom Bohn was working closely. When it appeared that Vandenberg would oppose the bill because of the objections of the National Retail Lumber Dealers Association, Bohn sought to convince the senator from Michigan that the objections of the NRLDA were unjust. Bohn was successful in his work with the Republican members of the Senate, for at the final vote a majority of Republican senators voted in favor of the bill.[11]

Woodbury was working closely with Morton Bodfish of the United States Building and Loan League. As the USBLL was in favor of a housing bill which would be restricted to the lowest income group and would also include a slum-clearance program, Woodbury made an effort to reach certain compromises with Bodfish that would insure nonopposition to the bill on the part of the USBLL. Woodbury was also corresponding with Herbert U. Nelson, but he did not entertain any hope of being able to bring the NAREB around to a position of nonopposition to the bill.

Charles F. Palmer, director of the Techwood Homes in Atlanta, Georgia, attempted to convince the leadership of the Chamber of Commerce of the United States that public housing was a worth-while program. Mr. Sam Clabaugh, chairman of the Housing Committee of the Chamber of Commerce, and Mr. Harper Sibley, president of the Chamber of Commerce, visited the Techwood Project on March 4, 1937. Palmer attempted to show them how the advantages of this type of project could be given to all the people in the country. After the visit Palmer

---

[10] Bohn to Wagner, March 5, 1937, Wagner Papers, S. 1685—1937.
[11] Statement of Ernest J. Bohn (personal interview).

wrote to Bohn to tell him that the officials of the Chamber had been to Techwood and that he thought that they were favorably impressed.

In the middle of March, E. Stuart Fitzpatrick, secretary of the Construction and Civic Development Department Committee of the Chamber of Commerce of the United States, decided that the time had come to hold a strategy meeting. The date of the meeting was March 18, 1937, the time was six o'clock in the evening, and the place was the Carlton Hotel in Washington. Present at this meeting were A. P. Greensfelder and Charles Lewis of the Construction and Civic Development Department Committee; Robert L. Davison and John H. Zink of the Special Housing Committee of the Chamber of Commerce; and a group of representatives of interested organizations and government agencies which included Morton Bodfish, Warren Bishop, Wilson Compton, J. M. Daiger, Fred Feiker, Edward J. Harding, Willard I. Hamilton, V. G. Iden, Edward C. Kemper, Walter R. McCornack, M. J. McMillar, Lawrence Mehren, and Charles F. Palmer. The discussion at this meeting centered around the Bodfish amendments. Mr. Samuel F. Clabaugh, chairman of the meeting, was authorized to appoint a small steering committee to review the suggestions which had been brought forward with reference to possible amendments to the Wagner bill, to report back to interested groups, and to arrange for presentation of points of view of the interested organizations at the hearings on the bill.

The steering committee was made up of Morton Bodfish, Wilson Compton, Edward J. Harding, and E. Stuart Fitzpatrick. The result of the deliberations of this committee was the proposed amendments of March 24. These were circulated among the interested organizations.[12]

---

[12] Minutes of Special Meeting on Housing, Chamber of Commerce of the United States, E. Stuart Fitzpatrick Files.

The NAREB attempted on a number of occasions to visit Wagner and discuss with him the housing program. Herbert Nelson wrote to Wagner on March 1, 1937 to tell him that he would be in Washington during the week of March 8 to 13 and that he would like to visit the senator.[13] Minna Ruppert, Wagner's secretary, replied to Nelson that the senator was absent from Washington because of a bad cold and that he would not be in his office during that week. Miss Ruppert told Nelson that she would be glad to arrange a meeting at some later date. Nelson also made a number of attempts to see the president.[14] On March 26, 1937 he wrote to the president to ask him for an appointment for himself and Paul E. Stark, president of NAREB. Nelson mentioned that most of the activity about housing was fruitless, except for some features of the FHA program.[15] The White House office replied that it was not possible to give him an appointment because of the pressure of business. From notations on the letter of Nelson, however, it would appear that the appointment was refused because Wagner did not approve of the president's having a conference with these opponents of his bill.[16]

The NAREB and the various state and city real-estate boards wrote frequently to the senators and representatives to protest against the housing bill. Senator Tydings received a letter of protest from C. Philip Pitt, secretary of the Real Estate Board of Baltimore. This letter was forwarded to Senator Wagner.[17] Wagner studied the letter and sent a reply to Tydings in which he stated that he had taken the utmost care to provide proper safeguards for the housing program (the real-estate board was

---

[13] Nelson to Wagner, March 1, 1937, Wagner Papers, S. 1685—1937.
[14] Ruppert to Nelson, March 2, 1937, Wagner Papers, S. 1685—1937.
[15] Nelson to Roosevelt, March 26, 1937, Roosevelt Papers, O.F. 63.
[16] Penciled notation on letter of Nelson to Roosevelt, March 26, 1937, "Wagner said NO!" (Roosevelt Papers, O.F. 63).
[17] Tydings to Wagner, March 11, 1937, Wagner Papers, S. 1685—1937.

asking for a limitation of $1,000 a year income for tenants
in the public-housing projects), but he found it impossible
to determine upon a definite income stated in so many dollars because of the great differences existing throughout the
country.[18] Wagner also sent a letter to Pitt, and attempted to
explain to him the difficulty of attempting to write legislation
calling for a sliding scale of standards for different sections of
the country. This letter was the start of a continued correspondence between Pitt and Wagner's office on the provisions of the
housing bill.[19]

The National Retail Lumber Dealers Association of America, under the direction of Frank Carnahan, sent many letters
to the members of Congress and to the president urging them not
to permit a program of public housing that was in competition
with private building. Because of the extreme position which it
took, the NRLDA did not find many supporters among the members of Congress. The position of the USBLL, which was satisfied with restrictions on the program, found a more sympathetic
reception from many senators and congressmen.

After the White House meeting on March 2, 1937, Senator
Wagner quietly left Washington for a vacation and rest at the
Bermudiana Hotel on the Island of Bermuda. Wagner had been
suffering from a type of the flu, and it was necessary for him to
get a rest and build up his strength for the busy year that lay
ahead of him. While Wagner was absent there was very little
activity in Congress concerning the housing bill. Keyserling
wrote to him on March 6 to tell him that the office was in good
order. Keyserling also indicated that the question of the reorganization of the Supreme Court had overshadowed everything
else on Capitol Hill.[20] In another letter of March 10 Keyserling

---

[18] Wagner to Tydings, March 16, 1937, Wagner Papers, S. 1685—1937.
[19] There is a series of letters of Pitt and Wagner written during March and April
(Wagner Papers, S. 1685—1937).
[20] Keyserling to Wagner, March 6, 1937, Wagner Papers, Chronological File.

told Wagner about the conferences that he was having with the members of the Treasury Department. Keyserling urged Wagner to remain a few more days in Bermuda to get a complete rest because there was no business in Washington that required his personal attention.[21] Wagner took Keyserling's advice and stayed a few more days. He returned to Washington on March 22.

Senator Black, chairman of the Senate Committee on Education and Labor, was also ill for many days during this session of Congress. The illness of these two important legislators, the sponsor of the bill and the chairman of the committee with jurisdiction over the bill, delayed the hearings and consequent Senate action on the bill. The supporters of the bill grew anxious as the weeks and months passed without any action.

It was finally decided to proceed with the hearings on the Wagner bill even though Senator Black would not be able to preside. Keyserling conferred with Senator Black's staff, and with Vinton and Bauer and the other housing experts in Washington, about the strategy to be employed during the hearings. Because of the extended hearings held during the previous two years, it was decided to make the Senate hearings that year as brief as possible. A smaller group of witnesses, mostly people who could explain the technical aspects of the bill, would be selected. The witnesses who represented the various pressure groups would be called upon to testify at the House hearings. On April 8 and 9 Keyserling sent telegrams to the group chosen to testify. This group included Stewart McDonald of the FHA; Coleman Woodbury of the NAHO, who would explain the financial provisions of the bill; Mrs. Simkhovitch of the NPHC; William Green of the AFL; John Fahey of the HOLC; Frederic A. Delano of the National Resources Committee; Charles Palmer of the Techwood Homes Project in Atlanta; and Secretary Ickes. Other housing experts such as Bohn, Vinton, Bauer,

---

[21] Keyserling to Wagner, March 10, 1937, Wagner Papers, S. 1685—1937.

Helen Alfred, Straus, and Langdon Post would be present at the hearings, ready to testify if it were necessary.[22]

Keyserling heard that a caravan of tenants from the Lower East Side Housing Conference were planning to come to Washington for the Senate hearings. Such a group had attended the Senate hearings in 1935, but Keyserling did not want them present at the Senate hearings this year. He sent telegrams to Post and to Simon Rifkind, who was a law associate of Wagner in New York, asking them to convince Mrs. Rosenman that it would be better to have the caravan of tenants come to Washington for the House hearings.[23] Benjamin Marsh, of the People's Lobby, wrote to Keyserling to ask for an opportunity to testify.[24] Keyserling told him to apply at Senator Black's office. Florence Stewart, of the Alley Dwelling Authority, also wrote to Keyserling asking for an opportunity to appear before the committee. To this request he replied that he would put her name on the list of witnesses and that he would inform her later of the time for her testimony before the committee.[25]

When the hearings opened on Wednesday morning, April 14, Senator Walsh was acting as chairman of the committee. He stated to those present that he had been chosen for this position because he had conducted the hearings on two previous occasions.[26] The only significant feature of the two days of hearings was the absence of any opposition to the bill. The reason for this lack of opposition was not immediately evident. All interested groups had received notification of the hearings. But shortly after the hearings were adjourned, subject to the call of the chairman, Herbert U. Nelson wrote to Wagner to protest the

---

[22] Telegrams and letters of April 8 and 9, 1937, Wagner Papers, S. 1685—1937.
[23] Keyserling to Post, and Keyserling to Rifkind, April 9, 1937, Wagner Papers, S. 1685—1937.
[24] Keyserling to Marsh, March 10, 1937, Wagner Papers, S. 1685—1937.
[25] Keyserling to Stewart, March 10, 1937, Wagner Papers, S. 1685—1937.
[26] *Hearings on S. 1685*, p. 1.

fact that the NAREB had not been given an opportunity to present its case to the committee. Wagner replied that one more day of hearings would be held within a week or two, and he would see to it that the NAREB had notification.[27]

By May 11 Senator Black was sufficiently recovered from his illness to resume his heavy schedule of work. On this day Black presided over a day of hearings set aside for the testimony of those opposed to the bill. The representatives of the New York real-estate associations and of the taxpayers' associations who had appeared before the committee at the previous hearings testified again at this hearing. But representatives of the NAREB, the USBLL, and the NRLDA did not appear.[28] It would seem that they had decided to wait for the hearings that were to be held before the House committee.

After the adjournment of the hearings on the afternoon of May 11, Keyserling and Vinton made a few changes in the provisions of the bill. On May 21 Keyserling and Vinton had another session to revise the bill. The changes made were concerned with the financial provisions of the bill. During these two weeks Keyserling had had some meetings with Dave Krooth of the PWA legal staff, and they attempted to work out a satisfactory plan for loans and annual contributions. The other changes concerned the appointment of personnel to the Authority subject to the civil-service laws and the appointment of one man as administrator of the Housing Authority who would administer the business of the Authority under the supervision of a board appointed by the president. There was also included in the section on standards a provision for slum clearance, which was incorporated in this draft in an effort to satisfy the demands of Senator Walsh.

---

[27] Nelson to Wagner, April 15, 1937, and Wagner to Nelson, April 16, 1937, Wagner Papers, S. 1685—1937.

[28] Proceedings of May 11, 1937; in *Hearings on S. 1685*, pp. 213-31.

On June 8, 1937 Wagner held in his office a special meeting
of the housing experts and the representatives of the PWA
Housing Division. Wagner had special Confidential Committee
Print No. 1, June 8, 1937 printed for this meeting. It was
hoped that the two rival groups could come to a working compromise on the question of administration and annual contributions. But no compromise was effected and no agreement had
been reached by Wagner's group and the members of the PWA
staff at the end of this meeting.[29]
Wagner attended a special meeting with the president and
his White House staff on June 18. The subject of this meeting was a revised financial plan for the housing bill. The president wanted a system of outright capital grants rather than a
system of annual contributions over a fixed period of years. As
a result of the meeting Wagner agreed to incorporate into the
bill a provision for outright capital grants as an alternate plan
of financial assistance. After Wagner's return from the White
House meeting Keyserling and Vinton drafted a new section
providing for the capital grants.[30] The bill, with this new section
on capital grants, was then sent to the printer and returned on
June 21, as Confidential Committee Print No. 2. The very day
the print was returned, it was decided by Keyserling and Vinton
to reword certain sentences in this new section on capital grants
and, more important, to place a limit on the amount of money
available for capital grants in a given year. A limit of $10,000,-
000 in capital grants was set for the years 1937 and 1938; with
these changes the bill was sent back to the printer and returned
the next morning as Confidential Committee Print No. 3, June
22, 1937.[31]

---

[29] See the account of this meeting in this study, Chap. 11, pp. 297-98.
[30] Memorandum of Vinton on front page of Confidential Committee Print No. 2,
June 21, 1937, Vinton Papers.
[31] Memorandum of Vinton on front page of Confidential Committee Print No. 3,
June 22, 1937, Vinton Papers.

This draft of the bill, Confidential Committee Print No. 3, June 22, 1937, was given to the members of the Senate Committee on Education and Labor to be used as a working copy in the amendment of the bill. Keyserling learned from the housing experts that the provisions for annual grants which in the Confidential Committee Print No. 3, June 22, 1937, called for a contract of twenty years limit should be revised so that the contract would not be so rigidly limited to twenty years. In Committee Print No. 3 the contract was to continue for twenty years, and then it would expire and come up for re-examination. In Committee Print No. 4 this sentence was revised so that the contract for annual contributions would be for a fixed but indefinite period. Another section was then added which stated that, if the contract was to extend over a period of more than twenty years, it was to be re-examined at the end of twenty years, and then again at the end of each ten years until the date of expiration. This revision was made in Section 10 of Confidential Committee Print No. 4, June 30, 1937.[32] This print was the one that was officially considered by the members of the Senate committee which met in executive session during the first two weeks of July.[33] Senator Wagner and his assistant were in complete control of the bill while it was being considered by the Senate committee. Concerning those sections of the bill which Secretary Ickes wanted amended, the section on administration and the section on demonstration projects, the committee members, especially Senator Walsh, were unanimously opposed to Secretary Ickes.

Senator Walsh wanted the bill amended so that slum clearance would be made a compulsory feature of the program. The amendment was made in his absence, and perhaps for this rea-

---

[32] This new clause was listed as (d) in this print. In the final version of the bill, after being amended, it was listed as (c).

[33] Memorandum of Vinton on front page of Confidential Committee Print No. 4, June 30, 1937, Vinton Papers.

son it was put in the section on standards and was not as rigid as Senator Walsh wanted it. Thus it was that Wagner, though not a member of the committee, received his bill from the committee almost in the form he wanted it. Keyserling was asked to write up the report to accompany the bill. This report was a seventeen-page booklet which explained all the provisions of the bill and expounded the arguments in its favor. It was considered to be one of the finest expositions of the housing problem and of government aid to solve the problem.[34]

There was some delay in reporting out the bill by the Senate committee. The public housers became worried, and Bohn went to see Senator Black. Black told him that he would report out the bill whenever Senator Wagner wanted it.[35] During this time Senator Wagner lacked his characteristic energy. In the opinion of the public housers he seemed to be letting the control of the bill drift away from him. It was known that Wagner was not well during these months, and it was just a matter of his not having the energy necessary to push the bill through all the operations of the legislative process. Bohn, Vinton, Bauer and Hushings of the AFL, and others interested in the bill went to Senator Wagner and urged him to action. Wagner gathered his strength and prepared for the last hectic weeks of the battle for the housing law.

Black reported out the bill on July 23, 1937. No important change had been made in the Confidential Committee Print No. 4, June 30, 1937, which Wagner had presented to the committee as the working copy of their report.[36] Wagner then con-

---

[34] Senate Committee on Education and Labor, *Creating a United States Housing Authority*, S. Rept. No. 933, to accompany S. 1685, 75th Cong., 1st Sess. (1937) (Washington: Government Printing Office, 1937). Hugh Johnson in his column in the *Washington Post* had high praise for this report.

[35] Memorandum of Bohn, July 15, 1937, National Association of Housing Officials. Housing Bill—1937.

[36] S. 1685 (Rept. No. 933), July 23, 1937.

sulted with majority leader Barkley, and they decided to begin the debate in the Senate on the housing bill on Monday, August 2. Wagner also consulted with Senator Walsh about his amendments to the bill. Wagner learned that Walsh was not satisfied with the provisions for slum clearance and that he would demand that provision for slum clearance be made compulsory by including it in the section wherein provision was made for annual contributions and capital grants. Walsh gave Wagner a copy of the type of amendments that he wanted on this subject. He also told him that he wanted the ratio of income to rent set at four to one, so that the program would make provision for persons in the lowest income groups.

In 1936, during the Senate debate on the Wagner housing bill, Senator Walsh as chairman of the committee reporting out the bill had been in charge of the debate. Because of the amended version of the bill, Wagner in 1936 did not consider it as his bill. In 1937 Wagner assumed complete charge of the bill. Senator Black was in favor of Wagner's directing the debate; and as the bill came out of the committee in the form in which Wagner desired, he was ready to assume full responsibility for the bill.

Before the debate began during the session of Monday, August 2, Wagner had read into the *Record* the amendments desired by Senator Walsh, together with an explanation.[37] Later that same day, however, when the debate was in progress, Wagner changed his mind about the Walsh amendments and proceeded as though he had not made any mention of them. The debate in the Senate concerned three important amendments. The first amendment affected the administration of the new Authority. This amendment was called the Logan amendment because of its introduction by Senator Marvel M. Logan of Kentucky. This amendment was discussed at length in the previous chapter

---

[37] *Congressional Record*, August 2, 1937, p. 7962.

of this study. The Byrd amendment, called after its sponsor, Senator Harry Flood Byrd of Virginia, placed a limitation of $4,000 per four-room unit, or $1,000 per room, on construction costs in the public-housing projects. The Walsh amendment, called after its sponsor, Senator David I. Walsh of Massachusetts, made slum clearance by demolition or by repair of existing slum quarters, the number of dwellings thus eliminated to be substantially equal to the number of new units to be constructed, a compulsory part of the public-housing program.

One feature of the debate in the Senate was the general objection made to the legislation by certain rural and southern senators, who claimed that such a bill would benefit only the urban population. This argument was brought up often during the four periods of debate, but for purposes of clarity it is necessary to consider the argument as a unit.

Senator King of Utah interrupted Wagner shortly after the debate had begun to ask him to explain whether this bill was for the benefit of New York and Chicago, or "for the benefit of the people throughout the United States." Senator Connally of Texas also expressed concern over the fact that southern rural areas would not benefit from the provisions of the bill.[38]

Senator Charles O. Andrews of Florida expressed another viewpoint of the rural mentality when he stated:

> I think we ought not to offer an inducement to people to come in [to the cities, such as New York] from our country or foreign countries or anywhere else and take advantage of our government in supplying them with homes.[39]

Wagner was quick to defend the immigrant. He said he was not interested in how long a person had lived in the United States; the person was a citizen and a human being. In the United States every citizen had equal opportunities and was

---

[38] *Ibid.*, p. 7967.
[39] *Ibid.*, p. 7978.

equal before the law. That, explained Wagner, was what we meant by the concept of our democracy.

Andrews replied:

> I fully agree with the Senator that this is a Democracy. The question I wish to ask the Senator is this: As a matter of fact, does the influx of population into New York City also largely come from the rural sections of the United States?

Wagner was a bit out of patience in answering Andrews.

> The Senator is talking about New York, and, of course, that is a favorite subject here. I do not find fault with that. It seems to me that only when I am speaking does New York become a favorite subject for everyone to say something about it. New York is not the only benefactor under this proposed program. I do not know how much New York will benefit.
>
> The application of the program is country-wide in other places where even worse conditions exist than in New York and which ought to be treated even before New York.[40]

At the end of the day's discussion Senator James H. Hughes of Delaware rose to make some remarks about these statements of the senators from the rural areas.

> I heard with a good deal of interest the discussion earlier in the day relating to rural communities. The Senator from Georgia [George] today addressed himself to the subject of rural communities. Is it not true, as a matter of fact, that if a Senator representing such communities supports this bill, he does so because of his broad interest in all the people of the country—people who need the housing provided under this measure—although it may not benefit his constituents in any way at all. He supports the bill, does he not, because those who need the help provided under it are all citizens of our country together, and whether we live in the country it is our problem as much as it is the problem of those who live in the city and represent a large city.[41]

---

[40] *Ibid.*
[41] *Ibid.,* p. 7992.

Another general objection to the bill was that too much money would go to New York or a few of the other large cities. Senator Alva B. Adams of Colorado and Senator Millard F. Tydings of Maryland were asking for a definite limitation on the amount of money that could be spent in any city during any one year. Wagner was tired of this type of sectional argument and lashed out at his opponents, saying:

> This work ought to be done where the evil exists, and I pointed out that when the legislation involving the A.A.A. came before us I not only voted for it, but I would have considered myself unpatriotic in that case had I suggested that there be a distribution according to population. However, if it will assuage the apprehension of the Senator that New York might get a larger share than the Senator thinks it ought to get, I am quite willing that the limitation be imposed upon New York, for instance.[42]

The rural group made a final desperate effort to limit the program when Senator Walter George of Georgia proposed an amendment that would limit the program to three years. George asked for the yeas and the nays on the ballot. The result of the vote was thirty-three yeas for the limitation to a three-year period and forty-seven nays against the limitation, with fifteen not voting.[43] This vote taken on the second day of the debate was a good test of strength and indicated that the bill would certainly pass in the Senate.

The Byrd amendment presents an interesting study of the genesis of a limiting amendment to a bill. It was well known that Senator Byrd was a "watchdog" of the Treasury. Throughout his long career in the Senate he had shown a keen interest in a balanced budget and the elimination of the waste of public funds. In Byrd's home state of Virginia, Rex Tugwell of the Resettlement Administration planned some experimental rural

---

[42] *Ibid.*, August 5, 1937, p. 8259.
[43] *Ibid.*, August 4, 1937, p. 8198.

communities. These projects came to the immediate attention of Senator Byrd because of two very evident features of the experiments. The first feature of the experiment was a certain radical social philosophy motivating the movement of hill people in Virginia to model farms. Byrd protested this feature of the program even before construction of the proposed project could be started.

> When Dr. George Mitchell was appointed regional Director I protested in person to him. This resulted in the changing of the original fantastic project, known as the C.B.I. Greene project, as it was proposed by Dr. Tugwell. It was there proposed that 28 mountain families would operate as a common unit on a cooperative system similar to those in Russia.[44]

The other feature of these experimental projects that came to Byrd's attention was the waste of money in their construction. The senator from Virginia started an immediate personal investigation of the cost of the projects in his home state. When Byrd asked for a statement from the Resettlement Administration and the Department of Agriculture on the cost per unit of the RA projects, he received contradictory sets of figures. He therefore applied to the General Accounting Office for the average construction cost per unit at the projects. The senator said that from the information available to him he estimated that the average cost would be between $6,000 and $8,000 per unit on the seven homestead projects in Virginia. The GAO reported to Senator Byrd that the average cost was $7,909.35 per unit on the seven projects in Virginia.[45]

Thus it was that Byrd was ready and determined to place construction-cost limitations on the public-housing bill when it came up for debate in the Senate. It happened that the limitation that Byrd was going to demand was exactly the type of amend-

---

[44] *Ibid.*, August 2, 1937, p. 7964.
[45] *Ibid.*, p. 7965.

ment that the NAREB and the USBLL were demanding. Senator Byrd had obtained his information independently of any help from the NAREB or the USBLL, and these two lobbies could advantageously appeal to the position taken by him in their efforts to convince other senators of the necessity of limiting the construction costs of the housing projects.

Early in the debate on Monday, August 2, 1937, Byrd asked Wagner to give him an estimate of the construction cost per family unit in a housing project. Wagner asked Byrd if he wanted an estimate of the cost per room unit. Byrd replied that he wanted the cost per family unit. Wagner told him that according to the figures he had available it was "$4,000 per family unit and $1,000 per room, on an average for the whole country." Byrd then asked:

> What assurance has the Senator that the same extravagances which existed under the R.A. at Tugwelltown, when that unit was built as a low cost housing unit, will not continue? At Tugwelltown the unit cost was $16,000 per unit, while up in New Jersey $20,163 per unit was spent. What guaranty can the Senator give that the same extravagance will not appear in connection with the program under his bill?[46]

Wagner answered that under this program the construction was to be done by the local housing authorities with money borrowed from the government, money that would have to be repaid with interest.

Senator Tydings interrupted Wagner to say:

> I should like to make an observation, if I may. I think the Senator from New York would be very wise, if he would espouse an amendment limiting the cost of these units to a fair price, because the Senator says he is just starting this thing; that this is more or less of an experiment. Assuming that the country wants it—and I know the Senator from New York wants it—it strikes me

---

[46] *Ibid.*, p. 7982.

that unless the first venture is encompassed with all the business safeguards we can throw around it, the whole program by maladministration will get into bad repute, and the program will be ended.[47]

Wagner replied:

I agree with the Senator on that point. I thought there were sufficient safeguards; but, after all, I do not think I have ever shown myself to be an adamant individual upon the floor of the Senate. If that is a desirable amendment, I shall not oppose it; but I should like to inquire a little more as to whether or not we are running a risk in imposing over a period of three years, a limitation such as the Senator proposed of $1,000 per room.

Byrd then told Wagner:

I simply took the Senator's own figure. If he wants to increase that figure, it is entirely agreeable to me.[48]

Senator Walsh entered the debate to say that he was in agreement with the Byrd amendment. Walsh also made the keen observation, in reply to a statement by Barkley that the authorities would be spending their own money and not the government's money, that the government subsidy would be linked to the cost of the project because rent would be determined by the cost of the project.[49] The Byrd amendment was not presented on that day; Byrd waited until Wednesday, August 4, to present it. The amendment read:

No contract for loans, annual contributions, capital grants, sale, lease, mortgage, or any other agreement or instrument made pursuant to this Act shall be entered into by the Authority with respect to any project costing more than $4,000 per family unit or more than $1,000 per room exclusive of the cost of the land and cost of renovating old buildings, less value of salvage.[50]

---

[47] Ibid.
[48] Ibid., p. 7983.
[49] Ibid.
[50] This amendment was incorporated into the bill as subsection (5) of Section 15 which was concerned with standards.

Senator Tydings asked for the yeas and the nays on this question. The Byrd amendment was passed by the slim margin of a single vote. There were forty yeas, thirty-nine nays, and sixteen not voting.[51]

Immediately after this vote the AFL, the LHC, the AFHA, and representatives of every other organization interested in the public-housing program tried to convince some of the senators to change their votes so that it would be possible to reconsider the amendment and raise the cost limitation on the construction of new dwelling units. These groups were convinced that the cost limitation was put at so low a figure that it would be impossible to construct units in the cities. The figure that Wagner had given was an *average* for the whole country; and besides this, the figure that Wagner had given to Senator Byrd was not recent enough to take into account the increased cost of labor and material in the large cities. Another consideration that the public housers wanted the senators to keep in mind was the fact that these structures had to be built far more substantially than ordinary homes because of the fact that provision was made for an amortization period of sixty years on the obligations of the projects.

The real-estate groups and the Savings and Loan League worked just as diligently to keep the absolute limitation in the bill. August 5, 1937 was a busy day for lobbyists and pressure groups on Capitol Hill. On the evening of August 5 the representatives of the public-housing groups met in the joint offices at the Hay-Adams House. Ernest J. Bohn, Warren Vinton, Langdon Post, and Catherine Bauer were the important leaders in attendance at this meeting. Post drew up a detailed statement based upon his experience with housing projects in New York City to prove the impossibility of constructing permanent (sixty-year-guarantee) dwelling units in a large city with a cost limitation

---

[51] *Congressional Record*, August 4, 1937, p. 8196.

of $1,000 per room or $4,000 per family unit. The next morning Post gave copies of this statement to Senate clerks and to pages who were to place them on the senators' desks in the Senate. This was certainly one sure way of getting the statement into the hands of the senators. This procedure, however, caused a furor among some of the Republican senators when they discovered what had been done, as it was against the rules of the Senate to distribute material of this kind to the desks of the senators on the floor of the Senate.[52]

While certain Republican senators were demanding an explanation of this breach of the rules, Republican Minority Leader Charles McNary sat back amused at the whole affair because he knew exactly what had happened. McNary lived at the Hay-Adams House and could not help overhearing housing discussion at breakfast and dinner; and, of course, he knew some of the housing-organization leaders there. He knew what was going on, yet he did not say a word about it during the discussion. Senator Wagner declared that he assumed full responsibility for the incident; but the senators knew that Wagner would neither have violated a Senate rule of this kind nor have cooperated in its violation and that his statement was merely an attempt to protect some one of the public housers.[53]

Senator Bridges spoke out during the debate about the pressure politics going on at that time.

> In a very constructive way he [Senator Byrd] has offered an amendment which was adopted by a majority of one vote. Immediately after the result of the vote was announced the steam roller started to operate. Lobbyists started to appear. They appeared in my office. They have operated on other Senators. Mail was distributed by Senate officials to the desks of various Senators—a very objectionable practice from my point of view.[54]

---

52 Statement of Ernest J. Bohn (personal interview).
53 Statement of Ernest J. Bohn (personal interview).
54 *Congressional Record*, August 6, 1937, p. 8359.

Senator Minton rose to make some remarks about Senator Bridges' statement.

> The Senator refers to a steam roller that he saw in operation around here. I wonder if he saw a little bit of a steam roller over on the other side, manned by an elephant. I noticed that all the Republican votes were for the amendment of the Senator from Virginia.[55]

Wagner and Barkley had decided to make a move for the reconsideration of the Byrd amendment. Senator McCarran of Nevada was chosen to make the motion. During the session on Friday, August 6, McCarran made the motion to reconsider the Byrd amendment.[56] A debate immediately followed this motion. Those sympathetic to the Wagner bill, such as Senator McCarran, Senator Joseph F. Guffey of Pennsylvania, Senator Homer T. Bone of Washington, Senator Sherman Minton of Indiana, and Senator Robert La Follette, Jr., of Wisconsin attempted to point out that the motion was not to eliminate a limitation of cost on the construction of dwelling units, but rather an attempt to get a realistic and workable limitation. Speaking against the motion to reconsider were Senator Tydings, Senator Vandenberg, Senator Bridges, and Senator Byrd. Byrd finally made the motion "to lay on the table the motion to reconsider." Majority Leader Barkley asked for the yeas and the nays on the question, and they were so ordered. The result of the votes was forty-four yeas to thirty-nine nays, with twelve not voting.[57] Those favoring limitation gained four votes from those who were absent at the previous vote on the amendment.

The Byrd amendment for an absolute limitation was thus sustained, and the Republicans, the southern Democrats, the NAREB, and the USBLL had won an important battle in their campaign to prevent a public-housing program.

---

[55] *Ibid.*, p. 8360.
[56] *Ibid.*, p. 8358.

[57] *Ibid.*, p. 8367

The background of the Walsh amendments was also a part of his personal political philosophy and his personal experience with public housing. Senator Walsh saw that the public housing constructed in Boston with PWA funds was not for the benefit of the poor working people living in the slums. After the construction of the new modern housing these workers continued to live in the slums, and middle-class people moved into the new PWA housing projects. The people in the middle class were the only class of people who could afford to pay the rents that were charged in the projects because of their high construction costs and small subsidy. Walsh was personally convinced that this PWA program was a misuse of government funds.

During the Senate debate on the Wagner bill in 1936 and during the hearings on the Wagner bills in 1935, 1936, and 1937, Walsh had always spoken for a slum-clearance program.[58] The PWA Housing Division staff was well aware of this fact; and when it was certain that the administration of the program would be placed in the Department of the Interior, Krooth and Gray visited Walsh in his office in an attempt to work out a compromise. The PWA Housing Division knew that it would be practically impossible in certain areas where there was an acute shortage of dwellings to attempt to limit the number of new housing units constructed to the number of slum units demolished or repaired. After a conference with Walsh in the first week of June, Krooth and Keyserling drafted a compromise

---

[58] An exchange of remarks between Senator Walsh and Stewart McDonald, Federal Housing administrator, during the hearings in 1937 well illustrates the thinking of Senator Walsh on this problem. One brief statement of Walsh from this exchange will summarize his personal philosophy:
"I believe Senator Wagner feels deeply on that subject [slum clearance for people in the low income group], and I do also. I do want some safeguard so we will not get into the situation where we will be dealing with influential low-income groups who have votes, and the poor widow, wash woman, orphans and others who have to live in these slums are forgotten" (*Hearings on S. 1685*, p. 79).

amendment to the paragraph on slum clearance that was already in Section 15 of the bill.[59] Walsh did not think that this paragraph in Section 15 accomplished the desired end.

> [Section 15.] The Authority shall be guided by these considerations. (2) In the case of a slum clearance project, or a low-rent-housing project which includes slum clearance, that substantially all of the dispossessed inhabitants will be provided for by the development of sufficient low-rent housing, within their financial reach, either upon the site to be cleared or in some other suitable locality, unless the clearance of the area will not make it impracticable for the inhabitants thereof to secure equivalent dwellings elsewhere at no higher cost to them or better dwellings elsewhere within their financial reach.

Keyserling and Krooth did not want to accept a slum-clearance program as opposed to a program of construction of new dwelling units on vacant land to increase the number of available dwelling units, so they were trying to incorporate into the language of the bill a slum-clearance provision that could be by-passed by the Authority. The amendment concerned the last sentence of the paragraph: "unless the Authority shall be satisfied that proper provisions will be made for otherwise rehousing such inhabitants." This amended clause was retained unchanged in the Confidential Committee Prints No. 1, June 8, 1937, No. 2, June 21, 1937, No. 3, June 22, 1937, and No. 4, June 30, 1937. This last print, No. 4 of June 30, 1937, was the print officially considered by the Senate committee in its executive sessions to mark up the bill prior to reporting it to the Senate.

Senator Walsh was absent when this section was considered by the committee. Walsh had made it clear to Wagner and to the committee that he was not satisfied with the very weak slum-clearance provision of Section 15, (2). He told the committee that he wanted a slum-clearance program that would be sub-

---

[59] Statement of David Krooth (personal interview).

stantially equivalent to the number of units constructed, and Walsh wanted this provision so stated that it would be a compulsory part of the program. Hence Walsh was angered at the Wagner group when he discovered that his amendment had not been considered. Walsh wrote a letter to the president to protest the lack of a compulsory slum-clearance provision in the bill. As the Wagner group and the PWA group had failed him, Walsh sought advice from John Ihlder. Ihlder provided Walsh with various statistics on slum clearance in Washington. He also gave the senator a series of photographs illustrating sections of Washington "Before Slum Clearance" and "After Slum Clearance."[60]

Walsh entered the debate on Monday, August 2, loaded with material. He had entered as a part of the *Record* his letter to the president and letters he had received from John Ihlder and other housing experts.[61] He opened his remarks by stating that it was not his intention, nor was it the intention of the committee, to put slum clearance among the ten standards to be considered before a project was to be begun.

> In the drafting of the bill, in my absence from the committee, this was inserted in the provisions which give the Board an option whether to act or not.[62]

Wagner replied to Walsh that he considered the provisions of the section on standards to be compulsory. Walsh stated that he was not willing to accept Wagner's interpretation. He ended the discussion with the statement that he would offer an amendment later which would make slum clearance a compulsory part of the program.

---

[60] Walsh hung these pictures on the walls of the Senate chamber and during the course of his speech on the necessity and advantages of the slum-clearance program, he invited his colleagues to examine them (*Congressional Record*, August 3, 1937, p. 8077).

[61] *Ibid.*, pp. 8089-91.

[62] *Ibid.*, August 2, 1937, p. 7969.

Before Walsh proposed his amendment he was drawn into the debate on the question of the income group to be served by the public-housing projects. Senator Vandenberg wanted to limit occupancy of the projects to the lowest income groups. He considered too high the ratio of income to rent of five to one. Vandenberg then mentioned that during the debate of the previous year he and Senator Walsh had set the ratio of income to rent at four times the rental.[63] Walsh rose from his desk to agree with Vandenberg's observation. He then went on to state:

> I did agree with the viewpoint of the Senator from Michigan in that respect, and I expect to offer an amendment along that line.

Wagner then asked him: "Is the Senator going to make it four times?"

Walsh replied:

> I am going to make it three or four, I want the people who get this subsidy to be not the low income group but the lowest of the low income group; and we have got to make the provision very low to bring that about.
>
> Take a tenement the rent of which is $25 a month. This bill would permit a man who gets $124 a month, if he had the political pull or influence with the authorities, to get into one of these houses and enjoy a subsidy as against the poor washerwoman with only $50 or $60 a month income.
>
> I know the Senator from New York and I are absolutely in accord as to the fundamental principle, but there is a difference as to how far we ought to go. The Senator from New York is disposed to be a little more liberal to the Authority than I am. That is the only difference between us.
>
> Let me say that I am convinced that unless we tighten it so that only the lowest income group—not the low-income but the lowest income group—can get these tenements and subsidies, we will have a housing scandal on our hands in the future.[64]

---

[63] *Ibid.*, p. 7986.
[64] *Ibid.*

On the next day, Tuesday, August 3, Walsh presented his amendments, which he drafted in such a way as to make slum clearance a compulsory part of the program. A *Provided* clause was inserted in sections 10 and 11, concerned with annual contributions and capital grants, which made these grants-of-aid contingent on a real slum-clearance program. If a number of new dwellings were to be constructed, unsafe and insanitary dwellings substantially equal in number must be "eliminated." This elimination could be accomplished in either one of two ways: by the demolition, condemnation, and effective closing of the dwellings or by their repair and improvement. The dwellings thus eliminated need not be on the same site as the newly constructed dwellings, but they must be situated in the same locality or metropolitan area.

> Section 10. (a) The Authority may make annual contributions . . . Provided, That no annual contributions shall be made, and the Authority shall enter into no contract guaranteeing any annual contribution in connection with the development of any low-rent housing project involving the construction of new dwellings, unless the project includes the elimination by demolition, condemnation, and effective closing, or the repair or improvement of unsafe and insanitary dwellings situated in the locality or metropolitan area, substantially equal in number to the number of newly constructed dwellings provided by the project.[65]

These amendments were adopted by the Senate on a voice vote without any opposition.[66] With the adoption of these amendments Senator Walsh was satisfied that the bill would clear the slums and bring the benefits of safe and sanitary housing to the poor washerwomen now living in the slums. This was precisely the type of amendment that the USBLL and the NAREB wanted put into the bill if there was to be a public-housing bill. Senator

---

[65] Walsh had the same clause, *mutatis mutandis*, inserted in Section 11 (a) which made provision for capital grants.

[66] *Congressional Record*, August 3, 1937, p. 8098.

Walsh, however, was not thinking of the interests of any lobby in fighting for these amendments. He acted as he did because of his personal interest in the slum dwellers and not because of any sympathy with either the USBLL or the NAREB. The Walsh amendments and the Byrd amendments are good examples of amendments that are definitely in line with the position taken by a lobby or pressure group but that are proposed independently of their efforts. The Congress of the United States is so large and is made up of legislators representing so many and such varied interests that almost any lobbyist or pressure-group representative can find a legislator who sincerely shares the interest and viewpoint of the lobby or pressure group. Such a wide diversity of interests in a two-party system of government is unique to the United States.

A good example of the manner in which an administration amendment is put into a bill is found in the case of an amendment proposed by Majority Leader Barkley which gave to the president the right to approve or disapprove of all contracts of loan or grants-in-aid made under the provisions of the bill. During a lull in the debate Barkley was recognized by the president. He proposed his amendment. The president immediately put the question to the house on a voice vote. And the amendment was passed.[67] The whole procedure took place so fast that visitors in the gallery, unacquainted with the legislative procedure, did not realize what had happened.

Finally, on the afternoon of August 6, 1937, the president of the Senate put the question: "Shall the bill pass?" Senators La Follette and Tydings asked for the yeas and the nays on the question, and it was so ordered. The vote on the Wagner bill in the Senate was sixty-four yeas, sixteen nays, and fifteen not voting. The details of the roll call were as follows:[68]

---

[67] *Ibid.*, August 4, 1937, p. 8179.
[68] *Ibid.*, August 6, 1937, p. 8373.

YEAS, 64

Adams	Clark	Lee	Overton
Andrews	Davis	Lewis	Pepper
Ashurst	Dieterich	Logan	Pittman
Barkley	Ellender	Lonergan	Radcliffe
Berry	Frazier	Lundeen	Reynolds
Bilbo	Gillette	McAdoo	Schwartz
Black	Green	McCarran	Schwellenbach
Bone	Guffey	McGill	Sheppard
Borah	Harrison	McKellar	Shipstead
Brown, Mich.	Hatch	Maloney	Thomas, Okla.
Brown, N. H.	Herring	Minton	Thomas, Utah
Bulkley	Hitchcock	Moore	Truman
Bulow	Holt	Murray	Vandenberg
Burke	Hughes	Neely	Van Nuys
Capper	Johnson, Colo.	Nye	Wagner
Chavez	La Follette	O'Mahoney	Walsh

NAYS, 16

Austin	Byrnes	Hale	Smith
Bailey	Connally	Johnson, Cal.	Steiwer
Bridges	George	Lodge	Tydings
Byrd	Glass	McNary	White

NOT VOTING, 15

Bankhead	Duffy	King	Smathers
Caraway	Gerry	Norris	Townsend
Copeland	Gibson	Pope	Wheeler
Donahey	Hayden	Russel	

Senator Wagner had won a victory for his bill in the Senate. He and his supporters had to turn their attention and efforts to the battle for the housing bill that was then going on in the House. Chairman Steagall had finally yielded to pressure and had scheduled hearings on the bill before his committee. Attention must now be turned to these final critical procedures in the legislative process.

CHAPTER XIII

The House Committee
Amends the Housing Bill

Various influential leaders of the public-housing groups had visited Representative Henry B. Steagall, chairman of the House Committee on Banking and Currency, during March and April to ask him to hold hearings on the housing bill which carried his name—the Wagner-Steagall housing bill. Steagall, however, did not appear to be any more interested in the housing bill in 1937, although during this year he was listed as its sponsor, than he had been in 1935 and 1936 when Representative Henry Ellenbogen had been sponsor of the bill. On May 8 Langdon Post, who was very disturbed over the delay in holding hearings before the House committee, made a special visit to Steagall's office and attempted to convince him of the necessity of holding hearings on the bill. Steagall did not give Post any promise that he would hold hearings on the bill before his committee, but he did tell Post that he was displeased with Senator Wagner's attitude toward him, mentioning that Wagner had never visited him to talk over the bill or the strategy to be employed in pushing it through Congress.

After this meeting Post wrote to Wagner to tell him that Steagall had been hurt by the senator's failure to communicate with him about the bill. Post asked Wagner to see Steagall and urge him to hold the hearings. Post warned Wagner that the public housers did not want Steagall to be able to give them the excuse at the end of the session that there was no time to hold hearings and that in consequence there was no possibility of House action on the bill.[1]

Post, in his capacity as chairman of the New York City Housing Authority, wrote to the president to urge him to ask Steagall to hold the hearings on the housing bill. Post informed the president that he had seen Steagall and that he was sure Steagall would hold the hearings if the president asked him to do so.[2] This letter was delivered to the president while he was en route to Fort Worth, Texas. McIntyre answered under instructions from the president, saying that the president would keep Post's request in mind.[3]

In response to Post's letter to him Wagner stated that he was waiting for favorable action on the bill by the Senate before he attempted to press Steagall for action in the House.[4]

The American Federation of Labor was also interested in getting the hearings before the House committee under way. The AFL considered the situation so critical that in addition to the work which Catherine Bauer and Boris Shishkin were doing "on the Hill" to get action on the bill, the National Legislative Committee of the AFL decided to assign their veteran lobbyist Bill Hushings the job of getting congressional action on the bill. On May 24 Bill Hushings talked with Keyserling, Senator Black, and Majority Leader Rayburn of the House about the progress of the bill. Hushings urged Rayburn to tell Steagall to have the hearings. Rayburn, who was party leader in the House at this time while Speaker Bankhead was absent in the South, could not promise Hushings any action on the part of the House. But Senator Black told Hushings that he would see Senator Wagner

---

[1] Post to Wagner, May 8, 1937, Wagner Papers, S. 1685—1937.
[2] Post to Roosevelt, May 8, 1937, Roosevelt Papers, O.F. 63.
[3] McIntyre to Post, May 11, 1937, Roosevelt Papers, O.F. 63.
[4] Wagner to Post, May 10, 1937, Wagner Papers, S. 1685—1937.

and report the bill out of the Senate committee whenever Wagner wanted it out. All agreed that the main obstacle of the housing bill was the fact that the bill had not received the "go ahead" signal from the White House.[5]

Bohn was also visiting various Democratic as well as Republican congressional leaders at the Capitol at that time, and he felt certain that Roosevelt was not as yet thoroughly convinced that the housing bill should be passed at that time. It was Bohn's opinion that there were other bills which the president was more interested in having enacted by Congress.[6]

During the month of June the weeks passed and there was no activity on the House side of the Capitol. During the first two weeks of July the Senate committee prepared to report out the bill, but Wagner did not push Steagall to hold the hearings. By July 13 Post could delay no longer in making a last desperate appeal to the president to intervene in favor of the bill. He wrote to the president to ask him to request Steagall to hold hearings so that the bill would have a chance of being passed at that session. Post cited the need for housing and the promise made to the public by the Democratic party to enact a housing bill. He also told the president that he was the only person who had power to get Steagall to hold the hearings. Post signed this letter in his capacity as president of the American Federation of Housing Authorities.[7]

Roosevelt took this request more seriously than he had Post's earlier request. The president's legislative program, especially the plan to reorganize the federal court system, had been badly beaten in Congress. If the president could have the public-housing bill enacted, he would have at least one New Deal law to his credit for that session. So it was that Roosevelt was now

---

[5] Hushings memorandum, May 24, 1937, American Federation of Labor, National Legislative Committee, Housing Bill—1937.

[6] Statement of Ernest J. Bohn (personal interview).

[7] Post to Roosevelt, July 13, 1937, Roosevelt Papers, O.F. 63.

ready to give his support to the housing bill.[8] On July 15 the president sent Post's letter and a memo to his administrative assistant James Roosevelt. He told him to talk with Steagall about the letter and to send a reply to "Tubby" Post.[9]

Congressman Steagall had left Washington during the third week of July and had returned to Alabama. This caused much alarm among the public housers. Ernest J. Bohn made a trip to Alabama, and to the neighboring states of Georgia and North Carolina, to obtain for the housing bill the support of prominent civic, church, welfare, and political leaders in these states. Senators and representatives from these states were generally opposed to the bill, and Bohn was urging various prominent leaders to exert pressure on their senators and representatives to support the bill. While Bohn was in Montgomery, Alabama, he heard that Steagall had left for a trip to Europe. On July 27 he sent a telegram to Keyserling telling him of his activities in these states in behalf of the bill and asking Keyserling to let him know immediately who was handling the housing bill in the House in the absence of Steagall.[10] Keyserling telegraphed Bohn to tell him that Steagall had returned to Washington.[11]

Steagall's return to Washington resulted from the pressure of the White House. When Wagner learned that Steagall had left Washington, he went to the White House for a conference with the president. After discussing the housing bill with Wagner the president finally decided that he would give the bill the "go ahead" signal. This decision of the president was made after he had received numerous protests and pleas from the various

---

[8] This was the common opinion of observers in Washington. Pearson and Allen in their syndicated column, "Washington Merry-Go-Round," for May 22, 1937 blamed the president and the Treasury Department for the lack of action with regard to the housing bill.

[9] F.D.R. to J.R., July 15, 1937, Roosevelt Papers, O.F. 63.

[10] Bohn to Keyserling, July 27, 1937, Wagner Papers, S. 1685—1937.

[11] Keyserling to Bohn, July 29, 1937, Wagner Papers, S. 1685—1937.

groups interested in the public-housing bill. The strong letter that Representative Beiter of Buffalo, New York, the assistant majority whip, sent to the president was typical of the protests being sent. Beiter first told the president that the bill would languish in committee unless the president acted. He then went on to point out that this bill was in accord with the presidential messages and with the plank in the Democratic platform of 1936. Beiter insinuated that the party control of the House would be in danger if no action was taken on the housing bill: "I do not want to go home without doing something about the housing problem and there seems to be a great deal of similar sentiment among my colleagues."[12] The AFL was also bringing to bear on the president the pressure of that great organization. Green and other leaders let it be known that they considered that the president had failed them in 1935 and 1936 and that, if he failed them in 1937 with respect to this housing bill, they would do something about it.[13]

Mike McDonough and Bill Hushings were sent by the AFL to discuss the housing bill with Speaker Bankhead on July 29. They were told on that day that Steagall was returning to Washington because of the decision of the White House. Bankhead had sent the telegram.[14]

When Steagall returned to Washington he found a letter from James Roosevelt waiting for him. It informed Steagall that the enclosed letter from Langdon Post (the one dated July 13) was sent to him in accordance with instructions from the president. Steagall was to read the letter and then he was requested to phone James Roosevelt and tell him what he thought about it.[15]

[12] Beiter to Roosevelt, July 8, 1937, Roosevelt Papers, P.P.F. 2694.
[13] Statement of Bill Hushings (personal interview).
[14] Hushings memorandum, July 29, 1937, American Federation of Labor, National Legislative Committee, Housing Bill—1937.
[15] J. Roosevelt to Steagall, July 27, 1937, Roosevelt Papers, O.F. 63.

Steagall phoned to James Roosevelt on July 29 and told him that he would like to come to talk with the president on Monday, August 2. He also told James Roosevelt that he planned to hold the hearings very soon. When the president received from James Roosevelt the memorandum of this conversation, he called Steagall by telephone and talked with him. The president in his penciled memorandum to McIntyre on this conversation with Steagall does not mention what he told Steagall,[16] but from subsequent action on the part of Representative Steagall the president must have convinced him that he wanted the bill reported out of his committee favorably and within a short time. Steagall had told Bohn and Krooth that this bill was socialism and would bankrupt the country; but that the boss wanted it, so he would put it through.[17]

Wagner sent a letter and a copy of the Senate report on the bill to each member of the House committee.[18] He also sent a letter and a copy of the Senate report to Chairman Steagall.[19] Wagner did not personally consult with Steagall, and Steagall resented this slight. Steagall did not seek any advice from Senator Wagner, but instead he consulted with Secretary Ickes and asked Ickes for an adviser from his PWA Housing Division. Ickes sent Dave Krooth as special adviser to Steagall.[20]

Steagall scheduled the first of the committee hearings for August 3. The rules and precedents governing the hearings before a House committee have been fully explained in Chapter 8. It will be sufficient for the purposes of this study to point out the specific pressure politics which were in operation during

---

[16] Penciled notation on memorandum of J.R. to the president, July 29, 1937, Roosevelt Papers, O.F. 63.

[17] Statements of Ernest J. Bohn and David Krooth (personal interviews).

[18] Wagner to members of the House Banking and Currency Committee, Representatives Goldsborough, Reilly, Hancock, and others, July 30, 1937, Wagner Papers, S. 1685—1937.

[19] Wagner to Steagall, July 31, 1937, Wagner Papers, S. 1685—1937.

[20] Statement of David Krooth (personal interview).

these hearings. Senator Wagner and his group of housing advisers from the various public-housing organizations had no influence with the House Committee on Banking and Currency or with Chairman Steagall in particular. Steagall selected his own witnesses from among the government agencies engaged in housing activities and from the list of those making application to the committee. His selection of witnesses demonstrated a partiality to Secretary Ickes and his supporters and to the representatives of the United States Building and Loan League and the Chamber of Commerce.[21] It will be remembered that before the more liberal Senate Committee on Education and Labor the partiality was in favor of the liberal labor and welfare groups.[22]

Mayor La Guardia, a former member of the House of Representatives, was Steagall's first witness. He was graciously presented to the committee by the chairman, who said that Mayor La Guardia needed no introduction to members of the House. But La Guardia was not so graciously questioned by

---

[21] The following persons testified before the House committee: Honorable Fiorello H. La Guardia, mayor of the city of New York; Honorable Stewart McDonald, administrator, Federal Housing Administration; Dr. Ernest M. Fisher, director of economics and statistics, Federal Housing Administration; Miles Colean, deputy administrator, Federal Housing Administration; Charles C. McGehee, deputy administrator, Federal Housing Administration; Honorable Everett Dirksen, representative in Congress from the state of Illinois; Honorable Henry Ellenbogen, representative in Congress from the state of Pennsylvania; Miles R. Frisbie, secretary, American Federation of Housing Authorities; Honorable Harold L. Ickes, secretary of the Department of the Interior; Morton Bodfish, executive vice-president, United States Building and Loan League; Samuel F. Clabaugh, president, Protective Life Insurance Company and director, Chamber of Commerce of the United States; Honorable Alfred Beiter, representative in Congress from the state of New York; J. C. deHoll, chairman of the Housing Authority, Birmingham, Alabama; Frank Carnahan, secretary, National Retail Lumber Dealers Association; Miss Josephine Goman, secretary, Detroit Housing Commission; Mrs. R. C. Bruce, apartment-house manager in New York City; Ernest J. Bohn, National Association of Housing Officials.

[22] See Chap. 7 of this study.

several members of the committee who were not in sympathy with his position, which was favorable to Secretary Ickes. After he had made a short introductory statement on the necessity of the bill and the universal support it had received from mayors throughout the country, Mayor La Guardia was questioned sharply by Hancock, Luce, Fish, and a few of the other more conservative members of the committee. The colorful mayor of New York had no difficulty in defending his position, despite the fact that he was on the witness stand from 10:20 A.M. until 12:55 P.M., when a recess was called by the chairman.[23] Steagall was holding the hearings before his committee during both the morning and the afternoon. Once Steagall had decided to take action, he drove his committee long and hard to report out an amended bill.

Steagall concluded the hearings with the afternoon session on Friday, August 6. He called the committee for an executive session on Monday morning, August 9.[24] During the executive sessions held during that week, the committee set to work to amend the Senate version of the bill in accordance with the various viewpoints represented by committee members. It was a difficult task for the committee to comprehend and evaluate all the technical problems, financial and administrative, involved in the bill. It was worthy of note that no witness who could qualify as an expert on the financial provisions of the bill testified before the committee. The fact that many parts of the bill were not understood by the members of the committee was brought out frankly by Representative Hancock during the debate in the House. Hancock claimed that there was not a single member who understood all its implications or who could adequately explain all the provisions of the bill.[25]

---

[23] *House Hearings on H. R. 5033 and S. 1685*, p. 42.
[24] *Ibid.*, p. 316.
[25] *Congressional Record*, August 18, 1937, p. 9249.

The committee did receive technical advice from the various groups interested in the housing bill, but it was partisan advice. The USBLL advised the House committee to retain the restrictive amendments of the Senate concerned with construction-cost limitation and slum clearance. The group further advised the committee to incorporate more restrictions on the local authority with respect to the use of the money loaned by the Federal Government. The league favored a rather substantial contribution from the local government to the subsidy given the housing project by the Federal Government.[26] The National Association of Real Estate Boards and the Chamber of Commerce of the United States advocated similar restrictive amendments. Neither of these organizations wished to see the Federal Government provide housing in competition with private industry. Their preference was for no public-housing bill; but if there had to be a housing bill, it should be safeguarded with many restrictions. Representative Hancock of North Carolina was in sympathy with these amendments. He also had the support of Representative Reilly of Wisconsin, another Democratic member of the committee, and of most of the Republican members on the committee.[27]

Representative McGranery was the spokesman for the public-housing groups. He supported the amendments which these groups sent to the committee. The leaders of the groups favoring public housing had several meetings at this time and agreed upon a series of amendments that they would ask the House to incorporate into the bill. Each group, such as the AFHA and the AFL, sent separate but identical copies of these amendments to each member of the committee. These groups also sent copies of these amendments to the president and requested him to use

---

[26] Bodfish to House Committee on Banking and Currency, August 10, 1937, Vinton Papers, Housing Bill—1937.

[27] Statements of Frank W. Hancock and Michael Reilly (*Congressional Record*, August 18, 1937, pp. 9251, 9246).

his influence with the members of the committee to have them adopted.[28] The leaders of the public-housing groups had prepared construction-cost charts on the various housing projects completed in New York City, and they demonstrated from these charts that it would be impossible to construct projects at a cost of $1,000 per room or $4,000 per unit. It was pointed out to the committee in these memoranda that a per-room cost of $1,400 or $1,500 would be sufficient for construction in the larger cities, but such a limitation would be too high for other areas. Therefore it was suggested that no set figures be included in the bill, but rather that the average cost in the locality for similar construction with the same type of building materials and the same labor conditions be used as the norm. It was emphasized that this norm would serve to prevent waste and extravagance and at the same time make the necessary provisions for adequate construction.

The other amendment that the public-housing groups deemed essential concerned Senator Walsh's amendment, which restricted the new units constructed to the number of slum units demolished or repaired. The memoranda stressed the fact that the "huddling together of two or even three families in one dwelling" was the most intolerable of all slum conditions and that this overcrowding would definitely result from the rigid operation of the Walsh amendment in areas where there was an existing shortage of dwelling units. If because of a shortage of dwelling units several families were crowded into space not intended for more than one, the very purpose of the Walsh amendment, slum clearance, would be defeated. The public-housing groups therefore urged that in certain areas where there was an insufficient number of dwelling units the demoli-

---

[28] American Federation of Housing Authorities to House Committee on Banking and Currency, August 10, 1937; American Federation of Labor to House Committee on Banking and Currency, August 10, 1937; Post to Roosevelt, and Shishkin to McIntyre, August 10, 1937, Roosevelt Papers, O.F. 63.

tion of the old buildings could be delayed until sufficient new dwellings had been constructed.[29]

In addition to these suggested amendments the committee received letters and telegrams from groups and individuals who advised them to vote one way or the other in the interest of the group or region. The Chamber of Commerce sent out a special bulletin at the end of July urging its members to write to their representatives and senators and make known to them their attitude toward the legislation. The official position of the Chamber of Commerce was opposition to the Wagner housing bill. While the Chamber of Commerce opposed the Wagner bill, it urged its members to support the Federal Housing Administration and the Federal Home Loan Bank.[30] Various real-estate boards, such as the New York Real Estate Board, sent letters to the senators and congressmen from their respective states urging them to defeat, or at least to drastically restrict, the housing bill.[31] Frank Carnahan of the NRLDA sent out letters at this time urging the congressmen to defeat the bill because it was in direct competition with private industry. Carnahan also made appeal to sectional prejudice when he warned members of the Congress that the benefits of the bill would go to the metropolitan areas and that the rural areas, though burdened with taxes, would not benefit from the legislation.[32]

---

[29] This was the argument that Catherine Bauer developed. It was adopted by the American Federation of Labor and also by the American Federation of Housing Authorities.

[30] *Special Bulletin No. 1836,* July 27, 1937. Washington: Chamber of Commerce of the United States.

[31] New York Real Estate Board to Wagner, August 5, 1937, Wagner Papers, S. 1685—1937.

[32] Carnahan to Wagner, July 29, 1937, Wagner Papers, S. 1685—1937. This same two-page letter with enclosures concerning the Federal Housing Administration program and a page from the *American Lumberman* describing a home that could be built with a FHA loan was sent to all the senators. Some senators, such as Senator Lonergan of Connecticut, sent their copies to Senator Wagner.

The AFL made an all-out effort to have the bill passed by the House committee. The National Legislative Committee, under the direction of Bill Hushings, listed the members of the committee whose vote was in doubt. This list was sent to President William Green, who sent a telegram to the labor leader in each district represented, telling him to wire the representative urging him to vote for the Wagner-Steagall low-cost housing bill. Green also requested the leader to see to it that the other officials and members of trade unions did the same. The list of representatives who were thus put under pressure by the National Legislative Committee of the AFL were Dudley A. White of Ohio, Republican; Hamilton Fish of New York, Republican; Michael Reilly of Wisconsin, Democrat; D. Worth Clark of Idaho, Democrat; Thomas F. Ford of California, Democrat; Clyde Williams of Missouri, Democrat; James A. Meeks of Illinois, Democrat; Herman Kopplemann of Connecticut, Democrat; and James I. Farley of Indiana, Democrat.[33]

For five days—from Monday, August 9, to Friday, August 13—the committee worked over the bill. By Friday afternoon the members of the committee favoring a restricted public-housing program judged that they were making satisfactory progress. Various amendments that Hancock and his colleagues had demanded were in temporary drafts of the bill. On Friday afternoon Steagall decided that there had been enough discussion and debate in the committee. He called in Krooth and a member of the Legislative Reference Service and told them to have the amended draft of the bill and the report to accompany the bill ready by midnight so that it could be sent to the printer and received back in printed form on Monday. Krooth and his associate took the amendments which had been adopted by the

---

[33] Telegram, Green to Balling of Norwalk, Ohio [Representative Dudley A. White's district], August 12, 1937, American Federation of Labor, National Legislative Committee, Housing Bill—1937.

committee and set to work to prepare the bill in accord with these amendments.[34]

The major changes in the House version of the bill as it was reported out of committee concerned administration, local contributions to the federal subsidy, construction-cost limitation, eligible income groups for occupancy of projects, slum-clearance provisions, and the limitation of obligations to be issued by the Authority. The Authority was placed under the jurisdiction of the secretary of the Department of the Interior, as had been done by the Logan amendment in the Senate; but the Authority was to be administered by a single administrator and an advisory board of nine members.[35] The personnel for the Authority could be selected without regard for civil-service regulations.[36] This last amendment was vehemently opposed by a number of mem-

---

[34] These facts gathered from the statement of Frank W. Hancock in the House during the debate (*Congressional Record*, August 18, 1937, p. 9249) and from statement of David Krooth (personal interview).

The following incident illustrates how complete was Ickes' control of the housing bill during the final stages of the legislative process. On August 10, 1937 John Ihlder, executive officer of the Alley Dwelling Authority of the District of Columbia, sent a letter to the president asking favorable consideration of an amendment to the Wagner-Steagall housing bill that would permit the Alley Dwelling Authority to share in the benefits of the bill. The amendment was referred by the president to the secretary of the Department of the Interior for his consideration and acknowledgment.

When the House reported out the bill a new section was added to the bill, Section 28, which specifically made provision for the Alley Dwelling Authority to receive funds from the president to carry on its work of slum clearance. There is no record in the files to indicate that Ickes actually sent a memorandum to Steagall telling him to include this amendment in the bill, but there is also no evidence that anyone else interceded for Ihlder and his group. It is also to be remembered that Mrs. Roosevelt was actively interested in the Alley Dwelling Authority, a fact that would induce Ickes, or anyone else, to give the amendment favorable consideration (Ihlder to Roosevelt, August 10, 1937 [with president's notation], Roosevelt Papers, O.F. 63).

[35] House Committee on Banking and Currency, *United States Housing Act of 1937*, H. Rept. No. 1545, to accompany S. 1685, 75th Cong., 1st Sess. (1937), Sec. 3 (a), (b), (c), and (d). Washington: Government Printing Office, 1937.

[36] *Ibid.*, Sec. 4 (a).

bers of the House who favored civil service, as will be seen from the summary of the House debate which is given in the last pages of this chapter.

The amendment to require local contributions in the form of cash, tax remissions, or tax exemptions to supplement the capital grant or annual contributions of the Federal Government was one for which the PWA Housing Division had shown some sympathy, though it was first proposed by the USBLL.[37] This provision was definitely in accord with the adopted amendments of Representatives Hancock and Reilly, though it did not go as far as some members of the committee desired.

The House committee amendment to the Byrd amendment on construction-cost limitation was a compromise between the demands of the USBLL and those of the public-housing groups. Two general limitations were put into the bill which prohibited projects of elaborate or expensive design and material.[38] This was what the USBLL had advocated throughout the campaign. They had plans for cheap public housing. The public-housing experts said that the type of construction that was advocated by the USBLL was so cheap that it would quickly deteriorate into slums and would not hold up for the sixty-year period of amortization. The second general limitation placed on construction of housing units stated that costs shall not exceed the average cost of similar dwellings in that locality constructed under the same building laws and the same labor conditions. This was the type of limitation that the public housers desired. They claimed that it would achieve the effect desired by all concerned.[39] A third limitation, which was Steagall's idea, was also placed in the

---

[37] *Ibid.*, Sec. 10 (a) and Sec. 11 (a). Howard A. Gray, director of housing in the Department of the Interior, wrote an article on this plan for *American City*. See Howard A. Gray, "Public Housing and Taxes," *American City* 52:93-97, April 1937.

[38] S. 1685 (Rept. No. 1545), August 13, 1937, Sec. 15 (5).

[39] Memoranda of AFL and AFHA to House Committee, August 10, 1937, p. 2.

bill.[40] It stated that "in each fiscal year, the average family-dwelling-unit cost (as herein defined) shall not exceed $5,000." The figure that Steagall used, $5,000, was in line with the memorandum sent to him by the AFHA and the AFL when they discussed the cost of construction in New York City. These groups had urged, however, that the second general limitation be the only one included in the bill. They were opposed to including in the bill any absolute figure that might not be applicable in all places or for any length of time.

The income group eligible for occupancy in the projects was limited to those whose yearly income did not exceed four times the yearly rental.[41] This ratio of four to one was in accordance with Senator Walsh's proposals and also with the proposals of the USBLL.

Senator Walsh's amendment providing for a limitation of new construction equivalent to demolition or repair of slum quarters was slightly modified. The language was changed so that the slum clearance was not a *part* of the housing project. In certain states the housing authority would have legal authority to make such provisions. It was stated that the Authority was to "make satisfactory arrangements for the elimination, etc."[42] This type of amendment did not satisfy the supporters of the Walsh amendment because they considered it too loose and vague. Likewise it did not satisfy the public-housing experts because they had advocated that language be included in the bill which gave the Authority the power to delay demolition where there was a housing shortage.

The limit of obligations issued by the Authority was cut from $700,000,000 to $500,000,000.[43] This amendment was in accord with the conservative policy of the House Banking

---

[40] Statement of David Krooth (personal interview).
[41] S. 1685 (Rept. No. 1545), August 13, 1937, Sec. 2 (1).
[42] *Ibid.*, Sec. 10 (a) and Sec. 11 (a).
[43] *Ibid.*, Sec. 20 (a).

and Currency Committee. Another amendment which Senator Tydings had discussed in the Senate, and one in which a number of legislators from the rural areas were interested, was included in the bill. It prescribed that not more than 10 per cent of the total amount of loans and contributions or grants shall be expended in any one state.[44]

These were the major amendments placed in the bill. When the draft was completed Steagall told Krooth that he was satisfied that it represented his views and those of the committee. Krooth together with a member of the Legislative Reference Service prepared the report in accordance with instructions from Steagall.[45]

The first and second paragraphs of the report illustrated the function of such documents.

> The Committee on Banking and Currency, to whom was referred the bill (S. 1685) to provide financial assistance to the States and political subdivisions thereof for the elimination of unsafe and insanitary housing conditions, for the eradication of slums, for the provision of decent, safe, and sanitary dwellings for families of low income, and for the reduction of unemployment and the stimulation of business activity, to create a United States Housing Authority, and for other purposes, having considered the same, report it back to the House with an amendment and recommend that the bill, as amended, do pass.
>
> The amendment strikes out all after the enacting clause of the bill (S. 1685) and inserts in lieu thereof new matter as appears in italics in the reported bill. Hearings were held by the Senate Committee on Education and Labor on S. 1685 and by your committee on the companion bill (H. R. 5033). The Senate Report (No. 933) sets forth the social and economic objectives of, and the need for, this legislation. There follows a summary of the important provisions of the bill as reported by your committee and the principal differences between it and the bill as passed by the Senate.[46]

---

[44] *Ibid.*, Sec. 21 (d).

[45] Statement of David Krooth (personal interview).

[46] S. 1685 (Rept. No. 1545), August 13, 1937.

When the committee met on Monday morning, August 16, they were presented with the printed copy of the amended bill and with the report, both dated August 13. Some of the members of the committee were angered at the arbitrary action of Chairman Steagall in printing the bill and report without further consideration by the committee. Steagall, however, told them that it was his duty to get out the bill and the report and that he assumed complete responsibility for them. The dissatisfied committee members did not fight Steagall in his own committee. They knew that they did not have a chance of winning a battle with the powerful chairman. On the floor of the House during the debate, however, certain of these members spoke out against Steagall. Representative Frank Hancock had this to say about Steagall and the committee amendment.

> The present bill has been considered under the most difficult circumstances. We have been prodded and urged, for the past ten days, to get out some kind of a housing bill, and that is about the best that we have done in presenting this measure. For the first week of our deliberations we were making real progress in the preparation of a housing measure which would really clear slums and assist in providing accommodations for the underprivileged, starting with the lowest income groups. Then almost suddenly last Friday afternoon, practically all of our work was set at naught by certain amendments proposed by the chairman at the request of the Housing Division of the Public Works Administration. The effect of these amendments could not be known until the bill was printed, for no member of the committee ever saw one of them, with the exception of the chairman, until the printed bills were available Monday morning of this week.[47]

Representative Jesse Wolcott made the following reference to Steagall's action:

> Mr. Chairman, much to my surprise the House Committee on Banking and Currency has the effrontery to strike out section 4 of

---

[47] *Congressional Record*, August 18, 1937, p. 9249.

the Senate bill which my amendment seeks to put back into the bill. [Section 4 (a) was concerned with the civil-service status of employees in the Authority.] . . .

Mr. Chairman, we understand and you understand that the only purpose of this action on the part of the majority members on the Committee on Banking and Currency is to give somebody an opportunity to appoint under the spoils system.[48]

As Wolcott stated, the Democratic majority on the committee followed the lead of their chairman and voted to approve the bill as Steagall presented it to them on that Monday morning, August 16, 1937. A meeting of the party leaders in the House was held to decide on the strategy to be used in pushing the bill through the House. Speaker Bankhead, Majority Leader Rayburn, Chairman of the Rules Committee O'Connor, and Steagall decided that the bill would be taken up on Wednesday, August 18, under a special rule. The rule would be so drafted that the debate would be concluded on Wednesday night and a vote on the bill would be taken before an adjournment. It was the opinion of the Democratic leaders that they had enough votes to pass the bill, especially as a number of Republicans, such as Jesse Wolcott and Everett Dirksen, would support the bill.

Wagner called a special meeting to be held in his office on Tuesday, August 17, to map out strategy for the presentation of certain amendments to the House that would bring the amended bill closer to the form in which Wagner drafted it. Bohn, Vinton, Post, Bauer, and Keyserling were present that morning to advise the senator. The public-housing groups wanted the income-to-rental ratio changed back to five to one. They also wanted the Byrd amendment on construction-cost limitation changed to a general statement in place of the definite figure of $5,000 in the House version and of $4,000 in the Senate version. Another very important change that this group of experts wanted made in the

---

[48] *Ibid.*, p. 9271.

bill concerned the Walsh amendment on a limitation of new construction making it substantially equivalent to the demolition or repair of slum dwellings. Every one of the public-housing groups wanted this amendment changed so that the Authority would have some discretion to delay the demolition of buildings where there was an acute housing shortage. They wanted to separate the housing-construction program from the slum-clearance program. They were convinced that these were two different programs and that one program should not be tied to the other. The group knew that they would have the active support of Representative Ellenbogen and Representative McGranery during the debate on the bill.[49]

The PWA Housing Division also held meetings to discuss the bill as reported by the House committee. Although the bill followed fairly closely the type of program that the PWA Housing Division desired and that it had advocated before the House committee, still there were two amendments that the PWA Housing Division wanted made in the House committee draft. The first concerned the ratio of income to rental. The PWA Housing Division wanted this changed from four to one as it was in the committee draft to five to one as it was in the original Wagner draft. Dave Krooth wrote to Keyserling and Bauer to ask them to support this amendment.[50] The PWA Housing Division was also interested in having the Walsh amendment on slum clearance modified in the same way as was advocated by the American Federation of Labor and the American Federation of Housing Authorities.

There was much activity on the part of the lobbies and pressure groups at this critical period during the life of the housing bill. It was the last effective opportunity that these groups had

---

[49] There are a number of telegrams and letters concerned with this meeting under date of August 16, 1937 (Wagner Papers, S. 1685—1937).

[50] Krooth to Bauer, and Krooth to Keyserling, August 18, 1937, PWA Housing Division, Housing Bill—1937.

to convince the legislators that certain changes should be made in the bill.[51] There was one more operation in the legislative process wherein the bill would be changed, the conference committee; but no group could count on having any specific amendment made at this time.

Steagall had "steam-rollered" the bill through his committee once the president had given him the "go ahead" signal.[52] The House Democratic leaders and the chairman of the Rules Committee had set up the machinery in the House so that the bill would be "steam-rollered" through that legislative body in a single day.

---

[51] Boris Shishkin of the Labor Housing Conference and the AFL was one of the lobbyists who made a special visit to see Steagall at this time. Shishkin had worked with Steagall during the preparation of the Glass-Steagall bill to reorganize the banks and he had the confidence of the chairman of the committee. He told Steagall of the necessity of making certain amendments in the bill, especially concerning the slum-clearance provisions. Steagall adopted the position of the AFL and the other public-housing groups, and the amendment to the Walsh amendment suggested by these groups was proposed by Steagall as a committee amendment during the debate in the House. The amendment that the public-housing groups desired was thus put into the bill (statement of Boris Shishkin, personal interview).

[52] In addition to the remarks that Hancock and Wolcott made about Steagall's procedure in the committee, which remarks were quoted above, Hancock also made this statement about Steagall's pressure. "Mr. Chairman, I regret that my views relative to this bill, in the form reported by our committee, are at variance with the views of a majority of my colleagues. As many members of this body know, I have for several years ardently favored a genuine slum reclamation and low-rent housing program. In early January I introduced a bill to commence, in a modest way, such a program, but, as things go here, it has been pigeonholed all these months. The present bill has been considered under most difficult circumstances. We have been prodded and urged, for the past ten days, to get out some kind of a housing bill, and that is about the best that we have done in presenting this measure" (*Congressional Record*, August 18, 1937, p. 9249).

The House Debate
on the Bill

Because the House of Representatives is a very large
body of legislators, there is not the freedom of debate in this
chamber that there is in the Senate. Important legislation is
ordinarily considered under a special rule which provides that
the debate shall be limited and that a decision on the bill shall
be reached within a definite time period. The Rules Committee
of the House thus exercises a controlling power over legislation.
If the Rules Committee refuses to give a rule to a committee
under which its bill will be considered, the bill is blocked from
consideration by the House. During the discussion of legislation
pending in the House, before the debate on the housing bill was
begun on the morning of Wednesday, August 18, Mr. John A.
Martin, of Colorado, made some comments on the power of the
Rules Committee, in the course of which he roundly condemned
the committee for arrogant and undemocratic action in setting
itself up as a superlegislative body.

> Mr. Speaker, yesterday, after I criticized the Committee on
> Rules regarding the wage and hour bill for its refusal to report
> the bill out, the gentleman from New York [Mr. O'Connor], chair-
> man of that committee, said, quoting the RECORD: I do not pro-
> pose to join my Democratic colleague from Colorado [Mr. Martin]
> and lambast my own party and put the responsibility on them.

Mr. Speaker, I did not lambast the Democratic Party. This is what I said, again quoting from the RECORD: The Democratic Party will be held responsible for it—

That is, responsible for the action of the Rules Committee in smothering the wage-hour bill. . . .

The country does not know anything about the Committee on Rules; it does not care anything about it, or know or care about individual members of Congress. All it knows is that the Democratic Party is in overwhelming control of this Congress and has failed to pass the wage-hour bill, and it will hold the Democratic Party responsible for it. . . .

Mr. Speaker, this is not the first time that the Rules Committee has arrogated to itself the power to pass upon the policy of legislation and has granted a rule for the consideration of legislation in the House, or refused to grant it, according to the views of individual members of the committee as to whether or not they favored such legislation. It has become a common practice on controversial legislation. In other words, the Rules Committee has set itself up as a superlegislative body over all the legislation of Congress, requiring a special rule in order that it may be brought up in the House and considered. That is precisely the position now occupied in the scheme of things in the House by the Committee on Rules.
. . .

As an illustration of however much parties may differ in their principles and objectives, they pursue the same methods once they gain power, is the change made by our party in the number of Members required to sign a discharge petition to take a bill from a committee and bring it before the House for consideration. As is well known, the 145 rule, being exactly one-third of the total House membership, was established by the Democrats of the House when they gained sufficient power in the Seventy-second Congress, cutting the number from 218, as the Republicans had it. The requirement of 218 names, being a majority of the total membership, was properly regarded as a rule designed to prevent the consideration of controversial legislation or any legislation not desired by the House organization. The 145 rule was a more democratic rule.

But no sooner had the party acquired complete and overwhelming control in the Seventy-third Congress than a caucus was called within a few days after the organization of that Congress for the purpose of changing back to the old Republican number,

218. The effort failed of the two-thirds vote necessary to make it binding on all the members and when the new membership was gotten somewhat better in hand, a second and successful effort was made, so now it requires 218 Members to take a bill from a committee.

There was no secret about the object of this change. It was not needed to control the Republican membership. . . .

Now in addition to this undemocratic change in the rules of the House, comes a Rules Committee bloated out of all resemblance to its small beginnings and proper proportions. . . .

The Rules Committee, consisting of 14 Members of the House, has become a superlegislative body. If 7 of its 14 members do not like the haircut of a bill, it matters not that the whole House and the whole country may be clamoring for it. The only way a measure can be taken from the committee is by a discharge petition and the signature of 218 Members, just as in the case of other committees. It is now too late in the session for this as a month or more must elapse. . . .[1]

After Mr. Martin had made his criticism of the Rules Committee, there were a few requests to extend remarks in the *Record,* the disposal of two reports, and then the speaker recognized Mr. John O'Connor of New York, chairman of the Rules Committee. He called up the resolution that he had prepared for the consideration of the housing bill.

HOUSE RESOLUTION 320

Resolved. That upon the adoption of this resolution it shall be in order to move that the House resolve itself into the Committee of the Whole House on the State of the Union for the consideration of S. 1685, an act to provide financial assistance to the States and political subdivisions thereof for the elimination of unsafe and insanitary housing conditions, for the eradication of slums, for the provision of decent, safe, and sanitary dwellings for the families

---

[1] *Congressional Record,* August 18, 1937, pp. 9231-33. Representative John Martin was an experienced legislator. He was a member of the Sixty-first, Sixty-second, Seventy-third, Seventy-fourth, and Seventy-fifth congresses. He was one of the young legislators who took part in the revolution against Speaker Joe Cannon in 1910.

of low income, and for the reduction of unemployment and the stimulation of business activity, to create a United States Housing Authority, and for other purposes, and all points of order against said bill are hereby waived. That after general debate, which shall be confined to the bill, and continued not to exceed 3 hours, to be equally divided and controlled by the chairman and ranking minority member of the Committee on Banking and Currency, the bill shall be read for amendment under the 5-minute rule as an original bill.

It shall be in order to consider without the intervention of any point of order the substitute committee amendment recommended by the Committee on Banking and Currency now in the bill, and such substitute for the purpose of amendment shall be considered under the 5-minute rule as an original bill. At the conclusion of such consideration the Committee shall rise and report the bill to the House with such amendments as may have been adopted, and the previous question shall be considered as ordered on the bill and the amendments thereto to final passage without intervening motion except one motion to recommit with or without instructions.[2]

After the reading of the resolution there was debate for one hour on the adoption of the resolution. O'Connor was recognized by the speaker; and before beginning his argument for the resolution and the passage of the housing bill, he announced that he had yielded thirty minutes on the resolution to the gentleman from Tennessee, Mr. J. Will Taylor, a minority member of the Rules Committee, who would represent the opposition to the resolution and the housing bill. The debate on the resolution was in reality a debate on the general principles of the housing bill. Two important principles were brought out during this debate. O'Connor stressed the fact that, since bad housing constituted a national problem, it should be corrected by means of federal legislation. Representative Taylor yielded his time to Representative Robert Luce of Massachusetts, who spoke against

---

[2] *Ibid.*, p. 9234. Galloway in *Congress at the Crossroads*, pp. 111-15, gives a short summary of the history of the Rules Committee and its controlling influence over legislation.

the bill because it appropriated money from the general tax funds for the benefit of a few metropolitan areas.

When the hour of discussion was concluded Mr. O'Connor was recognized by the speaker.

> Mr. Speaker, I move the previous question on the resolution to its adoption or rejection. The previous question was ordered. The resolution was agreed to.

Mr. Steagall was then recognized by the speaker.

> Mr. Speaker, I move that the House resolve itself into the Committee of the Whole House on the state of the Union for the consideration of the bill (S. 1685) to provide financial assistance to the States and political subdivisions thereof for the elimination of unsafe and insanitary housing conditions, for the eradication of slums, for the provisions of decent, safe, and sanitary dwellings for families of low income, and for the reduction of unemployment and the stimulation of business activity, to create a United States Housing Authority, and for other purposes.
>
> The motion was agreed to.
>
> Accordingly the House resolved itself into the Committee of the Whole House on the state of the Union for the consideration of the bill S. 1685, the low-cost housing bill, with Mr. Cooper in the Chair.
>
> The clerk read the title of the bill.
>
> By unanimous consent, the first reading of the bill was dispensed with.[3]

Mr. Steagall, as chairman of the House Committee on Banking and Currency, then opened the debate with a statement on the purposes of the bill. The technical material in the statement on the cost of the program to the government had been prepared

---

[3] *Congressional Record*, August 18, 1937, p. 9240. An interesting procedure takes place when the House resolves itself into the Committee of the Whole. The speaker leaves the chair and the mace (the symbol of authority in the House) is removed from its pedestal at the right hand of the speaker's chair by a sergeant at arms and placed in a holder on the floor to the right of the pedestal.

for him by the PWA Housing Division. As Steagall did not have
a complete understanding of the technical and financial aspects
of the bill, he did not desire to yield to anyone for questions;
but he finally yielded to his colleague on the committee, Mr.
T. Allan Goldsborough of Maryland.

> I yield first to the gentleman from Maryland, a member of
> the committee. I must hurry on. We are necessarily limited in this
> discussion. I am not responsible for it. I am doing the best I can.
>
> MR. GOLDSBOROUGH. The limit of the contribution, as a matter
> of fact, will be something over $11,000,000 a year over the
> 60 years.
>
> MR. STEAGALL. No; the gentleman is in error. Under the bill
> there could be a contribution of $20,000,000 a year. This is the way
> it is computed, according to the best figures I can get from experts,
> who know how to figure much better than I. Upon the basis not of
> $11,000,000 but $20,000,000 of annual contribution I have given
> the figures I have indicated to the House.
>
> MR. GOLDSBOROUGH. That could not be true, because the total
> amount of the contribution would be less than $700,000,000, and if
> this is averaged throughout the 60 years it would be something over
> $11,000,000. There is no question about that.[4]

This exchange of *facts* between Steagall and Goldsborough
gives a good indication of the grasp that the two senior members
of the committee had of the financial provisions of the bill.

Steagall finished his statement with an eloquent plea to all
the rural representatives to support this bill. He represented an
area which would not benefit from this legislation; but, he stated:
"I recognize that we are one people and the distress in one community involves every community in the United States."

When Steagall finished, Representative Jesse Wolcott of
Michigan, ranking minority member of the committee, rose and
addressed the chair.

---

[4] *Ibid.*, p. 9241. Mr. Goldsborough and Mr. James J. Lanzetta of New York had
risen at the same time to ask Steagall a question. Steagall yielded to Lanzetta
after his exchange with Goldsborough.

Mr. Chairman, I yield myself 15 minutes. Mr. Chairman, re-gardless of what action this Congress has taken in years gone by to give relief to the railroads, to the insurance companies, to farmers, to home owners, and to small industry, that alone is not a justifica-tion for passing this bill if this bill is not meritorious. Several wrongs cannot make a single right.

I am supporting this bill because I believe it is meritorious. I know there are many in the House and in the country who are in complete disagreement with me on the stand I have taken. If I cannot justify my stand, then I individually am responsible, for I speak for no one but myself in respect to this bill.[5]

After Wolcott had made an explanatory statement on the bill, he described the bill as a foundation upon which to build for the future. A number of members wished to ask Wolcott questions, and he yielded to them. In answering these questions about the specific provisions of certain sections of the bill Wolcott demonstrated that he had a better knowledge of the provisions of the bill than did Steagall. As the questions were still being proposed when his time had expired, Wolcott yielded to himself another five minutes to finish his statement.

Wolcott finished his statement and the chairman recognized Mr. Goldsborough, who was managing the majority side of the debate in the absence of Mr. Steagall from the House chamber. Goldsborough yielded fifteen minutes to Michael Reilly of Wis-consin. Reilly severely criticized the financial provision of the bill. He stated that he was of the opinion that the localities should make a larger financial contribution to the program. He ended his statement, nevertheless, by giving notice to the House that he would vote for the bill.

I am not satisfied with this bill; I think it has not gone far enough in placing financial responsibility for slum clearance on the cities; but legislation is the result of compromise; one cannot always have his way in the committee or on the floor of this House.

---

[5] *Ibid.*, p. 9242.

While the bill has not gone as far as I would have it go in the way of protecting the United States Treasury, still, it is a great improvement on the original bill, and I am going to vote for it.[6]

Wolcott yielded ten minutes to Mr. Taylor of Tennessee, who spoke against the bill on the grounds that it was unconstitutional. The political theory of the South was clearly expressed in his words.

> If this class of legislation falls within the scope of the general-welfare clause of the Constitution, then our founding fathers utterly failed in their attempt to protect either individual or States' rights. The power to handicap and tax the individual is, indeed, the power to destroy. That abuse is camouflaged and subterfuged in this bill. Our founding fathers realized the strength of unity and to preserve unity they proposed a union of the States; however, the colonists refused to join that union until their local self-government and individual rights were amply protected. If the colonists had thought Congress might ever place any such construction upon the welfare clause as is clearly implied in the pending measure, there would have been no union. If we pass this legislation and the courts uphold it, then Congress shall have all power except that granted the executive and the courts; and all other rights reserved to the individual and to the States will be of no avail, which in its final analysis means that the Constitution might as well be declared null and void and discarded.[7]

Taylor was reluctant to yield for any questions. He finally yielded to one of his friends from Kentucky, Mr. John M. Robison, for a question that set up an argument against the bill. Mr. William B. Barry of New York, who had been attempting to ask Taylor a question, was finally given an opportunity of proposing his question.

> MR. BARRY. Mr. Chairman, will the gentleman yield?
> MR. TAYLOR. I am sorry, I do not have time to yield.

---

[6] *Ibid.*, p. 9247.
[7] *Ibid.*

MR. BARRY. The gentleman has just yielded twice.

MR. TAYLOR. I have only ten minutes, and I shall not be able to finish in that time. However, I will yield to the gentleman.

MR. BARRY. The gentleman claims that this is legislation for a preferred class. Does the gentleman believe that any of the legislation we have passed to aid the farmers is justified, and, if so, wherein is any difference in principle involved?

MR. TAYLOR. We did have some hope of recovery in that legislation, but we have very little in this.

MR. BARRY. We gave $4,000,000,000 in subsidies to the farmers, but here you are going to get your money back.

MR. TAYLOR. I cannot yield further.[8]

When Taylor had completed his remarks, it was again time for the Democrats to speak on the bill. Goldsborough yielded ten minutes to Mr. Frank W. Hancock, Jr., of North Carolina, a Democrat, but one who was an opponent of the bill. Hancock expressed his opposition to the financial provisions of the bill. He claimed that they were unsound, and he called the attention of the members of the House to the fact that no representative of the Treasury Department appeared before either the Senate or the House committee to approve of the financial provisions of the bill. Hancock finished his ten-minute period and was given an additional five minutes. The burden of Hancock's argument was concerned with the fact that the lowest income group was not served by the bill, since the families in this group would not have sufficient income to meet the rent requirement.

> I am, of course, disappointed from the testimony presented to our committee, that no family with an income of $700 per annum or less could possibly meet the rent requirement. My hope and aim has always been that a measure of this kind would first benefit those who needed it most, and that would include the 15 or 20 per cent of our true American families who were in the lowest income brackets.[9]

---

[8] *Ibid.*, p. 9248.
[9] *Ibid.*, p. 9251.

Hancock was opposed to the lack of a provision demanding a substantial local contribution to the subsidy from the Federal Government for the project.

> I know that the municipalities, under the leadership of Mayor La Guardia of New York City, make the claim that no city in the United States with a population of over 50,000 is able to make any contribution toward this program. My answer to that is that if they are not willing to dig down in their treasuries and bear a part of the expense of this program they should not come to the Federal Treasury and "holler" for help. (Applause.) [10]

Hancock also used a jocose example to explain the subsidy provision of the bill.

> Here is a good friend of mine who wants to engage in a worthy, humanitarian enterprise. He is bent on doing something good for humanity. He has the idea but he is not willing to back it with his own money. I am interested in what he wants to do, and I am in a position to make some of his friends put up the money. So I say to him, "I will lend you $1,000 at 3 percent if you will use it in furtherance of this worthy enterprise." The contract is made, and I then say to my friend that if he will continue to use the project for which he has spent my money I will give him $35 per year to pay me the interest on the money I loaned him. This is a fair sample of the financial arrangement under this bill. (Laughter.) [11]

Fish had taken over as minority leader in the absence of Wolcott from the House chamber. He recognized Mr. Charles L. Gifford of Massachusetts for ten minutes to follow Hancock. Gifford was also an opponent of the bill. He attacked the security for the bonds issued by the Federal Government. He claimed that the buildings in the projects would not last for the sixty-year amortization period. People accustomed to living in the slums would not in Gifford's opinion, allow a house to last for twenty years. And the maximum life of a good house, Gifford

---

[10] *Ibid.*
[11] *Ibid.,* p. 9252.

claimed, was thirty-three years. Therefore the sixty-year period for amortization was absurd, and a sixty-year loan was unsound.[12] While Hancock and Gifford were making their attacks on the bill they were questioned by Representative Edward W. Curley of New York; but the questions did not penetrate to the heart of the argument and no specific refutation was made of the attacks on the financial provisions of the bill. The reason for this was simply that the only person who could explain the provisions was Representative Ellenbogen, and he was cut off from the debate by Steagall and the other members of the Committee on Banking and Currency.

Fish yielded himself fifteen minutes when Gifford had concluded his remarks. He asked for and received unanimous consent to proceed for six minutes out of order. He spoke of the necessity of withdrawing our citizens and our troops from the battle zones of China. Fish then spoke in criticism of the bill:

> We should try to take the population out of the cities and put them on land, with little homes of their own, where they become property owners, taxpayers, and good American citizens. I believe that would do more to offset radicalism, socialism, and communism in America than any one thing this Congress could do.
>
> MR. SHORT. Will the gentleman yield?
>
> MR. FISH. I yield to the gentleman from Missouri.
>
> MR. SHORT. Does not the gentleman from New York agree with the very able gentleman from North Carolina [Mr. Hancock] whose logic was irrefutable, that this bill absolutely prohibits individual ownership?
>
> MR. FISH. Absolutely.
>
> MR. SHORT. It regiments and communizes by throwing up army barracks in cities, such as you have out there at Tugwelltown and Greenbelt, and shacks that will be more collectivistic than anything I saw in all of Soviet Russia.
>
> MR. FISH. The gentleman believes in plain speaking. So do I.[13]

-----

[12] *Ibid.*
[13] *Ibid.*, p. 9254.

But Fish had opened his speech with a statement favorable to the bill, and he concluded his speech with what can certainly be called another favorable statement.

> The gentleman knows perfectly well this bill is going through. It is going through because many of us believe in slum clearance and low-cost housing for our lowest income groups, and this is the only bill before us, and it is probably the only way to get the results we want in the near future. The plan and scope of the bill has been approved by practically every newspaper in New York City and I propose to support it, although it is far from perfect and does not carry out my ideas of what a real housing program should be, and I fear the bill will be a disappointment to its most earnest well-wishers in failing to make much of a dent in slum clearance in the city of New York, particularly with the unfair and unfortunate 10-percent allocation limitation.[14]

Representative Thomas F. Ford of California was next recognized by Goldsborough. Ford pointed out that some of the members of the House went to great pains to tell everyone they were in favor of the bill, but that at the same time they wanted to limit the program so that it would be unworkable. The principal argument developed by Ford was the fact that the slums breed disease and crime and that these evils spread to other communities. Thus the slums constitute a national problem which must be attacked by federal legislation.

Representative Dudley A. White of Ohio followed Ford in the debate. He spoke against the bill, mentioning that the subsidy plan was an unsound financial scheme. Representative Brent Spence of Kentucky, a rural representative, spoke of the necessity of passing this bill because the slums presented a national problem that affected all areas of the country, even the rural areas.

Representative Everett Dirksen of Illinois was recognized by Minority Leader Wolcott. In his florid style Dirksen ex-

---

[14] *Ibid.*

plained how the slum problem could not be solved by the localities. He then went on to score the waste and inefficiency in the
resettlement projects, but declared that, despite this waste and
inefficiency, the government must act.

> As time goes on I fancy that we shall take the housing func-
> tion of Government for granted, even as now we take for granted
> the theory and function of social security. It is but another case of
> where our charitable impulses are on the march.
> As a former member of the Committee on Banking and Cur-
> rency, I labored with the first housing bill that came to that com-
> mittee. From that background and that experience I must confess
> dissatisfaction with some aspects of the pending measure. I feel
> certain, however, that when our housing venture is launched and
> the set-up made that many of the present objectionable features of
> the bill will be gradually softened and eliminated and the program
> established on a sound and workable basis.[15]

Representative Fred L. Crawford of Michigan, another Republican, was given eight minutes when Dirksen concluded his
oration. Crawford did not take his full time, but proposed a
series of questions to Steagall designed to bring out the fact that
the legislation would not provide dwellings for persons in the
lowest income bracket. The people who would be tenants in the
projects were people who would be able to pay rent, people not
on relief, but people with an income of over $700 a year. After
this series of questions Crawford yielded the balance of his time
to Steagall. The chairman then yielded the remaining time of
debate, fifteen minutes, to Representative Clyde Williams of
Missouri, who spent most of his time answering questions of his
colleagues concerning the type and size of cities that would
benefit by the legislation. At the end of this period the chairman
pounded the gavel and announced that the time for debate had
expired and that, as the clerk read the bill, amendments would
be in order at the end of each section.

---

[15] *Ibid.*, p. 9258.

The time of the gentleman from Missouri has expired. All time has expired. The clerk will read the House substitute for the Senate bill. Under the rule it will be considered as an original bill, and amendment will be in order at the end of each section of the House amendment to the Senate bill.[16]

Before proceeding to an examination of the amendment of the bill on the floor of the House, certain observations should be made concerning the debate that was conducted under the special rule. The first observation refers to the principle of selectivity used by the managers of the debate in choosing members of the House to engage in debate. Seniority of membership on the House Committee on Banking and Currency, the committee which had jurisdiction over the bill, was the basis for choosing the debaters. Fourteen members of the House were given an opportunity to argue the merits of the bill. Seven Democrats and seven Republicans were recognized. The seven Democrats were the ranking members of the House Committee on Banking and Currency. There were only six Republicans on the committee, so Representative Dirksen, a former member of the committee, was chosen to fill out the Republican list. Representative Taylor, of the Rules Committee, yielded to Representative Luce during the debate on the resolution, and Representative Luce yielded to Taylor during the debate on the bill. This is an example of the protocol observed during House debate.

Because of the practice of choosing debaters on the basis of their seniority on a committee rather than because of their ability and their understanding of the problem involved, the debate on the housing bill was a poor exposition of the problems involved in the legislation under discussion. The few members of the House who understood the bill, such as Ellenbogen and McGranery, were cut off from debate because of their lack of membership, or lack of seniority, on the committee. It would

---

[16] *Ibid.*, p. 9260.

seem that party responsibility would dictate that the best-prepared and most able members of the Congress be chosen to defend a bill designed to carry out decisions announced in the platform and legislative program of the party.

One glaring misunderstanding of the bill exhibited by Steagall and the other proponents of the measure was that concerned with the Walsh amendment. Senator Walsh proposed that slum quarters must be demolished, or effectively closed, or *repaired*.[17] Not once in the entire debate in the House did anyone give any evidence of understanding Walsh's provision for the repair and reconditioning of slum dwellings.

After the clerk read Section 1 of the bill Steagall, who was in charge of the proceedings, proposed a committee amendment to the wording of the section so that it would be explicitly stated that the housing contemplated in this bill would be for the benefit of those with low income "in rural or urban areas." The question was put on agreeing to the amendment. Representative Ellenbogen rose in opposition to the amendment. As Ellenbogen said when he started to speak, he was employing a parliamentary device in order to obtain the floor and discuss the bill. This was the first opportunity that this legislator, one of the principal authors of the bill under discussion, had to speak. He made an intelligent speech explaining the various major provisions of the bill and recounting the universal support that was manifested in favor of the bill. He then requested the House to remove the absolute and rigid limitations that had been put into the bill and replace them with general limitations which would not hinder the operation of the program. He mentioned in particular the limitation of income to rental ratio of four to one, the construction-cost limitation of $5,000 for each family dwelling unit, and the rigid requirement limiting new units constructed to the number of slum dwellings demolished. Ellenbogen was

---

[17] *Ibid.*, August 3, 1937, p. 8079.

stopped at the end of five minutes, which was the rule under which the House was then operating, and his request for unanimous consent to proceed was objected to.[18] Following Ellenbogen in making general statements on the merits of the bill were Representatives Edward Curley of New York, Alfred Phillips of Connecticut, and E. V. Izac of California. They proposed *pro-forma* amendments in order to have the opportunity to address the House. Debate on the section was closed under the five-minute rule, the *pro-forma* amendments were withdrawn, and the question of agreeing to the committee amendment was put to the House. The amendment was agreed to.[19]

The next section to be considered for amendment was Section 2, which contained the definitions. It was read in full, and then, as there were no committee amendments, an amendment was sent to the clerk by Representative Frank Crowther of New York. This amendment concerned the use of vacant land that had been cleared of slums for parks, playgrounds, garages, and so forth. Representative Wolcott, who was in favor of this type of amendment, proposed a similar amendment which was considered as a perfecting amendment to the Crowther amendment. There was a short discussion on the merits of the proposal; then Steagall asked unanimous consent that all debate on the amendment and all amendments thereto be closed. There was no objection, and a vote was taken on the amendments. Both the Crowther amendment and the Wolcott amendment were rejected.[20]

Representative Hancock then offered a perfecting amendment to the section which defined "acquisition cost." This amendment was accepted by Chairman Steagall, and was agreed to by the committee.[21]

---

[18] *Ibid.*, August 18, 1937, p. 9262.
[19] *Ibid.*, p. 9264. In this part of the debate, when reference is made to the committee, it means Committee of the Whole House on the State of the Union.
[20] *Ibid.*, p. 9266.
[21] *Ibid.*

Representative Case of South Dakota offered an amendment restricting the eligibility of tenants in the housing projects to citizens of the United States. Case gave a short speech in favor of this restrictive amendment. The amendment was accepted by a vote of seventy-six ayes to sixty-four noes (the division was called for by Ellenbogen). When the result was announced Representative Lanzetta of New York asked for tellers. The tellers were refused, and the amendment was agreed to.[22]

At this point Steagall wanted to close all amendments to the section; but Hancock and Ellenbogen refused to give consent, stating that they had important amendments to present to the committee. Hancock then presented his amendment, which would restore the limitation on construction costs to the figure of $4,000 per unit and $1,000 per room which Senator Byrd had put into the Senate version of the bill. This amendment was objected to by Representative Frank E. Hook of Michigan as a "definite effort to emasculate the bill."[23] Representatives Fish and McGranery also objected to this limitation. Steagall announced that he hoped that the amendment would be voted down. The vote (with Hancock demanding a division) was fifty-nine ayes to seventy-seven noes.[24]

---

[22] *Ibid.*, p. 9267. A vote by tellers means that the speaker, or chairman when the House has resolved itself into the Committee of the Whole House, appoints one member from each side to count the votes on his side of the House. *Hinds' Precedents*, Vol. 5, Secs. 5987-97, pp. 523-26, gives the rules and precedents on this method of counting votes, in which the members rise from their seats and walk down the center aisle to the well of the House and file past the teller counting the side of their choice. This method of voting has the advantage of indicating to the leadership, and to the lobby groups and the press, the specific support for and opposition to the bill without the members' names being recorded.

[23] *Congressional Record*, August 18, 1937, p. 9267.

[24] *Ibid.*, p. 9269. During the course of his argument in favor of his limiting amendment, Hancock digressed to speak about the appointment of Senator Black to the Supreme Court, and certain bills that were not passed by the Congress. No one raised a point of order that Hancock was speaking and proceeding out of order.

Ellenbogen was then recognized and proposed his amendment to set the ratio of income to rental at five to one rather than at four to one as had been done by the House committee. Wolcott objected to the amendment because it made the units unavailable to the lowest income group, the people who needed help most. Steagall also opposed the amendment and announced that he hoped that the committee would vote down the amendment. When the question was put by the chairman the amendment was rejected.[25]

The clerk then read Sections 3 and 4. When he finished Wolcott offered an amendment to Section 4 (a) which would put the agency under civil-service regulations. Steagall immediately opposed the amendment, saying that it put under civil service too many employees, including experts. He moved for the closing of all debate on the section and all amendments thereto. The motion was passed.[26] Representative Robert Ramspeck of Georgia, chairman of the House Committee on Civil Service, had attempted to get the floor to speak on the amendment. He was cut off from the debate by the action of Mr. Steagall. Ramspeck then attempted to get the floor by offering an amendment of his own, similar in language to that of Wolcott's. Steagall objected to this amendment on the ground that it was a repetition of Wolcott's amendment and hence out of order. The chair overruled the point of order. Tempers were warm in the House at this juncture. The entire Committee on the Civil Service was in a state of anger. Mrs. Edith Nourse Rogers of Massachusetts rose to make a barbed remark about the situation at that time.

> Mr. Chairman, is it not the custom when the death of a Member occurs to conduct some memorial or pay a tribute to that Member? I should think it ought to be in order to pay tribute to

---

[25] *Ibid.*, p. 9270.
[26] *Ibid.*, p. 9271.

the death of a great committee. I have the honor of serving on the Committee on the Civil Service, of which the gentleman from Georgia [Mr. Ramspeck] is chairman, and that committee is dead. It has been choked to death. (Laughter.)[27]

The chairman put the question of Representative Ramspeck's amendment, and it was rejected. The question was then put on Representative Wolcott's amendment, and it was rejected. Representative Fred L. Crawford of Michigan made a third attempt to put an amendment in the bill requiring civil-service status for the employees of the new agency, but it was also rejected.

As the clerk was reading Section 5, Representative Williams interrupted the reading to ask unanimous consent that the further reading of the section be dispensed with. This was a procedure that was employed when routine sections of the bill which did not contain any controversial matters were being read. It was a time-saver at an hour when the members were weary from the long hours in the chamber. But Representative Ramspeck objected to the motion.

An amendment to Section 5 was offered by Representative Thomas R. Amlie of Wisconsin which would permit the use of funds from the appropriations for the Authority to be used for research, experimentation, and so forth. This amendment was opposed by Hancock, who claimed that all the money should be used to put up the much-needed housing units. This amendment was also rejected.

When Section 6 was read, Representative White of Ohio wanted to amend it so that all transactions would be subject to the preaudit of the General Accounting Office. The preaudit would extend to the bonds and other obligations issued by the Authority, as well as to the expenses of the Authority. This was opposed by Reilly of Wisconsin, who pointed out that a preaudit of obligations was unknown in government agencies and that it

---

[27] *Ibid.*, p. 9272.

would be unworkable. This was the same type of amendment that was discussed in the Senate after Senator Byrd had brought to light the great waste on the Resettlement Administration projects.[28] The amendment was rejected by the Committee of the Whole House.[29]

Mr. Gifford then offered an amendment to strike out that section of the bill which gave to the president the authority to approve all housing projects. At the time that this amendment was debated the Republicans took the opportunity of making a few criticisms of the president's conduct of the Public Works Program. White asked Gifford a question.

> MR. WHITE. On the many P.W.A. projects dealing with housing, is it not true that the President has had the same authority of check?
>
> MR. GIFFORD. Yes; and ugly rumors persist about those people on whom he depends or on whose advice he acts, as to whether largesses be granted or withheld.
>
> MR. WHITE. Furthermore, is it not true that under these projects the cost of what was supposed to be low-cost housing projects has run as high as $26,000 per dwelling unit, in face of that kind of a check? So it is not any kind of a check at all.
>
> MR. GIFFORD. As far as the gentleman's remarks go, there are many smelly things happening lately without any shame exhibited on the faces of those responsible. We cannot investigate because our Rules Committee will not let us investigate. So book sales to corporations roll merrily on and anything goes with this administration, no matter how unsavory. I think by voting this amendment you would relieve your President of a great burden and also relieve some of us from the punishment we might receive in some of our congressional districts by withholding what might be our due and share of funds allocated.[30]

This amendment was rejected. After this vote Ramspeck obtained the floor by the use of a *pro-forma* amendment. He was

---

28 *Ibid.*, August 4, 1937, p. 8176.   30 *Ibid.*
29 *Ibid.*, August 18, 1937, p. 9274.

still angry because of the treatment he had received from Steagall. He spoke of the absurdity of the Democratic members' of the House of Representatives repudiating the express desire of the president regarding the civil service. Ramspeck said that the president had sent two distinct messages to the House requesting that no agencies be put outside of the civil service. Ramspeck then had a few words for Steagall.

> I have no quarrel with any Member of this House who does not agree with me about civil service, but I do quarrel with any man who takes what I consider to be unfair advantage of a member of his own party, the chairman of a committee, representing the subject matter under consideration, and put his own party in the hole, and denies to his own President the right to have considered properly on this floor the requests he has made regarding civil service. (Applause.) I resent that.[31]

Representative Fish saw a good opportunity for the Republicans to make some remarks about the Democrats, and he rose to take advantage of it.

> Mr. Chairman, I rise in opposition to the pro forma amendment and I do not propose to strike out the President on the question of civil-service requirements. I wish to make some comments, however, about the tactics of the chairman of the Committee on Banking and Currency in cutting off debate on the civil-service section and his statement. I have the highest regard for him. If I did not I would denounce him vigorously for his tactics here this afternoon. I think he was carried away by his enthusiasm for the patronage he saw just around the corner. He got up and told the Members of the House an entirely different version of the meaning and text of the bill. Striking out the civil-service requirements opens the bill wide for a paradise of spoilsmen and for a huge patronage grab of offices without the merit system at all.
>
> He told you an entirely different story and then cut off debate. You members on that side followed him, you did exactly what Members on our side would have done, followed your chairman,

---

[31] *Ibid.*

but you followed him up a blind alley and he gave you misinformation. You followed him up a blind alley against your own President who has come out in the public press demanding that the civil-service system be maintained in these bills. Here you are giving lip service to the President but actually you are knifing him in the back. Is there a conspiracy here of silence, or is there a conspiracy between the Democratic majority in the House to do one thing and have the President say the other? Is the President only shadow boxing with the merit system and giving lip service to it?[32]

Fish's remarks touched off a heated discussion on the question of the merit system. Representative Claude A. Fuller, chairman of the Democratic patronage committee, ridiculed the merit-system examinations and claimed that the Republicans supported the system because they wanted to get the government jobs.[33] Wolcott answered this charge by claiming that the actions of the Democratic party demonstrated that they were not sincerely in favor of the merit system. Representative Robert Luce of Massachusetts also made a few barbed remarks about the Democrats and their interest in civil service. Steagall then moved that all debate and all amendments to the section be closed. The motion was agreed to, and the clerk went on with the reading of Section 7. When the clerk concluded reading this section, Mrs. Rogers rose and made a *pro-forma* amendment "to strike out the enacting clause." She then launched out into a discussion of civil-service regulations and federal employees. When her time was concluded her motion was rejected.

There were no amendments offered to Section 8. Mr. Hancock offered an amendment to Section 9 which provided for an increase in the amount of the local contribution to the federal subsidy to the local projects, which local contribution was to be given in the form of tax exemption or cash or both. Mr. Phillips, a former mayor of Stamford, Connecticut, and Mr. James

---

[32] *Ibid.*
[33] *Ibid.*, p. 9276.

McGranery argued against the amendment, pointing out that all the testimony presented to the committee demonstrated that such a burden would make it impossible for the cities to operate the housing program. The amendment was rejected by a vote of fifty-one ayes to eighty-two noes, the division called for by Mr. Hancock.[34]

Mr. H. Jerry Voorhis of California then offered an amendment which would strike out the limitation of loans to 85 per cent of the cost of the development, thus allowing for a loan of 100 per cent on the cost of the development. Voorhis stated in his argument for the amendment that, as the government has a first lien on the property because of the 85-per-cent loan, it would be impossible for the local authority to borrow the other 15 per cent on a second lien. The Republican members of the House Committee on Banking and Currency, Gifford and Williams, opposed the amendment, and it was rejected by the committee.

The next amendment was offered by Representative Peter De Muth of Pennsylvania. It made provision for loans to individuals to construct single detached homes. Mr. Williams made a point of order that the amendment was not germane to the bill or any section of the bill. The ruling of the chairman, Mr. Jere Cooper of Tennessee, sustained the point of order.[35]

As the hour was growing late, Mr. Andrew May of Kentucky asked unanimous consent that the further reading of the bill be dispensed with. Mr. Ramspeck objected. Steagall then moved that the further reading of the bill be dispensed with, and that amendments might be offered to any part of the bill considered as read. Mr. Ramspeck objected that the motion was not in order. The chair sustained the point of order, and the clerk continued to read the bill.

---

[34] *Ibid.,* p. 9278.
[35] *Ibid.,* p. 9279.

Mr. Spence of Kentucky then proposed an amendment that the demolition of the slum dwellings might be delayed where there was a shortage of dwellings. He proposed the amendment as a committee amendment. It read as follows:

> . . . except that such elimination may in the discretion of the Authority be deferred in any locality or metropolitan area where the shortage of decent, safe, or sanitary housing available to low-income families is so acute as to force dangerous overcrowding of such families.

Steagall emphasized the fact that this was a committee amendment which the committee hoped would be adopted. Wolcott also rose to say that he would support the amendment. Ellenbogen made a plea for the amendment, and concluded his remarks with the statement that "this is one of the amendments that restores sanity to the bill and I hope it will be adopted." The amendment was agreed to.[36]

Hancock then presented an amendment which would require the demolition of slums "within a period of two years after the development of the low-rent housing project." Hancock claimed that the words "make satisfactory arrangements" used in this section did not make slum clearance mandatory, and he wanted to make sure that the slums were actually cleared. Reilly objected to the two-year period because it seemed to be an arbitrary period. He asked that the amendment be rejected. The amendment was rejected.

Mr. Wolcott then offered several perfecting amendments to the section which were accepted. Sections 12 and 13 were read by the clerk. No amendments were proposed to these sections. Mr. Kent E. Keller of Illinois then asked unanimous consent to dispense with the further reading of the bill. Ramspeck objected to the motion, saying: "I gave notice to the chairman of this committee when he cut me off from debate that this bill was

---

[36] *Ibid.*, p. 9280.

going to be read and it is going to be read. I object, Mr. Chairman."[37] The clerk read Sections 14 and 15, and when he concluded Hancock offered an amendment to reduce the limitation on construction costs to $4,000 per unit and $1,000 per room; the House version contained the limitation of $5,000 average per family unit. O'Connor objected vigorously to the amendment, and Steagall pointed out that the real limitation was not in a specific figure of $5,000, but in the general limitations that the projects could not be of elaborate design or materials and that construction costs could not be higher than construction costs in the locality for similar buildings constructed under similar local conditions. Steagall moved to close debate, which was agreed to. The amendment was defeated, fifty-nine ayes to ninety-seven noes; the division was called for by Hancock.[38]

There was a long debate about the meaning of a sentence in Section 16 (6) which required subcontractors working on a housing project to submit to the secretary of labor the number of persons on their payroll, the total number of man-hours worked, and so forth. Mr. Wadsworth claimed that the language as it was then in the section could mean that, if the Bell Telephone Company were a subcontractor on a housing project, it would have to submit the payroll, and so forth, of the entire system, whereas the intent of the law was that the payroll, man-hours worked, expenditures, and so forth on the project should be submitted to the secretary of labor. Fish then suggested that the section be amended to read "on the particular project." Wadsworth did not accept this suggestion of Fish, but reworded the section so that the contractor would be responsible for submitting the names of all the subcontractors. McGranery objected to this, saying that the subcontractors should furnish this infor-

---

[37] *Ibid.*, p. 9282.
[38] *Ibid.*, p. 9284.

mation so that there would be no danger of "kickbacks" and so forth, though he agreed that the information submitted should apply to the particular project. Steagall claimed that the language did mean the particular project; but many of the members did not agree with him. Fish again proposed that the words "on the particular project" be added to the sentence. This was acceptable to Wadsworth, and it was agreed to by Steagall. The amendment was proposed to the committee, and agreed to.[39]

The clerk read Sections 17, 18, and 19. Fish then proposed that the limitation of funds to be spent in any one state be raised from 10 per cent, as it was then in the bill, to 15 per cent, which would be a compromise between the 10 per cent called for by the House version and the 20 per cent called for by the Senate version. The amendment was rejected.[40]

Sections 22, 23, 24, 25, 26, 27, and 28 were read by the clerk, and no amendments were proposed to any of these sections. Mr. Keller again asked for unanimous consent that further reading of the bill be dispensed with, and again Mr. Ramspeck objected. Hancock then made one last attempt to amend the bill. He offered an amendment which would place two sections of the National Housing Act concerned with loans for private multi-dwelling homes into the bill. Wolcott objected that the amendment was not germane to the bill or to any section of the bill. Hancock defended his amendment, claiming that it would increase the housing facilities available for people in the low income bracket. Wolcott replied that the only thing that the Hancock amendment had in common with the bill was the word "housing." The chair then said that it was ready to rule on the point of order. After quoting some precedents from *Cannon's Precedents of the House* the chair ruled that the amendment was not germane.[41]

---

[39] *Ibid.*, p. 9286.
[40] *Ibid.*, p. 9287.

[41] *Ibid.*, p. 9288.

The clerk then read the last two sections of the bill. Since there was no debate or amendment to these sections, the chairman stated: "The question is on the committee amendment, as amended, to the Senate Bill." The amendment, as amended, was agreed to.[42] The chairman then stated that "under the rule the Committee will rise."

> Accordingly the Committee rose; and the Speaker having resumed the chair, Mr. Cooper, Chairman of the Committee of the Whole House on the state of the Union, reported that that Committee, having had under consideration the bill (S. 1685) to provide financial assistance to the States and political subdivisions thereof for the elimination of unsafe and unsanitary housing conditions, . . . to create a United States Housing Authority, and for other purposes, pursuant to House Resolution 320, he reported the same back to the House with an amendment adopted in Committee of the Whole.
>
> THE SPEAKER. Under the rule, the previous question is ordered.
> The question is on agreeing to the amendment.
> The amendment is as follows:[43] [There followed the amended text of the bill.]
> The amendment was agreed to.[44]
> The bill was ordered to be read a third time, and was read the third time.
> MR. LUCE. Mr. Speaker, I present a motion to recommit.
> THE SPEAKER. Is the gentleman opposed to the bill?
> MR. LUCE. I am.
> THE SPEAKER. The gentleman is a member of the committee reporting the bill.
> The clerk will report the motion to recommit.
> The clerk read as follows.
> Mr. Luce moves that the bill be recommitted to the Committee with instructions to report the same back forthwith with the following amendment:
> On page 39, strike out subsection (a) of section 4, and insert in lieu thereof the following:

---

[42] *Ibid.*
[43] *Ibid.,* p. 9289.
[44] *Ibid.,* p. 9292.

"The Administrator is authorized, in accordance with the provisions of the civil-service laws and the Classification Act of 1923, to employ and fix the compensation of such officers, attorneys, experts, and employees as may be necessary for the proper performance of the duties of the Authority under this Act at salaries fixed in accordance with the Classification Act."

MR. STEAGALL. Mr. Speaker, I move the previous question on the motion to recommit.

The previous question was ordered.

THE SPEAKER. The question is on the motion of the gentleman from Massachusetts to recommit the bill.

The question was taken, and the Speaker announced that the noes appeared to have it.[45]

Mr. Luce then demanded the yeas and nays on the motion to recommit. They were so ordered and the question was taken. There were 140 yeas, 221 nays, and 70 not voting. So the motion to recommit was rejected. The speaker then announced that the question was on the passage of the bill. Hancock demanded the yeas and nays. The speaker called for a vote on the yeas and nays, and 115 members rose to be counted in favor of the yeas and nays. They were so ordered. The question was taken and there were 275 yeas, 86 nays, and 70 not voting.[46] The result of the vote was announced. A motion to reconsider was laid on the table. Thus the Wagner-Steagall housing bill was passed, in its amended form, by the House of Representatives.

The special rule under which the housing bill was amended made it possible for the bill to be acted upon within a period of approximately nine hours. The House met at 11 A.M. on that day, and it was ready to consider the special rule shortly before twelve o'clock noon. The final vote was taken at nine o'clock in the evening. As was already mentioned above in this chapter, the debate on the bill was controlled by the House Committee

_____

[45] *Ibid.*
[46] *Ibid.*, p. 9293.

on Banking and Currency, which had jurisdiction over the bill, and only those members with seniority on that committee or who were acceptable to the ranking committee members were recognized by the chairman to debate on the bill.

The amending process is also in control of the committee insofar as the rule provides that the committee amendments are considered first, and the chairman has the power to move that all amendments and all debate on the amendments be closed. Committee amendments represent the majority view of the committee. Most of the committee amendments are perfecting amendments to correct mistakes and to clarify vague language in the committee bill as reported. Sometimes substantive amendments are offered by the committee. In the case of this bill, one such substantive amendment was offered. It was concerned with the Walsh amendment on slum clearance. For some reason Steagall did not put into the bill the amendment giving the Authority discretion to delay the demolition of slum dwellings; but immediately after the bill was reported out he decided to accept the amendment that was desired by the PWA Housing Division, the AFL, and the other public-housing groups. This was the only substantive committee amendment presented. Wagner and the public-housing groups and the PWA Housing Division were not successful in convincing the committee that they should change the ratio of income to rental back to five to one. This amendment was presented by Ellenbogen as an independent amendment. It was rejected by the Committee of the Whole.

The minority of the Committee on Banking and Currency presented a number of amendments to limit certain provisions of the bill, but not a single one of their amendments was accepted by the Committee of the Whole.

CHAPTER XV

The Wagner Housing Bill Becomes Law

Because the House of Representatives passed a different version of the housing bill than the Senate, it was necessary that the Senate either accept the amendment of the House or ask for a conference to compromise their differences in the two versions of the bill.[1] As the House had just passed an amended version of the Senate bill, there was no question of the House receding from its amendment and accepting the Senate bill.

Notice of the passage of the housing bill (S. 1685) with a House amendment was sent to the Senate on the morning of August 19. It was announced at the start of the meeting that the House had passed the bill and that "it requested the concurrence of the Senate."[2] Shortly thereafter the vice-president laid before the Senate the amended bill. Senator Walsh moved that the Senate disagree to the House amendment and request a conference with the House on the disagreeing votes of the two houses thereon, and that the chair appoint the conferees on the part of

---

[1] *Jefferson's Manual,* Sec. 46, "Conferences," gives a detailed outline of conference procedure. The edition of the *Manual* with annotations of House rules and procedures in *Rules and Manual of the United States House of Representatives,* Nos. 530-59, is an excellent treatise on the technicalities of the conference committee.

[2] *Congressional Record,* August 19, 1937, p. 9296.

the Senate.[3] This motion was agreed to, and the vice-president appointed Mr. Walsh, Mr. Copeland, Mr. Thomas of Utah, Mr. Borah, and Mr. La Follette managers on the part of the Senate at the conference.[4]

The House was informed of this action on the part of the Senate. When the chief clerk of the House had finished reading the message from the Senate, Mr. Steagall asked unanimous consent to take from the speaker's desk the housing bill (S. 1685), to insist on the House amendment, and to agree to the conference asked by the Senate. There was no objection to the request of Mr. Steagall. The chair then appointed as conferees Messrs. Steagall, Goldsborough, Reilly, Wolcott, and Fish.[5] The House conferees were chosen from the House Committee on Banking and Currency, to which the bill had originally been referred, and on the basis of seniority. They were the three senior majority members and the two senior minority members.

A special committee print showing the differences between the bill as amended by the House and as amended by the Senate was printed for the use of the conference committee. The conferees usually meet on the Senate side of the Capitol behind closed doors; rarely have members and others been admitted to make arguments. The proceedings were held in secrecy. The meetings of the conference committee are privileged, and meetings may be held while the house is in session.[6] As these confer-

---

[3] Senator Walsh, who was formerly chairman of the Senate Committee on Education and Labor and the ranking majority member, was acting as chairman of the committee because of the appointment of Senator Black to the Supreme Court.

[4] *Congressional Record,* August 19, 1937, p. 9297.

[5] *Ibid.,* p. 9358.

[6] In addition to the section in *Jefferson's Manual* concerned with the procedure in the conference committee, Cleaves' *Manual of the Law and Practice in Regard to Conferences and Conference Reports* (which is a Senate Document) is a guide for the members of the committee. This manual is incorporated in the *Senate Manual* (1953 edition), pp. 113-30.

ences are asked for at the end of the session, it is ordinary procedure that the meetings are crowded into the last days of a session of Congress.

The meetings on this particular bill were very rushed. The conference committee met for eleven and one-half hours on August 20 to compromise the House and Senate differences.[7] The Senate conferees were agreed that many of the provisions of the House amendment were improvements to the bill, and hence they would be acceptable to them. This was fortunate for the fate of the bill, because the House conferees were not in any mood to compromise away their amendment by accepting any Senate suggestions that would nullify its provisions. Steagall on his part had given notice to the House, when he asked that the House accept the invitation to conference, that the House should insist on its amendment.

The conferees accepted the House version of Section 1 which contained a declaration of policy, but omitted the statement of findings relative to the problems of the slums and the housing shortage which were in the Senate bill. This agreement provided a clear and brief statement acceptable without debate to both houses. Section 2 was concerned with definitions. The definitions of the House amendment, which were more brief and precise, were accepted by the conference with but one exception. The definition of low-income families which fixed the ratio of income to rental at five to one (income equal to six times the rental for families of three or more dependents) was accepted by the conference. This was a victory for the Senate and for the public-housing groups, such as the Labor Housing Conference. It was one of the few agreements of major importance that favored the Senate bill. The limited availability of housing to families of citizens of the United States (Representative Case's amendment) was omitted by the conference. The definition of average-family-

7 *Congressional Record*, August 21, 1937, p. 9636.

dwelling-unit cost, which the House had included in its amendment, was also dropped by the conference.[8]

The administrative provisions of the conference report followed the House amendment except that the advisory board of nine members was omitted by the conferees. The section now provided for a single administrator under the supervision of the secretary of the Department of the Interior. Senator Tom Connally and other senators expressed satisfaction with this conference amendment.[9]

Section 4 of the bill was concerned with appointments to the new agency and the job status of appointees. The whole question of civil service and of Senate confirmation of appointments was involved in this discussion. During the conference it was passed over to be considered at the end of the meeting.[10] Concerning the transfer of existing housing projects to the new Authority (Section 4 (d)), the conference combined the provisions of the Senate bill with the House amendment to reach a satisfactory compromise. The auditing requirements in the Senate bill (Section 6 (a)) were omitted by the conference. This was in line with the House amendment, which did not contain any such provisions for auditing.

The Senate bill (Section 7 (a)) provided funds for research and experimentation. No corresponding provision appeared in the House amendment. The conference agreement omitted such provision, but permitted the publication and dissemination of housing information by the Authority. With respect to the annual report to be made by the Authority to the Congress, the provision of the House amendment was adopted. The confer-

---

[8] Mr. Steagall submitted the conference report on August 20, 1937. See House Committee of Conference, *United States Housing Act of 1937*, Conf. Rept. No. 1634, to accompany S. 1685, 75th Cong., 1st Sess. (1937) (Washington: Government Printing Office, 1937).

[9] *Congressional Record*, August 21, 1937, p. 9581.

[10] *Ibid.*, p. 9587.

ence dropped Section 8 (b) of the Senate version, which related to review of administrative actions of the Authority. The House version contained no such provision.

With respect to the loans made by the Authority, the conference adopted a limitation of all loans to 90 per cent of the cost of the project. This was a compromise agreement which was in favor of the House amendment. The section concerned with the annual contributions was discussed at some length and a compromise was reached which required that local contributions make up 20 per cent of the annual contributions. The House amendment had required a contribution equal to 25 per cent. The House amendment had separated slum clearance from housing development. Senator Walsh's amendment in the Senate had made it a part of the project. The conference agreed to make slum clearance a part of the project, but it accepted the House amendment which gave to the Authority the power to defer such elimination or improvement of slum dwellings in case of an acute housing shortage in the area. Section 11, which was concerned with capital grants, was modified by the same compromise agreement that was incorporated into Section 10 concerned with annual contributions.

The House amendments to Section 10 (b) and (c), which provided for the use of the subsidy to pay obligations to the Authority and required examination of contracts at the end of the first ten years and every five years thereafter, were adopted by the conference in preference to the Senate provisions, which did not specify how the subsidy was to be used and which provided for examination of contracts at the end of twenty years and then every ten years thereafter.[11]

The Senate bill contained no provision for the disposal of federal projects transferred to or acquired by the Authority. The conference adopted the provisions of the House amendment

---

[11] S. 1685 (Conf. Rept. No. 1634), pp. 16-17.

394 The Wagner Housing Act

(Section 12) which made provision for the disposal of such projects. The House amendment contained no provision for acquiring property, which was provided for in the Senate bill. The House amendment also did not contain any provision for the subordination of securities or obligations of the Authority for which the Senate bill had made provision. The conference omitted the provisions in the Senate bill.

The Senate bill (Section 14) contained various standards relating to the making of loans, and so forth. They were not included in the House amendment, and the conference agreement does not include them. The Senate bill (Section 15 (4)) contained a provision for the maintenance of playground facilities in connection with housing projects. This provision was not included in the House amendment, although Wolcott offered an amendment on the floor of the House to make provision for them.[12] The conference agreement provided that any contract for a substantial loan might contain a condition requiring a playground or open play space when the Authority deemed it necessary for the health and safety of the children.

The section concerned with the limitation of construction costs was another of those important sections that demanded a real compromise. The Byrd amendment had set a limit of $4,000 in construction costs on a family unit and $1,000 on each room. The House amendment had made provision for general limitation of costs in line with construction costs for similar type of building in the locality, and it also specified that the projects could not be of elaborate or expensive design or material. The House amendment also contained a construction-cost limitation of $5,000 per family dwelling unit. The conferees made a compromise which provided that the construction-cost limitation should be $4,000 per family unit and $1,000 per room, except that in any city where the population exceeded

---

[12] *Congressional Record*, August 18, 1937, p. 9266.

500,000 the family-dwelling-unit cost limitation should be $5,000 and the per-room cost should be limited to $1,250. The conferees also adopted the general limitations included in the House amendment.[13]

The Senate bill (Section 20 (a)) had provided for an aggregate bond issue by the Authority totaling $700,000,000. The House amendment fixed the total at $500,000,000. The conference adopted the aggregate amount fixed by the House amendment. The Senate bill (Section 21 (d)) provided that no more than 20 per cent of the funds provided for in the act for loans, grants, contributions, and so forth should be expended within any one state. The House amendment had fixed the limit at 10 per cent. The conference agreement adopted the figure of the House amendment.

The House amendment contained an additional section to the bill (Section 28) to make specific provision for the District of Columbia Alley Dwelling Authority to share in the benefits of the bill. The Senate bill had no such provision. The conference adopted the provision made by the House amendment.[14]

It is now necessary to return to the discussion of the civil-service status of employees of the new Authority. It will be recalled that this subject started quite a heated debate on the floor of the House during the amendment of the bill. Fortunately for the student of this bill, the secret proceedings of the conference committee were discussed quite frankly by both Walsh and Steagall when they made their report to their respective houses. This subject involved the most bitterly contested sections of the bill, and neither side appeared willing to make a compromise. Senator Walsh felt so strongly on the necessity of including civil service in the bill that he was considering withdrawing from the conference when the House conferees would not compromise.

---

13 S. 1685 (Conf. Rept. No. 1634), p. 18.
14 *Ibid.*

It was only his conviction that the Senate wanted to enact the bill that kept Walsh and his Senate colleagues in the meeting.[15] During the Senate discussion of the report Borah stated that the "conference had reached the point where we had to yield, or have no bill. That was the definite position of the House."[16]

Senator Tom Connally and Senator Barkley wanted to know why the House was opposed to the civil-service status of the new agency and also why the House was opposed to Senate confirmation of appointees. Walsh stated that he discovered an unusual state of mind, or a new state of mind, in the House. In direct answer to Connally's question Walsh said:

> But behind it all, I believe, is a growing feeling that this power in the Senate [to approve appointees] tends to make those in authority consult the members of the Senate rather than the members of the House in the matter of appointments.[17]

Walsh said that after the struggle they had succeeded in getting at least the words "civil service" in the bill by providing that employees with salaries under $1,980 would have to be appointed in compliance with the civil-service laws, and that all the employees would be under the Classification Act. In return for that, Walsh said, the Senate conferees had to surrender the Senate power of confirmation in the case of all positions except those carrying with them salaries in excess of $7,500.[18]

There were certain senators who were not satisfied with this compromise. They did not like the idea of surrendering their right to confirm political appointments. Walsh warned them that this new state of mind on the part of the House would affect all future legislation passed by the Congress. Barkley, the majority leader, mentioned to Walsh that he was sure that Walsh could

---

[15] *Congressional Record*, August 21, 1937, p. 9585.
[16] *Ibid.*, p. 9586.
[17] *Ibid.*
[18] *Ibid.*

have convinced the members of the other body of the fallacy of the theory that the Senate wanted to control appointments to the detriment of the House. Walsh replied to Barkley that when he had talked on the preceding afternoon with "our distinguished and able leader" and given him a report on the proceedings in the conference committee, the conferees had not finished their discussion of the civil-service provisions of the bill. It was necessary to return to the meeting and spend the entire evening in conference. It was not as easy as Barkley had supposed. Walsh stated that he had never before been in a conference in which there was so much pleading to save the House conferees from having to face House members who would denounce them for restoring the civil-service requirement and for permitting any confirmation of employees on the part of the Senate.[19]

After this explanation of the great struggle in the conference, there were a few questions about how the program would operate in the South. Senator Bankhead, who had been selected to replace Hugo Black, newly appointed to the Supreme Court, was particularly anxious to know how Birmingham and Mobile could benefit by the program. Senator George also wanted to know about the provisions for local contributions. Wagner and Walsh both tried to demonstrate to them that the bill would operate for their benefit. Senator King then made the suggestion that action on the bill should be deferred until the next session of Congress. Wagner was quick to reply to this suggestion. The senator pleaded for action on the bill at the present time. He mentioned how many years he had spent fighting for the bill; he admitted that it was not perfect; but he pleaded that the bill be passed and the program started. The motion to accept the conference report was then put to the Senate. The motion was agreed to by a voice vote.[20]

---

[19] *Ibid.*, p. 9587.
[20] *Ibid.*, p. 9591.

Walsh was correct in his appraisal of the situation in the committee, for on the other side of the Capitol Steagall was having difficulty in convincing some of the members that the House conferees had not sold out to the Senate. Steagall presented the conference report to the speaker *pro tempore*, Rayburn, who was in the chair in the absence of Speaker Bankhead. Steagall then asked that the statement of the managers on the part of the House be read in place of the report itself.[21] Steagall had had this statement so prepared that it gave evidence, and justly so, that the House conferees had yielded to the Senate conferees on only a few minor points. When the statement had been read, Steagall gave a brief explanation of some of the changes in the House amendment. He was asked by Representative Case of South Dakota about the amendment restricting tenants of the housing projects to families of citizens of the United States. Steagall told him that it had been dropped in conference, but he should not fear that aliens would derive the benefits of this legislation.[22] There was a brief discussion of the limitation of construction costs, but Representative Alfred Phillips, who had argued against the limitation, stated that he would vote for the report.[23]

Steagall then attempted to justify the conference agreement which made provision for civil-service status for the new agency. He told the House that he had made a good bargain. The type of employee who would be employed in the new agency—architect, engineer, real-estate appraiser, and so forth—would not be within the $1,980 limitation. Hence only very few employees

---

[21] The same conference report is submitted by both the senior Senate manager and the senior House manager to their respective houses. The report is signed by all the conferees. The House rules require that the House manager also submit a written statement as an addition to the report (House Rule 29). According to the procedure in the Senate the senior conferee gives an oral statement to the members.

[22] *Congressional Record*, August 21, 1937, p. 9634.

[23] *Ibid.*, p. 9636.

would be appointed in compliance with civil-service laws. Stea-gall pointed out that only three classes of employees would be under civil-service law, and there were sixteen classes under civil-service classification. Therefore the House won its point with regard to thirteen classes of positions.[24]

Wolcott then took over and explained to the members the difficulty of enacting legislation. He mentioned how he had been told when he came to the Congress that legislation was a matter of compromise. He did not know what that meant until he had taken part in conference with the conferees of the Senate. "I did not fully realize what it meant," he said, "until the conference on this bill when, after spending 11-$\frac{1}{2}$ hours yesterday giving and taking, adding and subtracting, sparring for advantage back and forth, we finally succeeded in coming to an agreement on what I consider to be a better bill."[25]

Mr. Fuller, chairman of the Democratic committee on pa-tronage, was not convinced by anything that Steagall or Wolcott had said. He spoke his mind when he said:

> Mr. Speaker, this conference report is nothing but a cutthroat report which would require the House to do a thing that the House is clearly opposed to. If the conferees had wanted to treat this House fairly, they would have come in here with a favorable re-port on the question that the House had so decidedly voted upon.[26]

Steagall defended his position and that of the conference in his reply to Fuller. He again stated that the House gained thirteen classes under the Civil Service Classification Act and yielded three in order to bring in a conference report to the House at a time when the House desired the report in order to carry out the program so much desired by its members.[27]

O'Connor, chairman of the Rules Committee, made an at-tempt to placate both sides of the dispute by pointing out that

---

[24] *Ibid.*, p. 9634.
[25] *Ibid.*, p. 9636.
[26] *Ibid.*, p. 9637.
[27] *Ibid.*, p. 9639.

the conferees had arrived at as good a compromise as could be expected. Steagall finally moved the previous question. The speaker *pro tempore* announced that the question was on agreeing to the conference report. The question was taken on a division demanded by Mr. Ross Collins of Mississippi and Mr. Thomas O'Malley of Wisconsin. There were 128 ayes and 48 nays. Mr. Charles Faddis of Pennsylvania objected to the vote on the ground that there was not a quorum present. The chair counted 227 members present, which constituted a quorum. So the conference report was agreed to, and a motion to reconsider was laid on the table. Mr. Dewey Short of Missouri then demanded the yeas and nays. Mr. James Mead of New York stated that the gentleman's request came too late. The speaker ruled that the request came too late. The conference report had already been agreed to and motion to reconsider had been laid on the table.[28] In this routine and anticlimactic action Congress passed the Wagner housing bill. Although the Wagner housing bill was from several points of view the most important piece of legislation considered in the closing hours of the first session of the Seventy-fifth Congress, it was only one of sixty-five bills and joint resolutions which were rushed through Congress that same afternoon.

After it was announced to the Senate that the House had agreed to the conference report, the Wagner housing bill was enrolled on parchment by the Senate, which was the house that had originated the bill.[29] This copy was then examined by the Committee on Enrolled Bills to check the accuracy of the copy. While this is a joint committee, each house acts independently.

---

[28] *Ibid.*, p. 9640.

[29] The final stages of the legislative process concerned with enrollment and signing of bills is outlined in *Jefferson's Manual*, Sec. 48. The edition of the *Manual* with annotations printed in the *Rules and Manual of the United States House of Representatives*, Nos. 572-77, gives an excellent summary of these final procedures in the legislative process.

The next step is for the president of the Senate and the speaker of the House to affix their certificate to the bill signifying that it had been truly enrolled.[30] In the case of the Wagner housing bill, there was no time to get an enrolled copy ready before adjournment. Congress adjourned on Saturday afternoon, August 21. In order that the Wagner housing bill, and some sixty-five other bills, might be enrolled, signed, and sent to the president, a House Concurrent Resolution was approved shortly before adjournment which authorized the signing, and so forth, of these bills after the adjournment.[31] Over the week end the housing bill was enrolled and checked. On Monday, August 23, the speaker signed the bill and transmitted it to the Senate.[32] The president *pro tempore* of the Senate, Key Pittman of Nevada, acting in the absence of the vice-president, signed the bill that same day.[33] Then the housing bill, together with the sixty-five other bills of the Senate which had been duly signed by the presiding officers of the two houses under authority of the House Concurrent Resolution 26, were presented on August

---

[30] The Committee on Enrolled Bills was abolished under the Legislative Reorganization Act of 1946 and its responsibilities and powers were transferred to the Committee on House Administration.

[31] "House Concurrent Resolution No. 26. Resolved by the House of Representatives *(The Senate concurring)* That notwithstanding the adjournment of the first session of the seventy-fifth Congress, the President of the Senate and the speaker of the House of Representatives be, and they are hereby, authorized to sign any enrolled bills or joint resolutions duly passed by the two Houses and which have been examined by the Committee on Enrolled Bills of each House and found truly enrolled. Passed, August 21, 1937." The Congress adjourned *sine die* on Saturday, August 21, 1937 (50 Stat. 1113 [1937]).

[32] "The Speaker announced his signature to enrolled bills and joint resolutions of the Senate: . . . S. 1685 . . ." (*Congressional Record*, August 21, 1937, p. 9675). Though this signing took place on August 23, the notice of it and of all other business transacted after the adjournment on August 21, is placed at the end of the *Record* under date of August 21, 1937.

[33] "The President pro tempore (Key Pittman of Nevada), under the authority of House Concurrent Resolution 26, signed on August 23, 1937, the following enrolled bills and joint resolutions which had previously been signed by the Speaker of the House of Representatives: . . . S. 1685 . . ." (*ibid.*, p. 9610).

23, 1937, to the president of the United States by the Committee on Enrolled Bills.[34]

On September 1, 1937, President Franklin D. Roosevelt signed the housing bill, thus making it one of the public laws of the land.[35] The final act in the long legislative process was completed with the stroke of President Roosevelt's pen. The bill S. 1685 had at last become the United States Housing Act of 1937.[36]

---

[34] "The following enrolled bills and joint resolutions, heretofore duly signed by the presiding officers of the two Houses, under authority of House Concurrent Resolution 26, were presented on August 23, 1937, to the President of the United States by the Committee on Enrolled Bills: . . . S. 1685 . . ." (*ibid.*, p. 9612).

[35] "The President of the United States, subsequent to the final adjournment of the first session of the seventy-fifth Congress, notified the Secretary of the Senate that he had approved Acts and joint resolutions of the Senate as follows: . . . On September 1, 1937 . . . S. 1685 . . ." (*ibid.*, p. 9612). The National League of Women Voters and the National Federation of Federal Employees wrote to the president on August 23, 1937, requesting that he veto the housing bill because of a lack of an adequate civil-service provision (Roosevelt Papers, O.F. 2694).

[36] 50 Stat. 888 (1937).

Comparison of Provisions

of the

Wagner Bill of 1935

and the

Ellenbogen Bill of 1935

74th Congress   H. R. 7399
1st Session

IN THE HOUSE OF REPRESENTATIVES
April 10, 1935

Mr. Ellenbogen introduced the following bill; which was referred to the
Committee on Banking and Currency and ordered to be printed.

A BILL

To establish the United States Housing Authority, to provide modern, large-
scale housing for families of low income, to provide employment in the
building and allied trades, to stimulate and stabilize the building industry,
to increase consuming power, to further national recovery, and to promote
the public health, safety, morals, and welfare.

*Be it enacted by the Senate and House of Representatives of the United
States of America in Congress assembled,* That this Act may be cited as the
"United States Housing Authority Act."

It is hereby declared that there exists in the United States an acute
shortage of modern low-cost housing available to American families of low
income; that conditions in slums, blighted areas, and overcrowded homes in
both rural and urban districts seriously affect and menace the public health,
safety, morals, welfare, and economic stability of many communities in the
United States; that the inability of private capital and ordinary private
enterprise to provide decent, modern, and sanitary housing for low-income
groups or to engage in rehabilitation activities has seriously limited and
curtailed the potential effective market for the products of the construction
and allied industries, has contributed largely to the critical and wide-spread
unemployment existing in the building trades and allied industries, has sub-

404

74th Congress   S. 2392
1st Session

IN THE SENATE OF THE UNITED STATES

March 13 (calendar day, March 26), 1935

Mr. Wagner introduced the following bill; which was read twice and
referred to the Committee on Education and Labor.

A BILL

To promote the public health, safety, and welfare by providing for the elimination of insanitary and dangerous housing conditions, to relieve congested
areas, to aid in the construction and supervision of low-rental dwelling
accommodations, and to further national industrial recovery through the
employment of labor and materials.

*Be it enacted by the Senate and House of Representatives of the United
States of America in Congress assembled,*

TITLE I—SLUM AND LOW-RENT PUBLIC HOUSING

Declaration of Policy

Section 1. Congested and insanitary housing conditions throughout the
Nation which seriously affect the public health, safety, morals, and welfare
and undermine the standards of living of the American people are hereby
declared to exist. It is found that the correction of these conditions is impossible by private initiative and funds, and it is declared to be the policy
of Congress that the Federal Government must give its financial aid, by way
of grants, loans, and other assistance, so as to encourage local government
initiative and participation, in order to secure the gradual demolition of
existing insanitary and unsafe housing, and the construction of new housing
facilities in accordance with modern standards of sanitation, safety, and

In the House of Representatives

stantially restricted the consuming power of the American people, has materially reduced interstate and foreign commerce, and has contributed to the creation of slum districts and blighted areas; that the correction of these conditions is a matter of concern to and has become the responsibility of the Government of the United States; that it is hereby declared to be the policy of the Congress of the United States to employ the credit and funds of the Government of the United States to remedy these conditions and to construct, and aid in the construction, of modern large-scale housing, available for those families who in good as well as in bad times cannot afford to pay the price which will induce the ordinary and usual channels of private enterprise to build such housing; therefore there is hereby created and established the United States Housing Authority, which is hereby declared to be a permanent agency and instrumentality of the United States of America for the purpose of establishing adequate and permanent machinery for the building, construction, supervision, and control of such housing, of obtaining the ends herein recited, and for the purpose of absorbing the structure, functions, assets, and liabilities of the Housing Division of the Federal Emergency Administration of Public Works by taking over its powers, funds, and assets; and the necessity of the creation of such Federal Housing Authority in the public interest is hereby declared as a matter of legislative determination.

Definitions

Sec. 2. As used in this Act—

(a) The term "Board" means the Board of the United States Housing Authority created by this Act.

(b) The term "Authority" means the United States Housing Authority created by this Act.

(c) The term "project" includes any large-scale housing construction development, inclusive of the necessary streets, utilities, and site preparation, planned or undertaken for families of low income or for special groups, whether constructed and/or administered directly by the Authority or some other housing agency.

(d) The term "housing" includes urban and rural housing, dwellings, apartments, or other living accommodations intended to be rented or sold to families of low income or special groups, and all necessary or desirable appurtenances of large-scale housing construction, inclusive of administrative and community buildings and equipment, meeting halls, barns, and other farm buildings and farm equipment, garages, recreational and educational facilities, workshops, stores, restaurants, and facilities for group activities.

In the Senate of the United States

comfort to be available at a low rental to persons of low income. Therefore, there shall be created, authorized, and empowered the agencies and instrumentalities of the Federal Government as herein provided for the purpose of attaining the ends herein recited, and their necessity in the public interest is hereby declared as a matter of legislative determination.

Definition

Sec. 9. A "local public housing body", as used in this Act, means a State, territorial, county, or municipal housing corporation or authority, authorized and empowered by statutory enactment to clear slums and/or to provide housing at a low rental for persons of low income.

In the House of Representatives

(e) The term "construction" shall include all operations necessary for the planning, erection, and completion of a project including the reconstruction or repair of any existing building which may be allowed to remain.

(f) The term "large-scale" as used in connection with the terms "housing" or "project" or both (which terms are hereinabove defined) means a housing project planned and administered as a neighborhood unit, large enough to preserve its inherent character, and to constitute a safe long-time investment for public funds.

(g) The term "housing agency" shall include:

(1) States, counties, cities, and municipal subdivisions which are authorized to engage in housing activities.

(2) "Public housing agency" which shall mean any public regional, State, or local housing authority, board, or commission or similar agency, established under the laws of any State or created by any State, city, county, or municipal subdivision or chartered by the "Authority" under the provisions of this Act for the purpose of aiding, assisting in, promoting, constructing, or administering modern housing for families of low income or special groups.

(3) "Nonprofit housing agency" which shall mean any private association, cooperative or corporate body, established for the purpose of constructing or administering modern housing for families of low income or for special groups without initial investments of its own and not established or managed for the purpose of obtaining a profit.

(4) "Limited-dividend housing agency" which shall mean any private association, cooperative, or corporate body, which limits the return on its investment to a definitely limited rate established by the Authority or by State or by local law and which agrees to submit its management, accounting methods, and books to the supervision, inspection, and control of the Authority.

(h) The term "State" shall include any of the States of the Union, the District of Columbia, and the territories or possessions of the United States.

THE UNITED STATES HOUSING AUTHORITY

Sec. 3. (a) There is hereby created the United States Housing Authority (hereinafter referred to as the "Authority") which shall be an instrumentality of the United States, and shall have authority to sue and to be sued in any court of competent jurisdiction, Federal or State.

(b) The management of the Authority shall be invested in a Board of Directors consisting of three members who shall be citizens of the United

In the Senate of the United States

Division of Housing

Sec. 2. (A) There shall be established in the Department of the Interior a Division of Housing, under the supervision, direction, and control of a director, to be appointed by the President and with the advice and consent of the Senate and whose compensation shall be fixed in accordance with the Classification Act of 1923 as amended. The Director is hereby authorized and empowered:

In the House of Representatives

States, to be appointed by the President, by and with the advice and consent of the Senate. Not more than two of the members of the Board shall be members of the same political party. The first appointees shall be appointed to hold terms of two, four, and six years respectively. On the expiration of these terms each new member shall hold office for six years. Compensation shall be at the rate of $10,000 per annum, payable monthly out of the funds of the Authority. The members of the Board of Directors shall devote their full time to the business of the Authority and shall be eligible for reappointment upon the expiration of their term. In case of a vacancy arising from whatever cause a successor shall be appointed to serve during the unexpired portion of the term. No Board member shall be permitted to hold other public office during his term of service.

(c) The Authority shall be a permanent institution of indefinite duration. It shall have power to adopt, alter, and use a corporate seal; to make contracts, to own or lease such real estate as may be necessary for the transaction of its business; to select, employ, and fix the compensation of such officers, employees, attorneys, agents, and consultants, as shall be necessary for the transaction of the business of the Authority, without regard to the provisions of other laws applicable to the employment and compensation of officers or employees of the United States; to define their authority and duties, require bonds of them and fix the penalties thereof, and to dismiss at pleasure such officers, employees, attorneys, and agents; and to prescribe, amend, alter, and repeal, by its Board of Directors, the bylaws, rules, and regulations governing the manner in which its general business may be conducted and the powers granted to it by law may be exercised and enjoyed, including the selection of its chairman and vice chairman together with provisions for such committees and divisions and the functions thereof as the Board of Directors may deem necessary for facilitating its business under this Act. The Board of Directors of the Authority shall determine and prescribe the manner in which its obligations shall be incurred and the expenses allowed and paid. The Authority shall be entitled to the free use of the United States mail in the same manner as the executive departments of the Government. With the consent of any board, commission, independent establishments, or executive department of the Government, including any field service thereof, the Authority may avail itself of the use of information, service, facilities, officers, and employees thereof in carrying out the provisions of this Act. Decisions of the Board shall be by majority vote of its members.

The principal office of the Authority shall be located in the District of Columbia, but there may be established agencies and branch offices in any

In the Senate of the United States

(a) To accept and utilize voluntary and uncompensated services, except that a reasonable allowance shall be made for the necessary travelling and other expenses incurred by those rendering such service;

(b) To appoint and fix the compensation and allowances of such officers, experts, or consultants as are necessary to carry out the provisions of this Act and to prescribe their powers, duties, responsibilities, and tenure, and, in accordance with the civil-service laws and the Classification Act of 1923 as amended, to employ such other employees and assistants as may be required for the administration of this Act.

(B) All such compensation, expenses, and allowances shall be paid out of funds made available by this Act.

(C) The Division shall acquire sufficient quarters to establish adequate planning, research, and supervisory agencies at the seat of the government or elsewhere and may make such expenditures for rent, equipment, books, files, printing, binding, and such additional facilities for keeping permanent records of the Division as are necessary to fulfill the purposes of this Act.

In the House of Representatives

city or cities of the United States under rules and regulations prescribed by the Board.

Sec. 4. The Authority shall have capital stock of $1,000,000, which shall be subscribed by the United States of America, payment for which shall be subject to call in whole or in part by the Board of Directors of the Authority.

There is hereby authorized to be appropriated, out of any money in the Treasury, not otherwise appropriated, the sum of $1,000,000 for the purpose of making payments upon such subscription when called. Receipts for payments by the United States of America for or on account of such stock shall be issued by the Authority to the Secretary of the Treasury and shall be evidence of the stock ownership of the United States of America.

Sec. 5. (a) The Authority is authorized to issue bonds in an aggregate amount not to exceed $1,000,000,000 which may be sold by the Authority to obtain funds for carrying out the purposes of this Act or to be delivered in payment of its obligations as hereinafter provided. Such bonds shall be in such forms and denominations, shall mature within such periods of not more than fifty years from the date of their issue, shall bear such rates of interest not exceeding 4 per centum per annum, shall be subject to such terms and conditions and shall be issued in such manner and sold at such prices, as may be prescribed by the Authority, with the approval of the Secretary of the Treasury. Such bonds shall be fully and unconditionally guaranteed both as to interest and principal by the United States, and such guaranty shall be expressed on the face thereof, and such bonds, shall be lawful investments and may be accepted as security, for all fiduciary, trust, and public funds, the investment or deposit of which shall be under the authority or control of the United States or any officer or officers thereof. In the event that the Authority shall be unable to pay upon demand, when due, the principal of, or interest on, such bonds, the Secretary of the Treasury shall pay to the holder the amount thereof which is hereby authorized to be appropriated, out of any moneys in the Treasury not otherwise appropriated, and thereupon to the extent of the amount so paid the Secretary of the Treasury shall succeed to all the rights of the holders of such bonds. The Secretary of the Treasury in his discretion, is authorized to purchase any bonds of the Authority issued under this section which are guaranteed as to interest and principal, for such purpose the Secretary of the Treasury is authorized to use as a public-debt transaction the proceeds from the sale of any securities hereafter issued under the second Liberty Bond Act, as amended, and the purposes for which securities may be issued under such Act, as amended, are extended to include any purchases of the bonds of the Authority issued under this Act. The Secretary of the Treasury

In the Senate of the United States

Appropriation

Sec. 7. For the purpose of this Act there is hereby appropriated the sum of $800,000,000, to be used for the purposes and in accordance with the provisions of this Act, in addition to the funds received by the Division pursuant to the terms of section 5, such appropriation to be made out of any moneys in the Treasury not otherwise appropriated, and thereafter the Housing Division shall receive and have additional funds which may be necessary from time to time to carry out the purposes of this Act. The President may allocate to the Housing Division such funds as have been appropriated by other Acts and are available for purposes within the purview of this Act, and any sum or sums so allocated shall be deemed on account of and as a credit against the said $800,000,000 herein appropriated for the use of the Housing Division.

In the House of Representatives

may, at any time, sell any of the bonds of the Authority acquired by him under this section. All redemptions, purchases, and sales by the Secretary of the Treasury of the bonds of the Authority shall be treated as public-debt transactions of the United States. The bonds issued by the Authority under this section shall be exempt, both as to principal and interest, from all taxation (except surtaxes, estate, inheritance and gift taxes) now or hereafter imposed by the United States or any district, territory, dependency or possession thereof, or by any State, county, municipality or local taxing authority. The corporation, including its franchise, its capital, reserves, and surplus, and its loans and income, shall likewise be exempt from such taxation; except that any real property of the Authority, held under the provisions of this Act, shall be subject to State, territorial, county, municipal, or local taxation to the same extent, according to its value, as other real property is taxed, unless specifically exempted by State or local legislation. No such bonds shall be issued in excess of the assets of the Authority, including the assets to be obtained from the proceeds of such bonds, but a failure to comply with this provision shall not invalidate the bonds or the guaranty of the same. The Authority shall have power to purchase in the open market at any time and at any price not to exceed par any of the bonds issued by it. Any such bonds so purchased may, with the approval of the Secretary of the Treasury, be sold or resold at any time and at any price. The Authority shall have the power to pay with the bonds issued by it, at the prevailing market value, for any obligation incurred by it under the provisions of this Act. The Authority shall have the power to accept in payment of any obligation due to it the bonds issued by it at the prevailing market value.

POWERS AND DUTIES OF THE UNITED STATES HOUSING AUTHORITY

Sec. 6. The Authority is authorized—

(a) To plan, prepare, alter, and carry out a comprehensive, long-range program to meet the housing needs of all the American people and to rehabilitate slum and blighted areas and to aid and assist housing agencies in formulating similar programs.

(b) To supervise the building of any project under the provisions of this Act and to prescribe and alter such requirements as it deems proper for the type and standard of housing, manner of construction, the labor policies, the kind of materials to be used, and such other matters as it deems proper.

(c) To assume all the obligations and take over all the projects, assets, funds, equipment, records, files, and personnel of the Housing Division of the Federal Emergency Administration of Public Works, established under

In the Senate of the United States

Sec. 3. (A) It shall be the duty and power of the Director to formulate and execute, and to aid in the formulation and execution of, slum clearance and low-rent public-housing programs and projects, in accordance with the provisions of this Act and for such purposes:

(a) To prepare, and from time to time, alter, amend, amplify, and to execute a long-range slum-clearance and low-rent public-housing program for the United States;

(b) To encourage, aid, assist, and cooperate with local public-housing bodies to formulate and to execute slum clearance and low-rent public-housing programs and projects;

The Housing Division of the Public Works Administration

Sec. 5. The Housing Division of the Public Works Administration is hereby terminated as of June 15, 1935, and all its equipment, records, files,

In the House of Representatives

title II of the National Industrial Recovery Act, which assets, funds, equipment, and so forth shall be transferred within sixty days from the passage of this Act; after such transfer such Housing Division shall cease to exist. The Authority shall have the powers and privileges now enjoyed by said Housing Division of the Federal Emergency Administration of Public Works, and shall carry on the functions, projects, and enterprises now carried on by said Housing Division. The provisions of this subsection shall not be construed as limiting the powers of the Authority granted elsewhere in this Act.

(d) To engage in the construction and in the management of projects.

(e) To create and charter regional or local Federal housing authorities or corporations, to be designated as "Federal Housing Authority of   ", to which it shall delegate such of its powers as the Board of Directors shall determine, for the purpose of constructing or managing projects.

(f) To make loans and grants for the construction of projects on vacant land or in slums, or blighted areas, which loans shall be secured as hereinafter set forth: *Provided, however,* That no grant shall be in excess of 30 per centum of the combined cost of labor and materials of any program or project and that any interest charged on any such loan shall range from zero to not more than the cost of the money to the Authority plus 1 per centum. Such loans may be made to housing agencies only; in the case of all housing agencies, except limited-dividend housing agencies, such loans may be made up to 100 per centum of the total cost of the project.

(g) To acquire by purchase, condemnation, gift, or otherwise, and to lease and operate such real and personal property as it may find necessary or desirable for housing projects, to demolish buildings, to enjoy and exercise the power of eminent domain, in like manner as is now enjoyed and exercised by the United States of America.

(h) To sell, assign, grant, convey, and transfer to housing agencies for completion and/or administration, and operation projects begun, completed, or owned by the Authority.

In the Senate of the United States

statistical data, and funds are hereby transferred to the Division created by this Act, together with the personnel thereof, except that nothing in this section shall be deemed to controvert any of the provisions of section 2 of this Act.

Sec. 4. (A) If it be found that in any area within any of the several States, the District of Columbia, Hawaii, Alaska, Puerto Rico, the Canal Zone, or the Virgin Islands there prevails a housing condition the correction of which is contemplated by this Act, and no responsible local public-housing body exists, then the Housing Division shall, in the discretion of the Director, initiate and execute within such area a plan for the clearance of slums and the construction, operation, and maintenance of low-rent public-housing projects.

Sec. 3 (Cont'd)

(c) To make grants and loans to local public-housing bodies in connection with any program or project of slum clearance and low-rent public-housing: *Provided,* That no grant shall be in excess of 30 per centum of the cost of labor and materials employed upon such program or project, and that any interest charged on any such loan shall not be higher than the rate of interest specified in the bonds of the Federal Government having a term of ten years or more, last issued prior to the making of such loan. (Cf. Sec. 7)

Sec. 4 (Cont'd)

(B) To effectuate the purposes and provisions of the preceding clause, the Housing Division shall have the power and authority to acquire by purchase, gift, or the exercise of the power of eminent domain or otherwise, such real and personal property as it may find necessary or proper for the initiation and execution of slum-clearance and low-rent public-housing programs and projects; to erect, maintain, manage, administer, and operate the dwellings included in such programs and projects, and to enter into and make all contracts and expenditures necessary to initiate and execute such programs and projects; *Provided,* That whenever it shall appear to the satisfaction of the Director that a local public-housing body has been created, duly authorized and empowered, and is capable of taking over the initiation of such a program or project within any such area and fully and properly to execute the same, then the Director shall take such steps as may be necessary, upon such terms and conditions as he may prescribe, to enable

In the House of Representatives

(i) To acquire sufficient quarters to establish and maintain adequate planning, research, and administrative agencies in the District of Columbia or elsewhere and to make such expenditures for rent, furniture, equipment, books, files, printing, binding, and such other facilities as the Board of Directors may determine.

(j) To study, survey, analyze the social, sociological or economic, financial, legal and technical aspect of all matters affecting housing needs and problems; develop housing standards and carry out or assist in carrying out experiments; to collect, publish, distribute, and coordinate information pertinent to the problem of modern housing and relating to the activities of the Authority and of other housing agencies; to make new surveys, studies, or analysis as need shall arise.

(k) To conform to proper standards of health, sanitation, and safety, and to local official city or regional plans, building, housing, and zoning laws, except that a plan for a project may differ from those provisions of local ordinances which are applicable to the standard lot and block subdivisions which have prevailed hitherto: *Provided, however,* That the plan in the judgment of the Authority assures equal or greater provision for light, air, ventilation, safety, and amenity than the local ordinances require.

(l) To plan in advance for emergency public works programs, and have projects ready for rapid execution during periods of unemployment.

Sec. 7. The Authority shall have the right to make rules, regulations, bylaws, and requirements and stipulations for the purpose of effectuating the purpose of this Act and for the proper conduct of its affairs. It shall have the right to determine the amount of interest on its loans which may vary from project to project and from time to time on the same project in accordance with local conditions and acceptable regional or local indices of wages and living costs, the range being from zero to not more than the cost of the money to the Authority, plus 1 per centum per year. The loans made under the provisions of this Act shall be fully and adequately secured by a lien or mortgage on the project and the Authority may take over and administer or dispose of any property or project on which it obtained a lien or mortgage, whenever it becomes necessary to foreclose. The Authority shall have the right to make such loans for such period as it deems advisable, and may shorten, lengthen, or extend the period and make such other terms of amortization for each particular project as the circumstances may require, provided that the period of amortization for buildings shall not exceed fifty years and the period of amortization for land shall not exceed seventy-five years. It shall have the right to determine the type and

In the Senate of the United States

such local public-housing body to take over and execute such slum clearance
and low-rent public-housing program or project.

Sec. 3 (Cont'd)
(d) To investigate, study and survey the social, economic, financial,
legal, and other technical aspects of housing needs, conditions, and problems; to formulate standards; and to collect, publish, and distribute information relating to the creation and administration of local public-housing
bodies and to the construction, maintenance, and operating of slum clearance and low-rent public-housing programs and projects.

Sec. 3 (c) (Cont'd)
And provided further, That when a loan has been made to a local public-
housing body, in connection with any program or project of slum-clearance
and low-rent public housing, the Division shall be in the position of a
mortgagee not in possession and shall exercise no control over the acquisition of land, the construction, maintenance, operation, or management of
the property and dwellings, unless and until a default has occurred in the
payment of interest, amortization of principal, or otherwise in the faithful
performance of any of the obligations assumed or undertaken by the local
public-housing body to whom the loan has been made, but this proviso shall
not apply to any program or project already undertaken by any Federal
agency or authority previous to enactment of this Act;

In the House of Representatives

tenure of ownership or tenancy by the occupants of all construction projects under the provisions of this Act, and the method of change and transfer of such tenancy or ownership as it deems proper: *Provided,* That such rules, regulations, and bylaws are not required to be uniform for all construction projects and may vary from time to time and from project to project. The enumeration of the above-mentioned rules, regulations, and bylaws in this section shall not be deemed as impliedly excluding the right of the Authority to make all other necessary or appropriate rules, regulations, and bylaws which it considers necessary or appropriate for the effectuating of the purposes of this Act. Such rules, regulations, and bylaws are not required to be uniform, but on the contrary, may vary from project to project and from time to time on the same project.

Sec. 8. Skilled and unskilled labor employed on construction projects, undertaken or financed by the Authority, shall be paid the wage prevailing for such or similar labor in the locality or region where the particular project takes place.

Sec. 9. In order to facilitate the construction of low-cost housing accommodations on a large scale as quickly, efficiently and economically as possible, and employ as many workers of the building trades as possible with the funds expended, the Authority shall (a) give precedence to those housing agencies which are prepared with good projects which can be carried out with a minimum of friction and delay, and (b) favor projects where land costs are not higher than the use value of the site for a good modern housing project.

Sec. 10. The Authority shall make and publish a detailed annual report of its operations to Congress to be filed January 1 of each year. The report shall include a statement of the assets and liabilities of the Authority.

Sec. 11. The Authority shall include in its annual report to Congress a statement of the interest subsidies and of all grants allowed by it during the past year; such grants and interest subsidies shall be charged against the funds obtained under section 12 hereof. If such funds are not available, the total amount of such grants and interest subsidies is hereby authorized to be appropriated from the funds in the Treasury not otherwise appropriated: *Provided, however,* That such interest subsidies shall not exceed the sum of $5,000,000 for the first year of the operation of the Authority; $10,000,000 for the second year of operation and the sum of $20,000,000 for each subsequent year of operation. Any subsidy allowance which remains unspent in one year may be spent in any ensuing year in addition to the specific allotment for that year.

In the Senate of the United States

Industrial Recovery

Sec. 6. To further national industrial recovery and with a view to increasing employment quickly, the Director shall make available, as rapidly as is compatible with efficiency, the grants and loans prescribed herein, precedence being given to such local public-housing bodies as are prepared to put their plans into immediate operation.

In the House of Representatives

Sec. 12. The President may allocate to the Authority such funds as may be appropriated by other Acts and are available for the purposes within the purview of this Act.

PENALTIES

Sec. 13. (a) Whoever makes any statement, knowing it to be false, or whoever wilfully over-values any land, buildings, or project under this Act for the purpose of obtaining any loan, or extension thereof; of obtaining money, property or anything of value under this Act, or of influencing in any way the action of the Authority, shall be punished by a fine of not more than $100,000 or by imprisonment for not more than five years, or both.

(b) Whoever (1) falsely makes, forges, or counterfeits any note, debenture, bond, mortgage, or other obligation or coupon in imitation of or purporting to be a note, debenture, bond, mortgage, or other obligation or coupon issued by the Authority, or (2) passes, utters, or publishes or attempts to pass, utter, or publish any false, forged, or counterfeited note, debenture, bond, mortgage, or other obligation or coupon purporting to have been issued by the Authority, knowing the same to be false, forged, or counterfeited, or (3) falsely alters any note, debenture, bond, mortgage, or other obligation or coupon issued or purporting to have been issued by the Authority, or (4) passes, utters, or publishes, or attempts to pass, utter, or publish as true any false, altered, or spurious note, debenture, bond, mortgage, or other obligation or coupon issued or purporting to have been issued by the Authority, knowing the same to be false, altered, or spurious; or any person who wilfully for profits violates any other provisions of this Act shall be punished by a fine of not more than $100,000 or by imprisonment for not more than five years, or both.

(c) Whoever, being connected in any capacity with the Authority, (1) embezzles, abstracts, purloins, or wilfully misapplies any moneys, funds, securities, mortgages, or other things of value, either belonging to or pledged or otherwise entrusted to it, or (2) with intent to defraud the Authority or any other body, politic or corporate, or any individual, or to deceive any officer, auditor, or examiner of the Authority, makes any false entry in any book, report, or statement offered to the Authority, or, without being duly authorized, draws any order or issues, puts forth, or assigns any note, debenture, bond, mortgage, or other obligation, or draft, bill of exchange, mortgage, judgment, or decree thereof, or (3) with intent to defraud, participates, shares, receives, directly or indirectly, any money, profit, or benefit through any transaction, loan commission, contract, or any other act of the Authority, or (4) gives any unauthorized information concerning any future action or plan of the Authority which might affect the value of securities or

In the Senate of the United States

[No section comparable to Section 13 of the Ellenbogen Bill is to be found in the Wagner Bill.]

In the House of Representatives

mortgages or, having such knowledge, invests or speculates, directly or indirectly, in the land, construction, or materials going into the construction of any project under the provisions of this Act, shall be punished by a fine of not more than $100,000 or by imprisonment for not more than five years, or both.

(d) No individual, association, partnership, or corporation shall use the words "United States Housing Authority" or a combination of these four words as the name or a part thereof under which he or it shall do business. Every individual, partnership, association, or corporation, violating this prohibition shall be guilty of a misdemeanor and shall be punished by a fine not exceeding $1,000, or imprisonment not exceeding one year, or both.

SEPARABILITY PROVISION

Sec. 14. The right to alter, amend, or repeal this Act is hereby expressly reserved.

Sec. 15. If any clause, sentence, paragraph, or part of this Act or the application thereof to any person or circumstance, shall, for any reason, be adjudged by any court of competent jurisdiction to be invalid, such judgment shall not affect, impair, or invalidate the remainder of this Act, and the application of such provision to other persons or circumstances, but shall be confined in its operation to the clause, sentence, paragraph, or part thereof directly involved in the controversy in which such judgment shall have been rendered and to the person or circumstances involved.

Sec. 16. This Act shall take effect immediately upon passage.

In the Senate of the United States

Sec. 8. If any provision of this Act or the application thereof to any person or circumstances is held invalid, the remainder of the Act, and the application of such provision to other persons or circumstances, shall not be affected thereby.

Short Title

Sec. 10. This Act may be recited as the "Federal Public Housing Act of 1935."

Sec. 11. This Act shall take effect on June 15, 1935.

The Wagner Bill

of 1936

74th Congress   S. 4424
2d Session

IN THE SENATE OF THE UNITED STATES

February 24 (calendar day, April 3), 1936

Mr. Wagner introduced the following bill; which was read twice and referred to the Committee on Education and Labor.

A BILL

To provide financial assistance to the States and political sub-divisions thereof for the elimination of unsafe and insanitary housing conditions, for the development of decent, safe, and sanitary dwellings for families of low income, and for the reduction of unemployment and the stimulation of business activity, to create a United States Housing Authority, and for other purposes.

Be it enacted by the Senate and House of Representatives of the United States of America in Congress assembled,

FINDINGS AND POLICY

SECTION 1. There exist in urban and rural communities throughout the United States slums, blighted areas, or unsafe, insanitary, or overcrowded dwellings, or a combination of these conditions, accompanied and aggravated by an acute shortage of decent, safe, and sanitary dwellings within the financial reach of families of low income.

These conditions are inimical to the general welfare of the Nation by (a) encouraging the spread of disease and lowering the level of health, morale, and vitality of large portions of the American people; (b) increasing the hazards of fires, accidents, and natural calamities; (c) subjecting the moral standards of the young to bad influences; (d) increasing the

428

violation of the criminal laws of the United States and of the several States; (e) impairing industrial and agricultural productive efficiency; (f) lowering the standards of living of large portions of the American people; (g) necessitating a vast and extraordinary expenditure of public funds, Federal, State, and local, for crime prevention, punishment and correction, fire prevention, public-health service, and relief.

The failure to remedy the acute dwelling shortage has also produced stagnation of business activity in the construction, durable goods, and allied industries, thus impeding business activity throughout the Nation and resulting in widespread and prolonged unemployment with its injurious effects upon the general welfare of the Nation.

Private industry alone has been and now is unable to overcome the obstacles in the way of relieving the shortage of decent, safe, and sanitary dwellings for families of low income, and the several States and their political subdivisions have been and now are unable adequately to aid in remedying this condition without financial assistance.

It is hereby declared to be the policy of the United States to promote the general welfare of the Nation by employing its funds and credit, as provided in this Act, to assist the several States and their political subdivisions to alleviate unemployment and to remedy the unsafe and insanitary housing conditions and the acute shortage of decent, safe, and sanitary dwellings for families of low income that are injurious to the health, safety, and morals of the citizens of the Nation.

DEFINITIONS

SEC. 2. When used in this Act—

(1) The term "low-rent housing" means decent, safe, and sanitary dwellings within the financial reach of, and available solely for, families of low income, and developed and administered to promote serviceability, efficiency, and economy; and embraces all necessary or desirable appurtenances thereto, including administrative, educational, recreational, and other buildings and facilities.

(2) The term "families of low income" means families who cannot afford to pay enough to induce private enterprise in their locality to build an adequate supply of decent, safe, and sanitary dwellings for their use.

(3) The term "slum" means any area where dwellings predominate which, by reason of dilapidation, overcrowding, faulty arrangement or design, lack of ventilation, light or sanitation facilities, or any combination of these factors, are detrimental to safety, health, or morals.

(4) The term "slum clearance" means the demolition and removal of buildings from any slum area, and may embrace the adaptation of such area to public purposes, including parks or other recreational or community facilities.

(5) The term "development" means all undertakings necessary for planning, financing, land acquisition, demolition, and construction and equipment activity to the point of completion. Construction activity in connection with a low-rent-housing project may be confined to the reconstruction, remodeling, or repair of existing buildings. The development of a low-rent-housing project may include slum clearance. The development of a slum-clearance project may be confined to demolition and removal.

(6) The term "administration" means all undertakings necessary for management, operation, and maintenance.

(7) The term "demonstration project" means any project owned or administered by the Authority, whether or not developed pursuant to section 11.

(8) The term "public housing agency" means any State, county, city, or other govenmental entity or public body (excluding the Authority), which is authorized to engage in the development or administration of low-rent-housing or slum clearance.

(9) The term "public housing society" means any association, co-operative, or corporate body organized solely to promote and administer low-rent housing, whose members are persons of low income in need of such housing, whose officers and directors are the freely chosen representatives of such members, and which is operated, without possibility of direct or indirect financial profit, under the supervision and control of the Authority.

(10) The term "limited-profit housing agency" means any association, cooperative, limited dividend corporation, or other corporate body organized to develop or administer low-rent-housing projects, whose dividend rates, if any, capital structure, interest payments, and rental charges are regulated or limited by law or subject to the supervision and control of the Authority, and which submits its records to the inspection of the Authority to the extent necessary to carry out the provisions of this Act.

(11) The term "housing agency" means any public housing agency, public housing society or limited profit housing agency.

(12) The term "going Federal rate" means the average interest rate paid by the United States upon its bonded indebtedness.

(13) The term "State" includes the States of the Union and the districts, Territories, dependencies, and possessions of the United States.

(14) The term "Authority" means the United States Housing Authority created by section 3 of this Act.

UNITED STATES HOUSING AUTHORITY

SEC. 3. (a) There is hereby created a body corporate of perpetual duration to be known as the United States Housing Authority, which shall be an agency and instrumentality of the United States.

(b) The administration and all the powers of the Authority shall be vested in a board of directors (hereinafter referred to as the board) composed of five members. The Secretary of the Interior shall be a member ex officio. The other four members shall be appointed by the President, by and with the advice and consent of the Senate, and may be removed by the President, upon notice and hearing, for neglect of duty or malfeasance in office, but for no other cause. One of the four original appointive members shall serve for a term of one year, one for a term of two years, one for a term of three years, and one for a term of four years, but their successors shall be appointed for terms of five years each, except that any individual chosen to fill a vacancy shall be appointed only for the unexpired term of the member whom he shall succeed. The President shall designate one member to serve as chairman of the board.

(c) A vacancy in the board shall not impair the right of the remaining members to exercise all the powers of the board, and three members of the board shall at all times constitute a quorum.

SEC. 4. (a) The Secretary of the Interior shall not be entitled to any additional compensation for his service on the board. Each of the other four members shall receive a salary of $10,000 a year, shall be eligible for reappointment, and shall not engage in any other business, vocation, or employment. No officer or employee of the Authority shall participate in any manner in the deliberation upon or the determination of any question affecting his personal interests or the interests of any corporation, partnership, or association in which he is directly or indirectly interested.

(b) The Authority shall, without regard to the civil-service laws and the Classification Act of 1923, as amended, appoint and fix the compensation of such officers, attorneys and experts, contract for the personal services of such architects, engineers, appraisers, negotiators, and real-estate brokers, and employ such skilled and unskilled labor, and with regard to such laws appoint such other employees, as it may from time to time find necessary for the proper performance of its duties.

(c) The Authority may accept and utilize such voluntary and uncompensated services (not excluding reasonable allowances for necessary traveling and other expenses), and with the consent of the agency concerned may utilize such officers, employees, equipment, and information of any agency of the Federal, State, or local governments as it finds helpful in the performance of its duties.

(d) At the expiration of sixty days from the enactment of this Act the Housing Division of the Federal Emergency Administration of Public Works shall cease to exist, and all its obligations shall be assumed by the Authority and all its assets, equipment, records, and employees shall be transferred to the Authority, for the purposes of this Act. No employee shall acquire by such transfer a permanent or civil-service status, but within ninety days after such transfer the Authority may certify to the Civil Service Commission the names of such transferred employees as it desires to retain and as are required to be under the civil-service laws by the provisions of section 4 (b) of this Act. Upon such certification, said Commission shall provide for the inclusion of such employees within the Civil Service. All housing and slum-clearance projects undertaken by the Federal Emergency Administration of Public Works, all contracts and other property held by it in connection with such projects, and any unexpended balance of funds allocated to it for housing and slum-clearance projects shall likewise be transferred to the Authority at the same time, and the Authority may continue such projects. Any action taken by said Federal Emergency Administration of Public Works in connection with any such project is hereby adopted and ratified. The President may at any time in his discretion transfer to the Authority any other bureau or division of any department or agency of the Federal Government that is engaged in low-rent-housing or slum-clearance activities, and the Authority may continue such activities subject to the provisions of this Act.

SEC. 5. (a) The principal office of the Authority shall be in the District of Columbia, but it may establish branch offices or agencies in any State, and it may meet and exercise any of its powers at any place within the United States. The Authority may, by one or more of its officers or employees or by such agents or agencies as it may designate, conduct hearings or negotiations at any place.

(b) The Authority may foreclose on any property, or commence any action, to protect or enforce any right conferred upon it by any law, contract, or other agreement. The Authority may bid for and purchase at any foreclosure by any party, or at any other sale, any low-rent-housing project which it previously owned or in connection with which it has made a loan or grant pursuant to section 9 or a loan pursuant to section 10.

(c) The Authority may procure insurance against any loss in connection with its property and other assets (including mortgages), in such amounts, and from such insurers, as it deems desirable.

(d) The Authority shall sue and be sued in its own name, and all suits shall be brought in the Federal courts except where the Authority consents specifically to a different forum. Attorneys appointed by the Authority may, at the direction of the Authority, appear for and represent the Authority in any case in court.

(e) The Authority shall have an official seal, which shall be judicially noticed.

(f) The Authority shall be granted the free use of the mails in the same manner as the executive departments of the Government.

(g) The Authority, including but not limited to its franchise, capital, reserves, surplus, loans, income, assets, and property of any kind, shall be exempt from all taxation now or hereafter imposed by the United States or by any State, county, municipality, or local taxing authority.

SEC. 6. (a) The Authority may make such expenditures for the acquisition and maintenance of adequate administrative agencies, offices, vehicles, furnishings, equipment, supplies, and books, for attendance at meetings, and for such other facilities and services as it may from time to time find necessary for the proper administration of this Act. The Authority shall determine and prescribe the manner in which its obligations and expenses shall be incurred, allowed, and paid, and the manner in which accounts shall be audited, without regard to the provisions of any other law governing the expenditure of public funds.

(b) The provisions of section 3709 of the Revised Statutes (U.S.C., title 41, sec. 5) shall apply to all contracts of the Authority for services and to all of its purchases of supplies except when the aggregate amount involved is less than $300.

(c) The use of funds made available for the purposes of this Act shall be subject to the provisions of section 2 of title 3 of the Treasury and Post Office Appropriation Act for the fiscal year 1934 (47 Stat. 1489), and to make such provisions effective every contract or agreement of any kind pursuant to this Act shall contain a provision identical to the one prescribed in section 3 of title 3 of such Act.

SEC. 7. (a) The Authority may engage in research, studies, surveys, and experimentation and may publish and disseminate information pertinent to the various aspects of housing.

(b) In January of each year the Authority shall make an annual report to Congress of its operations, including loans, grants, and contributions made or contracted for, low-rent-housing and slum-clearance projects undertaken, and the assets and liabilities of the Authority.

SEC. 8. The Authority may from time to time make, amend, and rescind such rules and regulations as may be necessary to carry out the provisions of this Act.

ASSISTANCE TO LOCAL LOW-RENT-HOUSING AND SLUM-CLEARANCE PROJECTS

SEC. 9. (a) The Authority may make grants and loans to any public-housing agency to assist the development, acquisition, or administration of any low-rent-housing project by such agency.

(b) The value of the grant to a low-rent-housing project shall be that which is necessary, in the determination of the Authority, to assure the low-rent character of such project, but shall in no case exceed 45 per centum of its development or acquisition cost. Such grant may be paid, in whole or in part, in a lump sum. Any balance (of the total value of the grant) not so paid shall be paid in the form of fixed and uniform annual contributions, over a fixed period not exceeding sixty years, each such annual contribution to be payable out of any funds available to the Authority when such payment is due. Each such annual contribution shall be equal to the amount of the annual payment which such balance would yield over such fixed period of years in an annuity computed at the going Federal rate of interest at the time such grant is made. The Authority shall embody the provisions for such annual contributions in a contract guaranteeing such fixed and uniform payments over such fixed period.

(c) No loans pursuant to this section shall be made or be outstanding for any low-rent-housing project in an amount greater than the development or acquisition cost of such project, less the total value (at the time when made) of any grant pursuant to subsection (b) of this section. Any such loan shall bear interest at such rate, be secured in such manner, and be repaid within such period, not exceeding sixty years, as may be deemed advisable by the Authority.

SEC. 10. The Authority may make loans to limited-profit housing agencies to assist the development or acquisition of low-rent-housing projects: *Provided,* That not more than $25,000,000 shall be so loaned in any one fiscal year. Any such loan shall not exceed 85 per centum of the development or acquisition cost of the project involved, shall bear interest at not less than the going Federal rate at the time such loan is made, and shall be secured in such manner, and be repaid within such period not exceeding sixty years, as may be deemed advisable by the Authority.

DEMONSTRATION PROJECTS

SEC. 11. (a) The Authority may develop and administer low-rent-housing and slum-clearance demonstration projects in order to demonstrate to localities the benefits to be derived therefrom. No such demonstration project shall be commenced in any locality without the advice and at the request of either the local governing body, a public housing agency, a public housing society representing families needing the project, or a local committee of representative and responsible citizens.

(b) As soon as practicable the Authority shall sell its demonstration projects: *Provided,* That low-rent-housing projects shall be sold only to public housing agencies.

(c) Pending sale, the Authority may lease any low-rent-housing demonstration project in whole or in part to a public housing agency or a public housing society, or enter into contracts for the administration of any such project in whole or in part by any such agency: *Provided,* That a project shall be leased to or administered by a public housing society only with the consent of a public housing agency in the locality if such an agency exists: *And provided further,* That the tenants of such project shall not be limited to the members of such society. The provisions of section 321 of the

Act of June 30, 1932 (U.S.C., Supp. VIII, title 40, sec. 303 (b)), shall not apply to any such lease or contract.

(d) The Authority may dedicate land for parks, playgrounds, and other recreational facilities, for sewers, for the opening or widening of streets, for incidental improvements, or for any other public purpose, and may grant licenses and easements upon such terms as it deems reasonable.

(e) The Authority may sell or exchange at public or private sale, or lease, any real property (except low-rent-housing projects, the disposition of which is governed elsewhere in this Act) or personal property, and sell or exchange any securities or obligations, the retention of which is not desirable in performing its functions under this Act, upon such terms as it may fix. To facilitate the sale of such securities or obligations any other securities or obligations retained by the Authority may be subordinated to those sold.

(f) In connection with the development or administration of any low-rent-housing or slum-clearance project pursuant to this section the Authority may acquire real or personal property or any interest therein by purchase, eminent domain, gift, devise, lease, or otherwise. In the acquisition of any land or site the provisions of section 355 of the Revised Statutes, as amended, shall not apply, but the Authority may avail itself of the services of the Attorney General acting in accord with his powers under such section to procure information relating to the state of title. The Attorney General shall, upon the application of the Authority, institute condemnation proceedings in its name. The practice and procedure govering [sic] such proceedings by the United States shall be followed, and the Authority shall likewise be entitled to proceed in accordance with the provisions of an Act of Congress approved February 26, 1931 (46 Stat. 1421), and an Act of Congress approved March 1, 1929 (45 Stat. 1415). The Authority may enter into agreements to reimburse any State or political subdivision thereof for expenses incurred in the acquisition, by condemnation or otherwise, of property to be conveyed to the Authority for the development of a low-rent-housing or slum-clearance project.

(g) The acquisition by the Authority of any real property pursuant to this Act shall not deprive any State or political subdivision thereof of its civil and criminal jurisdiction in and over such property, or impair the civil rights under the State or local law of the inhabitants on such property; and insofar as any such jurisdiction may have been taken away or any such rights impaired by reason of any such acquisition (including the transfer of property to the Authority pursuant to section 4 (d)), such jurisdiction and such rights are hereby fully restored.

(h) The Authority may enter into agreements to pay annual sums in lieu of taxes to any State or political subdivision thereof with respect to any low-rent-housing or slum-clearance project owned by the Authority.

The amount so paid for any year upon any such project shall not exceed the taxes that would be paid to the State or subdivision, as the case may be, upon such project if it were not exempt from taxation thereby.

SEC. 12. Subject to the specific limitations or standards in this Act governing the terms of sales, rentals, leases, loans, grants, annual contributions, or agreements, the Authority may, whenever it deems it necessary or desirable in the fulfillment of the purposes of this Act, consent to the modification, with respect to rate of interest, time of payment of any installment of principal or interest, security, amount of annual contribution, or any other term, of any contract or agreement of any kind to which the Authority is a party or which has been transferred to it pursuant to this Act. Any rule of law contrary to this provision shall be deemed inapplicable.

STANDARDS

SEC. 13. In making any loan or grant for the development of a project pursuant to section 9, or any loan for the development of a project pursuant to section 10, and in undertaking any demonstration project pursuant to section 11, the Authority shall be guided by these considerations:

(1) In the case of a low-rent-housing project, that there exists in the community concerned a shortage of decent, safe, and sanitary dwellings within the financial reach of families of low income, which is not being remedied adequately by private enterprises;

(2) In the case of a slum-clearance project, that there exist in the community concerned slum areas that are not being remedied adequately by private enterprise, and that either (a) the clearance of the area will not make it difficult for the dispossessed inhabitants thereof to secure equivalent dwellings elsewhere at no higher cost to them, or (b) that such inhabitants will be provided for by the development of sufficient low-rent housing, within their financial reach, either upon the site to be cleared or in some other suitable locality;

(3) That the project conforms to a general program formulated by the Authority to distribute the benefits of this Act as widely as practicable throughout the United States, consistently with the needs of the several States and their political subdivisions;

(4) That the form of assistance to the project is an appropriate means of carrying out the purposes of this Act in the particular case, and that the amount of financial assistance to be afforded such project by the Authority will not be in excess of the amount necessary for such purposes;

(5) That the site on which a project is or shall be developed is suitable for the project and has been or will be purchased for a reasonable price.

SEC. 14. In order to insure that the low-rent character of housing projects will be preserved, and thus to protect private industry from the competition that would exist, either if such projects were made available to families able to afford decent, safe, and sanitary dwellings without public assistance or if such projects were withdrawn from the financial reach of families of low income, it is hereby provided that—

(1) When a loan or grant is made pursuant to section 9, and when a loan is made pursuant to section 10, the Authority shall retain the right (subject to any mortgage or other lien of a third party) to take possession of, administer, and dispose of the low-rent-housing project involved in the event of a substantial breach of the covenant (which shall be embodied in the deed, mortgage, or other contract providing for such loan or grant) to maintain the low-rent character of such housing project. Any such covenant shall run in the case of a grant for a period of sixty years, and in the case of a loan for a period equal to the maximum period allowed for the repayment in full of such loan: *Provided,* That no such covenant shall continue to run after the acquisition of such project in a bona-fide foreclosure under a mortgage or other lien held by a third party if the Authority has received actual notice in writing of such foreclosure proceedings at least thirty days before sale.

(2) When a loan is made pursuant to section 9 or section 10, the Authority shall retain the right, in the event of a substantial breach of the covenant (pursuant to paragraph 1 of this section) to maintain the low-rent character of the housing project involved or in the event of the acquisition of such project by a third party in any manner including a bona-fide foreclosure under a mortgage or other lien held by a third party, to increase the interest payable thereafter on said loan to a rate not in excess of the going Federal rate (at the time of such breach) plus 2 per centum per annum or to declare the unpaid principal on said loan due forthwith.

(3) When a grant or any part thereof shall be made payable in annual contributions pursuant to section 9 (b), the Authority shall retain the right, in the event of a substantial breach of the covenant (pursuant to paragraph 1 of this section) to maintain the low-rent character of the housing project involved, to reduce or terminate said annual contributions. In the event of the acquisition of such project by a third party in any manner including a bona-fide foreclosure under a mortgage or other lien held by a third party, such annual contributions shall terminate.

(4) When a lease or contract for the administration of a low-rent housing project is made pursuant to section 11 (c), the Authority shall retain the right to terminate such lease or contract in the event of a substantial breach of the covenant (which shall be embodied in such lease or contract) to maintain the low-rent character of such housing project.

(5) The Authority may also insert in any contract of loan or grant, contract of sale, lease, contract of administration, mortgage, or any other agreement or instrument made pursuant to this Act, such other covenants,

conditions, or provisions as it may deem necessary in order to insure the low-rent character of the housing project involved.

SEC. 15. In order to protect the financial position of the Authority, and to prevent Federal assistance to any low-rent-housing project in excess of that contemplated by this Act—

(1) The sale by the Authority of any low-rent-housing project shall be for a consideration, in whatever form may be satisfactory to the Authority, equal to at least 55 per centum of the development or acquisition cost of the project less such allowance for depreciation as the Authority shall fix. The amount by which such development or acquisition cost (less depreciation) exceeds the sales price shall be considered a grant pursuant to section 9 (b), and the project shall then become eligible for a loan pursuant to section 9 (c) and for annual contributions pursuant to section 9 (b).

(2) In the administration by the Authority of any low-rent-housing project, and in the leasing or administration under contract of any such project pursuant to section 11 (c), the Authority shall fix the rentals (which in the case of a lease pursuant to section 11 (c) means the rentals payable by the public housing agency or the public housing society to the Authority) at an amount at least sufficient to pay (a) all necessary and proper administrative expenses of the project (if administered by the Authority or administered under contract) ; (b) such sums as will suffice to repay, within a period not exceeding sixty years, at least 55 per centum of the development or acquisition cost of the project, together with interest at such rate as the Authority deems advisable.

SEC. 16. In order to protect labor standards—

(1) The provisions of the Act of August 30, 1935, entitled "An Act to amend the Act approved March 3, 1931, relating to the rate of wages for laborers and mechanics employed by contractors and subcontractors on public buildings" (49 Stat. 1011), and of the Act of August 24, 1935, entitled "An Act requiring contracts for the construction, alteration, and repair of any public building or public work of the United States to be accompanied by a performance bond protecting the United States and by an additional bond for the protection of persons furnishing material and labor for the construction, alteration, and repair for the said public buildings and public works" (U.S.C., Supp., 1934 edition, title 40, sec. 270 (a) to (d), inclusive), shall apply to contracts in connection with the development or administration of low-rent-housing or slum-clearance projects owned by the Authority and the furnishing of materials and labor for such projects: *Provided*, That suits shall be brought in the name of the Authority and that the Authority shall itself perform the duties prescribed by section 3 (a) of the Act of August 30, 1935, and section 3 of the Act of August 24, 1935.

(2) Any contract for a loan, grant, annual contribution, sale, lease, or administration with a housing agency shall contain a provision requiring that the wages prevailing in the locality, as determined by the Authority, shall be paid to all laborers and mechanics employed in the development or administration of the low-rent-housing or slum-clearance project involved.

(3) The Act entitled "An Act limiting the hours of daily services of laborers and mechanics employed upon work done for the United States, or for any Territory, or for the District of Columbia, and for other purposes," as amended (37 Stat. 137), shall apply to contracts of the Authority for work in connection with the development and administration of low-rent-housing or slum-clearance demonstration projects.

(4) The benefits of the Act entitled "An Act to provide compensation for employees of the United States suffering injuries while in the performance of their duties, and for other purposes" (39 Stat. 742), shall extend to officers and employees of the Authority.

(5) The provisions of sections 1 and 2 of the Act of June 13, 1934 (U.S.C., title 40, sec. 276 (b) and (c)), shall apply to any low-rent-housing or slum-clearance project financed in whole or in part with funds made available pursuant to this Act.

FINANCIAL PROVISIONS

SEC. 17. The Authority shall have a capital stock of $1,000,000, which shall be subscribed by the United States and paid by the Secretary of the Treasury out of any available funds. Receipt for such payment shall be issued to the Secretary of the Treasury by the Authority and shall evidence the stock ownership of the United States of America.

SEC. 18. There is hereby authorized to be appropriated, out of any money in the Treasury not otherwise appropriated, the sum of $51,000,000 for the fiscal year ending June 30, 1937, of which $1,000,000 shall be available to pay the subscription to the capital stock of the Authority, and there is authorized to be appropriated the sum of $75,000,000 for the fiscal year ending June 30, 1938, and the sum of $100,000,000 for each of the fiscal years ending June 30, 1939 and 1940, respectively. All such sums, and all receipts and assets of the Authority, shall be available for the purposes of this Act until expended.

SEC. 19. Any funds available under any Act of Congress for allocation for low-rent housing or slum clearance may, in the discretion of the President, be allocated to the Authority for the purposes of this Act.

SEC. 20. (a) The Reconstruction Finance Corporation shall make advances to the Authority from time to time upon its request, but not to exceed, in the aggregate outstanding, the sum of $100,000,000, which shall bear interest at a rate not exceeding cost plus one-eighth of 1 per centum per annum and shall be repaid in full by the Authority to said Corporation or its successor within a period of sixty years from the time when made. Such advances shall be available for the purposes of this Act until expended. The Authority shall apply toward such repayment the net income from, and the proceeds of the sale of, assets transferred to it pursuant to section 4 (d) of this Act, but the Reconstruction Finance Corporation shall not have a lien upon, nor exercise any control over, the administration or disposition of such assets. The amount of notes, debentures, and bonds or other obligations which said corporation is authorized and empowered to have outstanding at any one time, pursuant to section 9 of the Reconstruction Finance Corporation Act, as amended, is hereby increased by the sum necessary for such purposes, not to exceed $100,000,000.

SEC. 21. (a) In addition to obligation incurred pursuant to section 20, the Authority is authorized to issue obligations, in the form of notes, bonds, or otherwise, which it may sell to obtain funds for the purposes of this Act. The Authority may issue such obligations in an amount not to exceed $100,000,000 on or after July 1, 1936, an additional amount not to exceed $150,000,000 on or after July 1, 1937, an additional amount not to exceed $150,000,000 on or after July 1, 1938, and an additional amount not to exceed $150,000,000 on or after July 1, 1939. Such obligations shall be in such forms and denominations, mature within such periods not exceeding sixty years from date of issue, bear such rates of interest not exceeding 4 per centum per annum, be subject to such terms and conditions, and be issued in such manner and sold at such prices as may be prescribed by the Authority, with the approval of the Secretary of the Treasury.

(b) Such obligations shall be exempt, both as to principal and interest, from all taxation (except surtaxes, estate, inheritance, and gift taxes) now or hereafter imposed by the United States or by any State, county, municipality, or local taxing authority.

(c) Such obligations shall be fully and unconditionally guaranteed upon their face by the United States, as to the payment of both interest and principal, and in the event that the Authority shall be unable to make any such payment upon demand when due, payment shall be made to the holder by the Secretary of the Treasury with money hereby authorized to be appropriated for such purpose out of any money in the Treasury not otherwise appropriated. To the extent of such payment the Secretary of the Treasury shall succeed to all the rights of the holder.

(d) Such obligations shall be lawful investments, and may be accepted as security, for all fiduciary, trust, and public funds, the investment or deposit of which shall be under the authority or control of the United States or any officer or agency thereof. The Secretary of the Treasury is likewise authorized to purchase any such obligations, and for such purchases he may use as a public-debt transaction the proceeds from the sale of any securities hereafter issued under the second Liberty Bond Act, as amended, and the purposes for which securities may be issued under such Act, as amended, are extended to include any such purchases. The Secretary of the Treasury may at any time sell any of the obligations acquired by him pursuant to this section, and all redemptions, purchases, and sales by him of such obligations shall be treated as public-debt transactions of the United States.

(e) Such obligations may be marketed for the Authority at its request by the Secretary of the Treasury, utilizing all the facilities of the Treasury Department now authorized by law for the marketing of obligations of the United States.

SEC. 22. (a) Any money of the Authority not otherwise employed may be deposited, subject to check, with the Treasurer of the United States or in any Federal Reserve bank, or may be invested in obligations of the United States or used in the purchase or retirement or redemption of any obligations issued by the Authority.

(b) The Federal Reserve banks are authorized and directed to act as depositories, custodians, and fiscal agents for the Authority in the general exercise of its powers, and the Authority may reimburse any such bank for its services in such manner as may be agreed upon.

(c) The Authority may be employed as a financial agent of the Government. When designated by the Secretary of the Treasury, and subject to such regulations as he may prescribe, the Authority shall be a depository of public money, except receipts from customs.

PENALTIES

SEC. 23. All general penal statutes relating to the larceny, embezzlement, or conversion, or to the improper handling, retention, use, or disposal of public moneys or property of the United States, shall apply to the moneys and property of the Authority and to moneys and properties of the United States entrusted to the Authority.

SEC. 24. Any person who, with intent to defraud the Authority or to deceive any director, officer, or employee thereof or any officer or employee of the United States, makes any false entry in any book of the Authority or makes any false report or statement to or for the Authority, shall, upon conviction thereof, be fined not more than $1,000 or imprisoned for not more than one year, or both.

SEC. 25. Any person who shall receive any compensation, rebate, or reward, or shall enter into any conspiracy, collusion, or agreement, express or implied, with intent to defraud the Authority or with intent unlawfully to defeat its purposes, shall, upon conviction thereof, be fined not more than $1,000 or imprisoned for not more than one year, or both.

SEC. 26. Any person who induces or influences the Authority to purchase or acquire any property or to enter into any contract and willfully
fails to disclose any interest, legal or equitable, which he has in such property or in the property to which such contract relates, or any special benefit
which he expects to receive as a result of such contract, shall, upon conviction thereof, be fined not more than $1,000 or imprisoned for not more than
one year, or both.

SEC. 27. No individual, association, partnership, or corporation shall
use the words "United States Housing Authority", or any combination of
these four words, as the name, or part thereof, under which he or it shall
do business. Any such use shall constitute a misdemeanor, and shall be
punishable by a fine not exceeding $1,000.

SEC. 28. If any provision of this Act, or the application thereof to any
person or circumstances, shall be held invalid, the remainder of this Act,
or the application of such provision to persons or circumstances other than
those as to which it is held invalid, shall not be affected thereby.

SEC. 29. This Act may be cited as the "United States Housing Act
of 1936."

BIBLIOGRAPHY

1. Manuscripts and Documentary Sources

The core of the material used in this study consists of the papers of President Franklin D. Roosevelt, the Senate office files of Senator Robert F. Wagner, Sr., and the legislative files of the PWA Housing Division. The papers of President Roosevelt are preserved in the Franklin D. Roosevelt Library at Hyde Park, New York. This library is administered by the National Archives, but the papers of President Roosevelt are not official government papers. The papers used in this study were taken from the White House office files. Official File 63 was the file for preserving material directly concerned with the housing bills. Several sections of the President's Personal File and one section of the President's Secretary's File were also used. It is to be noted that the term "official file" does not make a file any more official than the other subseries of President Roosevelt's White House papers.

The office files of Senator Wagner were deposited at Georgetown University after the retirement of the senator from office. Two sections of these files, S. 1685—1937, which contained all the material on the housing bill, and the "yellows" (the carbon copies of the letters sent from Senator Wagner's office each day) or Chronological File for 1936 and 1937 contained most of the material pertinent to this study.

The files of the defunct PWA Housing Division are located in the offices of the Public Housing Administration of the Housing and Home Finance Agency in Washington, D.C. These files have been shifted from office building to office building as the various housing agencies of the government were reorganized. Much of the material originally contained in these files has been lost. However, there are a number of folders containing a partial legislative history of the housing bill which proved useful for the purposes of this study.

The papers and memoranda of prominent participants in the battle to enact the Wagner housing bill proved most useful to fill in the lacunae of the other files. Henry Ellenbogen, formerly a member of the House of Representatives and cosponsor of the bill with Senator Wagner, had in his files a number of memoranda that added materially to the completeness of this study. This material is in the chamber of Judge Ellenbogen in the Court House in Pittsburgh.

Warren J. Vinton, who served as a special adviser to the housing groups and who acted as secretary at the various meetings that the public-housing groups held, has preserved over the years a very complete file on the Wagner housing bills. Vinton was a trained research specialist and his material is especially valuable because it is annotated with dates, names, and other pertinent information. This material is in Vinton's office in Washington, D.C.

Ernest J. Bohn wrote numerous letters and memoranda during the three years that the housing bills were under consideration. This material was deposited by Bohn at the offices of the National Association of Housing Officials in Chicago.

The National Association of Housing Officials kept a complete file on the progress of the housing bills while they were under consideration by Congress. These files are concerned with the technical aspects of the legislation. There are a number of folders containing correspondence between NAHO and the officials of NAREB and USBLL concerning proposed amendments to the bills. These files are in the offices of NAHO in Chicago.

The files of the National Legislative Committee of the American Federation of Labor also furnished material for this study. These files outlined the activity of a lobby in attempting to convince Congress to give favorable consideration to a bill in which it has an interest. These files are located at the headquarters of the AFL in Washington. Also located at the headquarters of the AFL are the files of the Labor Housing Conference. These files contain correspondence between the LHC office in Washington and various labor unions throughout the country. The LHC was an interest group devoted to educating labor unions in the technicalities of housing legislation.

A small amount of material concerned with the first interest group devoted to the enactment of a housing law was found in the files of the

National Public Housing Conference. These files have been moved on several occasions and much material has been lost. The files are at present in the offices of the National Housing Conference (the organization dropped "Public" from the title some years ago) in Washington.

There was very little material in the National Archives. Some of the petitions and resolutions in favor of the bill that were sent to the Senate Committee on Education and Labor by various state and municipal governments are preserved in the Legislative Records section of the National Archives. No material pertaining to the housing bill (S. 1685) was deposited with the Archives by the House Committee on Banking and Currency.

Important material illustrative of the principles and attitudes of two important lobby organizations that opposed the Wagner bill were also studied. The minutes of the special housing committee organized by the Chamber of Commerce of the United States which functioned from November 1935 until the passage of the bill in 1937 were made available by Mr. E. Stuart Fitzpatrick. These records are preserved in the offices of Mr. Fitzpatrick at the headquarters of the Chamber of Commerce in Washington, D.C.

The National Association of Real Estate Boards made available their library of published material on housing, and more important for the purposes of this study, the minutes of the meetings of the Board of Directors held during the period of November 18, 1932 and August 23, 1937. This material is preserved at the headquarters of NAREB in Chicago.

There is a large amount of material pertaining to the various housing bills in the published material of the Government Printing Office. The various official drafts (as opposed to confidential committee prints, which are private prints and are not on deposit in any library though they are printed by the GPO) of the bills and the various proposed amendments are on file in the Legislative Reference Service of the Congressional Library. The printed testimony of the hearings before the Senate and House committees is also to be found in bound copy in the Legislative Reference Service. Committee reports to accompany bills reported by the Senate or House committee will also be found in the Legislative Reference Service. The *United States Statutes at Large* contain the text of the laws and resolutions pertinent to this study. The

Congressional Record contains the complete record of the debates and remarks on the housing bills. Certain reports concerned with government housing activities during World War I were used as background material; a report of a special committee appointed by the commissioner of the Bureau of Labor in 1892 concerned with the slums in cities of 200,000 or more population was also used for background information; these reports may be found in the Public Document Series of the Sixty-fifth and Fifty-second congresses.

The authoritative source material for the procedures of the legislative process is to be found in *Rules and Manual, United States House of Representatives,* which also contains an annotated edition of the Constitution and *Jefferson's Manual.* This manual is revised and printed for each congress. The rules of the House are annotated with rulings and precedents of the speaker with the appropriate references to *Hinds'* and *Cannon's Precedents,* where the text of the ruling may be found. *Rules and Manual of the United States Senate* contains the rules and standing orders of the Senate and Cleaves' *Manual of the Law and Practice in Regard to Conferences and Conference Reports,* in addition to a wealth of other historical material pertaining to the government. *Gilfry's Precedents, Decisions on Points of Order with Phraseology in the United States Senate,* though not as complete or large a work as *Hinds'* and *Cannon's* gives the necessary information about Senate practice and procedure.

The NAHO issued mimeographed bulletins periodically (on an average of twice a month) which contained information about the progress and development of the housing bill. It also contained information about the development of local housing authorities and the housing movement generally. *A Housing Program for the United States* was the title of a published report of a conference on housing that the NAHO sponsored in October of 1934. This report served as a working basis for the first drafts of the housing bill.

Public Housing Progress, issued twice a month, was the medium of propaganda used by the NPHC. It illustrates the methods of this pressure group in building up public support for the legislative measure that it was sponsoring.

The proceedings of the annual meetings of the AFL and the editorial comment of its magazine the *American Federationist* show the development of a policy with regard to the housing bill. These two sources give the official attitude of the organization with regard to the bill.

Material from the proceedings of the annual meetings of the National Conference of Social Work shows the official attitude of this interest group with regard to the housing bill.

Miscellaneous bulletins and letters of the NAREB, USBLL, NRLDA, and the Chamber of Commerce of the United States manifest the attitudes of these lobbies toward the housing bill. The editorial material from *National Real Estate Journal, Savings and Loan Journal, American Lumberman,* and *Nation's Business* also manifest the official attitudes of these associations toward the housing bill.

2. Personal Interviews and Personal Letters

In order to supplement the material in the various files, the author of this study had a number of interviews with the principal participants in the struggle to enact the Wagner housing bill. Mr. Leon Keyserling, who was Senator Wagner's administrative assistant, and Miss Minna Ruppert, who was the senator's private secretary, explained the organization and activity in the senator's office during the period when the housing bills were being considered by Congress. Judge Henry Ellenbogen, who worked with Wagner on the housing bill in 1935 and 1936 when he was a member of the House of Representatives, explained his contribution to the bill. Judge Ellenbogen also wrote a long personal letter to the author answering specific questions about the reasons for changes made in the Ellenbogen drafts of the bill in 1935.

Mr. David L. Krooth, who was on the legal staff of PWA at the time the housing bills were being considered and who was assigned by Harold L. Ickes to work on the housing bill and later to work with Chairman Steagall of the House committee, added much to the understanding of the relationship of the PWA to the other public-housing groups by the information he gave to the author in a number of interviews.

Warren J. Vinton explained a number of the technical aspects of the bill in a series of interviews. Ernest J. Bohn in his interviews with the author explained the part played by the various pressure groups in pushing the housing bill through the stages of the legislative process.

Mr. William Hushings, secretary of the National Legislative Committee of the AFL, explained the part played by the Federation in working for the enactment of the bill.

Catherine Bauer in an interview and in personal letters explained her part in the development of the housing policy of the AFL.

Ira S. Robbins, who drafted the first housing bill introduced by Senator Wagner, explained the circumstances of this action. John W. Edelman, who was associated with the American Federation of Hosiery Workers, explained how that organization was the first limited-dividend corporation to obtain a loan for the development of a housing project.

E. Stuart Fitzpatrick, who is secretary of the Construction and Civic Development Department Committee of the Chamber of Commerce of the United States and who served as secretary of the special housing committee of the Chamber of Commerce, explained the attitude of the Chamber of Commerce toward the Wagner bill. Mr. Fitzpatrick also made available the minutes of the meetings of these two committees, which are on file in his office in Washington.

Morton Bodfish in a personal interview explained his part in developing amendments to the Wagner bill. Material was also taken from the *Building and Loan Annals* published while Bodfish was executive vice-president of USBLL.

Herbert U. Nelson, executive vice-president of NAREB, discussed his opposition to the Wagner bill in a personal interview. His office in Chicago made available for research various source materials including minutes of the meetings of the Board of Directors of NAREB.

These were the principal interviews which furnished material for this study. There were a number of other interviews, some of which are mentioned in the footnotes, in which a participant explained a point of secondary importance concerning the bill.

3. Published Works

"Applications by Limited-Dividend Corporations for Housing Loans." *Architectural Record* 74:159-60, September 1933.

Ascher, Charles S. "Housing Officials Organize National Group." *Public Management* 15:372-73, December 1933.

Bailey, Stephen Kemp. *Congress Makes a Law*. New York: Columbia University Press, 1950.

Bauer, Catherine. *Modern Housing*. Boston: Houghton Mifflin Company, 1934.

Benton, Thomas Hart. *Thirty Years' View*. 2 vols. New York: D. Appleton Company, 1856.

Byrne, Thomas. *The Social Philosophy of Senator Robert F. Wagner*. Unpublished dissertation. Georgetown University, 1951.

"Cleveland City Council Calls National Conference on Slum Clearance." *Public Management* 15:252-53, August 1933.

"Costly Slums." *Business Week*, No. 245, May 12, 1934, p. 27.

Dillon, Mary Earhart. "Pressure Groups." *American Political Science Review* 36:471-81, June 1942.

Douglas, Paul. *Social Security in the United States*. New York: Whittlesey House, 1936.

Ebenstein, William. *The Law of Public Housing*. Madison: The University of Wisconsin Press, 1940.

Elliott, William Yandell. *The Need for Constitutional Reform*. New York: McGraw-Hill Book Company, 1935.

"Federal Aid Now Offered for Low-Cost Housing and Slum-Clearance Projects." *American City* 47:82, August 1932.

Finch, George A. "The Treaty of Peace with Germany in the United States Senate." *American Journal of International Law* 14:155-206, January 1920.

"First Housing Projects Approved by Public Works Administration." *Architectural Record* 74:164-67, September 1933.

Ford, James. "Housing for War Workers Engaged on Army and Navy Contracts." *Annals of the American Academy of Political and Social Science* 79:270-74, September 1918.

———— "The President's Conference on Home Building and Home Ownership." *Journal of Home Economics* 23:924-28, October 1931.

———— and others. *Slums and Housing*. 2 vols. Cambridge: Harvard University Press, 1936.

"Funds for Housing." *Saturday Evening Post* 194:20, July 30, 1921.

Galloway, George. *Congress at the Crossroads*. New York: Thomas Y. Crowell Company, 1946.

"Government Duty in the Housing Crisis." *Literary Digest* 67:20, October 23, 1920.

"Government Housing Chaos." *Nation* 108:84-85, January 18, 1919.

Gries, John and James Ford, editors. *President's Conference on Home Building and Home Ownership.* 11 vols. Washington: President's Conference on Home Building and Home Ownership, 1932.

Hitchcock, Curtice N. "The War Housing Program and Its Future." *Journal of Political Economy* 27:241-79, April 1919.

"Housing Campaign." *Business Week*, No. 251, June 23, 1934, p. 7.

"Housing Conference in Washington, D.C." *Monthly Labor Review* 38:624-26, March 1934.

"Housing Corporation and the Senate." *Outlook* 124:394-95, March 3, 1920.

"Housing Features of the National Industrial Recovery Act." *American City* 48:5, July 1933.

"Housing Post-Mortem in the Senate." *American City* 22:110, February 1920.

Ihlder, John. "Card Houses: Can the Federal Government Afford To Abandon Its Industrial Villages." *Survey* 41:519-21, January 18, 1919.

——— "Uncle Sam as Auctioneer." *Survey* 41:659-60, February 8, 1919.

Karlin, William. "New York Slum Clearance and the Law." *Political Science Quarterly* 52:241-58, June 1937.

Kefauver, Estes and Jack Levin. *A Twentieth-Century Congress.* New York: Duell, Sloan and Pearce, 1947.

Kohn, Robert D. "Housing in a Reconstruction Program." *Survey* 42:341, May 31, 1919.

Lasker, Loula D. "Heading Up the Housing Program." *Survey* 70:348-49, November 1934.

Lee, Frederic P. "The Office of the Legislative Counsel." *Columbia Law Review* 29:381, April 1929.

"Legal Aspects of the Housing Problem." *Monthly Labor Review* 12:925-33, May 1921.

McConachie, Lauros G. *Congressional Committees.* New York: Thomas Y. Crowell Company, 1898.

McCown, Ada C. *The Congressional Conference Committee.* New York: Columbia University Press, 1927.

Moffett, James A. "Back to Prosperity with Housing." *Scientific American* 152:234-35, 292-93, May, June 1935.

"New York's Law, the Only One under Which R.F.C. Aid Can Be Had, Fits Only New York Conditions. . . ." *Business Week*, No. 172, December 21, 1932, p. 18.

Nolen, John. "Government Housing." *New Republic* 13:212-13, December 22, 1917.

Parrish, Wayne W. "Housing Campaign Moves into High Gear." *Literary Digest* 118:8, July 28, 1934.

———— "Housing Program Faces Serious Obstacles." *Literary Digest* 118:28, August 4, 1934.

———— "New Deal's Far-Reaching Housing Program." *Literary Digest* 118:4, July 14, 1934.

———— "A Real Deal for the Home Owner." *Literary Digest* 118:6, July 21, 1934.

Parsons, Floyd W. "The Housing Shortage." *Saturday Evening Post* 193:34 ff., November 13, 1920.

Pryor, Flo. "Housing and the Hosiery Workers." *American Federationist* 42:734-38, July 1935.

Robinson, Harold. "Some Problems Confronting the Public Works Emergency Housing Corporation." *Cornell Law Quarterly* 19:548, June 1934.

Schaub, Edward L. "The Regulation of Rentals during the War Period." *Journal of Political Economy* 28:1-36, January 1920.

Smith, Alfred E. "A Housing Policy for New York." *Survey* 45:3-4, October 2, 1920.

———— "To Stimulate Low-Cost Housing: A Proposal for Limited Dividend Housing Corporations, Aided by Public Credit and with Power of Condemnation." *American City* 34:127-28, February 1926.

"Supreme Court and the Rent Laws." *Review* 4:430, May 7, 1921.

Tinkham, George Holden. "The Urgent Need for a Federal Bureau of Housing and Living Conditions in the Department of Labor." *American City* 22:222-23, March 1920.

Wayman, Dorothy. *David I. Walsh, Citizen-Patriot.* Milwaukee: Bruce Publishing Company, 1952.

Whitaker, Charles Harris. "Wanted—Ten Million Houses!" *Saturday Evening Post* 192:23 ff., May 8, 1920.

"Who Will Build Five Million Homes?" *Literary Digest* 66:17-18, August 28, 1920.

Wood, Edith Elmer. *The Housing of the Unskilled Wage Earner*. New York: The Macmillan Company, 1919.

────── "Is Government Aid Necessary in the Financing of Low-Cost Housing?" *American City* 40:99-100, March 1929.

────── *Recent Trends in American Housing*. New York: The Macmillan Company, 1931.

Young, Roland. *This Is Congress*. New York: Alfred A. Knopf, 1946.

cism of, 99; comparison of with 1935 Ellenbogen bill and report of Baltimore conference, 100-04; provisions of, 102-03; Senate hearings on, 104-11, 333; and controversy over control of housing, 108; and Federation of Architects, Engineers, Chemists and Technicians, 110; death of in committee, 111, 114; opposition of NAREB to, 138-40; reintroduced by Beiter and Kennedy, 144-45

Wagner bill of 1936, drafting of by Keyserling and Ellenbogen, 133-34; and AFL, 138, 150, 152, 154-55, 176, 238; revision and introduction of, 144-71; provisions of first draft of, 147-49, 151-53; criticism of by LHC, 151-52; revised draft of, 153-54, 157; interest of public in, 154-55; conference of housing officials on, 157-61; appropriations of, 163; introduction of in Senate, 164-67, 169-70; introduction of in House, 167-69; statement of NAHO on, 172; Senate hearings on, 172, 175-85, 333; opposition to and support of by various groups, 172-75, 188-89, 242-43; attitude of F. Roosevelt toward, 186, 188, 190; Senate debate and vote on, 187-88, 191-208, 333; killed in House committee, 210-34; preparations to pass in 1937, 235-50; passage of urged by AFL, 238; opposition of NAREB to, 242

Wagner bill of 1937, House hearings on, 231, 304-05, 340-47; suggestions of PWA for, 245, 251, 256-60, 288, 289, 290, 291-92, 293-95; not ready for opening of Congress, 247-48; perfected by technical experts, 251-73; provisions of Confidential Committee Print No. 1, 260-63; and the Department of the Interior, 261, 268, 272-73, 285, 287, 288-92, 296-98, 299-306; official comments on, 264; provisions of Confidential Committee Print No. 2, 265; conference of hous-

ers on, 265-68, 297-98, 320; introduction of in Senate, 269-73; effect of attempted reorganization of Supreme Court on, 270; effect of antilynching bill on, 270-71; attitude of F. Roosevelt toward introduction of, 271-72; copy of sent to Steagall, 272; introduction of in House, 272; opposition of the Department of the Treasury to, 272-73, 274-88; Senate hearings on, 282, 290-92, 293, 296, 307, 317-19, 333; and AFL, 287, 297, 301, 308, 330, 341-42, 344, 348-50, 351, 354, 358, 388; revised provisions of, 293-96, 298-99, 319, 320-22; PWA amendments to, 299-304; Senate debate and vote on, 301-04, 322-30, 331-32, 335-39; and Logan amendment, 302-05, 323-24; support of by housing groups, 307-13, 343; opposition of public groups to, 313-16; and Confidential Committee Print No. 3, 320-21; reported out of Senate committee, 322-23; and Walsh amendment, 323, 324, 333-38, 349-50, 354, 357-58, 374, 383, 388, 393; and Byrd amendment, 324, 326-32, 348-49, 353-54, 357, 374, 394-95; limitation of construction costs in, 327-32; provision of for slum clearance, 334, 337; House committee amendments to, 347-57, 358, 359 note, 388; and Alley Dwelling Authority, 352 note, 395; House debate and vote on, 360-88; selection of speakers on during House debate, 373-74; Senate-House conference on, 389-400; provisions of as agreed upon by Senate-House conference, 391-97; acceptance by Senate of Senate-House report, 396-97; acceptance by House of Senate-House report, 398-400; enrollment of, 400-01; signing of by Pittman, 401; signing of by F. Roosevelt, 402

Walker, John O., 76, 267

Walsh, David I., and Committee on Education and Labor, 93, 221; and

470   The Wagner Housing Act

hearings on 1935 Wagner bill, 104-05, 110-11; position of on public housing, 165-66, 184-85; and hearings on 1936 Wagner bill, 170, 175-85; reporting out of committee of 1936 Wagner bill, 190; and Senate debate on 1936 Wagner bill, 192-93; on Kruesi and Ryan, 204-05; removal of from chairmanship of Committee on Education and Labor, 221; on independent administration of housing program, 299; and debate on Logan amendment, 303; and provisions of 1937 Wagner bill for slum clearance, 319, 321-22, 323, 324, 333-38; and Byrd amendment, 329; and Ihlder, 335; request of for Senate conference with House, 389-90; and civil-service provisions of 1937 bill, 395-96; and Senate discussion of Senate-House report on 1937 bill, 397

Walsh, J. Irving, 25

Walsh amendment, 323, 324, 333-38, 349-50, 354, 357-58, 374, 383, 388, 393

Wank, Roland A., 76

War workers, 7-8, 10-11, 13

Washington (District of Columbia), 49. *See also* Alley Dwelling Authority

Washington Sanitary Housing Company, 6

Washington Sanitary Improvement Company, 6

Wayne (Pennsylvania), 49

West, Charles, 153, 288, 297, 298, 300

Whitaker, Charles Harris, 12 *note*

White, Alfred T., 5-6

White, Dudley A., 351, 371, 378-79

White House meetings on housing, 123-24, 145-47, 153, 156-57, 264, 271, 276-78, 320

Wilbur, Ray Lyman, 26-27

Williams, Clyde, 251, 372, 378, 382

Williams, J. W., 106, 118

Wilmerding, Lucius, 156 *note*, 255-56

Wilson, S. Davis, 177 *note*

Wolcott, Jesse, 356-57, 365-66, 375, 377-78, 381, 383, 385, 390, 399

Wood, Edith Elmer, 13-14, 55, 64, 76, 107, 145, 158, 178, 266

Wood, Elizabeth, 76

Wood, Reuben T., 94-96

Wood bill, 94-95, 97, 114

Woodbury, Coleman, 57, 65, 76, 81, 97, 140, 158, 172 *note*, 178, 237, 240-41, 251-54, 262, 265-66, 267, 271, 276, 305, 312, 313, 317

Woodside (New York), 35

World War I, 5, 7-8, 8-9

Wright, Carroll D., 7 *note*

Wright, Henry, 72-73, 76

Young, Roland, 222

Zink, John H., 142, 314

Ziprin, Sheba, 106